Getting Finance in South Asia 2010

Getting Finance in South Asia 2010

Indicators and Analysis of the Commercial Banking Sector

Kiatchai Sophastienphong

Anoma Kulathunga

THE WORLD BANK
Washington, D.C.

1818 H Street NW
Washington DC 20433
Telephone: 202-473-1000
Internet: www.worldbank.org
E-mail: feedback@worldbank.org

1 2 3 4 13 12 11 10

ISBN: 978-0-8213-8057-4
eISBN: 978-0-8213-8392-6
DOI: 10.1596/978-0-8213-8057-4
ISSN: 2079-8903

Cover illustration and design: W. Drew Fasick, The Fasick Group, Inc.

Contents

Foreword xi
Acknowledgments xiii
About the Authors xv
Acronyms and Abbreviations xvii

1. INTRODUCTION 1
Development Dimensions and Micro Indicators 2
Access to Finance 2
Performance and Efficiency 3
Financial Stability 3
Capital Market Development 4
Market Concentration and Competitiveness 4
Payment Systems Development 5
Savings Mobilization 6
Corporate Governance 6
The Methodology 7
Interpretation of Ranks 8
The Role of Microfinance in South Asia 11
Endnotes 12

PART I: ANALYSIS

2. PRUDENTIAL REGULATIONS FOR BANKS IN SOUTH ASIA 15
Capital Adequacy 16
Implementation of the Basel II Capital Adequacy Framework 17
Asset Quality 21
Income Recognition 22
Write-Off Policy 22
Exposure Limits 22
Directed Lending 23
Liquidity 23
Debt Restructuring Policy 23
Endnotes 24

3. THE GETTING FINANCE INDICATORS: COUNTRY PERSPECTIVE . . . 25
Afghanistan 26
Access to Finance 28
Performance and Efficiency 29
Financial Stability 29
Capital Market Development 30
Market Concentration and Competitiveness 30

Payment Systems Development 30
Savings Mobilization 31
Corporate Governance 31
Bangladesh 33
Access to Finance 35
Performance and Efficiency 36
Financial Stability 36
Capital Market Development 37
Market Concentration and Competitiveness 37
Payment Systems Development 38
Savings Mobilization 38
Corporate Governance 39
Bhutan 41
Access to Finance 42
Performance and Efficiency 43
Financial Stability 43
Capital Market Development 43
Market Concentration and Competitiveness 44
Payment Systems Development 44
Savings Mobilization 44
Corporate Governance 45
India 47
Access to Finance 49
Performance and Efficiency 50
Financial Stability 50
Capital Market Development 51
Market Concentration and Competitiveness 52
Payment Systems Development 52
Savings Mobilization 54
Corporate Governance 54
Maldives 57
Access to Finance 59
Performance and Efficiency 60
Financial Stability 60
Capital Market Development 61
Market Concentration and Competitiveness 61
Payment Systems Development 62
Savings Mobilization 62
Corporate Governance 63
Nepal 65
Access to Finance 68
Performance and Efficiency 69
Financial Stability 69
Capital Market Development 71
Market Concentration and Competitiveness 72
Payment Systems Development 72
Savings Mobilization 73
Corporate Governance 73

Pakistan 75
Access to Finance 78
Performance and Efficiency 78
Financial Stability 79
Capital Market Development 81
Market Concentration and Competitiveness 81
Payment Systems Development 82
Savings Mobilization 83
Corporate Governance 83
Sri Lanka 87
Access to Finance 89
Performance and Efficiency 90
Financial Stability 91
Capital Market Development 92
Market Concentration and Competitiveness 93
Payment Systems Development 93
Savings Mobilization 95
Corporate Governance 96
Endnotes 98

4. COUNTRY RANKINGS ON THE GETTING FINANCE INDICATORS . . 101
Composite Ranking 102
Annual Rankings 104
Five-Year Average Rankings on Micro Indicators 106
Access to Finance 106
Performance and Efficiency 106
Financial Stability 106
Capital Market Development 107
Market Concentration and Competitiveness 107
Payment Systems Development 108
Savings Mobilization 108
Corporate Governance 109
Endnotes 113

5. AN INTERNATIONAL PERSPECTIVE 115
Benchmark Comparison 115
Access to Finance 116
Performance and Efficiency 117
Financial Stability 117
Capital Market Development 119
Market Concentration and Competitiveness 119
Payment Systems Development 120
Savings Mobilization 121
Benchmark Comparison with Individual Economies 122

6. FINDINGS AND OBSERVATIONS 129
Access to Finance 130
Performance and Efficiency 130
Financial Stability 130
Capital Market Development 132

Market Concentration and Competitiveness 132
Payment Systems Development 133
Savings Mobilization 133
Corporate Governance 134
Impact of the Financial Crisis 135

PART II: INDICATORS

7. COMPILATION GUIDE FOR THE GETTING FINANCE INDICATORS FOR SOUTH ASIA 139
Access to Finance 139
Performance and Efficiency 141
Financial Stability 143
Capital Market Development 145
Market Concentration and Competitiveness 146
Payment Systems Development 148
Savings Mobilization 150
Corporate Governance 152
Endnotes 153

8. METHODOLOGY 155
Data Compilation 155
Choice of Indicators 155
Method for Country Rankings 156
Financial Indicator Scores 156
Corporate Governance Scores 157
Financial Soundness Ranking 157
Presentation of Data 157

9. MAJOR POLICY DEVELOPMENTS IN THE PRUDENTIAL REGULATIONS OF SOUTH ASIA, 2007–08 161
Afghanistan 161
Prudential Regulations 161
Other Policy Developments 162
Legislation Enacted 163
Bangladesh 163
Prudential Regulations 163
Other Policy Developments 167
Legislation Enacted 170
Bhutan 170
Prudential Regulations 170
Other Policy Developments 172
Legislation Enacted or Pending 172
India 173
Prudential Regulations 173
Other Policy Developments 177
Legislation Enacted or Pending 179
Maldives 180
Prudential Regulations 180
Other Policy Developments 181
Legislation Enacted or Pending 182

Nepal 182
Prudential Regulations 182
Other Policy Developments 184
Legislation Enacted 185
Pakistan 185
Prudential Regulations 185
Other Policy Developments 191
Legislation Enacted or Pending 192
Sri Lanka 192
Prudential Regulations 192
Other Policy Developments 195
Legislation Enacted 197
Endnotes 198

SPECIAL FEATURE

MANAGING THE IMPACT OF THE GLOBAL FINANCIAL CRISIS AND ECONOMIC SLOWDOWN 199
An Overview 200
The Crisis and South Asian Economies 200
Economic Impact 201
Policy Responses and Challenges 206
The Crisis and South Asian Banking Sectors 206
Impact on Banking 208
Policy Responses and Challenges 212
Endnotes 214

APPENDIXES

Appendix 1. Prudential Regulations in South Asian Countries, End of 2008 216
Appendix 2. Getting Finance Indicators for South Asia, by Country and Year, 2001–08 242
Appendix 3A. Getting Finance Indicators for Benchmark Economies, 2001–08 274
Appendix 3B. Data Sources and Notes for Benchmark Economies 296
Appendix 4A. Corporate Governance Matrix: Questionnaire Responses for South Asian Countries, 2008 299
Appendix 4B. Status of Corporate Governance of Banks in South Asian Countries, 2008 308
Appendix 5. Payment Systems in Place in South Asian Countries 309
Appendix 6. Annual Rankings on the Getting Finance Indicators for South Asian Countries, 2004–08 311

REFERENCES 315

INDEX 321

Foreword

The financial sector is crucial to any economy—it affects the business climate, investment climate, and economic growth. Well-functioning financial systems are not only critical for sustaining high economic growth paths—mobilizing savings from the public and allocating them to productive investments—but can also play a pivotal role in making growth more inclusive, allowing more people to contribute to growth and share in the benefits, and providing access to finance for all, which in turn is associated with more rapid growth, job creation, better income distribution, and poverty reduction. Furthermore, the financial sector can operate as a shock absorber or as an amplifier of external or internal shocks, as the recent global financial crisis has best illustrated. It is therefore critical to understand the weaknesses and vulnerabilities in the financial sector, and thereby to monitor and compare the financial sectors across economies and over time. However, the available data and analytic work based on these data often lack the robustness needed to objectively assess countries' financial sector development. Information is scattered, disparate, often limited to measuring only the size of the financial system, not allowing other dimensions of the financial sector to be compared over time or across countries.

These data availability and comparability issues have prompted the Poverty Reduction, Economic Management, Finance and Private Sector Development Department of the South Asia Region of the World Bank to embark on a regional initiative to develop standardized indicators to measure the depth and breadth of the financial sector. The Getting Finance Indicators that have been updated and enhanced over the past five years now encompass various dimensions of financial sector development including access to finance, performance and efficiency, corporate governance, and financial stability.

This is the fifth of a series of regional studies on Getting Finance Indicators for the South Asia Region. All Getting Finance Indicators covered in the fourth edition have been updated and two new development dimensions—namely, payment systems development and savings mobilization—have been added to the study. As under previous editions, each of these dimensions is represented by six microfinancial indicators. The coverage of the South Asian countries has been expanded to include Afghanistan, Bhutan, and the Maldives, while retaining the five South Asian countries with relatively more developed financial sectors (Bangladesh, India, Nepal, Pakistan, and Sri Lanka), thus bringing all the eight South Asian countries under study for the first time. Similarly, the coverage of the benchmark countries has been broadened to cover Malaysia, Thailand, Japan, China, the Republic of Korea, Italy, France, Germany, raising the total number of benchmark countries to 15.

Using the Getting Finance Indicators for the period 2001–08, the book provides an analysis of the strengths and weaknesses of the commercial banking sector of the eight South Asian countries. The analysis reveals that countries in the region have made significant development efforts under several different areas and have generally been expanding access to finance and improving performance and efficiency, market concentration and competitiveness, corporate governance, and savings mobilization. They are tightening prudential norms in line with international standards, and they are developing their capital markets and their payment systems, although much more needs to be done.

This initiative has over the years served to strengthen the financial risk assessment framework in the region. These indicators would be useful to supervisory authorities to monitor financial vulnerabilities and weaknesses, and also to draw comparative analyses with regional counterparts. The special feature on the impact of the global financial crisis on the financial sector adds a wealth of knowledge on how South Asian countries were affected by this financial meltdown and how they responded to it.

Ernesto May

Sector Director, Poverty Reduction, Economic Management, Finance and Private Sector Development
South Asia Region

Acknowledgments

The authors wish to acknowledge the invaluable contributions of many individuals.

We gratefully acknowledge the encouragement by Ivan Rossignol (Sector Manager, SASFP), comments and guidance received from Simon C. Bell (Sector Manager MNSED), and John F. Speakman (Lead Private Sector Specialist, SASFP). Several members of the World Bank country teams facilitated the research and operational visits and commented on the study, including Md. Reazul Islam and Richard Nash for Afghanistan; Shah Nur Quayyum, Sadruddin Muhammad Salman, and A. K. M. Abdullah for Bangladesh, K. R. Ramamoorthy for India; Shamsuddin Ahmad Suran Kc Shrestha and Sabin Raj Shrestha for Nepal; Imtiaz Ahmad Sheikh and Kiran Afzal for Pakistan; and Sriyani Hulugalle and Lohitha Karunasekera for Sri Lanka. We offer them special thanks.

We thank the representatives of central banks and other supervisory authorities who participated in this study and provided advice and insights based on their experience, including the following: Mohammad Zarhir and Farzana Rashid Rahimi (Da Afghanistan Bank); Md. Nazrul Huda, S. M. Rabiul Hassan, and Ashok K. Karmaker (Bangladesh Bank); Eden Dema (Royal Monetary Authority of Bhutan) and Dorji Phuntsho (Royal Stock Exchange of Bhutan); Ahmed Munawar (Maldives Monetary Authority); Pralhad Thapa and Rishikesh Bhatta (Nepal Rastra Bank); Surbir Paudyal (the Securities Board of Nepal); Jiva Nath Nepal (Bank of Kathmandu Ltd.); Yaseen Anwar, Saeed Ahmed, Lubna Farooq Malik, Muhammad Javaid Ismail, and Abdul Samad (the State Bank of Pakistan); and Ananda Silva, Janakie Mampitiya, Yvette Fernando, A. A. M. Thassim, Dhammika Nanayakkara, and Arjuna W. Mohottala (the Central Bank of Sri Lanka).

We benefited from the thoughtful and helpful comments received during the peer review process. We are indebted to Anjali Kumar (Lead Economist, IEGCG), Ranee Jayamaha (former Deputy Governor, Central Bank of Sri Lanka), Varsha Marathe (Senior Financial Sector Specialist, SASFP), Eliana Cardoso (Chief Economist, SAR), Ulrich Bartsch (Senior Economist–India, SASEP), Deepak Bhattasali (Lead Economist, SASEP), Hisanobu Shishido (Senior Economist–Nepal, SASEP), Sanjay Kathuria (Lead Country Economist–Bangladesh, SASEP), T. G. Srinivasan (Lead Country Economist–Afghanistan, SASEP), Luchia Chritsova (Consultant, CAIFI), Massimo Cirasino (Lead Financial Sector Specialist, CAIFI), Youssef Saadani (Consultant, MNSED), Thyra Railey (Lead Financial Sector Specialist, SASFP), and Kyoo-Won Oh (Consultant, SASFP) for providing invaluable inputs, advice, and insight.

To disseminate the main findings and recommendations of the fifth edition, the World Bank, jointly with the Asian Development Bank (ADB), organized a conference on "South Asia Getting Finance Indicators 2010" in Manila, Philippines in February 2010. This conference was designed to provide regulators from central banks, securities exchange commissions, and ministry of finance representatives in South Asia with insight into the key issues for the development of financial sectors in the region, an opportunity to share intraregional experiences, hear about ADB's experience in East Asia, and discuss other international best practices in bank management. More important, this forum provided a platform for the exchange of knowledge and expertise in financial sector development. In addition to World Bank and Asian Development Bank staff, those participating in the conference included the following: Muhebullah Safi (First Deputy Governor, Da Afghanistan Bank), Kapil Mani Sharma (Chief Program Officer, Public Enterprise Division, Ministry of Finance, Bhutan), Dorji Phuntsho (C.E.O. Royal Stock Exchange of Bhutan), Sangay Dorji (Head, NBFI, Royal Monetary Authority of Bhutan), Md. Nazrul Huda (Deputy Governor, Bangladesh Bank), Shitangshu Kumar Sur Chowdhury (General Manager, Offsite Supervision, Bangladesh Bank), Md. Yasin Ali (Member, Securities and Exchange Commission, Bangladesh), Amalendu Mukherjee (Joint Secretary for Banking Policy, Finance Division, Ministry of Finance, Bangladesh), Mr. Prashant Saran (Wholetime Member, Securities and Exchange Board of India), Aishath Asna Hamdi (Assistant Manager, Maldives Monetary Authority), Hawwa Latheef (Assistant Manager, Maldives Monetary Authority), Bahadur Min Shrestha (Chief Manager, Nepal Rastra Bank), Bimal Wagle (Joint Secretary, Ministry of Finance, Nepal), Mr. Mukti Nath Shrestha (Securities Board of Nepal), Mr. Yaseen Anwar (Deputy Governor, State Bank of Pakistan), Mr. Ananda Silva (Assistant Governor, Central Bank of Sri Lanka), and Mr. Namal Kamalgoda (Director of Research and Policy, Securities Exchange Commission of Sri Lanka).

We express our deep appreciation to Alison Strong for her excellent editorial support; Chie Ingvoldstad and Mariko Katsura for their research support; and Maria Marjorie Espiritu for her technical support and for organizing and managing the dissemination process.

About the Authors

Kiatchai Sophastienphong is senior financial sector specialist, Poverty Reduction, Economic Management, Finance and Private Sector Development at the World Bank, South Asia Region. Recently Mr. Sophastienphong has led the Financial Sector Assessment Program update mission to Sri Lanka; helped to design and implement restructuring and bank privatization programs in Bangladesh, Nepal, and Pakistan; and guided the dialogue on financial sector issues in several client countries at both policy and technical levels. He has designed the overall financial sector strategies for these countries and developed a program to implement them. Before joining the Bank, he held senior executive positions at the Bank of Thailand (the central bank) and two private commercial banks in Thailand. He also worked at the Asian Development Bank as senior financial economist in the Regional and Sustainable Development Department. In addition to the Getting Finance series, he recently coauthored the book *South Asian Bond Markets: Developing Long-Term Finance for Growth* (published by the World Bank). His research interests include bank restructuring and privatization, corporate debt restructuring, and bond market development. He received a BA and an MA in economics from the University of Cambridge, United Kingdom.

Anoma Kulathunga is a PhD candidate at the George Washington University Business School in Washington, DC, and a consultant at the World Bank. Before undertaking her doctoral studies, Ms. Kulathunga had worked for the Central Bank of Sri Lanka for 15 years. She received an MA in finance from the George Washington University and an MBA from the University of Sri Jayewardenepura, Sri Lanka. She is an associate member of the Chartered Institute of Management Accountants, U.K. In addition to the Getting Finance series, she recently coauthored a chapter in *Islamic Finance: The Regulatory Challenge* (published by John Wiley & Sons). Her research interests include financial sector development, Islamic banking, worker remittances, and international banking.

Acronyms and Abbreviations

AA	articles of association
a/c	account
ADB	Asian Development Bank
Af	Afghanis
AGM	annual general meeting
AR	annual report
ATM	automated teller machine
BB	Bangladesh Bank
BIS	Bank for International Settlements
BOD	board of directors
CAR	capital adequacy ratio
CBSL	Central Bank of Sri Lanka
CD	certificate of deposit
CEO	chief executive officer
CFO	chief financial officer
CITS	check imaging and truncation system
CMDA	Capital Market Development Authority (Maldives)
CR	concentration ratio
CRIB	credit information bureau
CRR	cash reserve requirement
CSE	Colombo Stock Exchange
DAB	Da Afghanistan Bank
DFI	development finance institution
ECAI	external credit assessment institution
ECS	electronic clearing service
FSV	forced sale value
G-8	Group of Eight
G-10	Group of Ten
G-20	Group of Twenty
GAAP	generally accepted accounting principles
GDP	gross domestic product
GNI	gross national income
HHI	Herfindahl-Hirschman Index
IAS	International Accounting Standards
IASC	International Accounting Standards Committee
ICAB	Institute of Chartered Accountants of Bangladesh
IFC	International Finance Corporation (World Bank Group)
IFRS	International Financial Reporting Standard
IMF	International Monetary Fund
IPO	initial public offering

km	kilometer
km^2	square kilometers
KSE	Karachi Stock Exchange
MICR	magnetic ink character recognition
MMA	Maldives Monetary Authority
MOF	Ministry of Finance
NECS	National Electronic Clearing Service
NEFT	national electronic fund transfer
NEPSE	Nepal Stock Exchange
NIFT	National Institutional Facilitation Technologies (network)
NPL	nonperforming loan
NRB	Nepal Rastra Bank
NRs	Nepalese rupees
Nu	Bhutanese ngultrum
OECD	Organisation for Economic Co-operation and Development
OFI	other financial institution
PICG	Pakistan Institute of Corporate Governance
PRISM	Pakistan Real Time Interbank Settlement Mechanism
PRs	Pakistan rupees
PSD	Payment Systems Department
RBI	Reserve Bank of India
Rf	Maldivian rufiyaa
RMA	Royal Monetary Authority of Bhutan
ROSC	Report on the Observance of Standards and Codes
Rs	Indian rupees
RTGS	real-time gross settlement
SAARC	South Asian Association for Regional Cooperation
SBP	State Bank of Pakistan
SEANZA	South East Asia, New Zealand, and Australia
SEBON	Securities Board of Nepal
SEC	Securities and Exchange Commission
SECP	Securities and Exchange Commission of Pakistan
SLIPS	Sri Lanka Interbank Payment System
SL Rs	Sri Lanka rupees
SME	small and medium-size enterprise
SWIFT	Society for Worldwide Interbank Financial Telecommunications
Tk	Bangladesh taka
TOR	terms of reference

Exchange rates for South Asian currencies

Country	US$1 equivalent
Afghanistan	50.00 Afghanis (Af)
Bangladesh	68.80 taka (Tk)
Bhutan	48.03 Indian rupees (Rs) 48.03 ngultrum (Nu)
India	48.03 Indian rupees (Rs)
Maldives	12.80 rufiyaa (Rf)
Nepal	77.00 Nepalese rupees (NRs)
Pakistan	82.90 Pakistan rupees (PRs)
Sri Lanka	114.80 Sri Lanka rupees (SL Rs)
European Union countries	0.68 euro (€)

Source: XE, http://www.xe.com/ (accessed September 19, 2009).

1

Introduction

The recent global financial meltdown was a revelation in one sense. Before the crisis there had been a belief that banks could never fail, a belief that encouraged overleveraging and excessive risk taking. The complexity of financial instruments, opaqueness of transactions, and sophistication of modeling techniques used by developed country financial institutions all combined to conceal the hollowness of their success. Many financial institutions largely ignored regulatory requirements or preempted them through the use of complex instruments and methods, while risk taking caused profits to rocket to unimaginable levels. Regulatory arbitrage became rampant in this environment. While financial institutions were in a mode of overexpansion, regulators visibly failed to enforce regulations—and the financial institutions took advantage of the regulatory anarchy. All this was an eye-opener for regulators in South Asia, as regulatory lapses and lack of enforcement can lead to potential instability in financial systems.

The ensuing crisis prompted an immediate reassessment of the regulatory framework and policies governing financial systems. A consensus emerged that greater market discipline and proactive supervisory regimes were essential to restore stability and confidence in financial systems and minimize systemic risks to national economies and the global economy.

For financial systems in developing economies, even those not directly affected by the crisis, the operating environment has changed significantly. As developed countries overhaul their regulatory and supervisory systems, they are changing international standards and practices. In response to the global changes taking place, developing countries too are redesigning regulatory frameworks and revamping policies. Thus, even the least affected financial systems are undertaking systemic changes to realign with the global market. Financial regulators in the developing world have expanded their resources and sharpened their tools. They are evaluating their supervisory systems, tightening their guidelines, monitoring the stability of the financial system, and taking prompt corrective measures where necessary.

Against this backdrop, the fifth edition of *Getting Finance in South Asia* provides a wealth of information for policy makers engaged in managing the financial crisis and formulating appropriate responses. This series stems from a regional initiative of the World Bank to develop standardized indicators for measuring the performance and soundness of financial sectors in South Asia. The previous editions included micro indicators to assess the development of the commercial banking sector through six dimensions—access to finance, performance and efficiency, financial stability, market concentration and competitiveness, capital market development, and corporate governance. The earlier editions also provided a time-series analysis, rankings by indicators of financial soundness, and a tool for benchmarking against selected high-income Organisation for Economic Co-operation and Development (OECD) member and nonmember economies and a comparator group of Asian economies (see World Bank 2004, 2005b, 2006d; Sophastienphong and Kulathunga 2008).

This fifth edition, in addition to updating the existing Getting Finance Indicators, provides a better assessment of financial stability and development in the region by introducing two additional dimensions—payment systems development and savings mobilization. More important, it includes data for three additional countries—Afghanistan, Bhutan, and Maldives—and thus for the first time encompasses the entire South Asian region. The report evaluates key prudential guidelines issued by the regulatory authority of each country to assess the comparability of data as well as to shed light on the country's level of regulatory development. It also expands the group of benchmark economies to allow comparison with diverse economies in Asia as well as the Western hemisphere. And it includes a special write-up on how South Asian countries and commercial banking sectors are managing the impact of the global financial crisis and economic slowdown.

Development Dimensions and Micro Indicators

The study analyzes indicators under eight development dimensions—access to finance, performance and efficiency, financial stability, capital market development, market concentration and competitiveness, payment systems development, savings mobilization, and corporate governance. For the first seven dimensions, aggregate financial ratios are collected over eight years, 2001–08, from the commercial banking sector of each country. Each of these dimensions is represented by six micro indicators. For the eighth dimension, corporate governance, a questionnaire was developed to evaluate such issues as ownership structure and influence of external stakeholders, investor rights and relations, transparency and disclosure, and board structure and effectiveness.

Comparability of the data is ensured to some extent by a compilation guide setting out definitions and concepts for compilers as well as for readers (see chapter 7). The definitions and rationale for the indicators used in previous editions remain the same.

Access to Finance

Access to financial services is important in raising the standard of living of poor people and underserved segments of society. In almost every part of the world, limited access to finance is considered a key constraint to private sector growth (see Beck, Demirgüç-Kunt, and Martinez Peria 2005). This is especially true in developing countries, where poor people have little influence over policy reforms and financial sector development thus often disproportionately benefits the rich.

In countries seeking to develop financial markets, it is important to measure and monitor the level of access to finance. The resulting knowledge provides a more balanced picture of financial outreach and, thus, helps policy makers and regulatory authorities better target their development efforts.

Initially, the study is analyzing access to finance using data relating to providers of finance (supply-side data). Building a more complete set of data would require collecting demand-side data as well, but this has been ruled out by time and resource constraints. Access to finance is measured using the following six micro indicators:[1]

- Demographic branch penetration (branches per 100,000 people)
- Demographic ATM penetration (automated teller machines [ATMs] per 100,000 people)
- Deposit accounts per 1,000 people
- Loan accounts per 1,000 people
- Geographic branch penetration (branches per 1,000 square kilometers)
- Geographic ATM penetration (ATMs per 1,000 square kilometers)

Demographic penetration indicates the availability of financial services to a given number of people. Geographic penetration indicates physical access to financial services in a given geographic area. And deposit and loan ratios show the use of such services.

Performance and Efficiency

The efficiency of banks is important for the robustness and resilience of the financial sector. The study uses traditional measures of bank efficiency to assess returns efficiency and cost efficiency.

Two of the most popular measures of efficiency are used to assess the scope for banks' earnings to offset losses relative to capital or assets, the sustainability of their capital position, and their efficiency in using capital or assets:

- Return on equity
- Return on assets

Two ratios measure banks' efficiency in terms of staff and operating expenses:

- Staff cost ratio (personnel expenses as a percentage of operating expenses)
- Operating cost ratio (operating expenses as a percentage of net interest earnings)

In addition, two ratios measure the earning strength and overall operating efficiency of the banking sector:

- Net interest margin (net interest earnings as a percentage of the average value of total assets)
- Recurring earning power (preprovision profits as a percentage of the average value of total assets)

Financial Stability

Maintaining stability in a financial system is key to achieving price stability and sustainable economic growth. In a stable financial system, markets function without disruptions, financial institutions can operate efficiently, and asset prices are realistic. To measure the stability of financial systems, the study uses ratios on capital adequacy, asset quality, and liquidity.

The two capital adequacy ratios measure the capacity of financial institutions to absorb losses and thus indicate their financial strength:

- Capital adequacy ratio (regulatory capital funds as a percentage of risk-weighted assets)
- Leverage ratio (total equity as a percentage of total on–balance sheet assets)

Two ratios measure banks' asset quality in terms of credit risk:

- Gross nonperforming loans (NPLs) ratio (gross NPLs as a percentage of total advances)
- Provisions to nonperforming loans ratio (loan loss provisions as a percentage of gross NPLs)

Finally, two ratios measure banks' vulnerability to loss of funds and liquidity mismatch in terms of liquidity risk:

- Liquid assets ratio (liquid assets as a percentage of total assets)
- Liquid assets to liabilities ratio (liquid assets as a percentage of liquid liabilities)

The study does not attempt to measure market risk, a third source of vulnerability, because of the lack of data across countries and over a reasonable period—a problem encountered in compiling data for previous editions.

Capital Market Development

The development of capital markets is a powerful indicator of the depth of the financial sector. By allocating funds for viable investment projects, healthy capital markets diversify the channels of financial intermediation, providing a counterweight to the banking business. Bond markets provide an alternative source of long-term finance for borrowers and allow lenders to convert illiquid assets into tradable securities. An active bond market allows credit risk to be spread over a wide range of investors and provides up-to-date information about a market player's creditworthiness. An active stock market suggests strong economic and institutional fundamentals.

To measure the level of capital market development in terms of depth, efficiency, and liquidity, the study uses the following ratios:

- Domestic bond market to equity market capitalization ratio
- Domestic public bonds outstanding to GDP ratio
- Trading value of top 10 stocks ratio (trading value of top 10 stocks as a percentage of total value of shares traded)
- Stock market capitalization to GDP ratio
- Stock trading value to GDP ratio
- Stock market turnover ratio (total value of shares traded as a percentage of average stock market capitalization)

Market Concentration and Competitiveness

The study examines the market structure of the banking sector to evaluate the banking system's proneness to instability and crisis. Greater concentration in the banking industry, by reducing competition and increasing cost, leads to lower efficiency and thus higher obstacles to receiving bank financing. Yet a highly competitive banking sector might be more prone to crisis—because of increased fragility resulting from intense competition—than a more concentrated one. Thus striking the right balance matters for the optimal functioning and stability of the financial sector.

To measure market concentration and competitiveness, the study uses the Herfindahl-Hirschman Index (HHI) and three concentration ratios. As part of guidelines for horizontal mergers, the U.S. Department of Justice and Federal Trade Commission (1997) issued HHI standards that are used as a measure of market concentration by the United States and many other countries as well as the European Union.[2] The study uses three variations of the K-bank concentration ratio, which, for reasons of simplicity and limited data requirements, is among the most frequently used measures of concentration in the empirical literature (see Al-Muharrami, Matthews, and Khabari 2006). Finally, the study uses two ratios measuring the relative activity and importance of the commercial banking sector.

The six micro indicators used to measure market concentration and competitiveness are as follows:

- Herfindahl-Hirschman Index (HHI)
- K-bank concentration ratio ($k = 3$), based on assets
- K-bank concentration ratio ($k = 3$), based on deposits
- K-bank concentration ratio ($k = 3$), based on loans
- Private credit extended by banks to GDP ratio
- Commercial banking assets to GDP ratio

Payment Systems Development

Safe and efficient payment systems are critical to the effective functioning of the financial system. Payment systems are the means by which funds are transferred between banks. The most significant ones, referred to by this study as systemically important payment systems, are a major channel for the transmission of shocks across domestic and international financial systems and markets—if the systems are not properly designed, managed, and regulated. Well-designed payment systems, by contrast, can contain the transmission of shocks and limit the adverse consequences of vulnerabilities in some participating banks or other systems.[3] Robust payment systems are therefore a key to maintaining and promoting financial stability. In the past few years a broad international consensus has developed on the need to strengthen payment systems by promoting internationally accepted standards and practices for their design and operation (CPSS 2001). The six indicators selected to measure the development of payment systems are standard ones used by the Committee on Payment and Settlement Systems of the Bank for International Settlements (CPSS various years).

The first two ratios measure the importance of cash and basic monetary instruments as a means of settlement used by nonbanks relative to the size of the economy:

- Notes and coins in circulation to GDP ratio
- Narrow money supply (M1) to GDP ratio

The next two ratios measure the importance of the real-time gross settlement (RTGS) system and retail payment system as interbank fund transfer systems relative to the size of the economy:

- Value of RTGS transactions to GDP ratio
- Value of retail transactions to GDP ratio

Two other ratios measure the participation of users in the RTGS system and retail payment system, with a high concentration indicating less participation:

- RTGS concentration ratio (of the five largest participants)
- Retail payments concentration ratio (of the five largest participants)

Savings Mobilization

Financial systems that are more effective at pooling the savings of individuals can profoundly affect economic development. Besides having a direct effect on capital accumulation, better savings mobilization can improve resource allocation and boost technological innovation (Levine 1999). The growth of output of any economy depends on capital accumulation, which in turn requires investment and an equivalent amount of savings to match it. Two of the most important issues in development economics, and for developing countries, are how to stimulate investment and how to bring about a higher level of saving to fund the increased investment (Thirlwall 2002).

The study uses six indicators to assess savings mobilization:

- Broad money supply (M2) to GDP ratio (an indicator of financial deepening)
- Real deposit interest rate (nominal deposit rate adjusted for inflation)
- Gross domestic savings to GDP ratio
- Reserve money to total deposits ratio (an indicator of financial intermediaries' efficiency)
- Loan to deposit ratio
- Worker remittances to GDP ratio

For all except the efficiency measure (reserve money to total deposits ratio) and the loan to deposit ratio, an increase in value would be expected to have a positive impact on savings.

Corporate Governance

Sound corporate governance creates an environment that promotes banking efficiency, mitigates financial risks, and increases the stability and therefore the credibility of financial institutions. Developing countries have much to gain by improving their corporate governance standards, still mostly in the development stage. The basic principles of sound corporate governance are the same everywhere: fairness, transparency, accountability, and responsibility. These are the minimum standards that provide legitimacy to banks, reduce vulnerability to financial crisis, and broaden and deepen access to capital.

Corporate governance scoring is challenging and must be approached with care. Unlike other forms of financial analysis, where quantitative measures can provide "hard" benchmarks, assessment of corporate governance is a largely qualitative exercise (see Standard & Poor's 2004). To assess corporate governance, the study developed a questionnaire on ownership structure and influence of external stakeholders, investor rights, transparency and disclosure, and board structure and effectiveness. The questionnaire is based on the good governance practices outlined by the OECD (see table 7.1 in chapter 7). Also underlying the questionnaire is a guidance paper issued in February 2006 by the Basel Committee on Banking Supervision, articulating eight principles to enhance corporate governance in banking and to guide the actions of the directors, managers, and supervisors of a diverse range of banks (see table 7.2 in chapter 7).[4]

Because the assessment of corporate governance is based on a series of straightforward questions, no definitions or guidelines are provided in the compilation guide for the questions or the resulting indicators. And because the collection of data for the analysis is confined to the simple questionnaire, the observations on corporate governance in this report should be viewed as preliminary at best.

The Methodology

This edition of *Getting Finance in South Asia*, like the previous ones, compiles annual aggregate data on the commercial banking sector of each country covered—this time for eight years, 2001–08. It assesses the development and soundness of financial sectors in South Asia through time-series analysis for each country, benchmark comparisons, and country rankings on financial soundness.

The impetus for the series came from the World Bank's identification of stable and efficient banking systems as essential for achieving the objectives of Country Assistance Strategies in South Asia. Standardized indicators to measure the vulnerabilities of the region's financial systems had not been fully developed. Thus, in 2002 the Poverty Reduction, Economic Management, Finance and Private Sector Development Department of the World Bank's South Asia Region launched a regional initiative to develop such indicators.

The first two editions used the indicators developed to analyze the financial performance and soundness of commercial banks, development banks, and nonbank financial institutions in five South Asian countries—Bangladesh, India, Nepal, Pakistan, and Sri Lanka. These editions provided time-series financial data, international best practices, and in-depth analysis of prudential norms—information useful to regulatory authorities in undertaking regional comparisons as well as comparisons with international norms (see World Bank 2004, 2005b). The third edition provided more focused analysis of the commercial banking sector. In addition, it used the financial and corporate governance indicators, now called the Getting Finance Indicators, to rank the South Asian countries on the basis of their financial soundness (see World Bank 2006d). The fourth edition added two more development dimensions and provided an international perspective through benchmark indicators for selected high-income OECD member and nonmember economies and a comparator group of Asian economies (see Sophastienphong and Kulathunga 2008).

This fifth edition, undertaken in the wake of the global financial crisis, has further broadened the assessment. Besides adding the three remaining South Asian countries and two more development dimensions, this edition expands the group of benchmark economies (box 1.1) and provides a comparison of key prudential norms and developments in such policy areas as corporate governance, payment systems, and implementation of the Basel II capital framework. It also provides

Box 1.1 Developing Benchmarks

Benchmarking is a useful diagnostic tool. By comparing data across countries, benchmarking makes it possible to identify gaps in performance as well as in guidelines. It also fosters healthy competition. The results of a benchmarking exercise can help channel resources efficiently to focused remedial action that improves systems and their performance.

To provide benchmarks for the South Asian countries, the previous edition used selected high-income OECD member and nonmember economies: Australia; Canada; Hong Kong, China; New Zealand; Singapore; the United Kingdom; and the United States. The choice of economies was based on two considerations: to include standard-setting countries (in the case of the OECD member countries) and to include members of the SEANZA (South East Asia, New Zealand, and Australia) group (in the case of the nonmember economies).[a] The choice was also influenced by the availability of data.

This edition expands the group of benchmark economies by adding China, France, Germany, Italy, Japan, the Republic of Korea, Malaysia, and Thailand. France, Germany, and Italy are included to provide comparisons with members of the European Union, while China, Japan, the Republic of Korea, Malaysia, and Thailand are added to strengthen the representation of high-growth Asian comparator economies.

a. SEANZA was formed to promote cooperation among central banks by providing intensive, systematic training courses for their staff. The original members were the central banks of Australia, India, New Zealand, Pakistan, and Sri Lanka. Joining later were those of Bangladesh; China; Hong Kong, China; Indonesia; the Islamic Republic of Iran; Japan; the Republic of Korea; Malaysia; Macao, China; Mongolia; Nepal; Papua New Guinea; the Philippines; Singapore; and Thailand.

composite five-year average country rankings and yearly country rankings on the financial soundness index for 2004–08 (see chapter 8 for details on the methodology). And, like the previous edition, the book includes a CD-ROM containing financial data from the eight South Asian countries for 2001–08 for use in analysis.

The rankings and analysis presented in this report are based mainly on data gathered from each country. The findings, interpretations, and conclusions therefore depend on the accuracy of these data as well as on the indicators selected. Also important to note is that countries are ranked using a simple averaging method, giving equal weight to each of the indicators included in the financial soundness ranking. Although weighting the indicators on the basis of objective criteria would have enhanced the value of the rankings, this was ruled out by time and resource constraints and by the need to review simple ranking results over a reasonable period to determine their usefulness.

While future editions will attempt to apply more complex ranking methods using weights, at this stage the rankings should be viewed as the results of a purely data-driven exercise. Even so, the results of the analysis point to the importance, in promoting and maintaining a stable financial system—a sound prudential supervisory framework; excellent corporate governance practices; broad access to finance; efficient payment systems; strong savings mobilization; and stable, efficient, and well-performing banks.

Interpretation of Ranks

Countries in South Asia began financial sector reforms as early as the 1980s. Early reform programs included initiatives to privatize and restructure public sector banks and develop capital markets. These were followed by reforms to liberalize the financial sector, strengthen prudential norms, revamp laws, build regulatory capacity, improve corporate governance, and develop market infrastructure and payment systems. While countries have undertaken varying degrees of reform, in most cases the reform programs have strengthened their financial systems and especially their banking sectors. Banks have become dominant players in the region's financial sectors and strong contributors to economic growth.

Many issues remain. But countries in South Asia continue to make financial sector reform a policy priority and are moving in the right direction. They also continue to adapt the reform process to emerging circumstances—as they did after the Asian financial crisis. In the wake of that crisis, South Asian countries accelerated their reform programs. They remained mindful of the fact that financial crises can occur at any time—and responded quickly to the current global financial crisis.

As the region's countries continue to respond to ongoing developments, they will need all the information they can get to evaluate the performance and soundness of their banking systems. Rankings can help countries gauge their position relative to others in the region and identify their strengths as well as areas needing improvement. This report ranks South Asian countries on each development dimension over the five-year period 2004–08 and overall (see chapter 4 for details).

In the overall ranking, India retains first place, reflecting its strong leadership in the growth and development of the region's financial sectors. Sri Lanka follows in second place, and Pakistan in third. Bangladesh and Maldives share fourth place, followed by Bhutan, Nepal, and Afghanistan. In the rankings on dimensions, low ranks are sometimes due to data being unavailable. This is especially so for Afghanistan, for which no data are available for one dimension—capital market development—and only partial data for the others.

Maldives ranks first in access to finance with a composite percentage score of 94 percent. It displaces Sri Lanka, which ranked first in the previous edition with a score of 93 percent. As explained in this report, however, the results for Maldives on the availability of bank branches and ATMs are skewed because the indicators fail to take into account the geographic dispersion of its population among atolls. Recognizing that access to finance remains a concern for its population, Maldives is initiating a mobile banking project. Sri Lanka ranks second overall in access to finance and leads in the use of financial services. Following in the ranking are India, Bangladesh, Bhutan and Pakistan (tied for fifth), and Nepal. Access is lowest in Afghanistan.

Maldives also ranks at the top in performance and efficiency (with a score of 93 percent), thanks to high values for returns, the net interest margin, and recurring earning power. These ratios have been mostly on the decline since 2006, however, a matter for concern. Ranking second is Pakistan (which secured first place in the previous evaluation with 80 percent), followed by Sri Lanka, Bhutan, Nepal, India, Bangladesh, and Afghanistan. Nepal saw a significant shift in 2008 as its banking sector finally emerged from a situation of negative equity. Banks in South Asia continue to enjoy high returns because of wide interest rate spreads, but with the economic slowdown and rising levels of nonperforming loans, these returns can be expected to decline. If nonperforming loans were to increase in the coming years, another concern for some countries would be the management of already high operating costs.

India once again leads the region in financial stability, with a score of 82 percent (down from 89 percent in the previous evaluation). The country's strengths are capital adequacy and better credit quality, resulting in lower levels of nonperforming loans compared with the rest of the region. Bhutan and Pakistan share second place, followed by Sri Lanka, Maldives, Bangladesh, Afghanistan, and Nepal. Bhutan recorded gains in its liquidity and capital ratios to secure the second-place ranking shared with Pakistan. Provisions for nonperforming loans are a concern for Maldives. They are also a concern for Nepal, where provisions fall far short of what is needed to cover the existing nonperforming loans. Afghanistan reported lower nonperforming ratios and high provisions. Liquidity has also been a concern for most countries in recent years, though it has been managed to some extent by their regulatory authorities.

India leads in capital market development with a score of 97 percent (up from the previous evaluation's score of 91 percent). Pakistan ranks second, followed by Sri Lanka, Bangladesh, Nepal, Maldives, Bhutan, and Afghanistan. Capital markets remain strongly in need of development. India has the region's most developed capital market. Both bond and equity markets are developed and provide long-term funding for companies. But in most of the region's countries banks still serve as the main funding source, even for long-term projects. Afghanistan lacks both a bond market and an equity market, and the central bank (Da Afghanistan Bank) operates a capital notes market for the government's funding needs. The country relies heavily on external funds for all its development efforts. Bhutan and Maldives have very small stock markets, and the Maldivian bond market has had just three issues by one company. Pakistan weathered a stock market crisis. The region's bond markets are dominated by government bonds or treasury bills, with corporate bond markets still at a nascent stage. Only India has been able to list government securities on its stock exchanges and benchmark on the yield curves.

India again ranks first in market concentration and competitiveness, with a score of 91 percent (up slightly from its previous score of 89 percent). Bangladesh ranks second, followed by Nepal, Pakistan, Maldives, Sri Lanka, Bhutan, and Afghanistan. In India, the top three banks hold less than 31 percent of assets, deposits, and loans, while in Sri Lanka these shares are around 50–55 percent. In Bhutan, with only two banks, market concentration is extremely high. Afghanistan ranks last because of lack of data. Nepal secures third place because of the influx of new banks. But while the new entrants have reduced concentration, they have not improved access or stability. Moreover, Nepal is faced with a situation in which too many banks are competing for deposits and loans, and heavy lending in the real estate sector has created a price bubble. To curb new entry, the central bank has temporarily stopped issuing banking licenses (six new licenses were issued in 2009, however). Another concern for countries is the increase in private credit extended by banks, which could pose credit risks. The previous edition of this report cautioned that rapid expansion of bank credit, if not coupled with systems for managing credit risk, would make banks vulnerable if economic activity were to slow. Today's economic slowdown was not on the horizon at that time. Now that it is a reality, banks should review their credit policies and existing loan portfolios carefully to ensure that credit risk is minimized. This situation is a concern for both Bhutan and Nepal, where credit bubbles could be in the making. In most countries banks have tightened their credit policies and, rather than profit seeking, have taken steps to consolidate their asset portfolios.

In payment systems development, Sri Lanka ranks at the top with a score of 94 percent. India comes second, followed by Pakistan, Bhutan, Bangladesh, Afghanistan, Nepal, and Maldives. For Bangladesh, Nepal, and Maldives, a lack of most of the data required affected their places in the ranking. While all countries in the region have retail payment systems for checks and other payment instruments, only Sri Lanka, India, and Pakistan have advanced payment systems. All three have real-time gross settlement systems for large-value, time-critical payments. Payment systems development, important in ensuring financial stability, is evaluated for the first time in this edition.

In savings mobilization, another dimension included for the first time, India leads with a score of 80 percent. Bangladesh ranks second, followed by Sri Lanka, Nepal, Pakistan, Bhutan, Maldives, and Afghanistan. Domestic savings can help sustain growth at times that external funding opportunities become uncertain. An important source in South Asia is worker remittances, which have continued unabated even in the economic downturn. Nepal has the highest remittances relative to GDP, while Maldives has negligible inflows. Afghanistan and Bhutan provided no data on remittances. As a result of persistent inflation, real deposit interest rates remain negative in all countries except India, which disrupts the savings market. All countries in the region have the potential to increase their savings rates.

In corporate governance, Pakistan ranks at the top with a score of 87 percent (up slightly from its previous score of 84 percent). India and Sri Lanka share second place, followed in the ranking by Bangladesh, Nepal, Afghanistan, Bhutan, and Maldives. Pakistan has issued comprehensive guidelines. Maldives did not supply some of the required data, which may have affected its place in the ranking. The questionnaire is based mostly on the availability of policy regulations, guidelines, and statutes. It does not show compliance and enforcement. Thus, it could be stated that these are the main areas on which the authorities should focus while also ensuring that the gaps in regulations and guidelines identified in the country analyses are corrected. Government influence in banking operations is another point of concern, since state-controlled public sector banks hold a significant share of banking assets in most countries. Other areas of concern are stakeholder rights, disclosure of beneficial ownership, minority shareholder rights, and adherence to international accounting and auditing standards.

The Role of Microfinance in South Asia

As in the previous edition, the analysis in this report is limited in coverage to commercial banks and ignores a range of other deposit-taking financial institutions, such as cooperative banks, microfinance institutions, and post office savings schemes. The findings on access to finance are therefore restricted to the commercial banking sector. Yet the microfinance movement is a significant force in financial inclusion in South Asia, providing access to financial services for a large number of people (table 1.1).

Recognizing this, most South Asian countries have regulations or guidelines in place for microfinance, and some have laws in the draft stage. Pakistan was the first country in South Asia to introduce a specialized law for microfinance, the Microfinance Ordinance of 2001, which paved the way for the creation of a microbanking industry and allowed commercialization of microfinance. The

Table 1.1 Selected Indicators on Microfinance in South Asia

	Afghanistan	Bangladesh	India	Nepal	Pakistan	Sri Lanka
Microfinance						
Institutions	10	274	288	47	28	23
Borrowers (thousands)	228	24,757	10,886	707	926	1,422
Borrowers as % of population	1	17	1	3	1	7
Borrowers as % of poor population	—	35	3	8	2	29
Credit unions						
Penetration (%)[a]	0.03	0.2	2.8	1.0	—	6.1
Members	4,766	157,047	20,000,000	172,830	—	860,611
Savings (US$ millions)	0.29	23.50	25,940	30.0	—	34.99
Loans (US$ millions)	0.81	19.93	15,770	27.0	—	23.25
Assets (US$ millions)	0.85	28.58	31,480	34.0	—	—
MSMEs (per 10,000 people)[b]	—	1	—	—	19	6

Source: Consultative Group to Assist the Poor (CGAP), "Country Maps," http://www.cgap.org/p/site/c/template.rc/1.26.2301/ (accessed September 15, 2009).
Note: No data available for Bhutan and Maldives.
a. Number of credit union members divided by a country's economically active population.
b. MSMEs = micro, small, and medium-size enterprises.
— = not available.

State Bank of Pakistan was the first South Asian central bank to issue regulations on branchless banking, aimed at extending the outreach of microfinance to underserved regions through cost-efficient, agent-based banking. India has introduced a draft microfinance law, while Sri Lanka has drafted one. Bangladesh passed the Microcredit Regulatory Authority Act in 2006.

Endnotes

1. In measuring access to finance, the analysis is confined largely to bank branches and ATMs. Throughout the period 2004–08 new financial services were provided in South Asia through mobile banking and agency banking and, more recently, by telecommunications and card service providers, some of which may have been routed through bank branches. It is important to note these new services and instruments even though their impact is not measured through these ratios.
2. HHI is calculated by squaring the market share of each bank and summing the squares. According to the guidelines, a banking industry is considered to be unconcentrated if HHI is less than 1,000, somewhat concentrated if HHI is between 1,000 and 1,800, and highly concentrated if HHI is more than 1,800.
3. For example, during the recent financial crisis almost all payment and settlement systems in the Group of Ten (G-10) countries showed great resilience and performed well even in the face of liquidity shortages in the market and extreme transaction volumes.
4. These guidelines focus on the fiduciary responsibilities of boards of directors and were updated in 2008/09 to strengthen the governance principles.

Part I

Analysis

2

Prudential Regulations for Banks in South Asia

Assessing the health of a financial system on the basis of financial indicators is fraught with technical and practical difficulties. The rules on loan classification and loan loss provisions vary from country to country, as do the capital adequacy guidelines—and this variation leads to differences in results. The data used for comparison are not always based on the same periods. The definitions and concepts underlying the data may differ from country to country—and while the compilation guide prepared for this study addresses this constraint, it is hard to ensure that the central banks submitting data strictly follow the guide. In addition, accounting principles and practices vary across countries. All South Asian countries have taken steps in recent years to bring their local accounting standards and practices into line with the International Accounting Standards, but the extent to which they actually follow these standards varies.

For all these reasons, it is important to compare key prudential guidelines in place in South Asian countries, to better understand the environment in which their commercial banks operate. This chapter reviews the main prudential guidelines implemented by the regulator of commercial banks in each country, which in all cases remains the central bank (table 2.1).

The review shows that South Asian authorities have made progress in aligning their prudential norms with international best practices. And as could be expected, countries with more sophisticated economic and banking environments have moved ahead. But the process is an evolving one. Capital adequacy norms need to be reexamined in light of the high-risk environment in which banks operate today. Credit risk management needs to be tightened through more stringent rules for nonperforming loans and provisioning. Risk management policies also need to be strengthened in such areas as market risk and interest rate risk. Most South Asian countries have been lagging in reporting and working to mitigate operational risks. Besides natural disasters, potential operational risks that could bring instability include fraud, human error, hardware and software problems, breakdown of processes and procedures, and lack of infrastructure for payments and settlements. The core banking operations of banks usually entail such market and operational risks, and it is to accommodate these risks that the Basel II Capital Accord requires that additional capital be maintained. In addition, liquidity

Table 2.1 Commercial Bank Regulator in South Asian Countries

Country	Regulator (central bank)
Afghanistan	Da Afghanistan Bank (DAB)
Bangladesh	Bangladesh Bank (BB)
Bhutan	Royal Monetary Authority of Bhutan (RMA)
India	Reserve Bank of India (RBI)
Maldives	Maldives Monetary Authority (MMA)
Nepal	Nepal Rastra Bank (NRB)
Pakistan	State Bank of Pakistan (SBP)
Sri Lanka	Central Bank of Sri Lanka (CBSL)

Source: Authors.

management needs to be improved, especially in foreign currency operations—an area that will be covered in a future edition of this report. South Asian authorities are aware of the need to further strengthen prudential regulations and are revising them in stages (see chapter 9 for a summary of developments in prudential regulations in each country in recent years).

Regulation and supervision are of primary importance in ensuring the stability of a country's financial system. Economic conditions have a heavy impact on banking sector operations, and an economic downturn can lead to a banking crisis, as occurred with the recent financial crisis. Efficient supervision techniques can help identify unstable situations through close monitoring and ensure that early preventive measures are taken. Benchmarking prudential norms against international standards can help bring greater stability and market discipline to financial institutions. At the same time, however, authorities need to be mindful that these standards are not designed to be a panacea.

Capital Adequacy

Regulators in South Asia have introduced prudential norms based on the Basel guidelines on capital adequacy, and they have been tightening these norms to bring them into line with international best practices. In accordance with the Basel guidelines, commercial banks in South Asia are required to maintain minimum capital ranging from 9 percent of risk-weighted assets in India (on a nonconsolidated basis) to 12 percent in Afghanistan and Maldives (see appendix table A1.1).[1] All South Asian countries use a minimum capital adequacy requirement that is higher than the international best practice of 8 percent.

To calculate capital adequacy, in most cases capital funds are divided into Tier 1 (core) capital and Tier 2 (supplementary) capital. In India, Pakistan, and Sri Lanka capital funds are further divided into Tier 3 capital, which consists of short-term subordinated debt that may be used for the sole purpose of meeting a proportion of the capital requirements for market risk. Tier 1 capital is required to be maintained at a minimum of 50 percent of total capital in all countries. In Afghanistan, India, Maldives, and Nepal the minimum for Tier 1 capital is set at 6 percent of total risk-weighted assets, while in Pakistan no limit is specified other than the requirement that Tier 2 and Tier 3 capital combined cannot exceed Tier 1 capital.[2] In Bangladesh, Bhutan, and Sri Lanka the Tier 1 capital adequacy requirement is 5 percent of risk-weighted assets.

South Asian regulators have also prescribed minimum paid-up capital for commercial banks. These amounts range from about US$6.25 million for Bhutanese banks to US$72.5 million for Pakistan banks. Bangladesh has different requirements for mainstream commercial banks (US$29.5 million) and Islamic commercial banks (US$14.5 million). Mainstream commercial banks in Bangladesh also have to maintain a total capital balance of not less than US$59 million.[3]

In all South Asian countries, Tier 1 capital includes paid-up common equity shares, share premium, retained earnings, statutory reserves, and general reserves (see appendix table A1.2). Such capital is considered freely and immediately available to meet claims against the bank. But there are also variations among countries in the composition of core capital that are worth noting. Bangladesh, Maldives, and Sri Lanka allow minority interests in subsidiaries to be counted. Bangladesh and Nepal allow dividend equalization funds to be part of core capital. India permits capital reserves representing surplus from the sale of assets to be eligible as Tier 1 capital. Both India and Sri Lanka allow specified perpetual debt instruments to be included, with India limiting this allowance to 15 percent of the previous year's Tier 1 capital. Nepal and Pakistan permit bonus share reserves. Nepal also includes capital redemption reserves, while Sri Lanka allows after-tax surplus from the sale of fixed and long-term investments. Common deductions from Tier 1 capital include goodwill, intangible assets, and equity investments in subsidiaries.

Tier 2, or supplementary, capital commonly consists of undisclosed reserves, revaluation reserves, general loan loss provisions, and hybrid instruments (such as unsecured subordinated debt and preference shares) that combine the characteristics of debt and equity and are available to meet losses. As with core capital, however, the definition differs across countries. Afghanistan, Bhutan, and Maldives include profits for the current year as part of Tier 2 capital. Bangladesh, Bhutan, Nepal, and Pakistan allow the exchange equalization or adjustment reserves to be counted as Tier 2 capital, while Bhutan allows research and development funds. India permits excess provisions toward depreciation on investment, and Bhutan, India, and Nepal allow investment fluctuation reserves. Sri Lanka allows minority interests arising from preference shares issued by subsidiaries. Bhutan, Maldives, and Pakistan do not allow preference shares to count as supplementary capital.

In all South Asian countries, Tier 2 capital cannot exceed 100 percent of Tier 1 capital, while in Pakistan and Sri Lanka Tier 2 and Tier 3 capital combined cannot exceed 100 percent of Tier 1 capital. All except Afghanistan and Bangladesh limit subordinated debt to 50 percent of Tier 1 capital. In Bangladesh, Pakistan, and Sri Lanka, up to 50 percent of the revaluation reserve arising from revaluation of bank assets is taken as Tier 2 capital, while in Nepal the asset revaluation reserve is allowed only up to 2 percent of total Tier 2 capital inclusive of this reserve. India allows 45 percent. All countries except Bangladesh limit general provisions to 1.25 percent of risk-weighted assets.

Implementation of the Basel II Capital Adequacy Framework

When the Basel Committee on Banking Supervision (of the Bank for International Settlements) published *International Convergence of Capital Measurement and Capital Standards: A Revised Framework* (commonly known as the Basel II Capital Accord) in June 2004, countries not part of the Group of Ten (G-10) were not expected to make adoption of the new framework a priority. The Basel II framework is aimed at building on a solid foundation of prudent capital regulation, supervision, and market discipline and further enhancing risk management and financial stability. Thus, the Basel Committee on Banking Supervision (2004a) encourages each national supervisor to carefully consider the benefits of the new framework in the context of its own domestic banking system and in developing a timetable and approach for implementation.

Afghanistan, Bhutan, and Maldives have not yet implemented Basel II, but they are compliant with Basel I. Bangladesh, India, Nepal, Pakistan, and Sri Lanka have embraced Basel II and are at various stages of implementation.[4] The differences in the pace at which South Asian countries are moving ahead with the adoption of Basel II standards, along with differences in the capital guidelines adopted by each country (see appendix table A1.3), lead to differences in the capital adequacy ratio. Countries that have adopted Basel II have had lower capital adequacy ratios, primarily as a result of greater capital charges for operational and market risk. Differences in the methods used to calculate the capital charges add to the disparities. These differences should be kept in mind when comparing the capital adequacy ratios of the countries.

In Afghanistan, Basel I is the current capital adequacy norm. The regulatory capital ratio for all banking institutions is above the minimum regulatory threshold (12 percent of risk-weighted assets). In planning for the transition to Basel II, Da Afghanistan Bank and the banking community will need to work together to address challenges, both tactical and operational. These include harmonizing goals; identifying and developing risk parameters, risk measurements, and ratings; improving lending processes; and addressing legal and regulatory preconditions and issues relating to accounting, disclosure, data management, supervisory resources, and training.

Bangladesh is materially compliant with Basel I, and in January 2009, Bangladesh Bank issued revised capital guidelines in line with Basel II. Under these guidelines, credit ratings for the purpose of the capital adequacy ratio are to be determined on the basis of risk profile assessments by external credit assessment institutions. While banks could use both the Basel I and Basel II frameworks to calculate their capital adequacy for 2009, beginning in January 2010 they will have to apply the Basel II framework alone. Under the initial implementation of Basel II, banks are to follow the Standardized Approach to calculate capital requirements for credit risk, the Standardized (Rule-Based) Approach to calculate those for market risk, and the Basic Indicator Approach to calculate those for operational risk. To ensure a successful migration to the new framework, however, both the regulatory authorities and the banking sector will need to address such issues as lack of capacity in credit rating agencies, gaps in the regulations for such agencies, lack of information, and the need to strengthen risk management tools and capabilities.

Bhutan uses Basel I as its capital adequacy norm. The country has not yet made any headway toward implementation of Basel II, given the size and functions of its banks and lack of expertise. But the Royal Monetary Authority of Bhutan is encouraging banks to develop their own internal credit rating systems and risk management techniques. Some financial institutions are already strengthening their internal controls and systems. One bank has formed a department to assess and manage risk.

India has issued comprehensive guidelines for implementation of Basel II. Foreign banks operating in India and Indian banks with operations outside the country have migrated to the Basel II framework since March 2008. All other commercial banks (except local area banks and regional rural banks) migrated to the new framework by March 2009.

All commercial banks in India (excluding local area banks and regional rural banks) are required to adopt the Standardized Approach for credit risk and the Basic Indicator Approach for operational risk. Banks are to continue to apply the Standardized Duration Approach for computing capital requirements for market risk. They need approval from the Reserve Bank of India to migrate to the Internal Ratings–Based Approach for credit risk and the Standardized Approach or Advanced Measurement Approach for operational risk. India recognizes that some challenges must be met before moving toward advanced techniques—relating mostly to issues in such areas as risk management, rating, capacity building, and corporate governance (Leeladhar 2007). The Reserve Bank of India is working toward addressing these issues.

Maldives is materially in compliance with Basel I, while Basel II remains a work in progress. The Maldives Monetary Authority issued new capital guidelines in 2009 allowing banks to apply the Basel II methods for computing capital requirements. Initially banks must use the Standardized Approach and Basic Indicator Approach to establish capital requirements (Pillar I) but must not have a leverage capital ratio less than 5.0 percent. The adequacy of a bank's capital remains subject to supervisory review (Pillar II) and market discipline (Pillar III), and higher capital levels may be required depending on the bank's risk profile and activities.[5]

Nepal issued a simplified version of the Basel II framework effective from 2008. On a trial basis and in anticipation of the transition to Basel II in 2009, banks were allowed to use Basel I in parallel with the new accord to report capital requirements. The new guidelines prescribe the use of a simplified standardized approach for credit risk, a basic indicator approach for operational risk, and an indigenous net open exchange model for market risk. This approach by Nepal Rastra Bank seems to be a practical one given the structure of banking operations in Nepal and the challenges faced by its banks, including lack of risk management tools and expertise; absence of credit rating agencies and internal ratings; and gaps in data, information, and disclosure practices. While the lack of external risk assessments means that the credit risk measurement is somewhat similar to the Basel I method, the expanded risk weights and recognition of risk mitigation techniques are welcome additions. The capital charge for operational risk is measured as a percentage of the previous three years' average income. Market risk is limited to foreign exchange risk measured by a net open position model. Although Nepal needs to address its challenges before moving toward more advanced approaches, its simplified, practical approach is a major step forward.

In Pakistan, all banks were required to adopt the Standardized Approach for credit and market risk and the Basic Indicator or Standardized Approach for operational risk beginning January 1, 2008. Banks were advised to adopt a parallel run of two years for the Internal Ratings–Based Approach on that date and to report their capital adequacy under Basel II while continuing to submit calculations based on Basel I until the State Bank of Pakistan (SBP) issues instructions to stop doing so. Banks in Pakistan have already made major advances in implementing the new framework, although many still face challenges in such areas as integrated risk management policy and collateral management. Banks have been hampered by the limited availability of external credit ratings of counterparts in Pakistan. The SBP is working with banks to meet these challenges and provide guidance.

Under the SBP's instructions, adoption of the Foundation or Advanced Internal Ratings–Based Approach for credit risk and the Internal Models Approach for market risk is optional and can be done only with prior written approval of the SBP. No bank has asked for permission to begin implementing the advanced approaches, although some of the larger banks can be expected to opt for these approaches in the next few years (SBP 2009b). Meanwhile, the SBP has required all banks to carry out internal risk ratings to force them to review their risk management systems and capabilities.

The Central Bank of Sri Lanka (CBSL) adopted the Basel II capital adequacy standards for all licensed banks effective January 2008. Accordingly, all banks are required to follow the Standardized Approach for credit risk, the Standardized Measurement Approach for market risk, and the Basic Indicator Approach for operational risk. Market risk has been incorporated into the capital adequacy ratio since 2006. By the end of June 2008 all commercial banks operating in Sri Lanka had switched to the Basel II framework. The capital adequacy ratios of the banking sector remain well above the minimum regulatory standards.

The CBSL will permit banks to shift to more advanced approaches once it ensures that they have the appropriate models and risk management systems. But issues relating to external rating agencies, risk management capacities in the banking sector, and gaps in data and information will need to be addressed first. The CBSL is addressing these issues through several efforts: implementing an integrated risk management framework for banks, issuing guidelines on maturity gap analysis, introducing regulatory limits on negative mismatches in asset and liability maturity profiles, and initiating draft guidelines on Pillar II of Basel II (CBSL, *Annual Report,* 2008).

Basel II requires that banks rate their corporate customers, and South Asian countries, especially those using advanced methods, should introduce this requirement. India has already started the process, but others have yet to follow. Basel II also requires that banks present losses due to operational risks on the basis of International Accounting Standards in their financial reporting. Banks using the Standardized Approach and those wishing to move to the Advanced Measurement Approach under Basel II should begin building up databases on operational losses and submit such data to the regulatory authorities.

While Basel II requires that loss data be reported on an International Accounting Standards basis, financial reporting standards tend to differ among South Asian countries. The central banks of Pakistan and Sri Lanka and some commercial banks in India and Maldives use International Accounting Standards. Banks in Afghanistan, which lacks a local accounting body, are required to follow International Accounting Standards. In some countries (Bangladesh, India, Nepal, and Sri Lanka), commercial banks adopt the accounting standards issued by their local accounting institution or body, which may or may not be on a par with international standards. Bhutan follows Indian accounting standards because it lacks a national accounting body.

Asset Quality

Using quantitative, time-based criteria, banks need to recognize nonperforming assets, then treat them appropriately with respect to the accrual of interest, classify them according to their ultimate collectibility, and make adequate provisions to cover potential losses on the basis of these classifications. The recognition of nonperforming assets stimulates collection efforts and helps reduce the possibility of loss.

International best practice is to classify a loan as nonperforming if the principal or interest (or both) is three months or more in arrears or if the loan continuously exceeds its approved limits (set by the lending bank, such as for value thresholds) for three months or more. Debt is classified as doubtful if past due for 3 months, substandard if past due for 6 months, and bad if past due for 12. Qualitative evaluations such as risk assessment, collateral, and repayment capacity may also cause a loan to be classified in any of these categories.

Commercial banks in South Asia classify advances that are in arrears for three months or more as nonperforming except in Afghanistan, where banks classify loans past due for two months as nonperforming. Banks across South Asia continue to classify nonperforming loans into different categories based on different time frames (see appendix table A1.4). Loans are classified in the substandard category if they are past due for a period ranging from 2–3 months in Afghanistan to 6–12 months in Sri Lanka. Loans are classified in the doubtful category if they are past due for a period ranging from 3–6 months in Afghanistan to 12–24 months in Bhutan. And loans are classified in the loss category if they are past due for a period ranging from 6 months or more in Afghanistan to 24 months or more in Bhutan. In most countries, a longer period applies under each category for long-term loans such as agricultural loans or long-term fixed loans. Regulations in all South Asian countries also require the use of qualitative criteria in the classification process.

Commercial banks in South Asia are required to classify nonperforming assets into different categories based on how long they have remained nonperforming and whether the amounts due are collectible and then to make provisions for them. All countries in the region except Afghanistan also require banks to provide for standard (or performing) loans, as part of general provisions. The rates range from 0.25 percent for standard priority sector loans in India to 5 percent for standard consumer loans in Bangladesh and unsecured consumer loans in Pakistan (see appendix table A1.5). In Afghanistan general provisions are encouraged for standard loans to nonfinancial institutions and other clients, while specific provisions of 5 percent are required for loans in the watch category (those past due for 31–60 days).

For substandard loans, provisions range from 20 percent to 25 percent. Exceptions are 5 percent for agricultural loans in Bangladesh, 6.25 percent for priority sector loans that are insured in Nepal, 10 percent for all substandard loans in India (and an additional 10 percent if unsecured), and 30 percent for high-exposure loans in Bhutan. For doubtful assets, all countries in the region except India have a 50 percent provisioning requirement. In India, provisions for doubtful assets are 100 percent of the extent to which the advance is not covered by the realizable value of the security as well as a percentage of the secured portion that depends on the period for which the advance has remained doubtful: 20 percent for up to one year, 30 percent for one to three years, and 100 percent for more than three years. Other exceptions are 5 percent for agricultural loans in Bangladesh, 12.5 percent for priority sector loans that are insured in Nepal, and 60 percent for high-exposure loans in Bhutan. For a loan in the loss category, all countries require 100 percent provisioning except Afghanistan, where the loan has to be written off in full. In India the loan has to be either written off or provided for at 100 percent. In all countries, provisioning is made after deducting the value of eligible security. The value that can be set off differs among countries.

In asset classification and provisioning South Asian banks therefore follow loan classification schedules that both differ among countries in the region and differ from international best practices. Further complicating the situation is that, contrary to international practice, classification schedules vary depending on the type of credit facility. This leniency in classification leads to lower provisioning requirements, resulting in a greater possibility of incurring losses on loans even when these requirements are met.

Income Recognition

South Asian countries have similar write-off policies. In all countries except Nepal, income on performing assets is recognized on an accrual basis, while income on nonperforming assets is realized only on a cash basis (see appendix table A1.6). In all countries, once a loan is classified as nonperforming, the interest accrued on it thereafter will be credited to an interest-in-suspense account and not credited as income; instead, the interest is recognized only on a cash basis. Further, all accrued but unpaid interest is to be reversed to an interest-in-suspense account. In Bangladesh, however, regulations do not specify whether this reversal should take place.

Write-Off Policy

The prudential regulations of Bhutan, Nepal, and Sri Lanka include no specific write-off provisions for nonperforming assets of commercial banks (see appendix table A1.7). Afghanistan requires assets in the loss category to be immediately charged off, while Maldives allows them to be written off at the end of the current calendar quarter but no later than 90 days after first being identified as a loss. Prudential regulations in Bangladesh, India, and Pakistan allow commercial banks to write off nonperforming loans at their discretion.

Exposure Limits

Banks face credit concentration risk when their credit exposures to an individual or group exceed a certain percentage of their regulatory capital. Prudential regulations set exposure limits with the aim of controlling this risk. Lower limits minimize the adverse effects of exposure and increase diversification benefits.

All South Asian countries have set detailed exposure limits in their prudential regulations, ranging from 15 percent of capital funds in Afghanistan, India, and Maldives to 50 percent of capital in Pakistan (see appendix table A1.8). In most countries the regulations also specify exceptions to the limits.

Directed Lending

Prudential regulations in Bangladesh, India, Nepal, Pakistan, and Sri Lanka clearly direct commercial banks to channel a certain portion of their credit portfolio to priority sectors (see appendix table A1.9). By contrast, the regulatory bodies in Afghanistan, Bhutan, and Maldives have issued no such guidelines. Most directed lending in developing countries is for priority sectors such as agriculture and for minority groups. Where such lending goes to low-return projects, it often results in low profitability and poor asset quality.

Liquidity

Prudential regulations in South Asia direct commercial banks to maintain certain statutory liquidity and cash reserve ratios (see appendix table A1.10). Statutory liquidity requirements range from 8 percent of total deposits in Nepal to 25 percent of average rufiyaa and foreign currency demand and time liabilities (excluding interbank liabilities and letter of credit margin deposits) in Maldives. Nepal reintroduced its statutory liquidity requirement to contain inflation. Afghanistan has two different ratios: the quick liquidity ratio and the broad liquidity ratio. Bangladesh has a statutory liquidity requirement of 18 percent for mainstream commercial banks and 10 percent for Islamic commercial banks. Cash reserve requirements range from 5 percent in Bangladesh, India, and Pakistan to 17 percent in Bhutan. In Sri Lanka, the previously high statutory reserve requirement has been gradually reduced to 7 percent.

Statutory liquidity and cash reserve requirements can have a favorable impact on banks' liquidity. But because they tie up funds, they can also have an adverse impact on banks' profitability by raising the cost of funds. In most cases, banks pass on such costs to customers. The high transaction costs that customers face as a result are among the critical obstacles to getting finance and enhancing access to finance. Statutory liquidity and cash reserve requirements are considered blunt monetary policy instruments, but with cascading effects on the transaction chain. No single ratio for statutory liquidity or cash reserves would meet the needs in all countries given the diversity in economic environments and growth capabilities. But the authorities need to be mindful of the effects of such requirements on transaction costs and access to finance and initiate action over time to reduce the ratios.

Debt Restructuring Policy

Prudential regulations for debt restructuring and rescheduling differ among the South Asian countries (see appendix table A1.11). In Afghanistan, which has issued no guidelines, banks are to follow International Accounting Standards and International Financial Reporting Standards. Bangladesh has issued guidelines on cash installments that need to be paid before restructuring is considered and has introduced a scheme for restructuring large loans. In Bhutan, restructuring is permitted only for loans that have been regularly serviced and are affected by genuine unforeseen financial constraints. India, which has issued detailed guidelines, allows restructured loans not to be classified under certain circumstances.

In Maldives, restructured loans include any new loan to repay or replace loans that are overdue, rescheduled, rolled over, or otherwise modified because of deterioration in the borrower's financial condition or an inability to repay the loan under the original terms. But all overdue interest is to be paid in cash at the time of restructuring. Nepal allows nonperforming loans to be reclassified as standard loans subject to a provision of 12.5 percent (or, for priority sector loans, 3.125 percent) and compliance with the terms of the restructured loan for two years. In Pakistan, restructured loans are to remain classified as nonperforming until the terms and conditions of the rescheduling or restructuring have been fully met for at least one year and at least 10 percent of the outstanding amount has been recovered in cash. Sri Lanka allows rescheduled loans to be reclassified as performing only if the borrower continues to comply with the terms of the rescheduling for six months.

Endnotes

1. The 12 percent capital adequacy requirement in Maldives is effective from 2009; the earlier requirement was 8 percent of risk-weighted assets. Similarly, in Pakistan the capital adequacy requirement was 8 percent of risk-weighted assets until December 2008. It was raised to 9 percent in 2009 and will be raised again, to 10 percent, in 2010.

2. In Nepal, the 6 percent Tier 1 capital adequacy requirement is effective from the 2009/10 financial year (which runs from mid-July to mid-July); previously it was 5.5 percent.

3. Minimum capital is prescribed in local currencies. The U.S. dollar equivalents are based on the conversion rates of September 19, 2009 (see the currency conversion table in the beginning of the report).

4. South Asian countries regularly exchange information on implementation of Basel II and on risk management through the SAARCFINANCE network, which operates under the South Asian Association for Regional Cooperation (SAARC), established in 1985. All eight South Asian countries are members. Their central bank governors and finance secretaries decided to establish the SAARCFINANCE network in 1998.

5. Maldives Monetary Authority, Prudential Regulation No. 01-2009 (Capital Adequacy).

3

The Getting Finance Indicators: Country Perspective

In the countries of South Asia, as in most developing countries, banks dominate the financial sector. Banking assets averaged more than 68 percent of GDP in 2008, ranging from around 14.3 percent of GDP in Afghanistan to 143.14 percent in Maldives. The region's capital markets are relatively undeveloped. The stock market is about a third of the size of the banking sector in all South Asian countries except India (where stock market capitalization is 116 percent of banking assets) and Pakistan (70 percent). In the region's bond markets, government bonds dominate while corporate bonds remain minimal. The government bond market is also around a third of the size of the banking sector, except in Pakistan (where domestic public bonds outstanding are 65 percent of banking assets) and Sri Lanka (54 percent).

In some South Asian countries, public sector banks control more than half the commercial banking assets. But in Afghanistan, Bangladesh, and Pakistan, private sector banks have taken the lead. And in Maldives, foreign banks dominate.

South Asian banks are relatively stable. Capital adequacy ratios exceed the statutory requirements in all countries except Nepal. Bank performance is satisfactory, with high interest margins and cost efficiencies. Gross nonperforming loans, while rising, have not reached alarming levels, and most countries have posted satisfactory levels of provisions. While the economic slowdown is likely to have an impact on asset quality, the region's banking systems are expected to continue to operate without significant disruptions.

All countries in South Asia have undertaken financial sector reform. They have made considerable improvements in prudential regulations, and the region is moving toward the adoption of higher capital standards. Similarly, the countries have taken steps in recent years to bring their local accounting standards and practices into line with International Accounting Standards, introduce corporate governance guidelines, strengthen supervisory capabilities, improve technological infrastructure, and modernize payment systems. These improvements continue to bear fruit, leading to an increasingly robust financial system. Issues remain in these areas, however, including improving compliance with and enforcement of prudential guidelines, corporate governance guidelines, and International Accounting Standards and managing credit, market, and operational risks.

The country analysis in this chapter provides a multidimensional perspective on the development of the region's financial sector over eight years, 2001–08. A benchmark comparison using data for 15 economies—high-income OECD member countries as well as nonmember Asian economies— enhances the value of the analysis (see appendixes 2–4 for the underlying data and chapter 5 for the benchmark comparison). Because the financial indicators give only a partial view of the dimensions considered, financial sector performance is examined, to the extent possible, in the context of the prudential guidelines issued, the compliance level, and other important developments (see chapter 2 for a comparison of regulatory frameworks in South Asian countries and chapter 9 for an update on major policy developments in 2007–08).

Afghanistan

Afghanistan ranks third among South Asian countries in area (652,100 square kilometers), fourth in population (28.14 million), and sixth in GDP (US$11.7 billion), according to 2008 data (table 3.1). With a gross national income (GNI) per capita of just US$370 in 2007, Afghanistan is classified as a low-income country. It is also classified as a heavily indebted poor country. Afghanistan's security situation, with conflict ongoing for more than three decades, has had an adverse impact on its fragile macroeconomic gains. Still, the macroeconomic framework is stable, though the country is heavily dependent on foreign aid.

High food and fuel prices led to steadily rising inflation, with a sharp increase from 12.9 percent in 2007 to 26.8 percent in 2008. This situation reversed in 2009, however, with inflation falling to an estimated −9.8 percent. The strict no-overdraft fiscal rule adopted by the Afghan government has restricted maneuverability in its monetary policy, already constrained by its limited policy tools. But the central bank has managed to keep the money supply within the target range by making judicious use of foreign exchange interventions.

GDP growth slowed from 12.1 percent in 2007 to 3.4 percent in 2008 because of drought, then rebounded to an estimated 15.7 percent in 2009 thanks mainly to good harvests. GDP growth is expected to be around 8.5 percent in 2010, in line with agricultural growth for a normal year. Agriculture accounts for about 36 percent of GDP. But illicit opium production, despite a recent declining trend, remains the main economic activity, accounting for around 30 percent of GDP.[1]

A current account surplus of 0.9 percent of GDP in 2007 deteriorated to a deficit of 3 percent of GDP in 2008, mainly as a result of high-priced imports. The current account improved slightly to an estimated 2.7 percent in 2009 and, thanks to rising export growth, is expected to improve further in 2010, though slowly.

Afghanistan has 16 commercial banks: 2 state-owned banks (generally referred to in this report as public sector banks), 9 privately owned banks (generally referred to as private sector banks), and 5 foreign banks. The private sector banks (mainly 2 of them) dominate the banking industry in terms of assets, deposits, and lending. Most of their deposits and loans are in U.S. dollars. The financial sector also includes 2 insurance companies and 15 microfinance institutions. In addition, there are more than 332 foreign exchange brokers and about 100 licensed money service providers (Pavlović and Charap 2009). The informal money transfer system *hawala* remains strong and active.

Table 3.1 Key Economic Indicators for South Asian Countries, 2008

Indicator	Afghanistan	Bangladesh	Bhutan	India	Maldives	Nepal	Pakistan	Sri Lanka	South Asia	World
Income group[a]	Low	Low	Lower middle	Lower middle	Lower middle	Low	Lower middle	Lower middle	n.a.	n.a.
Population (millions)	28.14	161.75	0.66	1,186.30	0.35	27.64	160.97	20.09	1,585.90	6,692.00
Surface area (km^2 thousands)	652.10	144.00	38.39	3,287.30	0.30	147.20	796.10	65.60	5,139.50	134,095.40
GNI per capita (US$, Atlas method)	370[b]	520	1,900	1,070	3,630	400	980	1,780	986	8,613
GDP (US$ billions)	11.70	84.20	1.39	1,206.69	1.26	12.28	164.56	39.60	1,521.68	60,917.00
Average annual GDP growth (%)	3.40	6.20	13.82	6.70	5.75	5.35	5.95	5.95	6.87	2.00
Annual inflation (%)	26.80	7.70	8.40	8.35	11.89	7.70	12.00	22.56	9.60	5.98
Gross domestic savings (% of GDP)	–1.18	20.10	34.80	37.70	—	11.50	13.25	14.13	28.42	24.19
Equity market capitalization (% of GDP)	—	19.26	13.14	106.05	20.60	28.12	36.05	11.08	45.10	59.36
Domestic public bonds outstanding (% of GDP)	—	18.42	3.14	36.24	4.51	13.55	33.13	29.07	—	—
Commercial banking assets (% of GDP)	14.30	57.04	63.74	91.80	143.14	69.05	51.38	53.39	—	—
Domestic credit provided by banking sector (% of GDP)	—	36.30	38.82	48.78	100.84	26.44	27.56	28.94	61.50[b]	162.50[b]
Deposit interest rate (%)	7.50	9.70	4.50[b]	—	6.50	2.30[b]	11.40	10.90	—	—
Lending interest rate (%)	14.90	16.40	14.00[b]	13.30	13.00	8.00[b]	14.60	19.00	—	—
Real interest rate (deposit, %)	–4.17	–1.58	–3.60	1.05	–0.65	–3.50	–12.63	–10.97	—	—
Commercial banks	16	43	2	77	6	28	36	22	—	—
Specialized banks	0	5	1	7	0	58	4	14	—	—
Nonbank financial institutions	0	29	0	364[c]	2	78	—	56[d]	—	—
Exchange rate/US$ (year-end)	52.14	68.92	48.46	48.46	12.80	77.65	77.65	113.14	n.a.	n.a.

Sources: World Bank, World Development Indicators database; International Monetary Fund, International Financial Statistics database, World Economic Outlook database; Asian Development Bank, statistical database, 2009a; Bhutan, National Statistical Bureau, 2009; South Asian regulatory authorities.

a. World Bank classification based on GNI per capita (Atlas method) in 2008: low income, US$975 or less; lower middle income, US$976–3,855 (see http://go.worldbank.org/K2CKM78CC0).

b. Data are for 2007.

c. Nonbank financial institutions permitted to accept deposits from the public.

d. Registered finance companies and specialized leasing companies.

— = not available, km^2 = square kilometer, n.a. = not applicable.

After the fall of the Taliban regime in 2002, banks were hardly in a position to act as intermediaries because of the lack of infrastructure and legal and regulatory frameworks. Since then, major rebuilding efforts have put into place legal and regulatory frameworks and other essential elements. In 2003, the Law of Da Afghanistan Bank and the Law of Banking in Afghanistan were enacted, reinstating Da Afghanistan Bank (DAB) as the central bank with the authority to conduct monetary policy and regulate banks and financial institutions. Ongoing development efforts are leading to observable improvements in bank operations and competitiveness. In addition, DAB is taking steps to improve the collection of data (available for most financial indicators only for the past few years) and policy coordination efforts.

Despite the volatile security situation, Afghanistan has shown progress in some areas of banking sector development. But challenges remain to be addressed. Access to financial services continues to be among the main constraints to development. Because of the limited banking network, credit penetration is low. While performance indicators for banks are favorable, high interest margins and low recurring earning power indicate vulnerability of earnings to interest rate shocks. For dilution of such risks, the earnings base should be diversified. Adequate capital and low nonperforming loans ratios are positive signs. But once the market matures and infrastructure and technology are in place, DAB would do well to move toward higher capital requirements. In addition, the liquidity situation warrants careful management.

Over the long term, capital market development should be considered as a vehicle for sustainable growth and efficient allocation of capital. Low domestic savings and underdeveloped capital markets force a reliance on external funding. Incentives should be provided to encourage savings. For avoidance of systemic risks, bank concentration should be reduced and healthy competition welcomed. Also important is to develop payment systems so as to improve efficiency and minimize settlement risks. Finally, corporate governance guidelines need to be augmented, and compliance and enforcement capabilities improved through training and development of the supervisory staff.

Access to Finance

Access to finance remains weak in Afghanistan. The country has less than one bank branch or automated teller machine (ATM) available for every 100,000 people or 1,000 square kilometers of land. This situation, while it continues to slowly improve, is far from satisfactory. In 2008 there were only 27 deposit accounts and 1 loan account per 1,000 people. The large share of private sector bank loans and deposits in U.S. dollars provides further evidence of the limited financial outreach to the public. In the absence of significant outreach by the banking sector, the hawala system continues to provide intermediary functions.

Microfinance institutions also provide financial access to the public. At the end of 2008, microfinance institutions were operating in at least 24 of the 34 provinces and had a client base of around 448,000, about 1.7 percent of the population. The Microfinance Investment Support Facility for Afghanistan—a private, nonshareholding company established by the government in 2003 and owned by the Ministry of Finance—provides funding and assistance to these institutions.

Performance and Efficiency

The overall performance of the banking system has improved since 2006 (figure 3.1). In 2007, both return on assets and return on equity were negative as a result of increased operating costs, provisions for loan losses, and taxes. The operating cost ratio jumped from 97.13 percent in 2006 to 101.79 percent in 2007. By 2008, the banking system's position had improved, with return on equity at 8.93 percent, return on assets at 1.77 percent, and the operating cost ratio falling to 83.87 percent. Interest income remains the major source of income for Afghan banks. Afghanistan posted the highest net interest margin in the region for 2008 at 7.12 percent.

Recurring earning power remains low at about 0.51 percent, denoting vulnerability in earnings strength and in the efficiency of the banking system. Moving toward a diversified earnings base that reduces interest rate risk will be necessary to ensure the long-term growth and stability of the banking sector.

Financial Stability

Banks are adequately capitalized and have low levels of gross nonperforming loans and high levels of provisions. In 2008 Afghanistan posted the region's best capital adequacy ratio, gross nonperforming loans ratio, and provisions to nonperforming loans ratio. The capital adequacy ratio is difficult to compare, however, since the region's more developed economies are following the more stringent Basel II guidelines.

Afghanistan, with a banking system still in its infancy, has not implemented Basel II but instead follows the Basel I accord. Banks are required to maintain a minimum regulatory (total) capital to risk-weighted asset ratio of not less than

Figure 3.1 Afghan Banks Improve Performance and Capital Levels

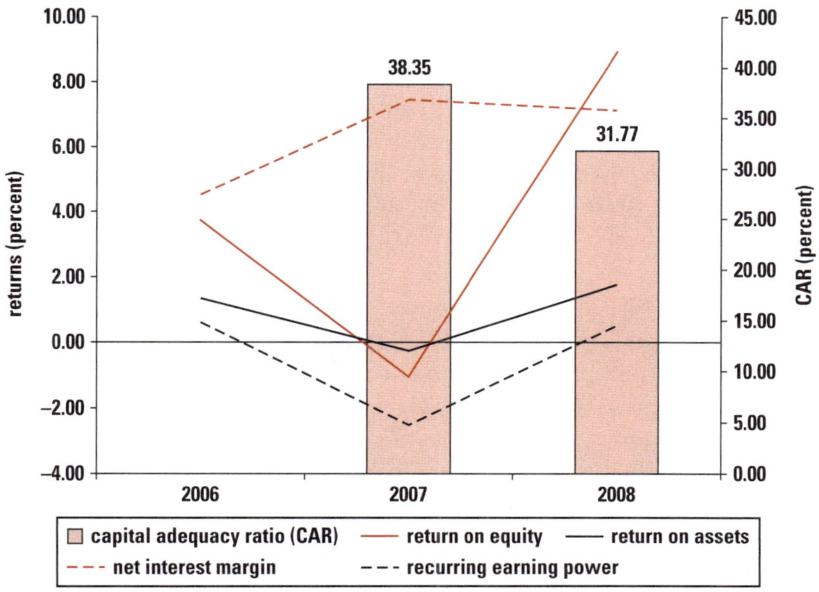

Source: Appendix table A2.9.
Note: CAR data are not available for 2006.

12 percent and a core (Tier 1) capital to risk-weighted asset ratio of 6 percent. The regulatory capital ratio of all banking institutions is above the minimum regulatory threshold (12 percent of risk-weighted assets). The aggregate ratio fell slightly between 2007 and 2008 to 31.77 percent. The leverage ratio continues to be low.

The gross nonperforming loans ratio remains low, dropping from 3 percent in 2007 to 0.90 percent in 2008. Provisions for nonperforming loans doubled, in part because of this drop. One reason for the low nonperforming loans ratio is the highly collateralized lending practices of Afghan banks. In addition, banks almost always prefer short-term lending.

Liquidity also remains low. The liquid assets ratio dropped marginally from 31.43 percent in 2007 to 23.80 in 2008. This suggests a need for banks to monitor the liquidity situation carefully to avoid liquidity risk.

Capital Market Development

The capital market in Afghanistan is extremely underdeveloped, with no stock exchange or bond market. The central bank, to meet the country's funding needs, established a capital notes market in 2005. Licensed commercial banks, money service providers, and foreign exchange dealers are eligible to participate in the primary auctions of these central bank securities. The primary and secondary markets for the capital notes have been established but are not automated.

Developing the country's capital market is critical to its future growth. Afghanistan will need to work toward establishing and strengthening the legal and regulatory framework for capital market institutions. In the meantime banks remain the only source of financing.

Market Concentration and Competitiveness

The commercial banking assets to GDP ratio has steadily increased, almost tripling in 2004–08. In 2008, the ratio was 14.30 percent. Data to assess market concentration are not available, but information suggests that private sector banks dominate the market. Two private sector banks account for more than 45 percent of assets and 66 percent of loans. These figures indicate that market concentration is high in Afghanistan. This leads to higher costs and lower competition, affecting efficiency. Moreover, if one of the two main private sector banks were to experience difficulties, this would have significant adverse consequences for the entire banking system.

Payment Systems Development

The Afghan payment system is still under development. While some banks offer their customers online banking, ATMs, and mobile banking services, most financial transactions are still paper based. Cash remains the dominant payment medium for the public. Since the banks are concentrated in Kabul, informal financial systems such as hawala operate in other areas. In addition, one telecommunications operator has provided mobile payment services since 2008.

Afghanistan has one payment system, a partially automated gross settlement system, for both large- and small-value transactions. There is no real-time gross settlement (RTGS) system in the country. Cross-border fund transfers through the Society for Worldwide Interbank Financial Telecommunications (SWIFT) have been available through DAB since 2003. The Afghanistan Fund Transfer System was implemented in 2004, and the Afghanistan Clearing and Settlement System in 2005. DAB, which operates the systems, offers their services to commercial banks and the banks' customers.

Notes and coins in circulation are low, kept at around 11 percent of GDP. DAB continually monitors the currency in circulation in an effort to contain inflation. The narrow money supply to GDP ratio rose slightly from 18.67 percent in 2004 to 21.38 percent in 2008. The value of retail transactions to GDP ratio dropped from 7.95 percent in 2007 to 4.91 percent in 2008. This ratio indicates the low level of noncash transactions in the country.

Savings Mobilization

Savings mobilization is weak, and Afghanistan continues to rely on external capital for its investment needs. The gross domestic savings to GDP ratio is still negative, though it rose from −35.77 percent in 2003 to −1.18 percent in 2008. The broad money supply averaged about 21 percent of GDP in 2004–08, indicating a lower level of financial deepening than in the rest of the region. The real interest rate in 2008 was −4.17 percent, pointing to a lack of incentives to shift income to savings.

The reserve money to total deposits ratio remains very high, though it has shown a declining trend. A lower ratio would indicate higher efficiency in financial intermediation and better incentives to save. The loan to deposit ratio is on the rise, indicating greater use of borrowing to fund activities.

Given the scarcity of capital in Afghanistan, one would expect the savings rate to be high, but this is not the case. The overall propensity to save is low. One main reason for the low savings rate is the lack of bankable projects. Another is the low interest rates, which banks keep low to avoid bringing in excess cash. Encouraging small and medium-size entrepreneurs would expand the demand for money, thereby raising interest rates and leading to higher savings.

Corporate Governance

Corporate governance is an area needing further development. The Law of Banking (2003), the legal foundation for banking regulations, subjects all commercial banks in Afghanistan to certain requirements, restrictions, and guidelines. Articles 22–26 of this law prescribe the corporate governance structure for banks. In addition, corporate governance guidelines issued by DAB in 2005 cover the following areas:

- Responsibilities common to both the board of supervisors and the management board
- Recommended makeup of the management board and qualifications for its members
- Responsibilities of the board of supervisors and its appropriate place in the governance of a bank in ensuring competent management
- Typical structure for a management board
- Selection of the board of supervisors
- Duties of the board of supervisors, including ensuring competent management, ensuring that appropriate plans and policies are in place, monitoring

operations, ensuring adequate internal controls and compliance with laws and decisions, overseeing the bank's financial performance, and preventing conflicts of interest

- Establishment of committees, including the audit committee; loan committee; investment, asset liability, and risk management committee; compensation committee; and nominations committee
- Conditions relating to banks that are subsidiaries of other companies

These guidelines are generally in keeping with Principles 3, 14, and 17 of the Core Principles of Effective Banking Supervision of the Basel Committee. DAB will monitor adherence to the guidelines through on-site supervision.

While the banking law prescribes ownership rights and structure, disclosure of investor rights, and board structure and effectiveness, the guidelines cover only corporate governance issues relating to the management of banks. They will need to be expanded to be comprehensive. The answers to the survey questionnaire on corporate governance reveal several areas needing further attention: disclosure requirements relating to ownership, government ownership, and special privileges; influence of external stakeholders such as labor unions and authorities; preemption rights of minority shareholders; disclosure requirements relating to ultimate beneficial ownership; and minority rights to appoint directors (see appendix 4A).

Setting up a local accounting body should be among the priorities, since a local standard-setting body could help ensure compliance and uniformity in accounting practices. While banks are required to adhere to international standards, some standards may not be applicable depending on a country's level of development, and some may need to be adapted to address country-specific issues. Another priority is to ensure effective monitoring of and compliance with the corporate governance guidelines through adequate training of both the examiners and the users.

According to the questionnaire answers, DAB approval is needed to acquire a qualifying holding of 20 percent or more in a bank. Banks are not required to disclose government ownership along with its special privileges. Whether external stakeholders such as labor unions and banking and securities regulators can influence the operations of banks is unclear. And there is no evidence that the preemption rights of minority shareholders are firmly protected.

Notwithstanding the requirement for DAB approval for acquisitions of qualifying holdings, it is unclear whether specific rules govern ultimate beneficial ownership or whether the ultimate owners need to disclose their holdings. The central registry kept by DAB for inspection by the public includes disclosures about the bank, but whether it includes disclosures about shareholders is unclear. Moreover, while the questionnaire answers indicate that shareholdings are generally disclosed in the audited accounts, no threshold limits for disclosure are given.

Procedures for shareholder meetings are defined. Voting procedures allow shareholders to vote by proxy, though the counting of votes need not be verified by a third party. Banks are not required to disclose special voting rights and caps on voting rights. Appointments and dismissals of members of the board of supervisors are subject to shareholder vote; however, government control is always present. There is no clear dividend policy prescribed by DAB; instead, this policy is at the discretion of individual banks. In the event of a legitimate takeover bid, DAB approval would be needed to change shareholdings. No guidelines are available to ensure minority shareholders' right to appoint directors; this again depends on a bank's rules.

Adherence to international accounting and auditing standards has been identified in recent studies as an area needing special attention. In the absence of a recognized local accounting body, the banking law is the source of most of the accounting and financial reporting requirements for banks. The banking law mandates adherence to International Accounting Standards and requires banks to make their annual audited financial statements available to DAB, their shareholders, and the public within three months after the end of the financial year, which must coincide with the calendar year.

Because there is no standard-setting body for accounting or auditing, there are no enforced accounting or auditing standards for the private sector. The Financial Supervision Department of the central bank is responsible for monitoring compliance with accounting, financial reporting, and statutory audit requirements in the financial sector (both banking and nonbanking). The department focuses on monitoring compliance with prudential norms, however, with little attention to general-purpose financial reporting.

All banks are required to set up audit committees, but the frequency of meetings, selection of auditors, and procedures can vary from bank to bank. Banks are also required to appoint an independent external auditor with qualifications and experience acceptable to DAB. These external auditors are allowed to perform nonaudit functions for banks. While DAB has issued guidelines on the appointment of internal auditors, internal auditing procedures, frequency of reporting, and similar operational issues can vary from bank to bank.

A bank's board of supervisors is required to have an uneven number of members, at least three and up to nine. The majority must be independent. The qualifications, roles, and responsibilities of board members are defined.

There are no policies on setting remuneration for board members. At annual general meetings, however, shareholders can appoint and dismiss members of the bank's board of supervisors, management board, and audit committee and also determine their remuneration. But shareholders may not tie such remuneration to the bank's financial condition or financial results. The compensation of the board of directors is disclosed on an aggregate basis in the audited financial statements.

Bangladesh

Among South Asian countries Bangladesh ranks second in population (161.75 million), third in GDP (US$84.2 billion), and fifth in area (144,000 square kilometers), according to 2008 data. In population density, Bangladesh ranks 11th in the world. With a GNI per capita of around US$520 in 2008, Bangladesh is classified as a low-income country. Poverty, political instability, and natural disasters such as floods and cyclones are among the main challenges Bangladesh is seeking to overcome through its development efforts.

Bangladesh has not been significantly affected by the ongoing financial crisis, as it has no direct links to toxic assets or failed institutions. But the country will nevertheless feel the economic impact because of its heavy reliance on exports to developed countries and on remittance receipts. Economic growth declined from 6.4 percent in 2007 to 6.2 percent in 2008, mainly because of the high cost of imports. The 2009 growth rate was marginally lower, at an estimated 5.9 percent. Lower prices for such imports as food and oil, a good harvest season, and strong remittances have helped sustain the growth rate. Projected growth for 2010 is 5.2 percent. Concerns about export vulnerability will remain, however, as the United States and the European Union, the main markets for ready-made garments, are still struggling with recession.

Overall, the economic situation appears to be favorable, but there are some concerns. Inflation has been creeping up, reaching 7.7 percent in 2008, mainly as a result of high-priced imports such as food and fuel. But the drop in food and fuel prices internationally led to a decline to an estimated 6.7 percent in 2009, and inflation is projected to be 6.5 percent in 2010. Current account balances remained positive in 2004–08, thanks mainly to growth in remittance inflows. Exchange rates were stable in nominal terms, and the country's international reserve position continues to grow. The fiscal deficit was kept below 4 percent of GDP over the five-year period. But the deficit was expected to increase in 2009 as a result of the stimulus package offered by the government to counter the economic slowdown. The fiscal situation needs to be managed carefully to prevent inflation from shooting up once again.

In Bangladesh, as in other developing countries, commercial banks dominate the financial sector. In 2008, commercial banking assets amounted to more than 57 percent of GDP. The country's financial sector includes 43 commercial banks, 5 development banks, and 29 nonbank financial institutions. The commercial banks consist of 4 state-owned banks (generally referred to in the report as public sector banks), 30 privately owned banks (generally referred to as private sector banks), and 9 foreign banks. The private sector banks have overtaken their public sector counterparts, securing a market share of about 52 percent of assets. But the four public sector banks continue to have a major impact because of their extensive branch network and 33 percent market share. With the aim of making the public sector banks more competitive and profitable, the Bangladesh government has undertaken management changes, turned them into limited liability companies, and divested shares. These restructuring efforts have yet to bear fruit, however.

Although the global financial crisis is not expected to have a significant effect on the banking system, Bangladesh needs to address the system's structural weaknesses to realize its full potential. While managing the reforms of the systemically important public sector banks, Bangladesh will also need to improve the profitability and efficiency, capital position, asset quality, and provisioning of all banks to strengthen the stability of the financial sector. Banks need to work on expanding their financial services to reach the public cost-effectively. To benefit from high net interest margins, banks should pursue cost efficiencies and improve performance.

Modernizing the banking infrastructure and payment systems would reduce systemic risks and increase efficiency. Recapitalizing public sector banks and some private sector ones would bring greater stability to the system. Improving market discipline requires strong enforcement of prudential regulations, and that will require clearly defining and standardizing key guidelines on capital requirements, disclosure requirements, accounting and auditing standards, and corporate governance. For expansion of funding options for economic growth, priority should be given to capital market development and domestic savings mobilization.

Bangladesh has low concentration ratios in its banking sector, and it should continue to maintain the competitiveness of the sector as financial sector reforms proceed (figure 3.2). The country has a deposit insurance scheme, one of only two in the region, under which deposits are insured up to Tk 100,000 (around US$1,450). And Bangladesh has a credit information bureau that is modernizing the credit information systems. Moreover, it has begun implementation of Basel II. Progress in these areas is paramount for continued financial stability and robustness.

Access to Finance

Indicators of access to financial services showed little change between 2001 and 2008. Branch penetration remained around 5 branches per 100,000 people and 47 branches per 1,000 square kilometers, while ATM penetration improved slightly to around 1 ATM per 100,000 people and 6 ATMs per 1,000 square kilometers in 2008. Lack of physical and technological infrastructure impedes financial outreach as well as growth potential in banking. The use of financial services offered by banks, as measured by loan accounts and deposit accounts per 1,000 people, increased marginally over the eight years. Low levels of use are common in developing countries, indicating both the inability of banks to reach the poor in a cost-effective manner and the lack of demand for such services because of poverty. In South Asia, where poverty is the main challenge, the use of financial services is low in all but a few countries.

Figure 3.2 Bangladesh Maintains Low Market Concentration in Banking

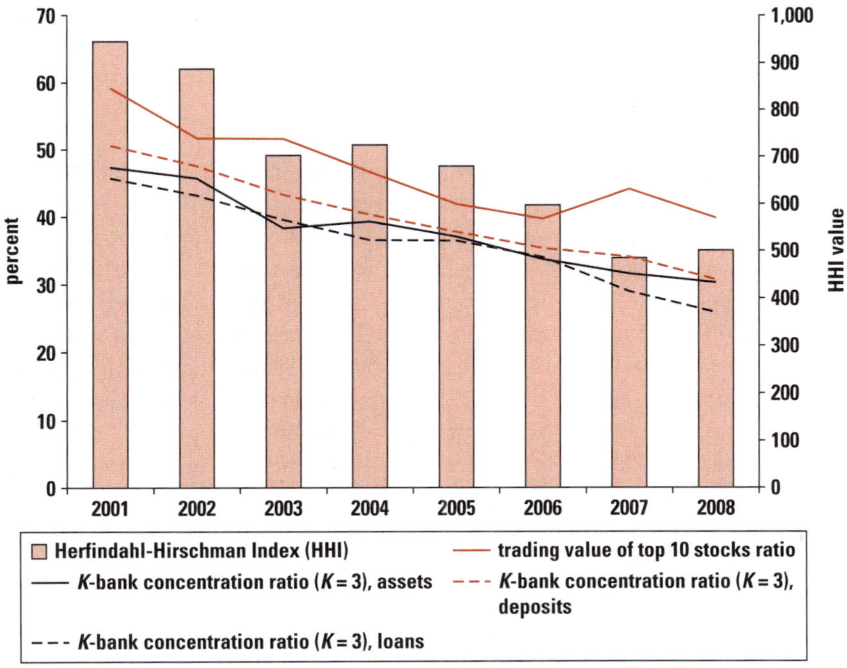

Source: Appendix table A2.10.

In Bangladesh, which has one of the biggest microfinance movements in the world, microfinance institutions play a notable role in providing financial services to the poor. It is estimated that these institutions have served more than 17 percent of the population (and about 35 percent of the poor population, based on national poverty estimates).[2] By mid-2008, outstanding microfinance loans amounted to about US$1.8 billion, nearly 3 percent of GDP. Microfinance institutions in Bangladesh are supervised by the Micro Credit Regulatory Authority under the Micro-Credit Regulatory Act, 2006.

Performance and Efficiency

Return on equity and return on assets in the banking sector have shown some improvement in recent years. In 2004, because of the charging of an accumulated shortfall of provisioning at one nationalized bank, both indicators turned negative for the entire industry. This position was later reversed, and by the end of 2008 the return on equity was 48.35 percent and the return on assets 2.63 percent. For public sector banks, however, these ratios are still negative.

The staff cost ratio held constant over the period studied, while the operating cost ratio showed a welcome declining trend. That ratio dropped by almost 62 percent between 2001 and 2008, to 88.9 percent. Because of overstaffing and efficiency issues, both staff and operating costs are much higher in the public sector banks than in the private sector or foreign banks.

For the banking industry as a whole, even with healthy growth in the net interest margin and in recurring earning power, returns remain lackluster, mainly because of the poor performance and high cost of the public sector banks. The present economic conditions will increase the number of delinquent loans and the provisioning needs, adding to the stress on returns. So it is important that banks aggressively pursue cost-efficiency improvements to benefit from the higher interest spreads. The restructuring of the public sector banks is expected to improve the earning capacity of the entire sector.

Financial Stability

The negative capital position of the public sector banks has affected the Bangladesh banking sector for a number of years. The capital adequacy ratio was below the statutory requirement of 10 percent in most years during the period. In 2008, the ratio exceeded the minimum for the first time, improving to 10.06 percent. In 2007, the public sector banks' cumulative losses had been transferred to a valuation adjustment account to be amortized over a 10-year period, improving their balance sheets in a narrow sense. With the better capital situation, the leverage ratio also improved to 6.21; this is still low by international standards, however. The gross nonperforming loans ratio dropped from 31.49 percent in 2001 to 10.79 percent in 2008, while the provisions to nonperforming loans ratio rose over the period to around 56.15 percent in 2008. Such improvements are a result of the reforms of the public sector banks, where regulatory changes have led to more streamlined loan recovery.

Although the capital position of the public sector banks improved after the valuation adjustments, bringing in additional capital is important to improve their viability. Thus, capitalization of public sector banks as well as some private sector banks should be actively pursued. To support this, Bangladesh Bank

(BB) doubled the minimum capital requirement for banks to Tk 4 billion and increased the capital adequacy requirement to 10 percent of total risk-weighted assets and the Tier 1 ratio to 5 percent. These regulatory reforms are a step in the right direction. Liquidity ratios show that Bangladesh banks do not have problems with liquidity issues.

As discussed in chapter 2, Bangladesh has decided to adopt the Basel II framework from 2010. This will mean additional capital charges for market and operational risk, putting greater pressure on banks already struggling to meet the existing compliance burden.

Capital Market Development

Development of capital markets is still at an early stage in Bangladesh. The country has two exchanges, Dhaka Stock Exchange and Chittagong Stock Exchange, both of which deal in equities, mutual funds, and debentures. Equity market capitalization increased sevenfold from 2001 to 2008, to 19.26 percent of GDP. Market liquidity improved, with the stock trading value at about 6 percent of GDP in 2008. The market turnover ratio was around 0.33. Ten or fewer stocks account for about 40 percent of the market capitalization. Public bonds outstanding typically average about 17 percent of GDP. And the bond market is about three times the size of the stock market on average. But the bond market is not developed and remains dominated by government bonds. The corporate bond market is virtually nonexistent.

In the absence of a developed capital market, banks become the only funding source for investment and economic growth. Thus, focusing on capital market development needs to be a priority for Bangladesh. Developing benchmark bonds, expanding the investor base, improving the market infrastructure, streamlining the regulatory framework and guidelines, and managing the market distortions created by government savings schemes are among the efforts needed to accelerate capital market development.

Market Concentration and Competitiveness

Market concentration is an area where Bangladesh has performed well. The top three banks account for less than 40 percent of assets, deposits, and loans. Moreover, Bangladesh had the region's best Herfindahl-Hirschman Index in all three years from 2006 to 2008. For 2008, the index was 500.56—well within the range for an unconcentrated banking industry (according to the norms, values less than 1,000). Low concentration can foster healthy competition.

Credit growth may be an area of concern, however. Private credit extended by banks increased by about 50 percent over the eight years to 36.30 percent of GDP in 2008. The commercial banking assets to GDP ratio in 2008 was 57.04 percent. If growth in deposits does not match the growth in private credit, banks will have to secure external funding to finance the credit growth. Bangladesh has a relatively high savings rate. But because government savings schemes offer better terms than banks, deposit mobilization by banks, while steady, has not shown dynamic growth. In the absence of a developed capital market, banks need to focus on securing deposits to finance their credit portfolio. At the same time, because of the private sector's heavy reliance on bank funding, credit growth will have to be monitored carefully to limit exposures to interest rate risk.

Payment Systems Development

BB has highlighted payment systems as a key area for development. Bangladesh has a manual clearing system, which is an end-of-day net settlement system. Four clearinghouses operate in the country: BB's clearinghouse in Dhaka and its branches in seven other cities; Sonali Bank's clearinghouses in 31 cities where there are no BB branches; the BB large-value check settlement system; and the BB foreign currency clearing system in Dhaka, which clears and settles foreign currency checks and payment orders. The settlement times are typically T+2, T+3, and even longer for regional checks. Bangladesh does not have an RTGS system.

BB is working toward a strategy for modernizing the payment systems and implementing an RTGS system in the future. In a move toward achieving this, the National Payment Systems Council was formed in 2007. Installation of the Bangladesh Automated Clearing House, with an automated check processing system and electronic fund transfer network, has already started. The automated check processing system and electronic fund transfer network are not yet operational. The implementation of payment reforms has been a slow process.

Bangladesh has reported few payment systems indicators, but those that are available suggest that the country, like most others in South Asia, has a large share of funds tied up in currency in circulation. The notes and coins in circulation to GDP ratio and the narrow money supply to GDP ratio both showed increasing trends over the period, hovering around 7 percent and 11 percent. The average ratio of currency in circulation to narrow money supply (about 60 percent) or even to broad money supply (15 percent) was high. Keeping funds tied up in currency in circulation limits lending activities and expansion of the economy. A modern payment system will improve the ability to use funds efficiently as well as keep the banking system liquid.

Savings Mobilization

Savings mobilization is an important concept for Bangladesh and for the other South Asian countries, the more so since their capital markets are not fully developed and external income is limited. Savings play an important part in capital formation and, in the long run, in economic growth and poverty reduction. Bangladesh compares well with the other South Asian countries in this respect. A measure of financial deepening, the broad money supply to GDP ratio has shown an increasing trend, reaching 49 percent in 2008. But as a result of high inflation, the real deposit interest rate turned negative in 2003 and continued the negative trend to peak at −3.16 percent in 2007. In 2008, the rate improved to −1.58 percent. Gross domestic savings average around 20 percent of GDP.

A measure of intermediary efficiency, the reserve money to deposits ratio held constant throughout the eight-year period at around 24 percent, while the loan to deposit ratio remained at around 81 percent. Declining trends in both would denote higher efficiency by the banking sector in mobilizing savings and allocating funds. In a favorable trend for savings, worker remittances have averaged around 7 percent of GDP. But concerns about a possible downturn in remittances remain, since more than 60 percent of the country's remittances originate from Gulf countries that have recently been suffering the effects of the global financial crisis. Overall, Bangladesh has good potential for savings mobilization given its good savings habits and constant stream of remittances. But to bridge the savings-investments gap, the banking sector should take steps to ensure continuity and improve efficiency, and thereby enhance financial deepening.

Corporate Governance

BB is continually working to improve corporate governance guidelines. Several key guidelines cover the following areas:

- Qualifications of bank directors and chief executive officers (CEOs) (fit-and-proper tests, selection procedures, and the like)
- Appointment of CEOs and advisers (moral integrity, experience and suitability, transparency and financial integrity)
- Authorities and responsibilities of the chairman, board of directors, CEO, and advisers (work planning and strategic management, lending and risk management, internal control management, human resources management and development, financial management, formation of supporting committees, appointment of CEO)
- Limits on the size of the board
- Responsibilities of the board
- Establishment of audit committees (financial reporting, internal and external audits, other responsibilities, organization, member qualifications, and meetings)
- Restrictions on lending to directors of private sector banks
- Dividend payments

No significant changes have been made since the guidelines were issued in 2003, and the responses to the survey questionnaire, first forwarded to the authorities in 2005, therefore remain largely unchanged (see appendix 4A). Examination of the questionnaire responses suggests a need to augment the guidelines with legal provisions governing beneficial ownership, minority shareholder rights, remuneration of directors, and roles and responsibilities of external and internal auditors. More attention is also needed in other areas. Full conformity with international accounting and auditing standards should be actively pursued. And while the regulatory authorities have started moving ahead with the process of infusing the banking system with a corporate governance culture and educating shareholders about their rights and responsibilities, much more needs to be done in these areas. The corporate governance analysis based on the answers to the questionnaire also led to the following observations.

The ownership structure is transparent. No individual or family can hold more than 10 percent of the shares of a banking company, and under the Bank Companies Act banks must disclose their shareholding structure in their articles of association. No legal provision seems to identify a threshold of share ownership to be disclosed to the general public. The government controls the nomination of directors for government-controlled banks, while the central bank regulates the remuneration of directors. The Companies Act protects the preemption rights of minority shareholders. There are no provisions to establish stakeholders' rights. Nor are there legal provisions governing the disclosure of beneficial ownership by shareholders other than the requirement that shareholders disclose their portfolios in their tax returns. But banks are required to submit reports to the Securities and Exchange Commission for shareholdings above 10 percent.

Investor rights appear to be in place when it comes to voting procedures and shareholder meetings. Shareholders receive adequate information in a timely fashion before shareholder meetings, and they are able to vote in absentia. No rules govern third-party verification of voting. Shareholders may vote on a range of issues, including related-party transactions. Special voting rights of individual shareholders other than the government are capped at 5 percent of the total votes.

In contrast, basic ownership rights need improvement. Shareholders can vote on appointments and dismissals of directors, and in the public sector banks it is evident that the government exercises control over such outcomes. As the regulator, BB has issued guidelines controlling the percentage of shares in a bank that any one shareholder may own. A clear dividend policy is in place, and structural defenses that can prevent takeover bids are not established. Minority shareholders cannot easily nominate a director, pointing to a need for legal provisions to safeguard their interests in the appointment of directors. Finally, no evidence shows that shareholders exercise any of these basic ownership rights.

Questionnaire responses on transparency and disclosure requirements indicate that financial statements are prepared annually and in accordance with local generally accepted accounting standards, which are in material conformity with International Accounting Standards. Yet other studies have revealed gaps remaining between the two sets of standards (see World Bank 2003; eStandardsForum 2009b).

The Institute of Chartered Accountants of Bangladesh (ICAB) is working toward improving harmonization with international standards. In December 2008, according to its 2009 action plan, the ICAB converged local standards with the new and updated *Handbook of International Standards on Auditing, Assurance and Ethics Pronouncements* (volume 1) issued by the International Auditing and Assurance Standards Board. In addition, in November 2008 the ICAB adopted its own clarity project, slated for completion by December 2009, to redraft national standards in line with the clarified International Accounting Standards (eStandardsForum 2009b). Preparation of accounting and auditing standards in line with international standards should be a priority.

Moreover, audit functions need to be defined in detail. Banks are required to appoint audit committees, but it is unclear whether the committees' mandate includes determining the process for selecting auditors. Contrary to internationally accepted standards, external auditors can perform other, nonaudit services for banks. While auditing standards are said to conform with international standards, here again other reports point to areas needing improvement (see World Bank 2003; eStandardsForum 2009b). And there are no provisions governing the roles and responsibilities of internal auditors.

Responses on the structure and effectiveness of boards of directors show that Bangladesh banks follow a unitary structure, with around 13 directors on average. A BB circular limiting the number of directors on a bank board to no more than 13 reduced the average, which in the recent past was around 20. The terms of bank directors are limited to six years, and their minimum qualifications are governed by the guidelines issued by BB. The roles and responsibilities of boards of directors are clearly defined.

Compensation policies need to be reviewed, however. Contrary to accepted standards, shareholders have no say on the remuneration of directors, and the board sets the remuneration of the bank's CEO with approval from BB. In addition, banks are not required to disclose the compensation of directors. There are no provisions for including performance-based compensation in directors' remuneration packages. Performance-based compensation has been widely accepted as a positive incentive in today's competitive world. But in light of recent events in the international financial world, where companies struggling with financial difficulties nevertheless paid large executive bonuses, guidelines on performance-based compensation packages should be reviewed carefully—and performance levels monitored.

Bhutan

Bhutan is one of South Asia's smallest countries, with an area of just 38,394 square kilometers and a population of only 0.7 million. Its GDP in 2008 was around US$1.4 billion. With a GNI per capita of US$1,900 in 2008, Bhutan is classified as a lower-middle-income country. After being governed by a monarchy for centuries, Bhutan held its first democratic elections and created its first democratically elected government in 2008.

Bhutan's economy is closely tied to that of India, its main trading partner as well as its largest donor. The value of its currency (the ngultrum) is pegged to the Indian rupee, and the Indian rupee (in denominations up to Rs 100) is accepted legal tender in Bhutan.[3] Inflation in India therefore has a direct impact in Bhutan. In 2008, when India's inflation rate jumped to 8.35 percent as a result of high oil prices, Bhutan's rose to 8.4 percent. In 2009, Bhutan's inflation rate was expected to go up to 9 percent, and in 2010, with economic recovery in India, Bhutan's rate is expected to match India's at around 4 percent.

Fluctuations in Bhutan's current account are caused by its fluctuating trade deficit with India, the sole recipient of hydropower exports from Bhutan and the source of most of its imports. India also funds power projects in Bhutan. Bhutan maintains a positive current account balance. It was 3.9 percent of GDP in 2008 and projected to increase to 5.5 percent in 2009 and 9 percent in 2010.

GDP growth was around 13.82 percent in 2008, driven by strong demand for hydropower from India and an increase in power generation capacity. The growth rate dropped to an estimated 6 percent in 2009 as a result of the economic slowdown in India, but it is expected to rise to about 6.5 percent in 2010. Bhutan had a fiscal surplus of 0.56 percent of GDP in 2007, and the newly elected government set an annual fiscal deficit target of about 5 percent of GDP. International reserves are healthy: in 2004–08, Bhutan had reserves equivalent to about 16 months of imports on average, the best record in the region. Overall, the economy seems to be on the way to recovery.

Bhutan's financial sector is small and underdeveloped. Its banking sector is very narrow, with just two commercial banks. One is a state-owned bank, and the other has a government stake. A development bank, an insurance company, and a pension fund make up the rest of the country's financial sector. The sector dominates the small stock exchange in Bhutan.

Bhutan has initiated reforms aimed at expanding and stabilizing its financial sector to help meet the needs of its small but rapidly growing economy. The Royal Monetary Authority of Bhutan (RMA), the regulatory authority for the sector, is encouraging new entrants to the market, which would reduce the dominance of government-owned financial institutions both in the financial sector and in the small capital market. Greater competition would also improve efficiency.

Bhutan's banking sector has been insulated from the global financial meltdown by its limited exposure. The main challenge for banks is to expand access to financial services and credit so as to support economic development. To reduce the cost and increase the timeliness of the provision of services, banks need to improve both cost and technological efficiency. Regulatory improvements would support better asset quality. Bhutan's high liquidity position has made liquidity management challenging (figure 3.3). Although the level of private credit is far from satisfactory for economic development, it grew rapidly in 2001–08, a situation that warrants careful monitoring by the authorities to prevent a credit bubble. The RMA, mindful of the high liquidity and the rapid increase in credit, raised the cash reserve requirement for banks in 2008 to slow the pace of private credit growth. This requires a very fine balance, however.

Promoting capital market development and domestic savings mobilization could provide effective funding options for investment, while modernization of the payment system would further reduce systemic risk. And two key areas that the RMA needs to focus on in its financial sector development efforts are developing a code of corporate governance for banks and streamlining accounting and auditing procedures.

Access to Finance

Lack of access to bank services is a serious impediment to development in the country. Over the period studied, Bhutan had on average six branches and one

Figure 3.3 Bhutan's Banking Sector Has High Liquidity

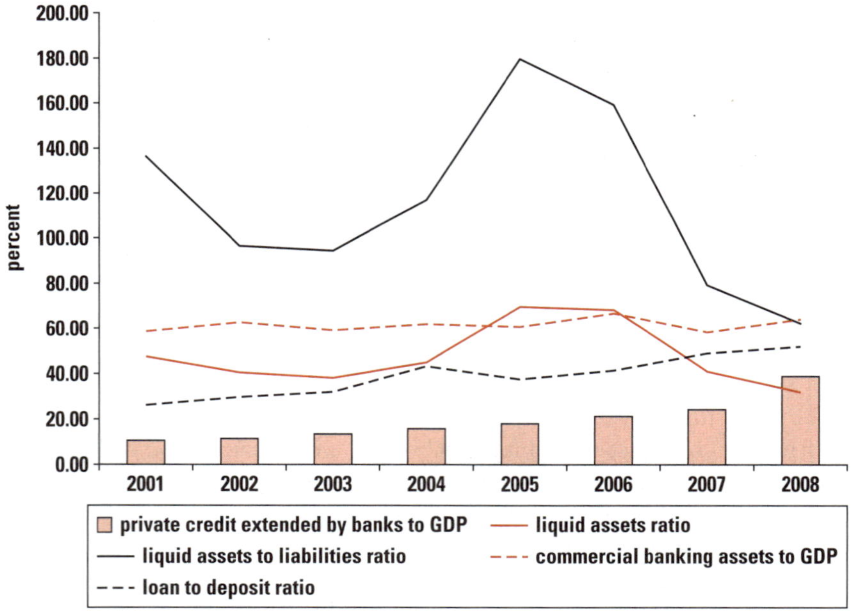

Source: Appendix table A2.11.

ATM per 100,000 people—and one branch and less than one ATM per 1,000 square kilometers. The low demographic and geographic penetration is mirrored in low rates of use of bank facilities. While use grew marginally over the period, in 2008 there were only 325 deposit accounts and 43 loan accounts per 1,000 people. The RMA has recognized the problem of poor access to bank and credit facilities and is trying to take remedial action to expand the banking sector. It has approved in principle three more licenses to start commercial banks. The new banks are now in the process of meeting the minimum requirements to obtain a formal banking license.

While the development bank provides loans to the rural sector and small and medium-size enterprises, the microfinance movement has not yet developed in Bhutan. In formulating a strategy to implement a microfinance system, Bhutan could look to other countries in the region, which provide success stories of the microfinance movement aiding economic development of the poor.

Performance and Efficiency

Return on equity and return on assets in Bhutan's banking sector have remained somewhat constant, dropping to 17.08 percent and 1.50 percent in 2008 despite the increasing trend in the net interest margin, which rose to 3.46 percent in 2008. One reason for the lackluster performance may be the rising staff costs, which amounted to 60.73 percent of total operating costs in 2008. The operating cost to income ratio declined, however—a favorable sign. Recurring earning power has also remained constant, averaging around 2 percent. For banks to benefit from higher margins, they need to improve cost-efficiency and reduce staff costs. To help further increase efficiency, Bhutan also needs to improve its technological infrastructure.

Financial Stability

Overall, the Bhutanese banking system is moderately stable. Bhutan is compliant with Basel I guidelines, and banks maintain capital adequacy ratios well above the statutory requirement of 10 percent. Because of growth in loan activities, the overall capital adequacy ratio dropped from 16.17 percent in 2007 to 13.93 percent in 2008. Bhutan has not yet made progress in implementing Basel II, given the simple structure of its banking system and lack of expertise. But the RMA is encouraging banks to develop their own internal credit rating systems.

Leverage is low in Bhutan, reflecting the relative inactivity in the banking sector. The leverage ratio in 2008 was just 0.08. Gross nonperforming loans averaged around 7 percent over the period, while provisions averaged around 47 percent. Although nonperforming loans are comparatively low, Bhutan's classification policies are rather lax. So the low nonperforming loans ratio does not provide a true picture of asset quality. For further improvement of asset quality, regulatory guidelines on asset classification and provisioning should be tightened.

Liquidity remains high. From time to time, the RMA uses monetary policy tools to sterilize liquidity. But given the shallow credit market, managing liquidity is a challenge for Bhutan.

Capital Market Development

Bhutan's capital market remains small and underdeveloped. At the end of 2008, the Royal Securities Exchange of Bhutan listed 19 companies and was operating with a market capitalization equivalent to 13 percent of GDP. The market is dominated by the four state-owned financial institutions. Besides equities, the exchange deals in treasury bills, government bonds, and RMA bills. But the market is very narrow and the instruments extremely limited. The domestic public bonds outstanding to GDP ratio was 3.14 percent at the end of 2008. No corporate bonds had been issued in Bhutan by 2008 (in 2009, however, the Royal Insurance Corporation of Bhutan Limited began issuing a corporate bond). Developing the capital market is important as a way to provide additional funding for investment and growth.

Market Concentration and Competitiveness

Since Bhutan has only two commercial banks, market concentration is extremely high. The Herfindahl-Hirschman Index for Bhutan averaged around 5,500 over the period, well above the 1,800 considered to denote a highly concentrated market. Commercial banking assets amounted to around 63.74 percent of GDP in 2008, having increased marginally over the period. However, private credit extended by banks increased by almost 267 percent between 2001 and 2008, from 10.61 percent of GDP to almost 38.82 percent. Bhutan should monitor this situation carefully to prevent a credit bubble. High credit growth in boom times exposes banks to credit risks if credit policies are not prudent and can have adverse consequences during an economic slowdown like that being experienced now by South Asian countries.

The limited access to financial services is a major impediment to growth and needs to be addressed in multiple ways. The RMA's steps to encourage new players to enter the banking system are an important move. Highly concentrated markets lack efficiency and are more fragile during times of crisis.

Payment Systems Development

Along with other aspects of the banking sector, Bhutan needs to develop payment systems. Today Bhutan has one system, an end-of-day net settlement system, for both large- and small-value payments. The clearing system is automated. The RMA operates the Bhutan Electronic Clearing House, which launched a check truncation system based on magnetic ink character recognition (MICR) in January 2007. Proposed bylaws for the clearinghouse are being developed. With financial assistance from the World Bank, the RMA is undertaking a project aimed at developing an electronic fund transfer and clearing system for Bhutan.

In Bhutan, unlike in most other developing economies, currency circulation is low. In 2008, notes and coins in circulation amounted to only 6.46 percent of GDP, and the narrow money supply to around 25.54 percent. While low currency in circulation often means that financial services, especially payment systems, are well developed, in this case it does not. Instead, it denotes limited use of currency in ordinary transactions, which curtails credit growth.

Savings Mobilization

Bhutan's average domestic savings rate is high relative to rates in the rest of the region. Gross domestic savings averaged around 44 percent of GDP in 2001–07 and reached 60.07 percent in 2007 (no data are available for 2008). Yet other indicators on savings mobilization are less positive. The broad money supply to

GDP ratio averaged around 48 percent of GDP in 2001–08, which could improve further. Since 2004, as a result of inflationary pressures, the real interest rate has turned negative. The reserve money to total deposits ratio was 61.42 percent at the end of 2008. The loan to deposit ratio remains low because of the limited lending activity. No information is available on worker remittances.

In the absence of a developed capital market, domestic savings would help Bhutan move away from a dependence on external funds and take charge of its development activities. Thus, to benefit from investment opportunities and foster development, Bhutan needs to focus on savings mobilization. Measures that would help create and maintain a constant stream of savings include improving access to financial services and managing inflation so that positive real interest rates can act as an incentive to save.

Corporate Governance

Corporate governance of banks is another area needing further development in Bhutan. The Financial Institutions Act, 1992 and the Companies Act, 2000 provide the legal foundation for banking regulations. In 2002, under the Financial Institutions Act, the RMA's division for financial institutions supervision issued prudential regulations relating to corporate governance that cover the following areas:

- Directors and chief executives (including duties, appointment, prohibitions, structure and duties of audit committee, and internal audit requirements)
- Code of ethics for directors and employees
- Submission of annual accounts
- Dividends and reserves
- Share capital ownership of banks and nonbank financial institutions
- Reporting requirements
- Guidelines for compliance officers

Yet there is no code of corporate governance or specific corporate governance guidelines for banks. Instead, bank directors are to comply with sections of the Companies Act relating to directors' responsibilities, appointment, eligibility, registration, term of office, resignation, conduct of meetings, vacancies, minutes of meetings, remuneration, and validity of proceedings.[4]

Analysis of the answers to the corporate governance questionnaire suggests that, overall, the practice and awareness of corporate governance are low in Bhutan (see appendix 4A). Since all financial institutions have a significant government stake, the government can influence management as both owner and regulator, a situation that should be remedied through privatization of these institutions. Basic shareholder rights are in place, as are the preemption rights of minority shareholders. Banks would benefit from improvements in such areas as provisions governing beneficial ownership, proxy voting rights, special voting rights, remuneration of directors, and disclosure requirements. Also key are building awareness on corporate governance and shareholder and investor rights, developing a code of corporate governance for banks, and streamlining accounting and auditing procedures.

Basic guidelines are in place on disclosing ownership structure and influence of stakeholders, but indirect or beneficial ownership is not clearly defined. Under the Financial Institutions Act, acquisitions of issued share capital above

20 percent in banks must be approved by the RMA, while acquisitions of 10 percent and above must be reported to the RMA. There are no apparent legal provisions identifying thresholds of share ownership that must be disclosed to the public. The government controls the nomination and remuneration of directors for government-controlled banks and financial institutions. Because of the significant government ownership stake in all financial institutions, this would mean that the government has substantial control over shareholder rights even as it acts as the regulator. The Companies Act protects the preemption rights of minority shareholders. There are no provisions to establish stakeholders' rights. Nor are there legal provisions governing the disclosure of beneficial ownership by shareholders except when filing taxes, and no thresholds are prescribed. There is no evidence that this reporting has been monitored or that action has been taken against violations.

Investor rights relating to voting procedures and shareholder meetings are met to a certain extent. Adequate information is disclosed to shareholders in a timely fashion before shareholder meetings. Shareholders are not able to vote in absentia. No rules govern third-party verification of voting. Shareholders may vote on a range of issues, though not on major or related-party transactions. But the RMA has provided regulatory guidelines on the conduct of related-party transactions. Special voting rights of individual shareholders need not be disclosed, nor are they capped.

In contrast, basic ownership rights are in place. Shareholders can vote on appointments and dismissals of directors, with the government exercising control over such outcomes in the government-controlled banks. A clear dividend policy is in place, and structural defenses that can prevent takeover bids are not established, though the government or the RMA reserves the right to approve such transactions. The ability of minority shareholders to nominate a director is not clearly defined. No evidence shows that shareholders exercise any of these basic ownership rights.

Bhutan does not have national accounting or auditing standards or a professional standard-setting body. Bank financial statements are prepared monthly, quarterly, and annually and in accordance with Indian generally accepted accounting principles, which are in material conformity with International Accounting Standards. But other studies on financial reporting and standards have revealed that reporting is confined to forms and schedules prescribed in the Companies Act, with limited nonfinancial disclosures (see World Bank 2006c). Until Bhutan has its own standard-setting institutions, it is important that the RMA issue detailed guidelines on disclosure requirements.

Banks are required to appoint audit committees to review internal and external audit functions as well as ensure compliance with laws and regulations. A panel of external auditors eligible to audit public companies in Bhutan is specified by the Royal Audit Authority, and the audit committees of the banks select their external auditors from this panel and get the RMA's consent. External auditors cannot perform other, nonaudit services for banks. Provisions governing the roles and responsibilities of the internal auditor are established. While auditing standards are said to conform with international standards, here again other reports point to areas needing improvement, such as a general lack of local standards and capacities that will need to be addressed in due course (see World Bank 2006c).

Responses on the structure and effectiveness of boards of directors show that Bhutanese banks follow a unitary structure, with around five directors on average. Board appointments are governed by eligibility criteria set out by the RMA in accordance with the Financial Institutions Act. The roles and responsibilities of boards of directors are clearly defined. Directors and employees are required to follow the code of ethics set out by the RMA in management and operations. For minimization of conflicts of interest, interlocking directorships in the financial industry are prohibited. No defined process is in place for director induction, training, and continuing education.

Compensation policies need to be reviewed. Contrary to accepted standards, shareholders have no say on the remuneration of directors, and the board sets the remuneration of the bank's CEO. The government determines the remuneration of the board. Moreover, disclosure of the compensation of directors is not required. Performance-based compensation systems are not in use. While such compensation systems are widely accepted as providing positive incentives, they should be implemented only after careful consideration.

India

India has had impressive economic growth over the past decade. Its GDP of US$1.2 trillion in 2008 makes India the 12th largest economy in the world. Its population of 1.18 billion makes it the second most populous country, after China. In South Asia, India ranks first in GDP (with 79 percent of the region's total GDP), area (3,287,300 square kilometers), and population. With a GNI per capita of US$1,070 in 2008, India is classified as a lower-middle-income country.

Spurred by expansion in industry and agriculture, annual GDP growth just before the global financial crisis averaged more than 9 percent. But rising oil prices and the onset of the financial crisis slowed the growth rate to 6.7 percent in 2008. This trend continued in 2009, when growth was expected to be around 6 percent. Recovery is expected in 2010, with growth projected to be 7 percent. The current account deficit rose from 1 percent of GDP in 2006 to 2.6 percent in 2008, driven in part by the export slowdown and higher world prices for oil. In 2009 the current account deficit improved slightly to an estimated 1.5 percent of GDP, and in 2010 it is projected to be 2 percent. On a positive note, India continued to attract remittances in 2004–08 at a level averaging around 3.17 percent of GDP. In addition, net annual portfolio flows returned to a positive US$8.5 billion in 2009, from a net annual outflow of US$9.3 billion in 2008.

On the fiscal side, inflation was creeping up as a result of international price increases, peaking at around 8.35 percent in 2008. The Reserve Bank of India (RBI) responded to this situation through the use of monetary policy tools. In 2009 inflation was expected to be around 2.5 percent. For 2010, when economic activity is expected to pick up, it is projected at 4 percent. The fiscal deficit jumped from 2.7 percent of GDP in 2007 to around 6.0 percent in 2008. This widening of the fiscal deficit stems from payment of wage arrears for the public sector under the Sixth Pay Commission proposals and the fiscal stimulus designed to counter the economic slowdown, and the trend was expected to continue in 2009.

The Indian rupee depreciated in 2008 as a result of the global financial crisis and the deleveraging activities that dried up capital inflows, slowing investment activity. Although both portfolio and foreign direct investment picked up modestly in 2009, India needs this pace to accelerate to meet its growing investment requirements. India enjoys one of the highest domestic savings rates in the region, averaging around 34 percent of GDP in 2004–08. Reserves are stable, with India maintaining import cover of 12 months on average in the past few years. Overall, India seems to have countered the economic slowdown, though it needs strong inflows of external capital, along with a continuation of its historically high savings rate, to accelerate investment.

India has a well-regulated and relatively stable banking sector and, unlike most countries in the region, a well-developed capital market. In 2008, the banking sector included 77 commercial banks: 27 public sector banks (8 state banks and 19 nationalized banks), 23 private sector banks (15 old private banks and 8 new ones), and 27 foreign banks. The RBI is the banking regulator and supervisor. In 2008 commercial banking assets amounted to around 91.8 percent of GDP.

India is one of the two countries in South Asia that offer an explicit deposit insurance scheme and was the second country in the world to establish such a scheme, in 1962 (the United States was the first, in 1933). Today, each depositor in a bank is insured up to a maximum of Rs 100,000 (US$2,084) for both principal and interest. A second important element for success in the banking sector is the Credit Information Bureau (India) Limited, incorporated in 2000 to provide credit information to member banks on both commercial and consumer borrowers.

The Indian commercial banking sector is relatively stable (figure 3.4), and it has weathered the second-round effects of the financial crisis thanks to a prudent regulatory framework and sound macroeconomic fundamentals. But some

Figure 3.4 **Indian Banks Are Stable and Well Capitalized**

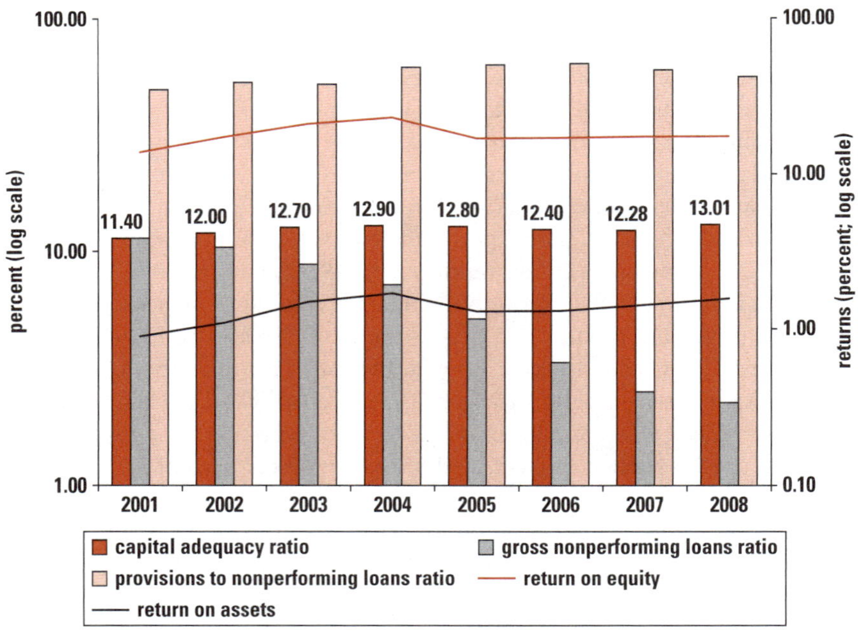

Source: Appendix table A2.12.

fundamental issues remain to be addressed. To promote financial inclusion, key to both human and economic development, banks should seek ways to increase access to the financial services and instruments they offer. In addition, banks should work to further improve their efficiency, achieving stable returns that enable them to further strengthen their provisions and capital cover. Concentration within banking segments should be monitored carefully. In corporate governance, addressing government ownership of banks, harmonization of standards and codes, and revision of statutes and guidelines would improve transparency and consistency. In addition, since India has performance-based compensation mechanisms in place, such mechanisms should be reviewed carefully given recent events in the international arena. Monitoring of performance levels also needs to be discussed.

The Indian capital market is far more developed than its regional counterparts. Yet there are several challenges to address. One is to develop the corporate bond market. With the massive infrastructure financing needs spurred by economic growth, there is huge untapped potential in the corporate bond market. Developing this market would also enable commercial banks to shift away from such long-term projects and better manage their risk portfolios. In developing the capital market, measures are needed to fill legal and regulatory gaps while at the same time not inhibiting market participants. Developing the corporate bond and equity markets while maintaining domestic savings and remittance levels would provide an enormous boost to economic growth.

Access to Finance

Access to financial services offered by the commercial banking sector continues to increase, though there is still room for improvement. Demographic penetration rose marginally in 2001–08, averaging around six bank branches and three ATMs per 100,000 people, though it is still low by developed-country standards. Geographic penetration has improved faster, averaging around 23 branches and 9 ATMs per 1,000 square kilometers in 2001–08 and growing to 26 branches and 13 ATMs per 1,000 square kilometers in 2008. Usage ratios are low, averaging 436 deposit accounts and 68 loan accounts per 1,000 people over the period, indicating a need to further improve access to bank branches and ATMs to match the pace of economic growth. Recognizing the need to increase financial inclusion, the RBI has taken policy measures to do so and has directed banks to make basic, "no frills" accounts available to certain parts of the population. Significant progress has been made in providing these basic accounts.

Besides commercial banks, 91 regional rural banks (predominantly in rural areas) and a large number of cooperative banks (98,343 rural and 1,770 urban) provide access to financial services to low-income and other disadvantaged groups. The regional rural banks are supervised by the National Bank for Agriculture and Rural Development, while most of the cooperative banks operate under the purview of state governments. The RBI regulates 53 scheduled urban cooperative banks, part of the group of 1,770 urban cooperative banks.

The microfinance movement in India has made great strides in providing financial access to the poor since its inception in the early 1990s. The main actors are self-help groups, with total loans outstanding of Rs 123.66 billion (US$2.6 billion) at the end of 2007, and microfinance institutions, with Rs 15.84 billion (US$330 million). For the self-help groups, commercial bank loans account for

Rs 87.60 billion (US$1.82 billion) of the loans outstanding. By March 31, 2007, there were 4.2 million self-help groups maintaining savings accounts with banks, with total savings of Rs 35.13 billion (US$731 million). These groups cover around 58 million poor households. Commercial banks hold the largest share of the self-help groups' savings (53.9 percent), followed by regional rural banks (32.9 percent) and cooperative banks (13.2 percent). (Note that this study does not include cooperative banks, regional rural banks, and microfinance institutions in its indicators on access to finance.)

Performance and Efficiency

Returns in the banking sector remained stable over the period, thanks to the relative stability of the net interest margin. The return on equity increased significantly between 2003 and 2004, mainly because of large profits realized on the trading of securities. The rate grew slightly in 2007 to end at 17.34 percent in 2008. Meanwhile, the return on assets showed an increasing trend. The net interest margin remained stable over the period at around 3 percent. Recurring earning power also appeared stable, with the ratio at 2.15 percent in 2008.

The operating cost ratio fell in 2007 to 71.05 percent but crept back up in 2008 to 76.03 percent. The staff cost ratio declined by almost 25 percent between 2001 and 2008, to 51.55 percent, as a result of automation and staff retirements.

Many countries in the region have reported better returns, interest margins, and earning power than India, but Indian banks are expected to be able to maintain stable performance levels even with the economic slowdown. While nonperforming loans are expected to increase as a result of adverse economic conditions, the restructuring of loans in the second part of 2008 and early 2009 should have eased bad loans, keeping returns stable. Even so, banks will have to keep nonperforming loan levels low and improve cost and return efficiency to maintain stability in returns.

Financial Stability

India's commercial banks are adequately capitalized. In 2008, all but two banks recorded capital adequacy ratios of more than 10 percent, above the 9 percent minimum capital requirement in India. All 27 public sector banks, along with 22 private sector banks and 26 foreign banks, showed capital adequacy ratios above 10 percent, while one local private bank and one foreign bank recorded ratios between 8 percent and 10 percent. In 2008, the aggregate capital adequacy ratio reported by the Indian banking sector was 13.01 percent. This capital adequacy reporting is under the Basel I framework. Foreign banks in India have followed the Basel II guidelines since March 2008, and all other banks were expected to follow suit by March 2009. In 2008, of the 77 banks in India, 41 had migrated to Basel II, and all 41 had capital adequacy ratios, reported under Basel II guidelines, exceeding the regulatory requirement of 9 percent.

The leverage ratio has continued to decline, reaching 10.63 in 2008. While leverage ratios in India are higher than those in most other South Asian countries, its banks may need to further augment their capital base. Since the onset of the financial crisis, the government has infused close to US$400 million in capital in some public sector banks to strengthen their capital position and is ready to do more in the coming year. As it is, banks are able to withstand the shocks to the system that may be caused by an increase in nonperforming loans.

The gross nonperforming loans ratio fell from 11.40 percent in 2001 to 2.25 percent in 2008. The provisions to nonperforming loans ratio stood at 56.18 percent in 2008. Provisions fell in 2007 and 2008. Because nonperforming loans may rise in the near future as a result of the economic slowdown, increasing the provision cover would be prudent. In the second part of 2008 and early 2009, the RBI allowed a large-scale loan restructuring process, covering around 4.5 percent of the loan portfolio, to counter the effects of the global financial crisis. Loan terms were restructured, and in some cases, loans that under normal circumstances would have been classified as nonperforming on time-based criteria (for example, because of late payments of interest) were classified as performing, depending on their recoverability. Since Indian banks are not directly exposed to the global financial crisis, no large-scale increase in nonperforming loans is expected.

Liquidity seems to have tightened over the period. The liquid assets ratio dropped slightly to 34.12 percent in 2008, though it remained significantly higher than in other countries in the region, while the liquid assets to liabilities ratio improved slightly to 146.23 percent. A rising loan to deposit ratio indicated increasing liquidity stress in the banking system and thus growing liquidity risk. The RBI countered this tight liquidity situation by easing the cash reserve requirement and other policy rates.

Overall, the outlook for the Indian banking system is for financial stability. With their current capital cushion, banks will be able to withstand the rising levels of nonperforming loans, and no dramatic increase in these levels is expected. But banks will be in a better position if provision levels are increased further and liquidity is prudently managed.

Capital Market Development

India's dynamic economic growth has paved the way for rapid development of its capital market over the past decade. Today India has a developed capital market for equities, bonds, and derivatives. Corporate governance has progressed, and the market infrastructure and regulatory framework have been improved. The stock market has developed rapidly, with market capitalization increasing from 29.40 percent of GDP in 2001 to 106.05 percent in 2008. Between 2007 and 2008, market capitalization increased by about 26.6 percent.

In 2008, however, the global deleveraging directly affected the Bombay Stock Exchange's Sensex index. As foreign investors liquidated their portfolios, the index fell by more than 52 percent at the end of 2007 to 9,788 at the end of October 2008. This negative trend did not last long, however. The index had recovered to 16,283 by October 2009 and is projected to rise further. Market depth has improved as well, with the trading value of the top 10 stocks declining from 72.90 percent of the total value of shares traded in 2001 to 26.78 percent in 2008. Market liquidity initially fell, then improved over the period: the stock trading value rose to 108.86 percent of GDP in 2008. The stock market turnover ratio improved steadily. In 2007 it increased slightly, but remained at an efficient level in 2008, at 1.13.

Government bonds dominate the bond market, with outstanding public bonds amounting to 36.24 percent of GDP in 2008. The corporate bond market is negligible at around 3.2 percent of GDP. The dominance of government bonds, accounting for more than 91 percent of the total bond market, is comparable to that in other South Asian countries. This dominance is likely to increase given the government's need to finance fiscal stimulus activities and the pay increase under the Sixth Pay Commission. India is the only country in South Asia to list government securities on the stock exchange and benchmark on the yield curve—an important step in bond market development.

The Securities and Exchange Board of India regulates the capital market. Trades take place mostly through electronic trading platforms, with same-day settlement for government debt securities and T+1 settlement for equity. Dematerialization is almost complete, and securities are traded only in dematerialized form. The dematerialization reforms have increased efficiency and transparency and reduced settlement costs for the investors. While the equity market is developed and stable, the corporate bond market is still at a comparatively nascent stage of development. Legal and regulatory gaps need to be filled to attract investors to this market.

Market Concentration and Competitiveness

India continues to lead the region in lowering market concentration in the banking sector. The Herfindahl-Hirschman Index declined steadily over the period to 535.63 in 2008. But when the banking sector is broken down by segment, it becomes clear that while the index shows a trend of declining market concentration among public sector banks, it shows an increasing trend among private sector banks and foreign banks. The data suggest that a few key players dominate these two segments, a situation that needs to be monitored carefully. The market shares of the top three banks in assets, loans, and deposits have remained steady at around 32 percent. Again, however, analyzing the banking segments separately shows higher concentration among private sector and foreign banks. Still, concentration is relatively low overall, indicating room for new entrants and healthy competition in the growing economy.

Private credit extended by banks increased rapidly, growing by almost 127 percent between 2001 and 2008 to 48.78 percent of GDP. Commercial banking assets also increased steadily, from 61.90 percent of GDP in 2001 to 91.80 percent in 2008. Commercial banks still hold the prime position in the formal financial structure. As the markets mature and corporate bond and equity markets grow, however, this can be expected to change.

The Indian banking sector is competitive and can expect efficiencies that will further lower intermediary costs. But the higher concentration in the private sector and foreign bank segments should be monitored. Private credit growth seems to have decelerated by 2009, possibly because of the economic slowdown. But because of the accelerated credit growth in previous years, credit risk will remain a concern. Prudential regulations and risk management systems should help manage this risk, however.

Payment Systems Development

India has a developed payment system that includes both retail- and large-value payment systems. The retail-value payment systems are automated or manual clearing systems with end-of-day net settlement. The retail payment system includes automated (MICR and non-MICR) check clearing, retail electronic fund transfer, and card payments. Today there are 71 MICR check processing centers functioning in the country. Where setting up MICR check processing was not found to be viable (the case in 1,064 clearinghouses), the settlement operations have been computerized so that settlement is done electronically even though the instruments are still sorted manually. High-value clearing is available at 24 major locations in the country. The threshold for high-value clearing is to be raised from Rs 100,000 to Rs 1 million (US$20,834) per transaction. Another clearing arrangement, "speed clearing," has been introduced at 53 locations, where outstation checks (those outside the main city or region) are now cleared on a T+1 or T+2 basis. To enhance the efficiency of the paper-based clearing systems, a check truncation system was implemented in February 2008 as a pilot project with the 10 banks in the National Capital Region (RBI, *Annual Report, 2008–09*).

Electronic fund transfer systems include the electronic clearing service (ECS), electronic fund transfer (EFT), and national electronic fund transfer (NEFT). ECS is available in 75 centers and operates on a T+1 settlement cycle. To enhance its efficiency, a new system, the National Electronic Clearing Service (NECS), which has centralized processing capabilities, was introduced in September 2008. By the end of March 2009, 114 banks with 26,275 branches were participating in the new system. NEFT is a nationwide electronic fund transfer system in which 89 banks with 55,225 branches participate. The transactions processed through the systems in 2008/09 totaled Rs 164,463 crore (US$34.3 billion) for the ECS (debits and credits) and NECS and Rs 251,956 crore (US$52.5 billion) for the EFT and NEFT (RBI, *Annual Report, 2008–09*). The total value of retail transactions relative to GDP has shown a declining trend, indicating increasing use of the RTGS system. In 2008 retail transactions amounted to 306.1 percent of GDP.

The RTGS system has been in operation since March 2004. This system is primarily for large-value transactions, with a minimum threshold of Rs 1 lakh (Rs 100,000). There were 55,006 RTGS-enabled bank branches by March 2009, with 11,494 branches added to the RTGS network in 2008/09. In that year the RTGS system processed 13.37 million transactions with a total value of Rs 323 trillion (US$6.73 trillion) (RBI, *Annual Report, 2008–09*). RTGS transactions have been increasing rapidly, reaching 1,024.69 percent of GDP in 2008.

The RBI assessment of the RTGS system reports that it is fully compliant with six core principles of the Committee on Payment and Settlement Systems of the Bank for International Settlements (BIS) and broadly compliant with core principles 3, 7, and 8 relating to management of credit and liquidity risk, operational reliability, and efficiency. To strengthen the regulation and supervision of the payment systems, a new law and two regulations came into effect on August 12, 2008: the Payment and Settlement Systems Act, 2007 (PSS Act 51 of 2007); Board for Regulation and Supervision of Payment and Settlement Systems Regulations, 2008; and Payment and Settlement Systems Regulations, 2008. India is presently making arrangements to implement RTGS second-generation modifications to its payment system from 2010 onward. This would further reduce the potential risks in the payment and settlement systems.

Besides the interbank and high-value check clearing systems and the RTGS system, two other systemically important payment systems are the Negotiated Dealing System and the Foreign Exchange Clearing System.

Both the notes and coins in circulation to GDP ratio and the narrow money supply to GDP ratio increased over the period to 11.17 percent and 21.06 percent, respectively, in 2008. Currency in circulation accounts for more than 53 percent of the narrow money supply. Heavy use of currency indicates a need for financial services or payment instruments—and while India has developed its payment systems, there is still room for expansion given the size of its population and geographic area. Conversely, the broad money supply indicator shows a higher level of financial intermediation (see the section on savings mobilization).

To promote more inclusive growth in the payment systems, India is expanding into such areas as mobile banking and prepaid smart cards. The RBI issued operating guidelines for mobile banking in October 2008 and policy guidelines for prepayment instruments in April 2009.

Savings Mobilization

Domestic savings are among the more important and more stable resources a country has at its disposal. India has enjoyed a consistently high domestic savings rate. In 2008, domestic savings amounted to 37.7 percent of GDP. The broad money supply is also high, at 76.45 percent of GDP in 2008, indicating efficient financial intermediation. The real deposit rate, which is adjusted for inflation, turned negative in 2003 but then turned positive again, and in 2008 it was around 1.05 percent. The reserve money to total deposits ratio has declined slightly and averages around 26 percent. The loan to deposit ratio rose steadily from 53.13 percent in 2001 to 73.88 percent in 2008, an increase of around 39 percent. Worker remittances have also been stable and were around 3.64 percent of GDP in 2008.

Overall, the savings situation in India is promising, with a sound savings culture, reliable remittance patterns, and incentives in the form of positive interest rates. Strong growth in domestic savings could be the solution for sustaining the dynamic economic growth observed in the past decade, especially in light of the capital outflows following the onset of the financial crisis. Indeed, India has been able to finance a significant portion of its investment needs through domestic savings (which amount to more than a third of GDP), an impressive feat for such a fast-growing economy. It is important that it take the steps necessary to maintain this advantage.

Corporate Governance

The Securities and Exchange Board of India regulates the corporate governance of listed companies across all sectors through Clause 49 of the Listing Agreements. Clause 49 provides guidelines on composition of the board of directors, composition and operations of the audit committee, remuneration of directors, board procedures, management, shareholders, and reporting requirements and compliance. In addition, the Banking Regulation Act, 1949, remains the foundation of the corporate governance framework for banks in India. Public sector banks are also governed by the statutes under which they are incorporated. These include the State Bank of India Act, 1955; the State Bank of India (Subsidiary Banks) Act, 1959, for the associate banks of the State Bank of India; and the Banking Companies (Acquisition and Transfer of Undertakings) Act, 1970/80, for nationalized banks.

Recognizing the importance of corporate governance to the efficiency of banks' operations, the RBI set up at least three committees to study different aspects of corporate governance.[5] On the basis of their recommendations, guidelines that can be implemented within the existing legislative structure are being issued while legislative amendments are being discussed. India has made good progress in these matters, though challenges remain in the implementation and enforcement of such regulations.

While the framework governing ownership, board composition and operations, and fit-and-proper criteria for the public sector banks is entrenched in the legal statutes that govern them, the RBI introduced a comprehensive policy framework for ownership and governance in private sector banks in February 2005. The broad principles underlying this framework are to ensure that ultimate ownership and control of commercial banks is well diversified, that key shareholders and directors and CEOs meet the fit-and-proper criteria, and that the board observes sound corporate governance principles. The RBI has also expanded the transparency and disclosure standards.

Detailed assessment of the responses to the corporate governance survey shows that existing provisions largely cover issues relating to ownership structure and influence of external stakeholders (see appendix 4A). There appear to be differences between the rules that apply to public sector banks and those applying to private sector banks, however.

The questionnaire responses also show that regulatory guidelines of both the RBI and the Securities and Exchange Board require disclosure of the shareholdings of promoters as well as the top 10 shareholders in the annual report, to which both shareholders and the market have access. The RBI disclosure threshold is 5 percent. For private sector banks, the threshold for disclosure is 1 percent. The government discloses its shareholdings only in public sector banks. In addition, the government appoints the chairman and managing director and the executive directors and nominates nonexecutive directors. The RBI, the regulator, is also represented on the board. But its earlier practice of nominating directors to the boards of all private sector banks has been changed, and the RBI now nominates directors only for selected private sector banks. Nominee directors include representatives of labor unions. Nonexecutive directors representing the government and the RBI do sometimes exercise influence over board decisions.

The prompt correction action regime does not discriminate on the basis of ownership. The regulator can initiate corrective actions proposed under the regime. Minority shareholders have preemption rights under the Companies Act. Legal provisions govern the disclosure of beneficial ownership of shareholders, but no thresholds are prescribed. Shareholders are required to disclose such ownership to the company.

The questionnaire responses indicate comprehensive coverage of investor rights relating to voting and shareholder meetings. Proxy voting is allowed, though electronic voting is not. Shareholders can demand a vote only if they hold a tenth of the total votes. Two independent parties are appointed by the chairman to assist in the polling process. The Banking Regulation Act caps individual voting rights at 10 percent for the private sector and 1 percent for the public sector. Shareholders can vote on a range of issues, including related-party transactions.

Government control over basic ownership rights once again warrants review. The government controls the appointment or dismissal of directors in public sector banks, while shareholders vote on such issues in private sector banks. There are no special provisions covering minority shareholder rights in electing board members. The RBI has given clear guidelines to commercial banks on broad parameters for declaring dividends. If these guidelines are not met, banks need to obtain prior approval from the RBI before recommending dividends to shareholders for approval. No structural defenses have been established to prevent takeover bids, but any transfer of shares exceeding 5 percent of total paid-up capital is subject to registration and regulatory scrutiny and to approval by the RBI.

Responses on transparency and disclosure suggest that policy improvements are needed on disclosure requirements, audit fees, and the internal audit function. Financial statements are prepared in accordance with generally accepted local accounting principles, which are in material conformity with International Accounting Standards. Considerable efforts have been made to align Indian accounting standards with the International Financial Reporting Standards. The Institute of Chartered Accountants of India uses the International Financial Reporting Standards in developing the national standards, departing from the international standards where justified. In recent years, the institute has issued and revised several accounting standards, significantly reducing the gap between the national and international standards. Differences remain, however (eStandardsForum 2007). A similar process is under way for local auditing standards. Financial reporting is done quarterly, semiannually, and annually. No provisions have been established requiring the disclosure of audit fees paid to external auditors.

The RBI has issued clear guidelines on the appointment of audit committees and has clearly delineated their roles and responsibilities. In private sector banks, these committees control the process of selecting external auditors; for public sector banks the central bank appoints auditors from a preapproved list. External auditors do not perform other, nonaudit services for the banks they audit. The RBI has issued clear guidelines on the roles and responsibilities of internal auditors. The internal audit function is performed by bank staff with the required professional qualifications and work experience. But internal auditors face no requirement to report to the board of directors rather than to management, raising questions about their independence.

Indian banks follow a unitary structure for their boards with around 8–12 members on average. The Banking Regulation Act governs requirements on the qualifications and experience of board members. The roles and responsibilities of the board are clearly defined, but tasks and objectives are not assigned to individual board members. Moreover, no provisions exist on formal and systematic training for directors, an issue that warrants attention.

Detailed guidelines are needed to harmonize the practices of local private and public sector banks for setting and disclosing the remuneration of directors as well as setting performance-based compensation policies. Compensation policies for public sector banks were reviewed by the RBI in March 2006. Executive directors of public sector banks will receive performance-based compensation for achieving targets, similar to their counterparts at private sector banks. In private sector banks, shareholders can vote on the remuneration of directors, while in public sector banks the government has the right to set remuneration. In addition, while private sector banks disclose directors' compensation in detail, public sector banks disclose only aggregate compensation.

The global financial crisis has prompted much debate in the international arena about executive compensation, stock options, and bonus practices. This would be a good opportunity for the RBI to review performance-based compensation policies in consultation with banks. The monitoring of performance also needs to be discussed.

Overall, India has made good progress in strengthening the corporate governance of banks. Some areas need further attention, however. One main issue is government ownership of banks and such underlying concerns as transparency, objectivity, and a level playing field. To address these concerns, differences in rules, regulations, and treatment between public and private sector banks should be minimized. To improve transparency and disclosure, accounting and auditing standards should be reviewed for consistency with international standards. The RBI, in consultation with banks, should also review compensation policies and the monitoring of executive performance. And banks should take an active part in incorporating corporate governance into their operations. To bring in some of the changes suggested by the consultative committees, the RBI could take steps to make necessary amendments to the legal statutes. Also important is to ensure proper enforcement of the guidelines. An efficient corporate governance system would provide both regulators and banks with the tools to improve robustness, reliability, and consistency—and thereby strengthen the credibility of the banking sector.

Maldives

Maldives has the smallest area (300 square kilometers), population (350,000), and GDP (US$1.26 billion in 2008) in South Asia. Yet it has the highest GNI per capita in the region at US$3,630 in 2008 and is classified as a lower-middle-income country. This was made possible by the remarkable economic growth achieved by Maldives in the past two decades.

The Indian Ocean tsunami in 2004, coupled with a decline in tourism revenue due to greater global uncertainties as well as high food and fuel prices, has taken its toll, however. Asset losses due to the tsunami amounted to around 62 percent of GDP. In 2006 reconstruction projects boosted GDP away from a negative trend, to 18 percent. But since then, despite a pickup in tourism and fishing, growth has lagged. In 2009, in the wake of the global financial crisis, the growth rate turned negative, dropping to an estimated −3.5 percent. The projection for 2010 is a conservative 3.5 percent, though it is hoped that the global economic slowdown will have waned by then.

As a result of expansionary policies, inflation crept up from 3.5 percent in 2006 to 11.89 percent in 2008 before declining to an estimated 4.5 percent in 2009. The soaring government expenditure pushed the fiscal deficit up to 13.57 percent of GDP by the end of 2008, and the deficit was expected to rise even higher by the end of 2009. The current account deficit dropped from 51.7 percent of GDP to an estimated 30 percent, but remains a matter for concern. Reserves have fallen to two months of import cover.

Overall, the fiscal situation is still critical, but Maldives is taking steps to address the situation. One priority was to stop monetizing the deficit, which was done in 2009. Maldives is also working to cut recurrent government expenditure to a sustainable level and obtain external financing. Because the country lacks domestic resources, its economic prospects will depend largely on an upturn in the world economy, at least in the near future.

The banking sector in Maldives consists of six commercial banks—one local bank in which the government is the majority owner and five foreign banks.

As in other countries in the region, banks dominate the financial sector; commercial banking assets in 2008 amounted to 143.14 percent of GDP. The financial sector also includes a leasing company, a housing finance institution, several insurance companies, money service businesses, and securities market intermediaries. The Maldives Monetary Authority (MMA) is the regulatory authority for banks as well as nonbank financial institutions, while the Capital Market Development Authority (CMDA) regulates the securities market.

The Maldivian banking sector is small but has the potential to grow. The authorities are working to expand the banking sector and capital market while improving financial outreach. These efforts, along with measures to address macroeconomic imbalances, should help ensure stability in the banking system, a key to stable and sustainable economic growth.

Although commercial banking assets tripled in 2001–08, and private credit provided by banks quadrupled over the same period, limited access to financial services remains one of the main impediments to financial inclusion and private sector development. The authorities are tackling this issue—which is caused by the geographic dispersion of the population—through a mobile phone banking project intended to provide branchless banking. Evaluation of the banking sector's performance reveals high but declining returns and rising operating costs, a trend that is a matter for concern. Maldivian banks have maintained stable capital adequacy ratios well above the minimum requirement (figure 3.5). Even so, increasing levels of nonperforming loans and declining provisions are another cause for concern. Asset quality should be improved through diversified lending and better credit information. A new credit information bureau should

Figure 3.5 Maldivian Banks Maintain Stable Capital Ratios

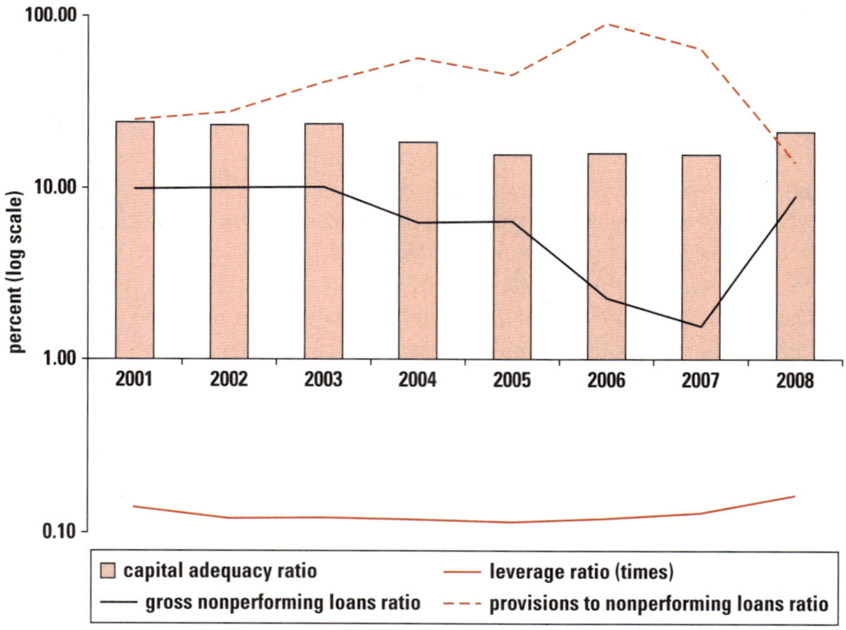

Source: Appendix table A2.13.

help by improving credit information and reducing costs. Another issue needing review is the high liquidity in the banking sector, which stems from high statutory reserve requirements.

The capital market remains undeveloped, making it difficult for banks to secure long-term funding—though development efforts are under way. The banking sector is narrow and concentrated. And the public sector seems to crowd out private sector credit, because of both macroeconomic imbalances and narrow capital markets. These areas need attention to expand capital markets and ensure a stable, competitive banking industry.

Maldives has a small but functional payment system, and efforts are under way to expand and modernize it, an important step toward improving the soundness of the financial sector. Although the domestic savings rate is high, the intermediation between savers and investors is inefficient. Steps are needed to create savings and investment opportunities and to improve interest rates by curbing inflation. Developing a stable domestic savings base to aid investment is important when the external economic and financial environment becomes uncertain.

Maldives has issued a corporate governance code as well as corporate governance regulations for banks, an important step. These guidelines are too new to assess their effectiveness. But issues that need to be addressed include the heavy government ownership in listed companies, transparency and disclosure principles with an emphasis on accounting and auditing standards, and compliance with guidelines and standards. Developing governance practices and compliance would improve transparency and accountability.

Access to Finance

Maldives leads South Asia in access to finance, mainly because of higher indicators of demographic and geographic penetration. Demographic penetration increased over the period studied—from 6 branches and 3 ATMs per 100,000 people in 2001 to 10 branches and 13 ATMs in 2008. Geographic penetration showed similar increases, growing from 57 branches and 27 ATMs per 1,000 square kilometers in 2001 to 103 branches and 130 ATMs in 2008.[6] Usage ratios also rose, reaching 965 deposit accounts and 142 loan accounts per 1,000 people in 2008.

But the story does not end there, because these penetration ratios do not take into account the geographic dispersion of Maldivians among the atolls of the country. This geographic dispersion poses a big challenge. According to a World Bank report (2008c, 3–4), "The Maldives may be one of the most difficult countries in the world in which to deliver financial services through traditional branch networks. . . . Its 300,000 people live on 198 scattered islands in 26 atolls, and 60 percent of the inhabited islands have less than 1,000 residents. . . . only 40 percent have bank accounts and this varies sharply between the outer atolls (35 percent) and Male (65 percent)." According to this report, the 2006 Investment Climate Assessment in Maldives identified access to finance as the biggest constraint to private sector development, followed by cost of financing—while in most South Asian countries finance typically ranks third or fourth.

Opening bank branches on all the islands clearly would not be cost-effective. Even microfinance, which has played a large part in the region in bringing access to financial services to mostly rural areas, would not be a feasible solution because of the high setup costs that would be involved. But mobile phone banking has good potential for delivering services across the country. Mobile phone penetration exceeds 100 percent, and the network provides full coverage of Maldives. With the assistance of the World Bank, the MMA has therefore initiated a mobile phone banking project that is expected to benefit the residents of the outer atolls especially. Even people in Male will benefit from the ability to conduct virtual transactions.

Performance and Efficiency

Although the Maldivian banking sector ranks high on performance indicators in South Asia, negative trends in 2007–08 are a matter for concern. Returns increased over much of the period studied, with the return on equity rising to 53.51 percent in 2006, and the return on assets to 6.36 percent. The two ratios then fell to 30.36 percent and 4.53 percent in 2008. The net interest margin and recurring earning power showed a similar declining trend. Meanwhile, operating costs rose from 30.60 percent of net interest earnings in 2006 to 36.30 percent in 2008. Staff costs amounted to almost half the operating costs in 2007, then dropped to around 33.6 percent in 2008. Even with these declining trends, the performance ratios are some of the highest in the region. But high banking costs and lower returns will adversely affect the performance and efficiency of the banking sector in the future.

One reason for the declining returns is the high concentration of lending in the economy's two main sectors—and thus the vulnerability to fluctuations in those sectors. The mainstays of the Maldivian economy are tourism, accounting for around 31 percent of GDP on average for the past decade or so, and fisheries, accounting for 7 percent. These two sectors accounted for 61.3 percent and 7 percent, respectively, of commercial bank lending in 2008. Housing construction loans represented another 8.7 percent of the total.

Commercial bank returns are falling because of declining growth in these activities. Growth in tourism arrivals dropped from 52.3 percent in 2006 to 12.3 percent in 2007 and just 1.1 percent in 2008. Growth was expected to fall to −11 percent in 2009, then pick up marginally to a projected 1 percent in 2010 and 2.5 percent in 2011. In the fisheries sector, total fish landings dropped by about 20 percent between 2006 and 2007 and did not increase in 2008 (Maldives, Ministry of Finance and Treasury 2009). Global uncertainties, the effects of the tsunami, the global financial and economic crisis, and high fuel prices are among the reasons for the slowing growth in these sectors. The concern is that neither industry is expected to see a robust turnaround in the near future.

Financial Stability

Maldives maintained a stable risk-weighted capital adequacy ratio of around 20 percent on average throughout the period studied (see figure 3.5). Even when performance ratios dropped in 2007, the capital adequacy ratio was around 15.58 percent—well above the then minimum requirement of 8 percent of risk-weighted assets. The minimum requirement was raised to 12 percent effective in 2009, a level that the average capital adequacy ratio also always exceeded during the period. In 2008, the capital position increased to 21.01 percent. Because Maldives adheres to Basel I guidelines, however, the capital cushion does not include charges against market risk or operational risk.

The gross nonperforming loans ratio fell from a high of 10.10 percent in 2003 to 1.56 percent in 2007, then jumped to 8.90 percent in 2008. At the same time, provisions for nonperforming loans dropped by nearly 50 percentage points—from 63.94 percent in 2007 to 14.02 percent in 2008. Although capitalization is high, growing levels of nonperforming loans and weak provisioning are a matter for concern. In today's uncertain economic environment, banks need to ensure that their capital base is not further eroded by a weak asset position. The banking sector's leverage position has been continually low, with equity just 16 percent of total assets in 2008, indicating the vulnerability of the capital position if more assets should go bad. Moreover, the liquidity position is high, though it declined considerably over the period. In 2008 the liquid assets ratio was around 22.60 percent.[7] The minimum reserve requirement is high, at 25 percent, and bank funds are tied up. This can have an adverse effect on the cost of funds, and the MMA should therefore take steps to reduce reserve requirements to facilitate credit expansion.

Overall, the capital position of Maldivian banks is stable, though the already rising levels of nonperforming loans and declining provisions could undermine this position. Maldives is grappling with outdated mortgage and property laws and lack of special debt recovery provisions, all of which play a major part in debt recovery and could have supported the management of nonperforming loans. Banks need to manage their liquidity positions well. Also important is to improve asset quality so as to minimize nonperforming loans. Maldivian authorities have taken an important step by initiating the creation of a credit information bureau with the assistance of the International Finance Corporation (IFC) of the World Bank Group. The exchange of credit information should help improve credit quality as well as reduce processing costs.

Capital Market Development

The capital market in Maldives is still very much at a nascent stage. The stock market has just four stocks listed. The corporate bond market has had only three corporate bond issues, by one company in 2006. The MMA has issued treasury bills to finance the budget deficit. Those outstanding in 2008 amounted to 4.51 percent of GDP. The stock market capitalization was around 20.60 percent of GDP in 2008. Market liquidity was around 3.19 percent of GDP. And turnover was about 0.014 times the average market capitalization, reflecting the low efficiency.

With the shallow capital market, banks lack access to long-term funding, which hampers their growth. While foreign banks can secure funding through overseas markets, the lack of local long-term funding will discourage domestic private sector banks from entering the market.

Maldives is working toward developing its capital market. The Maldives Security Depository, established in 2004, facilitates scripless trade sharing for the stock market. It operates a net clearing and settlement system with a payment-versus-delivery mechanism to minimize risk and to dematerialize the trades.

Market Concentration and Competitiveness

The Maldivian banking sector is narrow, leading to a heavily concentrated market. The Herfindahl-Hirschman Index showed an increasing trend over the period and averaged around 3,400. According to accepted norms, an index above 1,800 denotes a heavily concentrated market. The top three banks account for more than 90 percent of assets, deposits, and loans. There is little room for competition and, thus, little opportunity to reap intermediary cost efficiencies.

Commercial bank credit jumped from 23.57 percent of GDP in 2001 to 100.84 percent in 2008. But public sector credit seems to crowd out private credit as a result of macroeconomic imbalances as well as narrow capital markets. Commercial banking assets almost tripled as a percentage of GDP, growing from 50.92 percent in 2001 to 143.14 percent in 2008. But while banks' asset position increased, the narrowness of their lending activities, reflected in the heavy concentration in two sectors, needs to be addressed, perhaps in the medium to long term.

Payment Systems Development

The ratio of notes and coins in circulation to GDP increased gradually over the period, to 9.37 percent in 2008. The narrow money supply increased much faster, from 21.23 percent of GDP in 2001 to 37.75 percent in 2008. Currency in circulation is not very high as a share of narrow money. There is no evidence that funds are tied up in currency in circulation; instead, they are tied up in reserves because of the high liquidity requirements for banks. Even so, a modern payment system would improve efficiency in the use of funds and, more important in this case, provide access to financial services.

Maldives has a small but functional payment system for both large- and small-value transactions, an end-of-day net settlement system. The MMA operates a manual clearinghouse for the commercial banks. Maldivian authorities are modernizing the payment system through the mobile phone banking project. The project will develop an RTGS system allowing real-time settlement of large-value payments and minimizing settlement risk; an automated clearinghouse system, which is an image-enabled, faster clearing system; a mobile payment system using mobile phones to facilitate branchless banking; and an electronic fund transfer point-of-sale/ATM switch system, a continuously available, real-time, secure system enabling reciprocity and interoperability. This modernization project is expected to make the systems compliant with BIS Committee on Payment and Settlement Systems core principles and assist in efficient utilization of resources. It should also improve financial inclusion by overcoming the challenges of geographic dispersion in Maldives.

Savings Mobilization

Maldives has not aggressively pursued savings mobilization. The country has a high savings rate but lacks a strong savings culture. A measure of financial deepening is high—the ratio of broad money to GDP increased from 43.04 percent in 2001 to 76.51 percent in 2008—and is reflected in the high per capita income. The real deposit interest rate declined over the period as a result of inflationary pressures, from 3.24 percent in 2001 to −0.65 percent in 2008. The available data on gross domestic savings show that they averaged around 47 percent of GDP in 2001–04. The reserve money to total deposits ratio declined over the period to 44.67 percent in 2008, which is still too high. The loan to deposit ratio increased over the period by about 72 percentage points to 133.41 percent in 2008. Unlike most countries in the region, Maldives does not have significant remittance income; it averaged less than 0.5 percent of GDP throughout the period. Instead, Maldives has net remittance outflows because of the many expatriates in its labor force.

These indicators show that domestic savings are underused. While the financial deepening ratio is high, this can have a negative impact on economic growth when coupled with high liquidity and low credit. The high ratio of reserve money to total deposits indicates low efficiency in financial intermediation between savers and investors. And although bank credit is growing, the lack of real investments or diversified credit opportunities means that the credit is not supporting sustainable growth.

Moreover, even though domestic savings rates are high, negative real interest rates and lack of investment opportunities can drive the savings abroad (because Maldives has no exchange restrictions, both residents and nonresidents can freely import and export capital). Other countries in the region offer attractive rates, instruments, and opportunities to encourage foreign investment. The comparatively low gross capital formation in Maldives is evidence that domestic savings are underutilized.

Although foreign income and capital are important, domestic savings should be aggressively pursued. During times of crisis, when foreign income declines and global deleveraging induces capital outflows, domestic savings can sustain economic development. Maldives would therefore benefit from taking steps to create savings and investment opportunities and to improve real interest rates by curbing inflation.

Corporate Governance

The key legislation governing the financial sector is the Maldives Monetary Authority Act, 1981 (amended in 2007). Regulations for Banks and Financial Institutions, issued under the Maldives Monetary Authority Act of July 1988 (amended January 1, 1998), set out the framework within which all banks and financial institutions in Maldives must operate. Based on the provisions of the Companies Act, 1996 (amended in 1998), and the Maldives Securities Act 2/2006, the CMDA issued a corporate governance code for all listed companies—first for voluntary adoption beginning January 1, 2007, then for mandatory adoption (unless a company is expressly exempted) beginning January 1, 2008. The CMDA code covers the following areas:

- Board of directors—effectiveness; composition; nomination and reelection of members; separation of chairman and CEO; role of the board, chairman, and CEO; duties; training; board committees (nominating, remuneration, and audit)
- Remuneration—policy, evaluation of board performance, disclosure
- Management—constitution, roles and responsibilities, access to information
- Internal audit, external auditor, and internal control
- Company secretary
- Shareholder rights—communications, meetings, voting rights
- Disclosure—financial and nonfinancial statements
- Voluntary provisions—system to raise concerns, investor and media relationships, and disclosure of remuneration for individual board members

To complement this code, the MMA issued a corporate governance regulation setting additional standards for banks, effective May 2009. This regulation covers the following areas:

- Requirements—policies and committees, competent management, conflicts of interest, records, board meetings, board of directors, resident manager, branch visits
- Corrective measures—remedial measures and sanctions

Because the guidelines were issued very recently, assessing their effectiveness is difficult. But the answers to the survey questionnaire reveal several areas needing further attention: government control, voting procedures, minority shareholder rights, and transparency and disclosure principles with an emphasis on accounting and auditing standards (see appendix 4A). The main issue is the government control over most outcomes, stemming from state ownership in almost all listed companies. Anecdotal evidence suggests that companies are amending their articles to circumvent this control. The recently created local accounting body needs to be strengthened and compliance with international standards pursued. However, some standards may not be applicable in Maldives given its level of development, and some may need revisions to address country-specific issues. Streamlining accounting and auditing standards is very important. Also important is to ensure compliance with guidelines and standards. Thus training should be provided for the examiners as well as the users.

The survey responses show that ownership structure is clearly defined. Public companies are required to keep a registry of shareholders who directly or indirectly control more than 5 percent of shares (substantial shareholders), but there is no special requirement to disclose government ownership and its special privileges. The government controls the remuneration and nomination of the board. It is unclear whether external stakeholders such as labor unions and banking and securities regulators can influence the nomination and remuneration process for the board of directors. And there is no evidence that the preemption rights of minority shareholders are firmly protected. The Maldives Securities Act obligates any person acquiring more than 5 percent of the shares in a public company to send notice of that fact within 14 days to the company, the CMDA, and the stock exchange. A registry of such holdings is to be maintained. This registry is accessible to shareholders, and because the information is disclosed to the stock exchange, it is accessible to the market. Breach of these disclosure requirements can lead to fines or imprisonment, although how strictly these penalties are enforced is not known.

There are established procedures for shareholder meetings, though voting procedures need to be clearly defined. It is unclear whether banks provide detailed agendas and explanatory circulars along with notice of meetings. Voting procedures—such as ability to vote by proxy, third-party verification, and shareholder voting rights—are determined by banks' articles. Moreover, it is unclear whether banks are required to disclose special voting rights and caps on voting rights. Since all listed companies are state-owned enterprises, the government exerts considerable control over appointment and dismissal of board members. While some companies have defined dividend rules, a provision has been included in the listing rules to circumvent problems arising because of a company's lack of written dividend policies. There are no structural takeover defenses that would prevent a legitimate takeover bid. Nor are there guidelines to ensure minority shareholders' right to appoint directors; this depends on individual banks' rules.

Transparency and disclosure is an area needing special attention and development. While the CMDA requires companies to follow internationally accepted accounting and auditing standards, there is no evidence that this is happening. The frequency of reporting and the availability of financial statements to the public are unclear, although the CMDA is trying to ensure quarterly reporting. No information is available to discern whether external auditors are allowed to perform nonaudit functions. The CMDA code and MMA regulation include guidelines on audit committees and external and internal auditors, but it is unclear whether banks follow any of these rules. A local accounting body, the Certified Practicing Accountants of Maldives, or CPA Maldives, was formed in 2007 to develop a system of regulation governing the accountancy practice in Maldives.[8] It is hoped that this step will help lead to greater transparency and disclosure and ensure compliance.

Boards have a unitary structure with 7–10 members, depending on the size of the company. Qualifications, roles, and responsibilities for board members are defined. The CMDA code requires that training be made available to directors.

Under the CMDA code, board remuneration is to be determined on the basis of a remuneration policy disclosed in the annual report. What role shareholders can play in determining board remuneration is not specified. Board remuneration can be tied to performance if the bank's remuneration policy allows this. If performance-based compensation mechanisms are in place, they should be monitored carefully. Whether directors' compensation is disclosed on an aggregate basis in the audited financial statements is unclear. No information is available to determine whether banks follow any of these rules on determining board remuneration.

Nepal

Nepal has the fourth largest area (147,200 square kilometers) in South Asia and the fifth largest population (27.6 million) and GDP (US$12.3 billion), according to 2008 data. With a GNI per capita of US$400 in 2008, the lowest reported in the region for that year, Nepal is classified as a low-income country.

Nepal has been relatively insulated from the global economic slowdown. And the peace accord signed between the Maoists and the other political parties in 2007, after a decade-long civil insurgency, has raised hopes that higher economic growth would be possible. The 5.35 percent GDP growth recorded in 2008 was the highest in the eight-year period studied—almost 2.6 percentage points higher than in 2007—thanks to a good crop season aided by a better monsoon as well as to higher tourism arrivals and stronger remittance income. In 2009, with industrial growth slowing as a result of uncertainties and labor unrest, GDP growth fell to an estimated 3.8 percent, and the projection for 2010 is a moderate 4 percent. Strong remittance inflows helped maintain the high consumption demand and thus growth momentum over the period.

Inflation in Nepal, influenced by price levels in India because of the currency peg, rose from 6.4 percent in 2007 to around 7.7 percent in 2008. In 2009, the rate rose further, to an estimated 12.8 percent, as a result of higher food and fuel prices, price hikes in India, and a wage hike in the public sector. The central bank, Nepal Rastra Bank (NRB), has expressed an intention to follow a tight monetary policy; but because of the accommodative stance taken, money growth reached nearly 30 percent in 2008 and 2009. NRB reintroduced the statutory liquidity ratio to curb inflation and also uses the cash reserve ratio to manage the money supply for bank lending, but these turned out to be ineffective in the absence of a tighter monetary policy. In 2007, higher remittances increased import demand and led to a trade account deficit but kept the overall current account in balance or in surplus. Helped by the growth in remittances, the current account had a surplus of 2.9 percent of GDP in 2008 and an estimated 3 percent in 2009.

Prudent fiscal management has kept the fiscal gap at a sustainable level over the years. The budget deficit was 1.61 percent of GDP in 2008, rose to an estimated 1.8 percent in 2009, and is projected to be around 2 percent in 2010. The NRB statute limits lending to the government through ways and means accounts or temporary overdraft accounts. There is a penalty on government borrowings above the limit. This may be a useful macroprudential indicator for fiscal discipline for other countries in the region.

The high volume of remittances has raised the standard of living of recipients. But the growing dependence on remittances increases economic vulnerability to a prolonged global slowdown. Remittances have also raised the demand for real estate and helped create a real estate bubble. NRB is rightfully concerned about a possible bursting of this bubble, which could create a severe liquidity crisis, and has cautioned banks about the adverse consequences of funding the real estate bubble. Further regulatory action and a tighter monetary policy stance are probably needed to manage the situation toward a soft landing (NRB has recently directed banks to gradually reduce their real estate exposure; see the section on financial stability).

Nepal's banking sector in 2008 consisted of 28 commercial banks: 3 public sector banks, 21 private sector banks, and 4 joint venture banks (generally referred to in this report as foreign banks). As in other countries in the region, banks dominate the financial sector; commercial banking assets amounted to 69.05 percent of GDP in 2008. The financial sector in 2008 also included 58 development banks, 78 finance companies, 12 microcredit development companies, 16 savings and credit cooperatives, 46 nongovernmental organizations, 117 government postal savings banks, and 16 insurance companies. In addition, there are 7,240 cooperatives licensed by the Nepalese government to conduct business as financial institutions. The capital market remains at an early stage of development in Nepal.

NRB regulates and supervises all financial institutions except government postal banks, cooperatives, and insurance companies. The government regulates the postal banks and cooperatives, the Insurance Regulatory Authority of Nepal (Bheema Samithi) regulates the insurance companies, and the Securities Board of Nepal (SEBON) regulates the capital market.

Nepal established a credit information bureau in 1989 under the Nepal Bankers Association, an important step toward ensuring credit quality. Efforts to improve the bureau's performance are ongoing with the assistance of the IFC. The country does not have a deposit insurance program, which is a concern given the large number of financial institutions and the importance of the banking sector in development activities.

Nepal's banking sector, with little exposure to foreign banks, is expected to emerge unscathed from the global financial crisis. Both the banking sector and the financial sector are expanding rapidly. But this expansion has not brought greater financial access to rural areas and some regions. Restructuring of ailing public sector banks has made these banks profitable for the first time in recent years. More remains to be done, however, with enormous negative net worth raising questions about sustainability and the public sector banks continuing to affect the performance of the entire sector because of their size. NRB is expected to decide on a future course of action.

The banking sector's performance levels were nevertheless high (figure 3.6), though higher interest spreads denote greater risk taking. Rapid entry of new banks has increased competition and led to aggressive deposit solicitation and risky lending practices. Fueled by remittance income, banks continue to funnel money into real estate ventures, creating a real estate bubble. Excessive exposure to real estate and rising asset prices are a major concern, especially since most banks lack a substantial capital cushion. In the absence of a developed capital market, a stable banking sector is critical to sustainable economic growth.

The payment system needs to be further developed. Automation and legal and regulatory improvements would bring both stability and efficiency to the system. Nepal lacks a strong savings culture, probably because of a lack of financial facilities. While the steady stream of remittance income has helped bridge the savings-investment gap, better savings habits would help overcome an overreliance on external funds for development. The corporate governance

Figure 3.6 Nepalese Banks Improve Performance with Lower Operating Costs

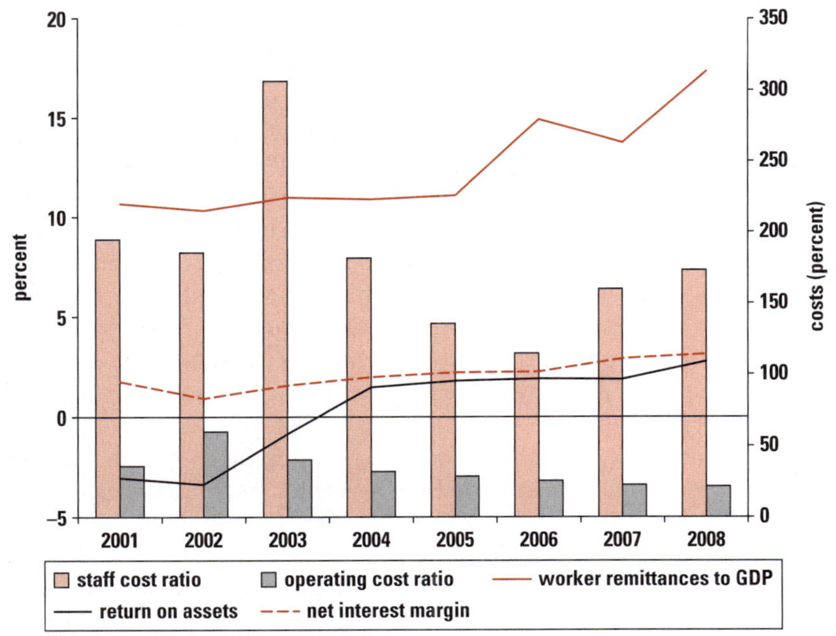

Source: Appendix table A2.14.

of banks deserves immediate attention, especially given the intense competition and greater risk taking being observed in the market. There is a need to improve governance standards, ensure compliance through effective enforcement, and encourage banks to undertake more meaningful implementation of the corporate governance regulations.

NRB has made efforts to address many of the issues highlighted here and to advise the banking sector over the years. The restructuring of public sector banks, an ongoing effort that has helped ease the pressure on the entire banking sector, is among its successful interventions. Other ongoing efforts include moving toward the adoption of Basel II, introducing a comprehensive corporate governance code for banks, and developing the payment system. But NRB has a serious capacity issue, especially given the many new entrants to the banking and financial sector. It needs both human resources and expertise to improve supervision and address new issues that arise with globalization and financial innovation. Building up its capacity would help NRB address banking sector challenges as well as ensure sustainable economic growth.

Access to Finance

Access indicators show no significant improvement in the provision of bank facilities over the period studied. The number of bank branches averaged around two per 100,000 people and barely three per 1,000 square kilometers over the eight years, while the number of ATMs in both cases averaged less than one. Thus, only about 0.002 percent of the population has access to a bank branch and only 0.001 percent to an ATM. Usage ratios were also low: deposit accounts averaged 111 per 1,000 people over the period, while loan accounts averaged 17 per 1,000. In 2008 deposit accounts were lower, at 107 per 1,000 people, while loan accounts increased to 25 per 1,000. According to these measures, use of commercial bank facilities is limited to less than 11 percent of the population for deposits and only around 2.5 percent for loans.

This situation warrants immediate attention. The number of commercial banks grew over the period—from 13 at the beginning of 2001 to 28 by the end of 2008—while commercial banking assets more than doubled, from US$3.3 billion to US$7.4 billion, or nearly 70 percent of GDP. But this financial deepening and widening has not happened in an equitable way. Banks have favored the developed central region and cities over the less developed regions in setting up their operations. More than 47 percent of the 555 commercial bank branches in operation in 2008 were located in the central region—and nearly 22 percent (120 branches) in the city of Kathmandu (NRB, *Annual Bank Supervision Report, 2008*). While countless studies have shown a positive correlation between financial depth and economic development, access to finance is also an important concept in social inclusion.

Beyond commercial banks, other financial institutions (not included in this study) also provide financial access in Nepal—including savings and credit cooperatives, nongovernmental organizations, rural development banks, and microcredit development banks. Collectively, these financial institutions held around 2.8 percent of the total assets in the entire financial system, about US$256.8 million, in 2008. Their loans granted amounted to around 2.5 percent of total loans (US$127.1 million), and their deposits to around 0.9 percent of total deposits (US$59.5 million). These institutions serve only a fraction of the market compared with commercial banks, which hold around 80.2 percent of total assets, 78.3 percent of total loans, and 83.7 percent of total deposits. Thus, commercial banks should lead the way in designing strategies to ensure financial inclusion.

Performance and Efficiency

Nepal's banking sector still suffers from the poor performance of two of the public sector banks as well as massive nonperforming loan losses by the private sector banks that eroded the capital base. The two public sector banks were incurring huge losses that affected the entire industry. After a massive restructuring, these banks have managed to stay profitable since 2004. The consolidated return on equity turned positive in 2008 for the first time in eight years, shooting up to an unrealistic 503.55 percent. The reason for this unusually large ratio is that the negative equity position turned positive during 2008, making the average equity for the year much smaller. In 2007, the return on equity had been −78.70 percent. The return on assets turned positive in 2004 and rose steadily, reaching 2.77 percent in 2008.

A rising net interest margin and falling operating costs have contributed to the profitability of Nepalese banks. The net interest margin almost doubled over the period, to 3.13 percent in 2008. Interest income accounted for around 69 percent of revenue earned in 2008. Recurring earning power dropped to −0.01 percent in 2003, then recovered steadily to 2.34 percent in 2008. The interest rate spreads of the public sector banks—which were high in 2004 and 2005, denoting higher risk taking—have since declined. The sector's operating costs declined steadily over the eight-year period, while staff costs dropped until 2006, then increased slightly. Staff costs increased substantially in 2009 as a result of a doubling of public sector wages. In 2008, operating costs amounted to 21.56 percent of income, while staff costs amounted to 172.89 percent of operating costs. Nepal had the best operating cost ratio in the region in 2004–08.

While the restructuring of the two public sector banks has produced positive results, the work is not yet done. The hard-earned gains need to be maintained if the banking industry is to stabilize in the future. The third public sector bank also suffers from huge cost inefficiencies and is also undergoing restructuring. Once this restructuring process is complete, the next course of action for the three banks should be undertaken without undue delay.

Financial Stability

The banking sector's consolidated capital adequacy ratio remained below the regulatory capital requirement of 10 percent throughout the eight-year period studied.[9] The continued losses and huge negative net worth of the public sector banks and the erosion of reserves due to the heavy nonperforming loans in the private sector banks continued to affect capital. But thanks to restructuring of public sector banks and growth in the capital base of private sector banks, the capital adequacy ratio turned positive in 2008, at 4.04 percent, for the first time since 2001.

The capital base of the public sector banks remains negative because of their huge negative net worth. But the situation is improving. To rid the public sector banks of their toxic reserves, the next step after restructuring will need to be determined soon—whether to recapitalize the banks through privatization or to liquidate the banks to get rid of the negative capital base and restructure them. Either alternative would need the approval of NRB as the regulator.

In 2008, two public sector banks and one private sector bank posted negative capital adequacy ratios due to negative capital funds, while one private bank posted a ratio below the regulatory requirement. All 4 foreign banks, the other 2 public banks, and the other 18 private banks had capital adequacy ratios above the minimum requirement—but 10 of these banks had ratios very close to the minimum requirement. In addition, while banks were scheduled to adopt the local model of the "Basel II minus" approach, developed in line with the more complex Basel II approach, by the 2008/09 financial year, banks were reporting capital adequacy ratios under Basel I guidelines for 2008 and no capital charges were therefore made for market and operational risk. The volatility of capital positions combined with the absence of additional capital charges could undermine the stability of these banks because of the procyclical behavior of the banking system.[10] So it is important to examine the viability of these institutions in adverse economic situations through sensitivity analysis and stress testing. In addition, the possibility of mergers and consolidations to improve stability should be considered.

Because of the negative capital, the leverage ratio turned negative in 2004, returning to a positive level in 2008 at 0.02. The gross nonperforming loans ratio fell by about 79 percent between 2001 and 2008 to 6.08 percent. Aggressive recovery and write-down procedures that developed with the restructuring process, more efficient supervision, and regulatory changes were among the reasons for this. Greater credit expansion, soaring values of land used as collateral, and loan restructuring also played a major part. But recovery of loans continues to be an issue in Nepal because of archaic mortgage and property laws and lack of special debt recovery provisions and commercial courts. While a reduction in nonperforming loans is a positive sign, the decreasing provision for such loans is a concern. Provision cover dropped from 30.59 percent in 2001 to 8.16 percent in 2008, in part because of higher collateral values. Liquidity ratios dropped over the period, though they have been on the rise since 2007 because of large remittance flows. The liquid assets ratio dropped by nearly half between 2001 and 2008, to 11.80 percent. The liquid assets to liabilities ratio followed a similar pattern.

The main concerns for the stability of the banking sector are the unresolved capital volatility, the excessive exposure to real estate lending, and rising asset prices. Fueled by the steady stream of remittances and the resulting liquidity, the real estate market has soared. Given the higher interest rate spreads, banks have competed aggressively for real estate lending. This is believed to have created a bubble situation. If remittance inflows slow, real estate prices could plummet, and the ensuing liquidity crisis combined with banks' overexposure to the bubble could throw the system into disarray. Recognizing this, NRB has cautioned banks about overexposure to the real estate bubble and also has taken monetary policy measures to contain the liquidity in the market. More recently, NRB directed banks to reduce their real estate exposure to 40 percent by July 2010, 30 percent by July 2011, and 25 percent by July 2012. Implementing risk-based supervision is also part of the solution, but NRB is hampered by constraints in human resources as well as expertise. NRB has temporarily contained the surge of new entrants by not issuing new banking licenses. More comprehensive measures may be needed to take control of the situation.

Capital Market Development

Nepal's capital market is still at an early stage of development. The country has one stock exchange, the Nepal Stock Exchange (NEPSE). The exchange has 23 member brokers who operate on the trading floor in accordance with the Securities Exchange Act, 2006, as well as rules and bylaws of the exchange. In addition, there are 17 merchant banks that work as issue managers, portfolio managers, underwriters, and share registrars. The NEPSE trading system (the NEPSE Automated Trading System, or NATS) is a fully automated, screen-based trading system with T+3 settlement, introduced in August 2007. Settlements are done on a paper-versus-payment basis, as there is no central depository system. Shares (equity and preference), debentures, government bonds, and mutual funds are traded through the stock exchange.[11] The financial institutions dominate the stock market with limited involvement by the real sector. There are only a few institutional investors and few participants.

The bond market in Nepal consists of a government securities market and a corporate securities market. To meet financing needs, the government issues short-term treasury bills and national savings certificates. The lack of a benchmark yield curve in the government bond market hampers risk management efforts by investors and thus may discourage new entrants. But the treasury bill market operates relatively efficiently. The corporate bond market is limited to a few private placements. There is no active secondary market or benchmark yield curves and, thus, no market pricing of corporate bonds.

The Nepalese institutional investor base is too narrow to support an active bond market. But the secondary market is not yet open to nonresident Nepalese or foreign institutional investors. Attracting foreign investors will require such actions as undertaking legal and regulatory reforms, developing market infrastructure (a central depository system, scripless systems, credit and research information, securities rating), developing accounting and auditing standards and uniform reporting standards, and enhancing corporate governance. Also important is to strengthen SEBON so that foreign investors have confidence in the regulator overseeing the capital market. As part of the strengthening process, SEBON would benefit from greater operational autonomy to conduct its affairs and attract professionals to its workforce, improving efficiency.

A review of capital market development indicators over the eight-year period reveals that the equity market is developing faster than the bond market. While the domestic public bonds outstanding to GDP ratio declined slightly, stock market capitalization more than doubled to 28.12 percent of GDP in 2008. But the stock market remains narrow and inefficient. The top 10 stocks accounted for nearly 92.5 percent of the total trading value in 2008. The stock market turnover ratio averaged only around 0.05 over the period, indicating relative inefficiency. Market liquidity improved over the period, with the stock trading value increasing from 0.59 percent of GDP in 2001 to 1.68 percent in 2008. The large remittance inflows have driven the demand for stocks and thus the stock market activity. But the high level of liquidity in the market, focused on a limited set of securities, may warrant painful readjustments in the future if not monitored carefully.

It is important that capital market development be actively pursued. Because of the lack of a developed capital market to meet long-term funding needs, banks continue to dominate the financial market, and maturity mismatches will therefore continue. Developing a stable capital market would improve efficiency in the banking sector by increasing competition, thus contributing to the banking system's stability in the long run.

Market Concentration and Competitiveness

Nepal's banking sector is not concentrated. With the influx of new entrants, all concentration ratios declined rapidly over the eight-year period. The Herfindahl-Hirschman Index dropped to 712.01 in 2008 (according to accepted international norms, index values less than 1,000 indicate an unconcentrated industry). All of the three-bank concentration ratios also declined, and in 2008 the top three banks held no more than 35.26 percent of assets, 30.98 percent of deposits, and 26.22 percent of loans. Private credit extended by banks remained stable over the period at around 28 percent of GDP (26.44 percent in 2008). Commercial banking assets also remained stable, averaging around 68 percent of GDP over the eight years.

Nepal's financial sector had a significant number of new market entrants in the eight-year period. The number of commercial banks rose from 13 in 2001 to 28 in 2008, while the total number of financial sector institutions increased from 98 to 238.[12] Commercial banks hold more than 80 percent of total financial assets. And while total banking assets grew by nearly 28 percent in 2008, the assets of private commercial banks increased by almost 41 percent.

The big increase in the number of players in the market raises concerns. Most new banks compete aggressively for deposits and engage in high-risk lending activities, as evidenced by the rapid expansion in the real estate sector. While the loan to deposit ratio in the banking sector as a whole was around 82.6 percent in 2008, the ratio for the seven new banks that started operations in 2007–08 was around 88.8 percent. Even though the banks compete aggressively, their low capital levels may cause problems. Overreliance on short-term deposits, which are likely to depend on remittances, could pose problems for the stability of the banking system. NRB is trying to control this situation, including through the stopgap measure of temporarily halting the issuance of new banking licenses. Over the medium to long term, other actions will need to be taken, including revising regulations, enhancing supervision capacity, introducing risk-based capital requirements, and improving credit rating and credit information systems.

Payment Systems Development

Cash is the dominant payment instrument in Nepal. Notes and coins in circulation averaged around 12.5 percent of GDP throughout the period. The narrow money supply increased from 15.99 percent of GDP in 2001 to 18.80 percent in 2008. As would be expected, currency in circulation as a share of narrow money was high, averaging around 65 percent.

Nepal has one retail payment system for both large- and small-value transactions, an end-of-day net settlement manual clearing system. In addition, Nepal has more than 10 check clearinghouses managed by NRB, located at regional and district levels. These clearinghouses clear and settle transactions relating to paper-based instruments such as checks, drafts, and payment orders. Manual settlement times are usually T+3, but regional clearing done on a collection basis can take 7–15 days. Moreover, since NRB is not electronically connected, each regional clearinghouse needs additional time to clear checks. In addition, banks have to maintain different regional accounts in each center, creating possible unwinding risk as well as inefficiencies.

Automated clearing facilities are not available in Nepal. Nor is there an RTGS system. But NRB is discussing the possibility of formulating a payment system master plan that will include an RTGS system. Payment systems development also involves such aspects as payment instruments, securities settlement, infrastructure, legal and regulatory issues, and awareness building.

Savings Mobilization

The broad money supply to GDP ratio was high throughout the period and around 60.35 percent in 2008, indicating adequate liquidity in the market. The real deposit rate turned negative in 2003 as a result of inflation and continued on a negative trend, registering −3.50 percent in 2008. The reserve money to total deposits ratio was fairly high at around 34.30 in 2008, denoting relative inefficiency in financial intermediation. Nepal's loan to deposit ratio was also high, averaging around 81 percent of GDP over the eight-year period.

Nepal's domestic savings rate has been the second lowest in South Asia after Afghanistan's. In 2008, gross domestic savings were around 11.5 percent of GDP. The high intermediary ratios and negative interest rates do not provide incentives for the public to save.[13] While low domestic savings can hamper growth, high remittances have helped overcome the savings-investment gap in Nepal. Worker remittances amounted to 17.38 percent of GDP in 2008 and were expected to be higher in 2009. Because of the large remittance inflows, the banking sector remained liquid throughout the period. Recognizing the importance of this, the RBI and NRB established the India-Nepal Remittance Corridor in 2008 to speed remittance inflows to Nepal. As long as remittance income keeps growing, savings will not be an issue for Nepal. Even so, it is important to develop a domestic savings base to avoid overreliance on foreign capital or income. When remittance-originating countries suffer prolonged economic slowdowns, as perhaps in the present situation, there is no guarantee that remittance inflows will continue unabated.

Corporate Governance

Financial institutions in Nepal are governed by a legislative framework provided by the Nepal Rastra Bank Act 2058 (2002), Bank and Financial Institution Act 2063 (2006), Company Act 2063 (2006), and Supervision Bylaws 2059 (2002). Directives are issued under the legislative framework to ensure compliance. The Securities Act 2063 (2007) also provides necessary guidelines for companies.

Recognizing the importance of corporate governance, NRB issued guidelines, effective from June 2005, as part of the unified directives relating to banks and financial institutions. Important areas covered include the following:

- Code of ethics for directors
- Duties and responsibilities of board of directors
- Appointment of the chief executive
- Code of ethics for employees
- Audit committee

- Prohibition on extending credit to directors, shareholders, or employees or to firms related to directors, promoters, or shareholders
- Prohibition on extending credit against assets of directors or family members as collateral

NRB assesses the corporate governance systems of banks as part of its on-site supervision. This supervision in past years identified serious lapses in corporate governance that contributed to the deterioration of public sector banks and some private sector ones. Weak corporate governance in some private sector banks is a growing concern because of the intense competition and high-risk activity observed. Moreover, NRB's resource constraints along with the large number of financial institutions hamper its efforts to ensure compliance.

Thus, corporate governance in Nepal's banking sector appears to need immediate attention. Governance standards need to be improved and a comprehensive governance code developed for banks, with compliance ensured through effective enforcement. Banks need to be encouraged to undertake meaningful implementation of the code, making corporate governance part of their culture. Adoption of the Basel II accord would be an important step toward a better corporate governance framework. To ensure the soundness of the banking industry, NRB and the banks should continue to work toward achieving a transparent, effective corporate governance system. Important areas needing greater attention include broadening investor rights, increasing disclosure, improving adherence to international accounting and auditing standards, and strengthening the effectiveness of boards.

Responses to the corporate governance survey remain unchanged since 2005 (see appendix 4A). Analysis of the responses suggests a need for greater transparency and disclosure of share ownership and beneficial ownership and for legal provisions establishing the rights of external stakeholders and minority shareholders. The regulatory guidelines contain no provisions on the disclosure of ownership. Although the central bank requires disclosure of shareholdings above 0.5 percent, this requirement is seldom enforced. Thus, in practice the public has no access to such information. There are no provisions establishing the rights of external stakeholders, such as whistleblower rules. Nor are there rules or regulations protecting the preemption rights of minority shareholders or legal provisions governing the disclosure of beneficial ownership.

Clear provisions and guidelines establishing shareholders' rights, including their right to attend and vote at shareholder meetings, need to be formalized. Also important is to examine the practices of shareholders to see whether they in fact exercise their rights. Information is disclosed to shareholders in a timely fashion before shareholder meetings; shareholders can vote in absentia, by proxy or by post; and third-party verification of voting is permitted. But shareholders are unable to vote on a range of issues, including related-party transactions. Banks are required to disclose special voting rights and caps on voting rights in their memorandum of association and articles of association.

Shareholders can vote on appointments to the board of directors, though the board itself appoints some members. For the government-controlled banks, the government can appoint directors. No clear dividend policy is in place; instead, the policy is set by the board and approved at the annual general meeting. There are no specific structural defenses that can prevent a takeover bid other than the legal requirement for regulatory approval of any transfer of promoters' shares. Nor is there any specific provision to ensure that minority shareholders can elect directors.

Banks' financial statements are prepared in accordance with generally accepted local accounting principles. Other studies have found that accounting and auditing standards are still being issued and do not yet fully conform to International Accounting Standards (see World Bank 2005a). Still, to the extent that NRB has issued guidelines, it is safe to conclude that banks are meeting the reporting standards to a certain extent. Financial reporting is done quarterly, and banks are required to disclose audit fees paid to external auditors.

Nepal's auditing standards appear to be at the development stage, according to other reports (see World Bank 2005a). It is advisable that NRB issue detailed guidelines on the appointment of both external and internal auditors. The central bank has issued guidelines on the appointment of audit committees as well as on their primary roles and responsibilities. But it is unclear whether the audit committees have control over the selection process for external auditors. Moreover, the guidelines do not cover the frequency of their meetings and other pertinent details. They do, however, prohibit external auditors from performing other, nonaudit services for the banks they audit. External auditors are appointed with the approval of the annual general meeting. Central bank guidelines require that the internal auditor be appointed by management and report to the audit committee.

NRB has issued detailed guidelines on the structure of boards and on the directors' roles and responsibilities. These guidelines appear to be adequate as long as they are strictly enforced. Banks in Nepal follow a hybrid structure, with boards having five to nine members on average. The guidelines do not specify detailed requirements for directors' qualifications and experience, though they do outline such requirements for the CEO. Directors are not required to attend any special training on their fiduciary duties and responsibilities, pointing to a need for developing a systematic training program. Shareholders can vote on the remuneration of directors. Compensation of directors can be linked to performance and must be disclosed in detail. Where performance-based mechanisms are in place, NRB should review them carefully.

NRB has continued to review and improve the legal and regulatory framework for the financial sector. Recent additions include the Bank and Financial Institution Act (2006); Insolvency Act (2006); Secured Transaction Act (2006); Company Act (2006); Asset (Money) Laundering Prevention Act, 2008; and Bank and Financial Institutions' Prompt Corrective Action Bylaws, 2008. Deposit and credit guarantee acts are to follow. As regulators, NRB and SEBON need to coordinate to ensure the compliance that is key to good corporate governance. Boards of directors should ensure that their bank adopts a corporate governance culture in its day-to-day operations. And boards should have a clear understanding of their role in corporate governance so that they can ensure that their bank's policies and practices are consistent with the corporate governance culture.

Pakistan

Pakistan's macroeconomic environment is affected by a volatile security situation as well as external balance uncertainties resulting from the global economic slowdown. The deteriorating security and political situation has affected every economic sector. Despite massive external aid, the real sector failed to pick up in 2008/09. The global economic slowdown has added to the uncertainties by casting doubts on the continuation of remittance flows, exports, and foreign investment. While the overall economic situation remains volatile, stabilization efforts have shown positive results.

Pakistan has the third largest population (161 million) and the second largest area (796,100 square kilometers) and GDP (US$164.6 billion) in South Asia, according to 2008 data. With a GNI per capita of US$980 in 2008, Pakistan is classified as a lower-middle-income country along with Bhutan, India, Maldives, and Sri Lanka. The country's economic slowdown began in 2008, when GDP growth declined to 5.95 percent, down from 6.8 percent in 2007. In 2009, the rate dropped to an estimated 2 percent. Sectors such as exports and manufacturing contracted, resulting in an overall slowdown. Moderate gains are expected in 2010, with growth projected at 3 percent, thanks largely to fiscal stimulus spending in the form of a planned public expenditure program, favorable agricultural output, and modest growth in industry and services.

The surge in world prices of food and oil pushed inflation to double digits—to 12.0 percent in 2008 and an estimated 20.8 percent in 2009. Even when oil prices and demand dropped, food price inflation appears to have kept the consumer price index at a high level. In 2010, inflation is projected at around 10 percent, but Pakistan will be vulnerable to reemerging upward pressure on oil and commodity prices. The current account remained in deficit throughout the period, increasing to 8.4 percent in 2008. Although exports contracted in 2009, a sharp reduction in imports and a steady stream of remittances helped limit the current account deficit to an estimated 5.3 percent. This trend is expected to continue in 2010, with the deficit projected at 4.8 percent. As a result of the global and domestic uncertainties, foreign investment rapidly declined. International reserves fell, and by the end of 2008 Pakistan's import cover had dropped to three months. This position reversed in 2009 with disbursements from the International Monetary Fund (IMF).[14]

The fiscal deficit increased over the period, with lower-than-projected tax collections leading to a drop in revenue. The deficit rose from 4.35 percent of GDP in 2007 to 7.56 percent in 2008. Concerns about revenue collection prompted the authorities to cut fiscal spending to reduce the budget deficit. But the global economic slowdown and the resulting expansion in the fiscal spending program will initially push the deficit higher.

Pakistan's banking system consisted of 36 commercial banks in 2008: 4 public sector banks, 25 local private banks (generally referred to in the report as private sector banks), and 7 foreign banks. In addition, four specialized banks and two microfinance banks also operate. The private sector banks dominate the banking sector—and banks dominate the financial sector. In 2008, commercial banking assets amounted to around 72.1 percent of total financial assets, or around 51.38 percent of GDP. The State Bank of Pakistan (SBP) is the banking regulator.

Pakistan's commercial banks have managed to weather the global financial crisis without much impact. But the economic slowdown that followed the onset of the crisis has affected bank performance (figure 3.7). Analysis shows that while the overall performance of banks is stable, several areas need attention. Rural areas remain underserved by banks, although nonbank institutions have

Figure 3.7 **Pakistan's Banks See Volatility Return**

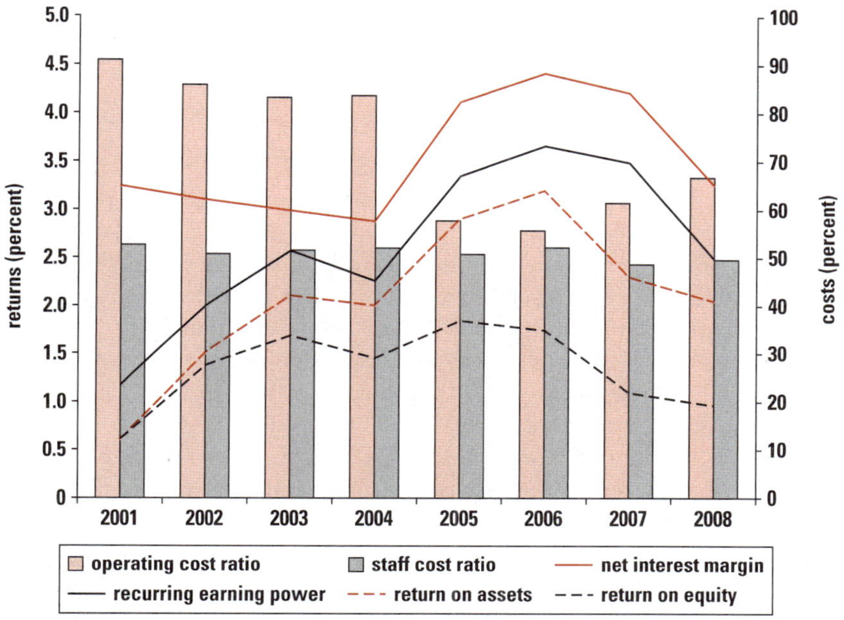

Source: Appendix table A2.15.

undertaken schemes to address this. A related issue is the lack of focus on savings mobilization. Even with steady remittance flows, Pakistan has not tapped the full potential of domestic savings as a means to finance investment. While bank performance levels have been high, this could change if the economic downturn continues, as seen in the volatility of returns in 2007–08. Nonperforming loans will rise as the economic slowdown affects the corporate sector as well as small and medium-size enterprises. High nonperforming loans and greater provisioning and write-offs would erode banks' capital cushion. Capital adequacy levels are strong thanks to the proactive regulatory guidelines and better-than-average returns, and implementation of Basel II could further improve financial stability. But the liquidity situation needs to be monitored.

Development of the capital market slowed after the stock market crash in 2008. The stock market is showing signs of recovery. But capital market development should nevertheless be a priority because limited options for long-term financing will affect economic development. Another area needing renewed focus is corporate governance. The guidelines for corporate governance of banks appear to be comprehensive. But compliance and enforcement need further review.

The SBP has developed a 10-year strategic plan for financial sector development. The plan addresses such issues as savings mobilization and poor access to banking facilities in underserved areas. It also addresses the need to establish a deposit protection scheme. According to the strategy paper, although the government protects all bank deposits under the Banks (Nationalization) Act of 1974, it cannot continue to do so because private sector banks now dominate the banking sector (SBP 2009b). The SBP has submitted a draft act to establish a deposit protection scheme to the Cabinet for consideration and is ready to launch the scheme subject to necessary legislation.

Pakistan established a credit information bureau in 1992, an important step in managing credit risk. In 2003, the bureau began offering credit information online, the first in the region to do so. Further development of the credit information bureau is planned under the SBP's 10-year strategy.

Access to Finance

Access to financial services through commercial banks remains low in Pakistan. Demographic branch penetration changed little over the eight-year period and was still around five branches per 100,000 people in 2008. The performance on geographic branch penetration was similar, with 11 branches per 1,000 square kilometers in 2008. For ATMs, however, both demographic and geographic penetration increased, to two ATMs per 100,000 people and four ATMs per 1,000 square kilometers. The use of services as measured by deposit accounts actually dropped, from 196 accounts per 1,000 people in 2001 to around 155 in 2008, though loan accounts increased from 16 per 1,000 people to 31.

Overall, both access and usage indicators remain far from satisfactory. Moreover, the distribution of branches between urban and rural areas is disproportionate. Urban areas have around two-thirds of the branches, though rural areas have two-thirds of the population. To promote the opening of branches in rural areas, the SBP introduced the Annual Branch Licensing Policy, which requires commercial banks with 100 or more branches to open at least 20 percent of their branches in rural underserved areas.

Nonbank institutions (not covered by this study) also provide financial facilities to the public. Pakistan Post provides savings and remittance services through its network of 13,419 branches, managing more than 3.6 million savings accounts and selling savings certificates. Because of its extensive branch network, some microfinance institutions have collaborated with Pakistan Post to provide financial services to the underserved. In addition, financial institutions have been permitted to collaborate with telecommunications companies in providing financial services as a way to improve access. Pakistan's microfinance movement is growing. In 2001, Pakistan passed the Microfinance Institutions Ordinance to outline a regulatory framework for microfinance through commercial banks and established microfinance banks under the purview of the SBP. Pakistan was the first country in South Asia to introduce a special law for microfinance. In addition, the SBP has issued separate prudential regulations for microfinance banks. The National Microfinance Growth Strategy aims to increase the number of active microfinance borrowers to 3 million by 2010 and to 10 million by 2015. By December 2008, the number of borrowers had grown to 1.7 million (Pakistan Microfinance Network 2009).

Islamic banking is growing fast in Pakistan and plays an important part in financial inclusion. By December 2008, there were 6 Islamic banks operating 384 branches and 12 conventional banks (with 130 branches) offering Islamic banking (table 3.2).

Performance and Efficiency

Pakistan's banks saw an upward trend in performance indicators until 2006. In 2007 and 2008, however, return ratios declined and cost ratios rose (see figure 3.7). The return on assets dropped from 3.20 percent in 2006 to 2.05 percent in 2008, while the return on equity dropped from 34.90 percent to 19.30 percent.

Table 3.2 Selected Indicators on Islamic Banking in Pakistan, December 2008

Indicator	Value
Total assets	
In PRs billions	276
In US$ billions	3.3
As % of total for banking industry	4.9
Total deposits	
In PRs billions	202
In US$ billions	2.4
As % of total for banking industry	4.8
Financing and investment	
In PRs billions	187
In US$ billions	2.3
As % of total for banking industry	4.4
Institutions	
Islamic banks	6
Conventional banks with Islamic banking divisions	12
Branches	514
Performance and stability indicators	
Return on (average) equity (%)	5.31
Return on (average) assets (%)	0.69
Nonperforming financing to total financing (%)	2.3
Provisions to nonperforming financing (%)	67.6

Source: SBP 2009a.
Note: Data are provisional.

A similar pattern occurred for the net interest margin (3.26 percent at the end of 2008) and recurring earning power (2.49 percent). While all return ratios declined, the operating cost ratio rose from 55.66 percent in 2006 to 66.82 percent in 2008. These trends were expected to continue in 2009.

While the trends are negative, the performance indicators remain strong. Because of the low cost of funds, the net interest margin is still high. As noted, private sector banks dominate Pakistan's banking sector, and the large banks have performed better than the industry average. If the economic downturn continues, however, the banking sector could be affected. In addition, some banks, with regulatory consent, deferred until 2009 writing off part of the equity losses suffered when the stock market crashed in 2008. These losses further reduced returns in 2009. Even so, the high interest margins have enabled banks to weather the fluctuations. Banks should monitor their rising operating costs and take appropriate corrective action to mitigate the impact. With the volatile economic situation, it is important for banks to keep costs low and improve their margins.

Financial Stability

Even with performance indicators declining, Pakistan's banking sector managed to keep the capital adequacy ratio above the 8 percent statutory minimum capital requirement. The capital adequacy ratio was 13.80 percent in 2007, the highest in the period, then fell to 12.20 percent in 2008. One reason for banks' strong capital position is that the SBP issued prudential guidelines increasing both the minimum regulatory requirement and the minimum paid-up capital requirement. Accordingly, banks had to increase their minimum paid-up capital from PRs 5 billion (US$60.42 million) in 2007 to PRs 6 billion (US$72.5 million) by the end of 2009—and will have to increase it further to PRs 10 billion (US$120.83 million) by 2013. The minimum regulatory requirement was raised from 8 percent of risk-weighted assets in 2008 to 9 percent in 2009 and will be raised to 10 percent in 2010. These regulatory changes, by compelling banks to increase their capital base, have helped them weather the adverse financial situation.

Adopting Basel II capital guidelines has also helped. All banks and development finance institutions in Pakistan are using the Standardized Approach for calculating credit and market risk. Two foreign banks have opted for the Standardized Approach for calculating operational risk, while the rest are using the Basic Indicator Approach (SBP 2008). Even though adopting Basel II reduces capital adequacy ratios because of additional charges for operational and market risk, 21 banks reported capital adequacy ratios over 15 percent in 2008 (when 8 percent was the minimum regulatory requirement), while 13 banks had ratios between 10 percent and 15 percent. Two banks reported ratios between 8 percent and 10 percent (see SBP 2008).

The leverage ratio increased to 9.35 in 2007, then fell slightly to 9.23 in 2008. The gross nonperforming loans ratio fell progressively from 19.6 percent in 2001 to 5.7 percent in 2006. The ratio then climbed to 6.3 percent in 2007 and 7.6 percent in 2008. Nonperforming loans to the small and medium-size enterprise sector seem to be on the rise, while the corporate sector accounts for the bulk of the nonperforming loans. Nonperforming loans in agriculture actually fell in 2008, probably because of the good crop season. The provisions to nonperforming loans ratio rose over the period until 2007, when it was 88.20 percent, then fell to 81.10 percent in 2008. Although provisions increased in absolute terms in 2008, the rise in nonperforming loans outmatched the rise in provisions. In addition, because of the high level of nonperforming loans in 2008, the SBP reinstated the practice of allowing up to 30 percent of the forced sales value of mortgaged property (commercial as well as residential), liquid assets, and stocks in the calculation of the loan values on which the provisions are made. This helped further reduce loan loss provisions.

Both liquidity ratios declined over the period until 2007, when they rose, then continued to fall in 2008. The liquid assets to total assets ratio fell from 33.82 percent in 2007 to 28.74 percent in 2008, while the liquid assets to liabilities ratio dropped from 57.07 percent in 2007 to 50.79 percent in 2008. Economic uncertainties resulted in a severe liquidity shortage in 2008. The SBP reduced the cash reserve requirement from 9 percent to 5 percent, freeing up liquidity for the banking sector.

While the accelerated economic growth rates have abated, the larger capital base, the higher returns resulting from high interest margins, and the timely revisions of regulatory guidelines have helped Pakistan's banks manage the economic slowdown and maintain stability. If the slowdown continues, however, nonperforming loans will grow as adverse market conditions affect the corporate sector as well as small and medium-size enterprises. High levels of nonperforming loans and increased provisioning and write-offs would erode banks' capital cushion and affect their stability. Banks as well as the authorities should therefore monitor the situation carefully and take early corrective action.

Capital Market Development

Pakistan's stock market had a remarkable growth spurt before the market meltdown experienced by the Karachi Stock Exchange (KSE) in May 2008. *BusinessWeek* dubbed it "the best-performing stock market in the world" in 2002.[15] The stock market capitalization grew by a staggering 473 percent between 2001 and 2007, from 8.06 percent of GDP to 46.2 percent. On December 26, 2007, the market closed high: the KSE-100 index was at 14,814.85, and the market capitalization close to PRs 4.56 trillion (around US$76 billion). On April 18, 2008, the KSE-100 index reached 15,676.34, the highest level recorded.

But as a result of political and economic uncertainties, the market fell sharply starting in May 2008. By December 31, 2008, the index had dropped to 5,865.01 and the market capitalization to PRs 1.86 trillion (US$23.50 billion). The authorities took measures to counter the market crash, including introducing floor prices and even closing the stock exchange temporarily in 2008. The market turned around, however, and by October 15, 2009, the KSE-100 index had climbed to 9,845.73 and the market capitalization to PRs 2.86 trillion (US$34 billion).

Pakistan has two other stock exchanges, in Lahore and Islamabad. The exchange in Lahore recorded a market capitalization of PRs 2.71 trillion (US$33 billion) on October 15, 2009, and the one in Islamabad a market capitalization of PRs 1.59 trillion (US$19 billion).

Overall, the market has shown little gain. The trading value of the top 10 stocks fell from 20.02 percent of the total value of shares traded in 2006 to 6.81 percent by the end of 2008. Market liquidity is tight, with the stock trading value at around 0.14 percent of GDP in 2008. And market efficiency is very low, as shown by the stock market turnover ratio of just 0.004. The bond market is also still developing, with the corporate bond market not yet a major factor. The domestic public bonds outstanding to GDP ratio averaged around 33 percent over the eight-year period.

Pakistan has vast potential for capital market development. It has raised money in international capital markets through eurobonds, global depository receipts, and exchangeable bonds. Once the economy stabilizes, it is hoped that the development of its capital market will pick up.

Market Concentration and Competitiveness

Pakistan managed to reduce the concentration ratios in its banking sector over the eight-year period. The Herfindahl-Hirschman Index declined to 741 in 2008 (values less than 1,000 indicate an unconcentrated industry, according to internationally accepted norms). The three-bank concentration ratios also declined over the period, and in 2008 the top three banks held 38 percent of assets, deposits, and loans on average. Low concentration promotes competition. Also favoring healthy competition is the dominance of private sector banks in Pakistan's banking sector. In addition, the higher paid-up capital requirements imposed by the SBP have helped weed out unsuitable market entrants (though this also means a need for more comprehensive programs to improve financial outreach, especially in rural areas).

Yet Pakistan also shows the same trends of increasing levels of commercial banking assets and bank credit to the private sector that have been observed throughout South Asia. Where a developed capital market is lacking (or, as in Pakistan, has gone through a market meltdown) and external financing flows out, commercial banks become the main providers of capital—and in some cases even the sole providers. In Pakistan private credit extended by banks increased over the period until 2007, then fell slightly to 27.56 percent of GDP in 2008. Commercial banking assets increased sharply until 2007 before decreasing in 2008 to 51.38 percent of GDP.

This situation needs to be monitored carefully, especially since Pakistan's banking sector still operates with relatively high interest margins. If interest rates were to rise, banks would face maturity mismatch issues. And since banks constantly roll over short-term funding, private sector firms are highly vulnerable to interest rate fluctuations and other restrictions imposed by banks. Once the economy recovers and the capital market again starts to develop, it is hoped that the private sector will have a greater range of funding opportunities available for development activities.

Payment Systems Development

Pakistan's payment system has both retail and large-value components. The small-value retail payment system is a semiautomated, end-of-day net settlement system, provided by the National Institutional Facilitation Technologies (NIFT) network. Pakistan has an RTGS system to handle large-value payments.

Set up by a consortium of banks and a private company, the NIFT network serves more than 4,500 branches of 40 banks (including the SBP) in 100 major cities of Pakistan. It offers four major clearing services: intercity clearing, overnight clearing, same-day high-value clearing, and local U.S. dollar clearing. In 2008, the network cleared 60.27 million checks with a value of PRs 21 trillion through its clearinghouses. The system processed PRs 137,369 billion of paper-based transactions and PRs 13,893 billion of e-banking transactions. Clearly, paper-based transactions still dominate, though e-banking is growing fast. The SBP is developing a strategic plan to reform the retail payment system, with an agenda that includes promoting e-banking as well as mobile banking.

Notes and coins in circulation were maintained at around 11 percent of GDP over the eight-year period. In 2008, currency in circulation amounted to around 28 percent of the narrow money supply and around 25 percent of the broad money supply. The narrow money supply was 39.73 percent of GDP. Cash is clearly the preferred mode of payment. The value of retail transactions grew to 1,444 percent of GDP in 2008. The retail payment system is concentrated. According to the retail payments concentration ratio for 2008, the system's five largest participants accounted for 79 percent of the retail payment transactions.

In July 2008, the SBP launched the RTGS system, the Pakistan Real Time Interbank Settlement Mechanism (PRISM), which operates under the Payment Systems and Electronic Funds Transfer Act enacted in 2007. The system is designed to handle all large-value payments in Pakistan, including interbank money and securities market transactions, the domestic leg of foreign exchange transactions, and net settlement positions from retail (NIFT) and bank card clearings (ATM switch operators). The high-value transactions are cleared through PRISM using SWIFT financial messaging. In 2008, the value of RTGS transactions amounted to around 389.75 percent of GDP, indicating the importance of having a real-time payment system for high-value transactions. The RTGS concentration ratio in 2008 was 32.39 percent, showing that RTGS transactions are not concentrated among a few participants.

Recognizing the importance to financial system stability of minimizing settlement risk, the SBP is drafting detailed settlement rules for PRISM participants. Creation of a national payment council is also being discussed.

Savings Mobilization

The broad money supply to GDP ratio hovered around 46 percent over the eight-year period, indicating that financial deepening could be further improved to increase the liquidity in the market. High inflation drove the real deposit interest rate down sharply, to a huge −12.63 percent in 2008. The domestic savings rate is low, dropping to 13.25 percent in 2008, indicating a weak savings culture in Pakistan. The reserve money to total deposits ratio is high, pointing to inefficiencies in financial intermediation. The loan to deposit ratio is very high, showing that banks continue to rely on borrowings rather than savings. Remittances improved only marginally over the period, but they remain a stable source of income.

Analysis of these indicators reveals that present conditions do not provide incentives for domestic savings. Indeed, domestic savings remained low over the period even with increased external capital, robust bank performance, and strong remittance receipts. A big part of the explanation may be the low access to financial services. As noted, the distribution of formal financial services leaves rural areas relatively underserved, and the use of financial services as measured by deposit accounts per 1,000 people dropped over the period. One reason for this may be the growing dominance of private sector over public sector banks. The more profit-oriented private sector banks may find that providing financial services in rural areas is not feasible because of its greater cost.

The SBP's 10-year strategy for financial sector development reflects its understanding of the potential of the banking industry to support economic growth and development by promoting domestic and foreign savings and investment. Under this strategy, the SBP plans to implement a financial inclusion program that will, among other things, encourage banks to meet the needs of underserved sectors, including through outreach programs for agriculture, housing, microfinance, and small and medium-size enterprises (SBP 2009b). The strategy is expected to improve savings mobilization, allowing it to be an important element in financial market and economic development.

Corporate Governance

The Securities and Exchange Commission of Pakistan (SECP), established by the Securities and Exchange Commission of Pakistan Act, 1997, as the regulator of capital markets and the controller of corporate entities, issued the country's first code of corporate governance in March 2002. The SECP code was later incorporated into the listing regulations of the three stock exchanges and thus applies to all listed companies. Its main objectives are to stimulate company performance while limiting the abuse of power, promote corporate accountability and protection of investor interests, safeguard minority interests, promote transparency in operations and decision making, and encourage directors to discharge their fiduciary responsibilities diligently and transparently.

Several other corporate governance initiatives followed. In 2004, the SECP initiated the establishment of the Pakistan Institute of Corporate Governance (PICG) to provide training and build awareness on corporate governance issues. In 2006 the International Finance Corporation launched a project aimed at improving corporate governance practices in Pakistan. And in 2007 the Association of Chartered Certified Accountants Pakistan, in association with the IFC, the SECP, and the PICG, conducted a survey of corporate governance practices in Pakistan. The survey targeted locally listed companies, large companies not locally listed, and financial institutions.

The SBP, as the banking sector regulator, issued prudential regulations (G1–G4) requiring all commercial banks and development finance institutions to comply with the SECP code of corporate governance. It also issued a handbook of corporate governance to promote compliance and good corporate governance practices in the banking sector. Among the key areas covered by the regulations and handbook are the following:

- Board of directors—qualification and eligibility, election, appointment of directors by the SBP, board independence, board responsibilities and powers, board meetings, loans and remuneration, and dealings
- Management—appointment, qualifications, requirement to attend board meetings, and fit-and-proper test
- Financial disclosure—frequency of reporting, responsibility for financial reports and corporate compliance, disclosure of interest by directors holding company shares, corporate ownership structure, and divestiture of shares by sponsors and controlling interests
- Auditor—guidelines, qualification and disqualification, tenure, reading and inspection of auditor's report, signature on audit report, and prohibition on auditors' holding shares
- Audit committee—composition, meetings, terms of reference, reporting procedure, and internal audit

Through guidelines G1–G3, the SBP amended two parts of the corporate governance code issued to banks—the fit-and-proper test and the responsibilities of boards of directors, management, and compliance officers—and added guidelines (G3) on contributions and donations for charitable, social, and public welfare purposes. In addition, guideline G4 makes it mandatory for all banks and development finance institutions to have themselves rated by a credit rating agency that is on the approved panel of the SBP. The key amendments in G1 and G2 cover the following:

- Broadening the scope of the fit-and-proper test to include sponsors and strategic investors in addition to directors, CEOs, and key executives of banks and development finance institutions
- Requiring prior clearance in writing from the SBP for the entry of sponsors and strategic investors and the appointment of directors and the CEO
- Requiring prior approval in writing from the SBP for acquisitions of 5 percent or more of the shares of a bank or development finance institution
- Further clarifying the scope of responsibilities of the board of directors and management

- Increasing the mandatory requirement for independent directors and restrictions on family and executive directors in banks
- Emphasizing that the board is to remain independent of management by focusing on policy making and providing general direction to the bank or development finance institution rather than getting involved in day-to-day operations, including credit decisions

Some of these amendments would improve self-governance; others, such as the requirement to obtain SBP approval for acquisitions of 5 percent or more of the shares in an institution, need to be reviewed. Other areas to focus on include greater transparency and disclosure, greater accountability, further disclosures on beneficial ownership, safeguards on stakeholder rights, greater clarification of board responsibilities, and greater emphasis on self-governance for institutions.

Analysis of the answers to the corporate governance questionnaire finds that Pakistan has legal provisions covering most aspects of banks' ownership structure and the influence of stakeholders (see appendix 4A). The provisions relating to beneficial ownership could be further strengthened through greater disclosure requirements, however. The SBP regulatory guidelines—along with the Banking Companies Ordinance of 1962 and the Companies Ordinance of 1984—require disclosure of share ownership, with the threshold set at 10 percent, through means available to both the market and the public. In addition, banks must disclose shareholdings of 3 percent or more to the SBP. As noted, share acquisitions of 5 percent or more require the SBP's prior approval. Government ownership is also publicly disclosed.

Only the board and the company can appoint bank directors, though the government can nominate directors of government-controlled banks. There are provisions establishing the rights of stakeholders such as labor unions, though no details were available for an assessment. The State Bank Act limits the issuance to banks of any directive by the government or a quasi-governmental body that is inconsistent with the policies, regulations, and directives issued by the SBP. The preemption rights of minority shareholders are protected under the guidelines, but it is unclear whether this is monitored.

The SBP requires disclosure of beneficial ownership of shareholders—including information on the sponsor shareholders, with the threshold set at 3 percent. But this information is not available to the public. In addition, the SECP code requires disclosure of shareholdings of directors, the CEO, and their spouse and minor children; associated companies, undertakings, and related parties; public sector companies and corporations; and shareholders holding 10 percent or more of the voting interest in the company. Banks are to disclose this information in their annual accounts.

Investor rights relating to voting and shareholder meetings appear to be in place. Adequate information is disclosed to shareholders in a timely fashion before shareholder meetings. Shareholders can vote in absentia, though postal and electronic voting is not used, and voting is verified by a third party. Shareholders can vote on a normal range of issues, including related-party transactions. Banks are required to disclose special voting rights and caps on voting rights.

While basic ownership rights exist, regulatory control over share transactions and management changes needs to be reviewed. Appointments and dismissals of directors are subject to vote by shareholders, although the SBP has the power to remove directors and managers. The government can appoint directors to government-controlled banks only by virtue of its shareholdings. A clear dividend policy is in place. There are specific structural defenses that can prevent a takeover bid, including the requirement for prior approval by the SBP for share acquisitions of 5 percent or more of total paid-up capital. In addition, the central bank must approve any change in bank management. For a privatization, it assesses prospective investors to determine whether they meet its fit-and-proper test for owners and managers. All companies are encouraged to protect the interests of minority shareholders. In addition, under the fit-and-proper test, 25 percent of board members must be independent.

The questionnaire responses show that provisions for transparency and disclosure meet the main criteria, though the internal audit function has room for improvement. Banks' financial statements are prepared in accordance with International Accounting Standards (IAS). All these standards apply in Pakistan except IAS 39 and IAS 40, which are deferred for the time being for financial institutions. Financial reporting is done quarterly, semiannually, and annually. Audit fees paid to external auditors must be disclosed.

The SBP has issued guidelines on the appointment of audit committees that clearly outline their roles and responsibilities, which include controlling the selection of auditors. External auditors are not permitted to perform other, non-audit services for the banks they audit. No bank can retain the same auditors for more than five years. The SBP has also issued guidelines relating to internal auditors. Under these guidelines, the fit-and-proper test devised for key executives applies to the head of internal audit. Internal auditors are independent and report to the audit committee, though the frequency of such reporting is not defined.

Banks in Pakistan follow a unitary board structure with a minimum of seven directors. Board members' qualifications and experience are governed by the fit-and-proper test outlined in the prudential guidelines. The board's roles and responsibilities are clearly defined; however, its tasks and objectives are not individually assigned, and this matter is instead left to the board. The SECP code recommends orientation courses for directors. In addition, the SBP's prudential guidelines urge that all board members attend at least one to two weeks' training at an institution such as PICG within the first year of joining the board. No information on formal or systematic training was available for assessment, however. Developing a systematic training program for directors is important.

The remuneration of directors is subject to a shareholder vote at annual general meetings, and banks are required to disclose the compensation of directors in detail. The remuneration paid to board members is linked to the meetings they attend, and no periodic, fixed remuneration is paid. There are no provisions for performance-based compensation. For assurance that banks can attract and retain qualified and competent directors, a review of compensation policies is needed. In addition, the recent financial meltdown and the underlying issue of executive compensation packages have highlighted the need for the authorities to discuss compensation policies with commercial banks and to set clear guidelines if the banks decide to link compensation to performance levels. In addition, performance levels will need to be monitored.

Pakistan has issued comprehensive guidelines in most areas of corporate governance. But the success of governance procedures depends largely on the commitment of banks. Their approach to corporate governance needs to go beyond simple compliance with legal requirements. Two other key issues are disclosure and accountability, emphasizing the importance of regulatory surveillance and enforcement.

Sri Lanka

Sri Lanka's economy has remained resilient over the past few decades in the face of a 30-year war, a devastating tsunami, escalating prices, and weak reserves. Challenges on many fronts led to particular volatility in 2008. Escalating oil and food prices caused the already high inflation to soar and the current account deficit to widen further. Foreign reserves plummeted in the second part of the year. The second-round effects of the global financial crisis appeared to compound these effects. While Sri Lanka had no direct exposure to toxic assets, the impact on the real economy through weak growth in export markets, along with a slowdown in domestic demand and external capital outflows resulting from the deleveraging activities of foreign investors, decelerated economic growth. But the end of the armed conflict in May 2009 brought renewed hope of sustainable peace and economic development.

Based on 2008 data, Sri Lanka ranks sixth in the region in population (20 million) and area (65,600 square kilometers) and fourth in GDP (US$39.6 billion). With a GNI per capita of US$1,780 in 2008, Sri Lanka is classified as a lower-middle-income country. Its economy has felt the effects of global trends. Between January 2003 and May 2008 South Asia suffered a huge loss of income from a severe terms-of-trade shock as a result of the surge in global commodity prices. Sri Lanka had a GDP loss of around 10.2 percent—around 7.7 percent on energy and 2.3 percent on food (World Bank 2008b). The current account deficit increased from 4.3 percent of GDP in 2007 to 9.3 percent in 2008. Inflation soared from 10 percent in 2006 to 15.8 percent in 2007 and 22.56 percent in 2008. Worker remittances, averaging around 7.6 percent of GDP, prevented a further slide in the current account balance. Meanwhile, the fiscal deficit hovered around 7 percent of GDP (because the government adjusted food and energy prices to world market prices, the deficit did not widen further). The overall impact was a slowdown in GDP growth from 7.7 percent in 2006 to 5.95 percent in 2008.

In 2008, the global financial crisis added to the decelerating effects on the economy. Global deleveraging resulted in a rapid outflow of external funds, exacerbated by the intervention of the Central Bank of Sri Lanka (CBSL) in the foreign exchange market in a bid to sustain the rupee's peg to the U.S. dollar. Foreign reserves dropped from US$3.5 billion in 2007 to US$1.8 billion at the end of 2008, and import cover fell to two months. The government countered the deteriorating situation by curbing expenditure, mainly by reducing the public sector wage increase, limiting imports, and easing monetary policy.

These actions paid dividends. The import limits and the easing of world food and energy prices improved the terms of trade, and inflation eased. Foreign reserves were improved by an IMF Stand-By Arrangement, a sovereign bond issue, and the return of investors.[16] Remittances continued to support reserves as well as the current account. In 2009, the current account deficit was expected to be around 3 percent of GDP, and inflation around 5 percent. Postwar reconstruction is also expected to boost the economy. The real sector is expected to rebound in 2010, and if fiscal consolidation takes place as planned, GDP growth is expected to be around 4 percent in 2009 and 6 percent in 2010.

Sri Lanka's banking system in 2008 consisted of 22 licensed commercial banks: 2 state banks (generally referred to in the report as public sector banks), 8 domestic private banks (generally referred to as private sector banks), and 12 foreign banks. The financial system also included 14 licensed specialized banks (8 national and 6 regional development banks) and 56 nonbank financial institutions and specialized leasing companies. The CBSL is the regulatory authority for the banking sector as well as nonbank financial institutions. The Securities and Exchange Commission (SEC) of Sri Lanka regulates the securities market.

The stability of the banking sector depends on six systemically important banks, two public sector banks and four private sector banks. These six banks held around 78 percent of commercial banking assets in 2007. The two public sector banks dominate, accounting for more than 42 percent of the total commercial banking assets. But the private sector banks are beginning to compete for dominance. In 2008, banks accounted for around 47.5 percent of total financial assets, an amount equivalent to around 53.39 percent of GDP.

In Sri Lanka, as in most other South Asian countries, the banking sector has been hit by the second-round effects of the global financial crisis through the impact on real sector activities. Timely regulatory actions and focused responses by the banking community appear to have helped the country's banks navigate the economic uncertainties. Analysis of the indicators for the eight-year period 2001–08 supports this premise.

The analysis also identifies the banking system's strengths and weaknesses. Access to financial services is among the highest in the region and already improving in the war-affected areas of the North and East. The profitability of banks improved over the period, though the economic slowdown is expected to lead to rising levels of nonperforming loans and thus falling returns. This suggests a need for banks to focus on reducing operating costs. Banks are relatively stable. The capital adequacy ratio is maintained above the minimum regulatory requirements, and all banks had switched to the Basel II framework by June 2008. Banks would benefit from further capital enhancements, however. The capital market continues to develop, though the private bond market remains limited. In the banking sector, market concentration is high. Development of the payment system has been laudable (figure 3.8). But savings mobilization remains below the potential for the country, pointing to a need to identify and counter barriers to saving.

Sri Lanka has taken important steps to improve corporate governance in the banking sector by issuing mandatory guidelines. More work is needed, however, to make the guidelines more comprehensive and effective. Important needs are to expand disclosure requirements and strengthen compliance and enforcement. Equally important is for the banking sector to incorporate the best practices of corporate governance. In other moves that will also support better corporate governance, Sri Lanka has made credit rating mandatory for all banks and implemented Basel II guidelines.

Sri Lanka has a credit information bureau (CRIB). In 2008, CRIB launched the Credit Information Management Systems, allowing more comprehensive credit reports. CRIB has the authority to issue credit reports to individuals as well as to financial institutions.[17] In addition, Sri Lanka has voluntary deposit insurance

Figure 3.8 **Sri Lanka Moves toward a Cashless Society**

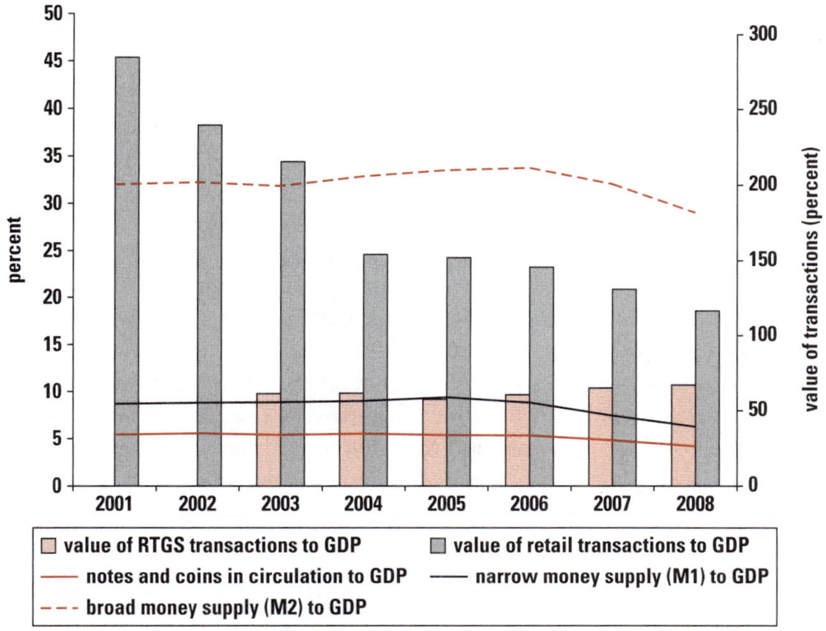

Source: Appendix table A2.16.
Note: There are no RTGS values for 2001 and 2002; the RTGS system started in 2003.

coverage, established in 1987, though it has seldom been used. The CBSL is working toward implementation of a comprehensive deposit insurance scheme, which should further strengthen the stability of the financial system.

Access to Finance

Sri Lanka arguably has the highest access to banking services in the region. Maldives has higher demographic and geographic penetration ratios. But as observed in the analysis of that country, the calculation of these ratios is skewed because it does not take into account the dispersion of the population among atolls (which are not supported by banking services). A recent World Bank study (2008a) reported that around 59 percent of households in Sri Lanka have access to financial services, the highest share in the region.[18]

Geographic and demographic penetration of bank branches and ATMs rose over the period. Demographic penetration increased to about 9 branches and about 6 ATMs per 100,000 people in 2008. Geographic penetration similarly increased, reaching 18 branches and 15 ATMs per 1,000 square kilometers in 2008. Moreover, the distribution of the branch network across the country is fairly equitable. Among the 25 districts in Sri Lanka, 7 districts accounting for 54 percent of the population have 64 percent of the branches, while the other 18 districts, with 46 percent of the population, have 36 percent of the branches. The 5 districts in the Northern and Eastern Provinces, where the war was mainly waged, account for an estimated 13 percent of the population and 9 percent of the branches. Some of these areas came under full government control only after May 2009. But reconstruction efforts are already under way to provide better banking facilities to these areas, and penetration ratios were expected to rise in 2009.

The usage indicators confirm the increase in financial access over the period. Deposit accounts per 1,000 people grew by around 44 percent from 2001 to 2007, then dropped slightly in 2008 to 1,304.31. Loan accounts per 1,000 people grew by around 6 percent over the same period, though the ratio dropped by 11 percent in 2008 to 240.37. The economic slowdown in 2008 appears to have slowed the growth in the use of banking facilities. But new branch openings by all major banks as part of the development in the north and east should rectify this in 2009 and beyond.

Besides the main branches of commercial banks, there were 3,332 other banking outlets in 2008, such as extension offices, pawn centers, student savings units, and pay offices. These outlets provide limited though valuable banking functions. In addition, the 15 licensed specialized banks had a network of 423 main branches and 221 other banking outlets in 2008.

The microfinance industry provides another important means of access to finance in rural areas. In Sri Lanka, microfinance is channeled mainly through cooperative institutions, Sanasa and thrift and credit cooperative societies, and Samurdhi banking societies.[19] A survey conducted in 2006/07 by the German Agency for Technical Cooperation revealed that there are around 10,000 active microfinance providers in Sri Lanka: 1,038 Samurdhi societies; 1,687 cooperative rural banks and women's development cooperatives; 3,794 active Sanasa and thrift and credit cooperative societies; and 2,500 other microfinance institutions, nongovernmental organizations, and the like. Almost 90 percent of these operate in rural areas. According to the survey, in 2007 Sri Lanka's microfinance industry accounted for around SL Rs 42 billion (US$400 million) in deposit accounts and SL Rs 68.8 billion (US$655 million) in loan accounts. To establish a regulatory and supervisory framework for the industry, the CBSL has drafted the Micro-Finance Institutions Act, which is now under revision. (For more information on microfinance in Sri Lanka, see GTZ ProMis 2009.)

Performance and Efficiency

Bank returns improved over the eight-year period, with the return on assets growing faster than the return on equity. The return on assets increased by around 140 percent to 2.01 percent in 2008. The return on equity remained relatively stable over the period and was around 27.64 percent in 2008. Both the net interest margin and recurring earning power showed robust growth in 2001–08. The net interest margin grew by 35.75 percent to 4.48 percent in 2008, while recurring earning power grew by 46.66 percent to 2.40 percent.

The operating and staff cost ratios declined over the period, helping to improve profitability. The operating cost ratio fell by 41.84 percentage points to around 76.82 percent in 2008. The regional average, however, was 60.25 percent. One reason for the higher operating costs in Sri Lanka is the high tax on financial services.[20] Staff costs fell from 46.21 percent of operating costs in 2001 to 42.74 percent in 2008. The two public sector banks have higher operating costs on average than the private sector banks, in part because of their extensive branch networks.

The return ratios were expected to decline in 2009 as the economic slowdown led to increases in nonperforming loans and reductions in banks' fee-based activities. All return ratios are strong, however, and banks should be able to withstand moderate reductions. If nonperforming loans were to increase significantly or interest margins to fall, however, banks' profitability will be affected. Because of their high operating costs, banks have been unable to increase their capital cushions even with high interest margins. To counter the effects of the economic slowdown on profitability, banks are expected to work to reduce costs and increase efficiency.

Financial Stability

Maintaining financial stability in the wake of the global financial meltdown is of prime importance to commercial banks as well as regulatory authorities. Lack of exposure to toxic assets and failing financial institutions in the developed world minimized the direct effects of the financial meltdown on Sri Lanka's banks. A bigger concern is the resulting economic slowdown, which could affect the quality of their asset portfolios and the growth of their business. Thus far, timely regulations and prudent management have played a big part in maintaining the stability of the financial system.

The capital adequacy ratio improved over the period, ending at 12.62 percent in 2008. By the end of June 2008, all commercial banks had switched to the Basel II capital computation method. Because of the additional capital charges on operational risk under Basel II, the capital adequacy ratio fell from 2007 levels by about 96 basis points. But the ratio remained above the minimum regulatory requirement throughout the period.

The leverage ratio increased over the period, and in 2008 equity was around 13.15 times total assets. The increase in the leverage ratio matched the trend in the capital adequacy ratio. But this also points to the need for banks to increase their capitalization levels. The gross nonperforming loans ratio fell by about 66 percent from 2001 to 2007. With the economic slowdown, this ratio is creeping back up. From 2007 to 2008, the nonperforming loans ratio increased by 1.30 percentage points, to 7.92 percent. The provisions to nonperforming loans ratio increased over much of the period, then fell slightly to 61.41 percent in 2008. In 2009 nonperforming loans were expected to be higher.[21] Banks should be able to withstand moderate shocks. In the present economic situation, however, banks need to expand their capital base to absorb possible losses that might occur with an increase in nonperforming loans.

A threat to the stability of the financial system arose at the end of 2008, when unauthorized finance business conducted by a subsidiary of one of the systemically important banks caused a run on deposits and liquidity stress for the parent bank. The CBSL stepped in immediately and successfully managed the situation by changing the board of directors, appointing one of the large public sector banks as the managing agent, and providing collateralized borrowings, mainly from the central bank. These measures restored public confidence and averted the bank's collapse. This incident justifies the call for banks to enhance their capital base.

The stringent monetary measures introduced in 2007 and the absorption of rupee liquidity through foreign currency sales led to tight liquidity in the market. In the second half of 2008, the CBSL relaxed its monetary policy and provided adequate liquidity to the market by lowering its statutory reserve ratios and repo and reverse repo rates numerous times. Overall, liquidity in the banking system has been fairly stable. At the end of 2008, liquid assets amounted to around 20.11 percent of total assets and to 23.46 percent of liquid liabilities, slightly higher than the regulatory requirement of 20 percent. Liquidity has been managed well except in the one bank that faced liquidity stress.

Overall, the outlook for financial stability is favorable, though the need to increase the capitalization of banks should be examined in the light of the economic situation. Nonperforming loans need to be monitored diligently, and credit quality needs to be maintained while pursuing stable credit growth.

Capital Market Development

Sri Lanka has one stock exchange, the Colombo Stock Exchange. The exchange is fully automated, with a central depository system, an electronic clearing and settlement system for share transactions, and an automated trading system. A debt securities trading system implemented in 2003 supports secondary trading of government securities. The exchange calculates two main price indexes, the All Share Price Index and the Milanka Price Index, as well as the Total Return Index. Price indexes are calculated for each of 20 business sectors. Equity and debt securities can be listed on either the main board (for larger companies) or a secondary board, Diri Savi, with much more relaxed listing requirements (for small to medium-size companies and start-up companies). At the end of December 2008, the exchange had 236 companies listed and a market capitalization of SL Rs 488.81 billion (around US$4.3 billion).[22]

The stock market capitalization improved until 2006, then declined from 2007 onward. In 2008, the market capitalization was 11.08 percent of GDP, having lost around 60 percent of its 2006 value. Moreover, the market became increasingly concentrated, especially after 2005; the trading value of the top 10 stocks accounted for 67.3 percent of the total in 2008. Market liquidity fluctuated over the period. A market liquidity measure, the stock trading value to GDP ratio, fell between 2005 and 2008 to around 2.5 percent. Market efficiency as measured by the stock market turnover ratio also fluctuated, rising in 2007 and 2008 to end the period at 0.17. Low turnover ratios denote relatively low efficiency.

Many factors drove the market decline in 2008. They include the impact of the global financial crisis, the deleveraging activities of foreign investors, and the country's economic slowdown. Domestic reasons for the market decline include court reversals of privatization deals for some blue chip companies, the high interest rates, and declines in company performance. But the equity market appears to have weathered these conditions. Today, investors are trying to reap peace dividends from the end of the war. And a sharp decline in interest rates has diverted funds back to the equity market.[23]

Government bonds dominate the bond market in Sri Lanka. In 2008, the domestic public bonds outstanding to GDP ratio was 29.07 percent. While the opening of treasury bill and bond auctions to foreign investors (allowed to purchase up to 10 percent) brought in funds in 2007 and early 2008, there has been a net outflow from treasury securities since then because of the financial crisis. The corporate bond market remains very small. The largest issue in 2008 was by a public sector bank.

The capital market in Sri Lanka is still very small compared with other markets around the world. But with the end of war, the stock and bond markets should grow, providing a stable source of long-term funding for the economy and an alternative to bank funding.

Market Concentration and Competitiveness

Market concentration is very high in Sri Lanka's banking system. While all concentration ratios have been declining, the three largest banks still held around 50 percent of banking assets, deposits, and loans in 2008. Moreover, as noted, the six systemically important banks hold more than 75 percent of commercial banking assets. The Herfindahl-Hirschman Index in 2008 was 1,198.75 (denoting a moderately concentrated industry, according to international norms).

The private credit extended by banks to GDP ratio increased over much of the period, a concern because of possible credit risks. With the economic slowdown, however, banks have tightened credit, and the ratio dropped by nearly 18 percent between 2006 and 2008, to 28.94 percent. The commercial banking assets to GDP ratio also increased over the period until 2006, then started to decline. In 2008, commercial banking assets amounted to 53.39 percent of GDP. High commercial banking assets and private credit along with high concentration ratios are a concern if interest margins start to drop, and this combination needs to be monitored carefully. Better risk management practices would help lessen the impact.

Some have argued that for a small country like Sri Lanka, having 22 banks is not operationally efficient and that banks should therefore pursue mergers and consolidations. But having fewer banks that are too big to fail also can have adverse consequences, especially in an economic downturn like the one countries are experiencing today. Having fewer banks does not guarantee lower operating costs. For example, India's commercial banking sector serves a population and geographic area 50 times the size of those served by Sri Lanka's—and has 3.5 times as many commercial banks and 13 times as many branches. Yet it has an operating cost ratio quite similar to that of Sri Lanka's banking sector.

So it can be argued that reducing the number of banks will not necessarily reduce operating costs. What is more important is to identify what contributes to higher operating costs, such as higher-than-average taxes, and work to reduce those costs. Conversely, increasing the number of banks to serve a policy objective—such as expanding access to financial services or increasing social inclusion—may also fail to achieve the desired results, as evidenced by Nepal. Thus, the right number of banks for a country is a policy decision that warrants careful consideration.

Payment Systems Development

Sri Lanka has three systemically important payment systems—a check-based retail payment system, a high-value and time-critical RTGS payment and settlement system, and the automated trading system operated by the stock exchange, which settles private equities. A strong institutional, legal, and regulatory framework has been developed to back these payment systems. Sri Lanka has gone further in payment system reforms than most countries in the region. These reforms have increased efficiency while minimizing risk and have improved financial access—all important concepts for economic development.[24]

The retail payment system consists of a check imaging and truncation system (CITS); the Sri Lanka Interbank Payment System (SLIPS), operated by LankaClear Pvt. Ltd.; and a retail check clearinghouse, jointly owned by the CBSL and the banks and also operated by LankaClear. LankaClear has a main operating center in the capital city of Colombo and 11 regional centers. The CITS, an interbank check clearing system, ensures T+1 settlement for checks deposited from almost anywhere in the country. By using check imaging, this system provides faster and more efficient settlement and minimizes risk. LankaClear also clears interbank payments. SLIPS is an end-of-day net settlement system. LankaClear sends the end-of-day net balances of SLIPS through the RTGS system for settlement. In 2008, LankaClear cleared around SL Rs 19.5 billion (US$170 million) of checks daily through the CITS, while the daily average for SLIPS clearing was SL Rs 979 million (US$8.5 million). Retail payment system transactions totaled SL Rs 5,221 billion (US$45.4 billion) in 2008.

Another clearing system handles U.S. dollar checks drawn within the country. This clearing is done by a commercial bank where other banks hold settlement accounts. This settlement system is not systemically important, handling only SL Rs 26 billion (US$226 million) in transactions in 2008.

In 2008, the CBSL initiated the establishment of a common payment switch, owned and operated by LankaClear, to clear all account-based electronic transactions between banks from their own accounts and on behalf of their customers. Many cash and check transactions and SLIPS transactions are expected to be shifted to the common payment switch, which will go live in mid-2010. LankaClear received the certification authority for the financial sector in 2009 and can therefore certify digital signatures for other countries in the region as well.[25] This is a commendable achievement. It will enhance the efficiency of the retail-value payment system and reduce the cost of transactions for banks and their customers through automation.

In September 2003, the CBSL established the RTGS system, which it operates, to process large-value and time-critical fund transfers. The CBSL provides collateralized intraday liquidity at no charge to all banks and primary dealers for RTGS settlements to be returned at the end of the day. In 2008, transactions with a total value of SL Rs 25.13 trillion (US$218.5 billion) were settled through the RTGS system.

The RTGS system is part of an integrated system, known as LankaSettle, that includes the securities settlement system LankaSecure, also operated by the CBSL. LankaSecure consists of a scripless securities settlement system and scripless securities depository system. LankaSecure maintains central records of ownership and transfers securities between security holders' accounts. The system handles government securities in scripless form. Settlement of securities takes T+3 to T+4. The total value of scripless securities holdings at the end of 2008 was SL Rs 1,713 billion (US$15 billion). The payment and securities messages are transmitted through the system using SWIFTnet, an internationally accepted online messaging system provided by SWIFT. In 2005, LankaSecure introduced an Internet-based information service, LankaSecureNet, that enables account holders to obtain detailed information on their accounts using the Internet.

Sri Lanka was the 16th country in the world to receive Red Book status for modernized payment systems from the BIS Committee on Payment and Settlement Systems.[26] Among the countries of South Asia, Sri Lanka as well as India and Pakistan have engaged in major payment reforms, and Sri Lanka was the first in the region to operate an RTGS and scripless securities settlement system with a SWIFT link (Jayamaha n.d.). In 2006, the CBSL established the National Payments Council, the highest decision-making body for payment and settlement systems, with representation of all stakeholders. Following a recommendation by the council, a local SWIFT service bureau, Lanka Financial Services Bureau Ltd., was established in 2008 to manage the SWIFT service facilities. The service bureau saves substantial foreign exchange while providing an efficient service to institutions participating in the RTGS and scripless securities settlement system. Moreover, according to the CBSL, the RTGS system was expected to conform to 9 of 10 BIS Committee on Payment and Settlement Systems core principles for systemically important payment and settlement systems by the end of 2009.

Payment system indicators for Sri Lanka show increasing use of the new secure systems. Both the notes and coins in circulation to GDP ratio and the narrow money supply to GDP ratio are lower in Sri Lanka than in the rest of the region's countries, and fell marginally over the period, denoting lower use of currency. In 2008, these two ratios were 4.22 percent and 6.29 percent, respectively. Currency in circulation accounted for more than 67 percent of the narrow money supply and around 14.5 percent of the broad money supply. The value of retail transactions to GDP ratio dropped by nearly 60 percent over the period, while the value of RTGS transactions to GDP ratio increased, indicating a shift toward the RTGS system. In 2008 the value of RTGS transactions amounted to around 67.11 percent of GDP. Similarly, the retail payments concentration ratio fell over the period, while the RTGS concentration ratio declined slightly in 2008. Since the RTGS system is quite new, the effects will be observable in the long run.

Savings Mobilization

Savings mobilization is important in any developing country, especially if its capital market is not fully developed. High savings allow a country to move away from overreliance on external funding. In Sri Lanka, however, savings remain below their potential.

The broad money supply averaged around 32 percent of GDP over the period, and declined to 29.07 percent in 2008, indicating a potential for greater financial deepening. As a result of inflation, however, the real deposit interest rate remained negative throughout the period. In 2008, the unprecedented inflation rate of 22.6 percent drove the real interest rate to a new low of −10.97 percent. High inflation inhibits domestic savings. This situation was expected to change beginning in 2009, however, with inflation back to normal levels.

The reserve money to total deposits ratio averaged around 21 percent, dropping to 19.03 percent in 2008. Lower levels of reserve money indicate greater efficiency in financial intermediation, which aids savings mobilization. The loan to deposit ratio rose by around 12 percent over the period, to 88.78 percent in 2008. The increase in this ratio shows that banks are relying on borrowings rather than deposits for their funding needs. Remittances remained steady throughout the period, averaging around 7.6 percent of GDP and providing an important stable flow of funds to the country. Several steps have been taken to ensure a steady flow of remittances. The CBSL has dedicated a bond to attracting diaspora savings and facilitated the opening of bank branches and exchange houses in countries that are important sources of remittances. In addition, the government offers tax holidays on the income of those who send remittances.

Sri Lanka has almost all the preconditions to promote savings—stable financial institutions, a strong regulatory framework, relatively high financial access through the banking network, and prudent savings habits. But for macroeconomic reasons, actual savings fall short of the potential. While the end of the war should provide an impetus for saving, investment policy is also important. Today domestic savings are used mainly to fund the government deficit, which puts upward pressure on inflation and further inhibits saving. A better alternative would be to channel domestic savings toward capital investments.

Corporate Governance

Under Monetary Law Act No. 58 of 1949, the CBSL has a mandate to secure financial system stability in Sri Lanka, while its Monetary Board is authorized to make rules and regulations as deemed necessary. And under Banking Act No. 30 of 1988 (last amended by No. 46 of 2006), the Monetary Board is empowered to issue directions to licensed commercial banks on the way in which any aspect of their business is to be conducted.[27] Under these legal provisions, the CBSL issued Banking Act Direction No. 11 of 2007, Corporate Governance for Licensed Commercial Banks in Sri Lanka, in December 2007, to be implemented from January 2008. A revision in April 2008 amended the provisions on executive directors and transitional provisions for founding directors, incumbent chairmen, and executive directors. The direction covers the following key areas:

- Responsibilities of the board
- Composition of the board
- Fit-and-proper criteria for directors
- Management functions delegated by the board
- Separation of the duties of the chairman and the CEO
- Board-appointed committees
- Related-party transactions
- Disclosures
- Transitional and other general provisions

Banks have a responsibility to adopt the guidelines set out by the CBSL not just as guidelines but also as part of their banking culture. Following is a detailed analysis of the corporate governance standards in Sri Lanka based on the responses to the survey questionnaire (see appendix 4A).

Under the guidelines and regulations issued by the Colombo Stock Exchange, publicly listed companies must disclose the share ownership of their top 20 shareholders in their annual reports, available to both the market and the general public. In addition, banks must disclose holdings of 5 percent and above to the CBSL monthly. Government ownership is disclosed in the same manner. Only the board of directors and the company can appoint directors and decide on their remuneration at annual general meetings. For government-controlled banks, however, the government can nominate directors. To be appointed as a director, a person must satisfy the fit-and-proper criteria. Even though rules protect the preemption rights of minority shareholders, no provisions establish stakeholder rights.

Among these guidelines, one of the most significant is the requirement, aimed at achieving broad-based ownership of banks, that large shareholdings of single shareholders, beneficial owners, or groups be reduced to 15 percent within a period determined by the Monetary Board of the CBSL. Because of its restrictiveness, this cap may create a strong incentive for shareholders to disguise their interests through nominees or associated parties, despite the legal provisions outlawing such agreements. The definition of significant ownership should be broadened and clearly defined, with legal provisions to ensure proper disclosure and to encompass exertion of control regardless of the size of the shareholding, and a suitability test should be introduced. The Monetary Board of CBSL should be explicitly empowered to prevent the exercise of voting rights by a party that fails the suitability test. These material ownership rules do not apply to government, public corporations, or statutory bodies.

Investor rights relating to voting procedures and shareholder meetings need further strengthening. Adequate information is disclosed to shareholders in a timely fashion before shareholder meetings, and shareholders can vote in absentia, but electronic voting is not available. No provisions exist for third-party verification of voting. Although major transactions of a bank should be approved by the shareholders by a special resolution unless otherwise specified in the articles of association, there is no evidence that shareholders must vote on related-party transactions. Disclosure of special voting rights and caps on voting rights is not required.

Basic ownership rights also need improvement, particularly with respect to shareholders' right to vote on the operations of banks, rights of minority shareholders, and regulatory and government control of share transactions. Board appointments and dismissals are not subject to a shareholder vote and are controlled by the government in public sector banks. The ability of minority shareholders to appoint directors depends on banks' internal rules. A clear dividend policy is in place. There are structural defenses against takeover bids, including a requirement for prior approval by the CBSL and the Ministry of Finance for the acquisition of a material interest in a bank (10 percent or more of its shares). In addition, the SEC requires any investor acquiring more than 30 percent of a listed company to make an offer to all other shareholders.

Banks' financial statements are prepared in accordance with generally accepted local accounting principles, which are in material conformity with International Accounting Standards.[28] Financial reporting is done monthly, quarterly, and annually, and audit fees paid to external auditors must be disclosed. The CBSL has issued clear guidelines on the appointment of audit committees and defined their roles and responsibilities. The audit committee makes recommendations on the selection of external as well as internal auditors. External auditors are not permitted to perform other, nonaudit services for the banks they audit. Guidelines on internal auditors have been issued, but improvements could be made. Internal auditors are independent, reporting to the audit committee, but the frequency of such reporting is not clearly defined.

Banks in Sri Lanka follow a hybrid board structure with around 5–11 members on average. Board members' qualifications and experience are governed by the fit-and-proper test criteria set by the prudential guidelines. Board committee requirements are presented in the SEC governance rules as well as the CBSL guidelines. The CBSL rules require boards to have audit, selection, remuneration, and risk management committees and to specify that the committees must be chaired by a nonexecutive director and include at least one independent director. The CBSL should enhance the guidance on the significance and responsibilities of the committees and the key role they play in the governance structure of a financial institution.

The roles and responsibilities of boards are clearly defined, and their tasks and objectives are defined and individually assigned. In addition, the corporate governance code details the need for systematic training for directors. Banks are permitted to disclose merely the aggregate compensation of their directors in their annual reports. No information is available on whether banks offer performance-based compensation to their directors or whether shareholders can vote on directors' remuneration—practices that should be incorporated into policy. If banks decide to link compensation to performance, however, the authorities need to discuss their compensation policies with them and set clear guidelines in light of the recent global financial meltdown and the issues related to executive compensation packages.

The CBSL has taken important steps to strengthen corporate governance in the banking sector. These include implementing Basel II, introducing mandatory corporate governance standards, and requiring credit ratings for better disclosure. But the corporate governance guidelines issued to banks could be further improved. Disclosure requirements and detailed guidelines are still needed on many issues, such as stakeholder rights, special voting rights, rights of shareholders to vote on bank operations, and minority shareholder rights. Other important issues include regulatory and government control of share transactions and the absence of beneficial ownership restrictions on government, public corporations, and statutory bodies. These issues should be reviewed, and necessary changes incorporated into regulatory guidelines and legal statutes to ensure compliance as well as enforceability.

Endnotes

1. According to World Bank estimates, Afghanistan produces and trades more than 90 percent of the world's illicit opium.

2. CGAP, "Country Maps," http://www.cgap.org/p/site/c/template.rc/1.26.2301/ (accessed in November 2009).

3. Denominations above Rs 100 (that is, Rs 500 and Rs 1,000) are not legal tender in Bhutan.

4. Financial Institutions Act, 1992, Part III, Article 11, Organization and Administration.

5. The three committees are the Patil Committee (chaired by R. H. Patil) to assess Indian standards relative to international standards and codes; the Verma Committee (chaired by M. S. Verma) to advise on banking supervision; and the Ganguly Committee (chaired by A. S. Ganguly) to study board effectiveness.

6. The actual numbers of branches and ATMs are lower. Because the geographic penetration ratios are calculated for 1,000 square kilometers and the area of Maldives is only 300 square kilometers, the actual numbers of branches and ATMs are multiplied by 1,000/300 to arrive at comparable ratios.

7. In September 2009, the MMA started open-market operations to mop up excess liquidity in the banking system. The treasury instruments to carry out these transactions were generated by securitizing outstanding balances in the government overdraft account at the MMA (known as the ways and means account), converting them to medium- to long-term government bonds with maturities of 2–10 years. This process was completed by January 2010, and under the medium-term macrofiscal plan the government will not resort to overdraft financing of the deficit. The next two key steps are establishing a proper auction system to sell government securities (rather than the current practice of offering instruments with amount and price predetermined) and obtaining a sovereign debt rating.

Establishing a proper auction system would also give rise to a reference yield curve, which would support the development of the corporate debt market.

8. Certified Practicing Accountants of Maldives official Web site, http://cpamaldives.org/page.php?display=about.

9. The minimum regulatory capital requirement was reduced to 10 percent of risk-weighted assets effective for the 2009/10 financial year, with the Tier 1 core capital requirement at 6 percent of risk-weighted assets. Previously (until the 2008/09 financial year) the minimum capital requirement had been 11 percent, and the Tier 1 requirement 5.5 percent. The financial year for banks in Nepal is from mid-July to mid-July.

10. *Procyclicality* is defined as the property of exaggerating or exacerbating the cyclical tendencies of aggregate economic activity (see SEMP 2009).

11. See Nepal Stock Exchange official Web site, http://www.nepalstock.com/about/index.php (accessed in November 2009).

12. In 2001, Nepal's financial sector consisted of 13 commercial banks, 7 development banks, 45 finance companies, 7 microcredit development banks, 19 savings and credit cooperatives, and 7 nongovernmental organizations. In 2008, as noted, there were 28 commercial banks, 58 development banks, 78 finance companies, 12 microcredit development banks, 16 savings and credit cooperatives, and 46 nongovernmental organizations (NRB 2008).

13. Policies such as interest rate ceilings, liquidity requirements, and reserve requirements can cause financial repression and may prevent intermediaries from functioning at their full capacity. McKinnon (1973) and Shaw (1973) argued that a repressed financial sector discourages both savings and investment because rates of return fall. Because reserves carry no interest, when reserve requirements are high, the interest spread widens and the cost of capital increases.

14. In fall 2008, the IMF supported the stabilization program embarked on by Pakistan through a Stand-By Arrangement of US$7.6 billion, deemed necessary given the sizable external imbalances and risk of large capital outflows. In August 2009, the IMF raised the support to US$11.3 billion to address increased risks and financing needs. The program is aimed at restoring financial stability through a tightening of fiscal and monetary policies, to reduce inflation and strengthen foreign currency reserves, among other things (see http://www.imf.org/external/np/country/notes/pakistan.htm).

15. "Guess Who Has the Hottest Stock Market," Up Front, *BusinessWeek*, September 23, 2002, http://www.businessweek.com/magazine/content/02_38/c3800022.htm#B3800024 (accessed November 19, 2009).

16. Sri Lanka's debut sovereign bond, floated in October 2007, was three times oversubscribed. The entry into the international capital market was made at the peak of the subprime crisis, when investor confidence had fallen significantly, but the investment community accepted Sri Lanka's credit story. A second sovereign bond, floated in October 2009, was 13 times oversubscribed. These two bond issues greatly improved the country's foreign reserves situation.

17. The CRIB Act was amended in 2008, enabling significant changes in the ownership of shares of CRIB. The CBSL reduced its 51 percent shareholding to 19.9 percent, paving the way for other public sector credit institutions to jointly hold 51 percent. CRIB also went live with its new data transmission facility, which allows online data submission and continuous evaluation of customer credit profiles. Sri Lanka's CRIB, ranked among the best in South Asia, can now provide not only negative but also positive information on borrowers as well as protect customers by permitting them to obtain credit reports directly from CRIB.

18. The World Bank study (2008a) reports that in Bangladesh 32 percent of households have access to financial services; in Bhutan, 16 percent; in India, 48 percent; in Nepal, 20 percent; and in Pakistan, 12 percent. No data are available for Afghanistan and Maldives.

19. *Sanasa* is the Sinhala acronym for the movement of thrift and credit cooperative societies, a microfinance cooperative network covering all provinces of Sri Lanka. Samurdhi is a donor-funded poverty alleviation program introduced by the Sri Lanka government in 1996. Samurdhi banking societies, the microfinance arm, have enhanced access to credit for poor families while promoting the savings and investment habit.

20. Banks in Sri Lanka are taxed at a rate close to 60 percent in addition to a debit tax on withdrawals.

21. Even with special debt recovery laws, commercial courts, and parate execution powers for banks, recovering loans backed by real estate will be difficult in Sri Lanka.

22. Information from Colombo Stock Exchange official Web site, http://www.cse.lk/ (accessed November 20, 2009).

23. Sri Lanka's stock market recorded unprecedented growth during the last quarter of 2009, with the All Share Price Index reaching 3,344.89 and the Milanka Price Index rising to 3,809. Market turnover and capitalization have been high, in part because of foreign investment in Sri Lankan shares.

24. The information in this section was drawn mostly from CBSL (*Annual Report, 2008*).

25. To promote public confidence in the authenticity, integrity, and reliability of data messages, electronic documents, electronic records, and other communications, the CBSL requested LankaClear to be the certificate service provider for the financial sector. Under the guidance of the CBSL, LankaClear therefore launched Sri Lanka's first certificate authority under the brand name LANKASIGN, in accordance with Electronic Transaction Act No. 19 of 2006 and Computer Crimes Act No. 24 of 2007, which affords legal protection against liability arising from electronic fraud.

26. A Red Book is a BIS Committee on Payment and Settlement Systems publication documenting all payment systems in a particular country in a structured format.

27. Banking Act Direction No. 11 of 2007, Corporate Governance for Licensed Commercial Banks in Sri Lanka, issued by the CBSL on December 26, 2007.

28. IAS 32, IAS 34, and International Financial Reporting Standards are yet to be introduced, however.

4

Country Rankings on the Getting Finance Indicators

Comparisons with other countries in the region can help in assessing the financial soundness of banking sectors in South Asia. For this purpose, the countries are ranked on the Getting Finance Indicators using a simple-average ranking method. The rankings should help in identifying where performance is strong and where improvements are most needed—and where each country is in the development process.

While useful, the rankings are purely data driven and do not fully capture the strengths and weaknesses of banking systems. The underlying data provide comparability, are easily available, and cover a range of years—and are therefore an integral part of any regional comparative study. But assessing the health of financial systems on the basis of a limited number of micro indicators imposes many technical and practical limitations (caveats reflected in the interpretation of the results). Assessment of financial sector development has many aspects and needs to take into account such important factors as market conditions, monetary policy, the state of the economy, the regulatory and supervisory framework, and the structure and capacity of the financial system. But while the rankings developed in this chapter cannot provide a full picture of the financial soundness of a banking system, they can serve as one tool in a full-scale financial sector assessment.

Two types of rankings are presented: a composite ranking based on the average scores for the five years 2004–08 and annual rankings for each of those years. The rankings are based on six micro indicators for each of seven financial dimensions—access to finance, performance and efficiency, financial stability, capital market development, market concentration and competitiveness, payment systems development, and savings mobilization—and responses to the questionnaire used to assess the eighth dimension, corporate governance. In the composite ranking, the countries are ranked on each of the eight dimensions across the five-year period to arrive at a composite score for each dimension. These composite scores are then averaged to produce an overall composite score. In the annual rankings, the countries are similarly ranked on financial indicators, and the scores within each dimension are added to arrive at the aggregate score for that dimension. (See chapter 8 for a description of the ranking methodology.)

Composite Ranking

In the five-year average composite ranking, India retains the top position with an overall composite score of 0.75—or a composite percentage score of 75 percent (table 4.1). The Indian commercial banking sector scores high on all dimensions except performance and efficiency. India's composite percentage score dropped from 80 percent in the previous edition of the report.

Sri Lanka secures second place with a composite percentage score of 70 percent (up from 65 percent in the previous edition), displacing Pakistan thanks to better scores on access to finance, payment systems development, and savings mobilization. Pakistan drops to third place with a composite percentage score of 62 percent (down from 67 percent in the previous edition). Yet it still scores high on corporate governance policy, performance and efficiency, financial stability, and capital market development.

Bangladesh and Maldives tie for fourth place with composite percentage scores of 57 percent. For Bangladesh, this rank is the same as in the previous edition, while Maldives is included for the first time in this edition. Bangladesh's strengths are market concentration and savings mobilization, while Maldives scores high on access to finance and performance and efficiency.[1]

Bhutan, also included for the first time, secures sixth place with a composite percentage score of 48 percent. Bhutan's financial stability ratios indicate moderate overall stability.[2] With the inclusion of three new countries, Nepal drops to seventh place with a composite percentage score of 47 percent (up from 42 percent in the previous edition). Nepal scores well on market concentration thanks to less concentrated markets—and fairly high on savings mobilization.[3]

Afghanistan is in eighth place with a composite percentage score of 28 percent. Data understandably are unavailable for many of the indicators, a situation that Da Afghanistan Bank is working to remedy by issuing guidelines and strengthening its structure and systems.

A radar graph shows each country's relative strengths and weaknesses based on the rankings (figure 4.1). India leads the countries with scores ranging from 0.97 on capital market development to 0.48 on performance and efficiency. Afghanistan ranks lowest, with scores ranging from 0.63 on corporate governance to 0.13 on market concentration and competitiveness (a dimension in which Afghanistan lacks data for most indicators).

A second radar graph highlights the relative performance on different dimensions by the countries as a group (figure 4.2). All countries had relatively high scores on corporate governance—ranging from 0.87 in Pakistan to 0.54 in Maldives—and on performance and efficiency—ranging from 0.93 in Maldives to 0.26 in Afghanistan.[4] By contrast, most countries had relatively low scores on capital market development—ranging from 0.97 in India to 0.13 in Afghanistan—and on payment systems development—ranging from 0.94 for Sri Lanka to 0.23 in Maldives.

The two radar graphs show that development levels differ among countries as well as among dimensions. How far each country has progressed in developing its financial sector depends on many aspects. While the region's countries have some similarities, they also form a diverse group with different strengths and weaknesses. The varied results presented in the radar graphs underscore the impossibility of introducing uniform financial sector development policies or reform programs in all the countries.

Table 4.1 Composite Ranking on the Getting Finance Indicators for South Asian Countries, 2008
(five-year average composite ranking)

Dimension	Afghanistan	Bangladesh	Bhutan	India	Maldives	Nepal	Pakistan	Sri Lanka
Access to finance								
Composite score (aggregate score/240)	0.13	0.58	0.48	0.70	0.94	0.31	0.48	0.89
Dimension rank	**8**	**4**	**5**	**3**	**1**	**7**	**5**	**2**
Performance and efficiency								
Composite score (aggregate score/240)	0.26	0.45	0.51	0.48	0.93	0.50	0.73	0.64
Dimension rank	**8**	**7**	**4**	**6**	**1**	**5**	**2**	**3**
Financial stability								
Composite score (aggregate score/240)	0.41	0.48	0.70	0.82	0.56	0.22	0.70	0.58
Dimension rank	**7**	**6**	**2**	**1**	**5**	**8**	**2**	**4**
Capital market development								
Composite score (aggregate score/240)	0.13	0.61	0.36	0.97	0.38	0.58	0.74	0.70
Dimension rank	**8**	**4**	**7**	**1**	**6**	**5**	**2**	**3**
Market concentration and competitiveness								
Composite score (aggregate score/240)	0.13	0.78	0.32	0.91	0.58	0.69	0.56	0.52
Dimension rank	**8**	**2**	**7**	**1**	**5**	**3**	**4**	**6**
Payment systems development								
Composite score (aggregate score/240)	0.25	0.36	0.38	0.53	0.23	0.24	0.39	0.94
Dimension rank	**6**	**5**	**4**	**2**	**8**	**7**	**3**	**1**
Savings mobilization								
Composite score (aggregate score/240)	0.29	0.57	0.48	0.80	0.43	0.52	0.49	0.53
Dimension rank	**8**	**2**	**6**	**1**	**7**	**4**	**5**	**3**
Corporate governance								
Composite score (aggregate score/40)	0.63	0.71	0.60	0.78	0.54	0.68	0.87	0.78
Dimension rank	**6**	**4**	**7**	**2**	**8**	**5**	**1**	**2**
Total score	2.23	4.52	3.82	5.99	4.57	3.73	4.96	5.58
Overall composite score (total score/8)	0.28	0.57	0.48	0.75	0.57	0.47	0.62	0.70
Composite percentage score	28	57	48	75	57	47	62	70
Overall rank	**8**	**4**	**6**	**1**	**4**	**7**	**3**	**2**

Source: Table 8.1.

Figure 4.1 South Asian Countries Have Varying Strengths and Weaknesses in Their Commercial Banking Sectors
(five-year average composite score, 2008)

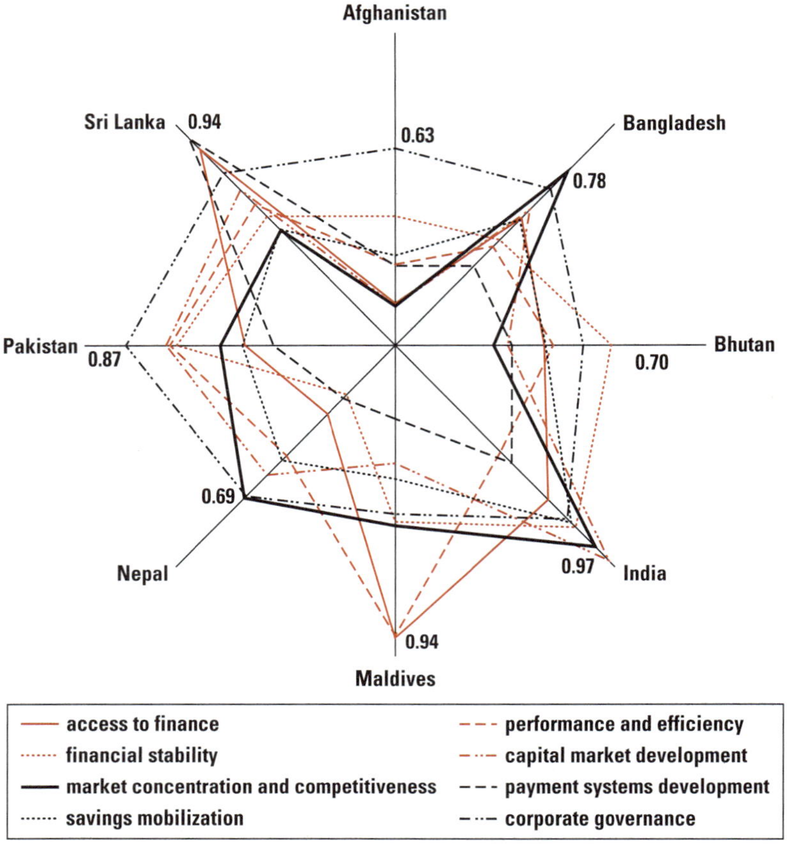

Source: Table 8.1.

Annual Rankings

Annual rankings for each of the five years from 2004 to 2008 make it possible to observe year-to-year changes in rankings. In the overall ranking, there was no change over the five years in the first two positions, with India remaining in first place and Sri Lanka in second (table 4.2). Maldives occupied third place in 2004, but Pakistan moved up to third place in 2005 and remained there through 2008. Maldives dropped to fourth place in 2005, then to fifth place in 2008, when Bangladesh moved up from fifth place to fourth. Nepal and Bhutan also switched places, with Nepal moving up to sixth place while Bhutan dropped to seventh. Afghanistan occupied eighth place throughout the period.

A comparison of the 2008 annual ranking with the 2008 composite ranking (covering 2004–08) shows no difference in the first three places—held by India, Sri Lanka, and Pakistan. Bangladesh holds fourth place in the 2008 annual ranking but shares that place with Maldives in the composite ranking. For Maldives, strong performance in the first four years (2004–07) offset weaker performance in 2008

Table 4.2 Annual and Composite Rankings on the Getting Finance Indicators for South Asian Countries, 2004–08

	Afghanistan	Bangladesh	Bhutan	India	Maldives	Nepal	Pakistan	Sri Lanka
Annual rankings								
2004 rank	8	5	6	1	3	7	4	2
2005 rank	8	5	6	1	4	7	3	2
2006 rank	8	5	6	1	4	7	3	2
2007 rank	8	5	6	1	4	7	3	2
2008 rank	8	4	7	1	5	6	3	2
Composite rankings								
2008 rank (2004–08)	8	4	6	1	4	7	3	2
2006 rank (2001–06)	a	4	a	1	a	5	2	3

Sources: Appendix 6; table 8.1; Sophastienphong and Kulathunga 2008.
a = Not included in the data set.

Figure 4.2 South Asian Countries Have Focused Most on Corporate Governance and on Performance and Efficiency
(five-year average composite score, 2008)

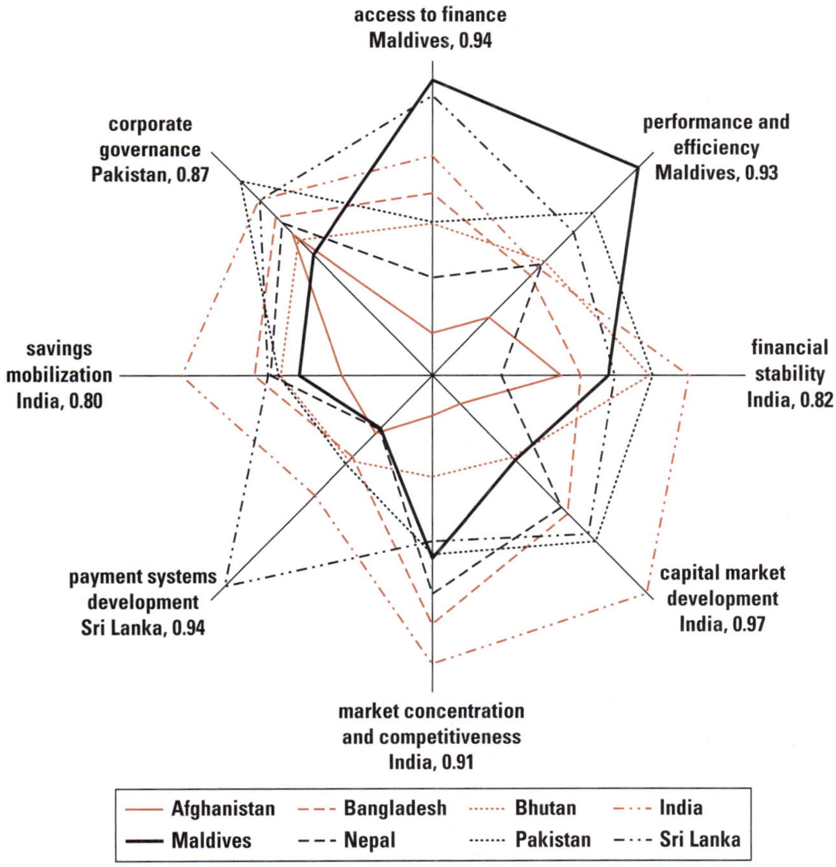

Source: Table 8.1.

to push it up to the shared fourth place. Similarly, Bhutan's performance in the first four years pushed that country up to sixth place in the composite ranking and pushed Nepal down to seventh.

Also interesting is to compare the 2008 composite ranking with the previous edition's 2006 composite ranking (covering 2001–06). In the 2006 composite ranking, India again held first place, while Pakistan was in second place (with a composite score of 0.67) and Sri Lanka in third (0.65). There was no difference in ranking for Bangladesh, while Nepal was in fifth place in the 2006 ranking, which did not include Afghanistan, Bhutan, and Maldives. Differences between the two rankings reflect not only changes in performance levels but also the different time periods covered and the inclusion in this edition of two new dimensions—payment systems development and savings mobilization.

Five-Year Average Rankings on Micro Indicators

Much more important than each country's place in the rankings are the factors underlying those rankings. Discovering what explains the rankings can help countries identify the areas needing further attention. Based on the five-year average composite ranking exercise, the following analysis provides a more complete picture of how each country performed on the micro indicators within each development dimension and therefore the key areas on which to focus.

Access to Finance

Maldives and Sri Lanka both have high scores on indicators of access to finance (figure 4.3). Yet in Maldives access to finance is an issue because of the dispersion of its population among atolls. India scores well on all access indicators, while the scores for Pakistan suggest a need to focus on the use of financial services—the provision of loans and mobilization of deposits. Bangladesh scores low on demographic penetration for both branches and automated teller machines (ATMs), while Bhutan scores low on geographic penetration. Nepal's scores suggest a need to work on all aspects of access to finance, though increasing the number of players in the market has not provided the desired effect. Afghanistan scores lowest on all indicators.

Performance and Efficiency

Maldives ranks first in performance and efficiency, with the best scores on all indicators except the operating cost ratio (figure 4.4). Pakistan and Sri Lanka also have high scores on performance indicators, though they too need to monitor operating costs. Nepal has the best operating cost ratio in the region but high staff costs. Bhutan's performance ratios are fair, while India has relatively low ratios but with less volatility expected. Bangladesh's ratios are improving, with operating costs falling over the years. Afghanistan has also shown improvement over the short period since it started to collect all data.

Financial Stability

India leads the region in financial stability (figure 4.5). Pakistan follows with good provisions, though nonperforming loans need to be managed carefully.

Figure 4.3 **Maldives and Sri Lanka Score Highest on Access to Finance**

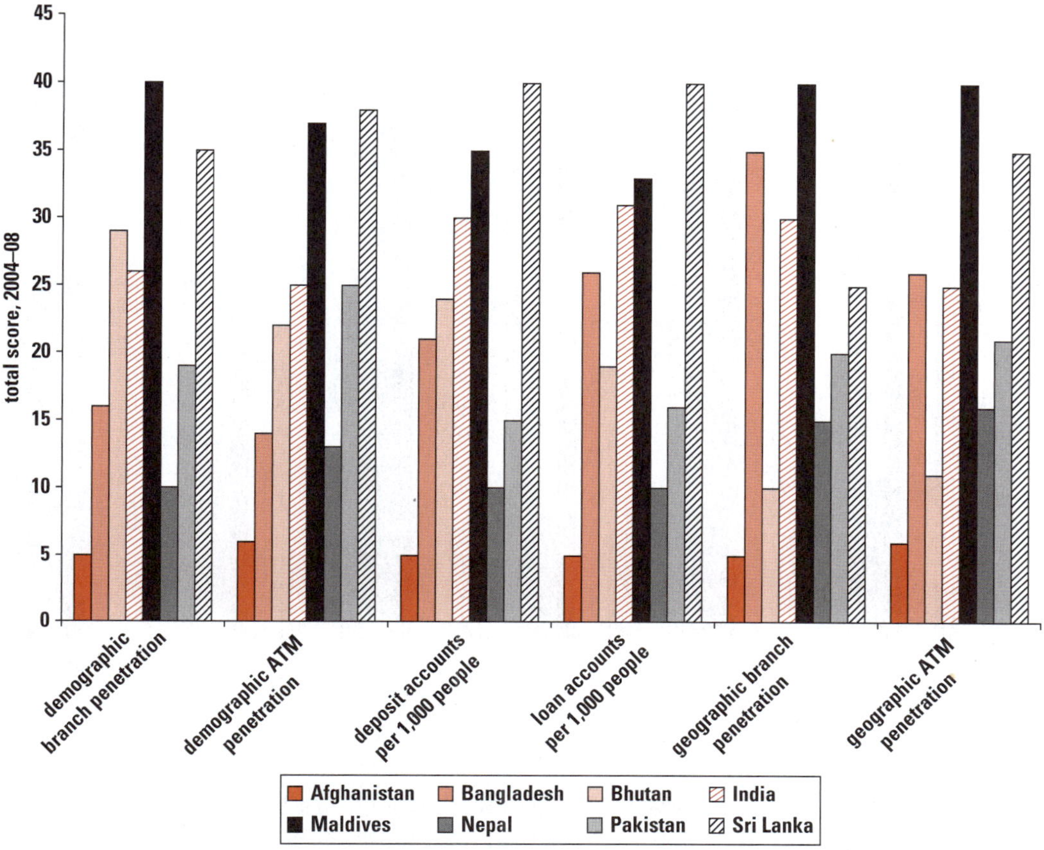

Source: Table 8.1.

Bhutan shows high ratios but has lax capital and provisioning policies. While Maldives ranks a close second on the nonperforming loans ratio, it nevertheless needs to focus on this aspect. Sri Lanka needs to manage liquidity as well as focus on nonperforming loans. Bangladesh needs to further improve capital. Afghanistan reports high provisions and low levels of nonperforming loans. Nepal urgently needs to improve capital as well as focus on provisions.

Capital Market Development

India has a developed capital market with higher market capitalization (figure 4.6). Pakistan and Sri Lanka need to focus on developing their bond markets, while all other countries need to focus on developing capital markets more broadly.

Market Concentration and Competitiveness

India has the lowest bank concentration ratios, indicating healthy competition, followed closely by Bangladesh (figure 4.7). Most South Asian countries need to

Figure 4.4 **Maldives Ranks First in Performance and Efficiency**

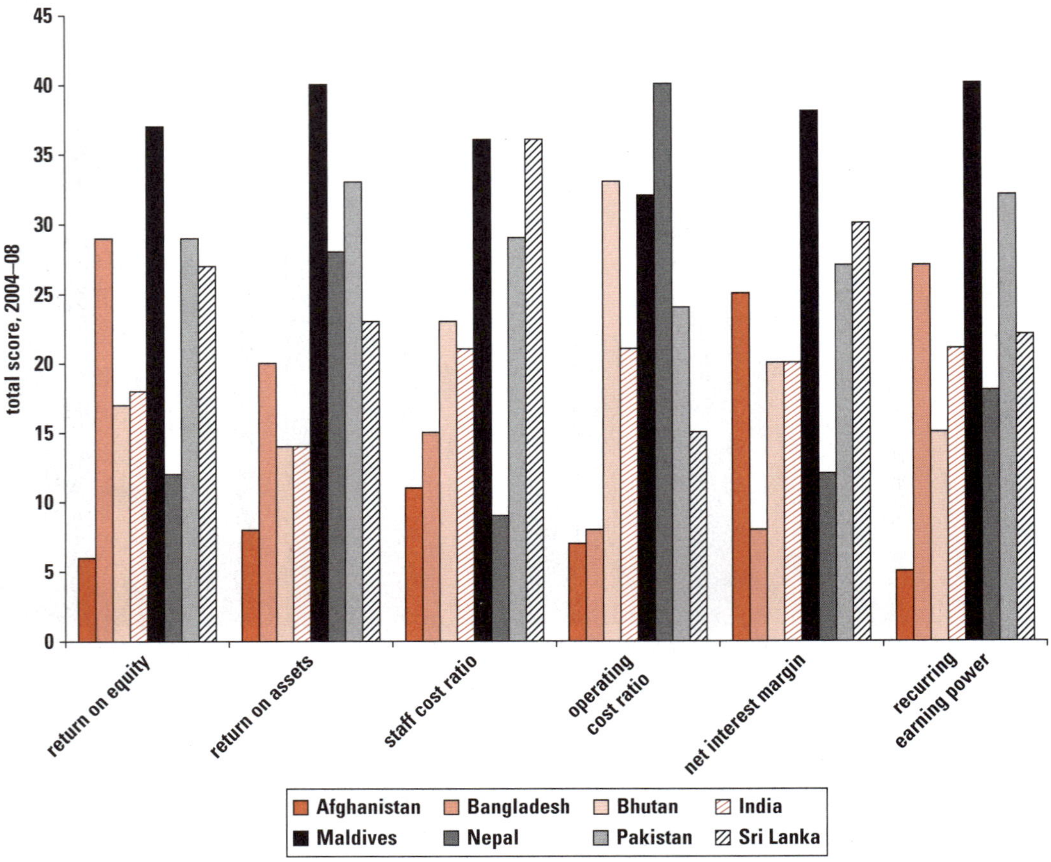

Source: Table 8.1.

focus on private credit extended by banks because of the credit risks that rising levels could pose—even as they need to expand financial services. Bhutan (with only two banks) and Sri Lanka have high concentration ratios. Afghanistan lacked the data to calculate concentration ratios.

Payment Systems Development

Payment systems development is an area on which most countries in the region need to focus. Most lack payment and settlement systems for high-value transactions. Only India, Pakistan, and Sri Lanka have real-time gross settlement (RTGS) systems (figure 4.8). But some retail payment systems in the region are automated net settlement systems.

Savings Mobilization

India leads in savings mobilization with relatively high financial deepening ratios, positive real interest rates, and high domestic savings rates (figure 4.9). Bangladesh

Figure 4.5 **India Leads in Financial Stability**

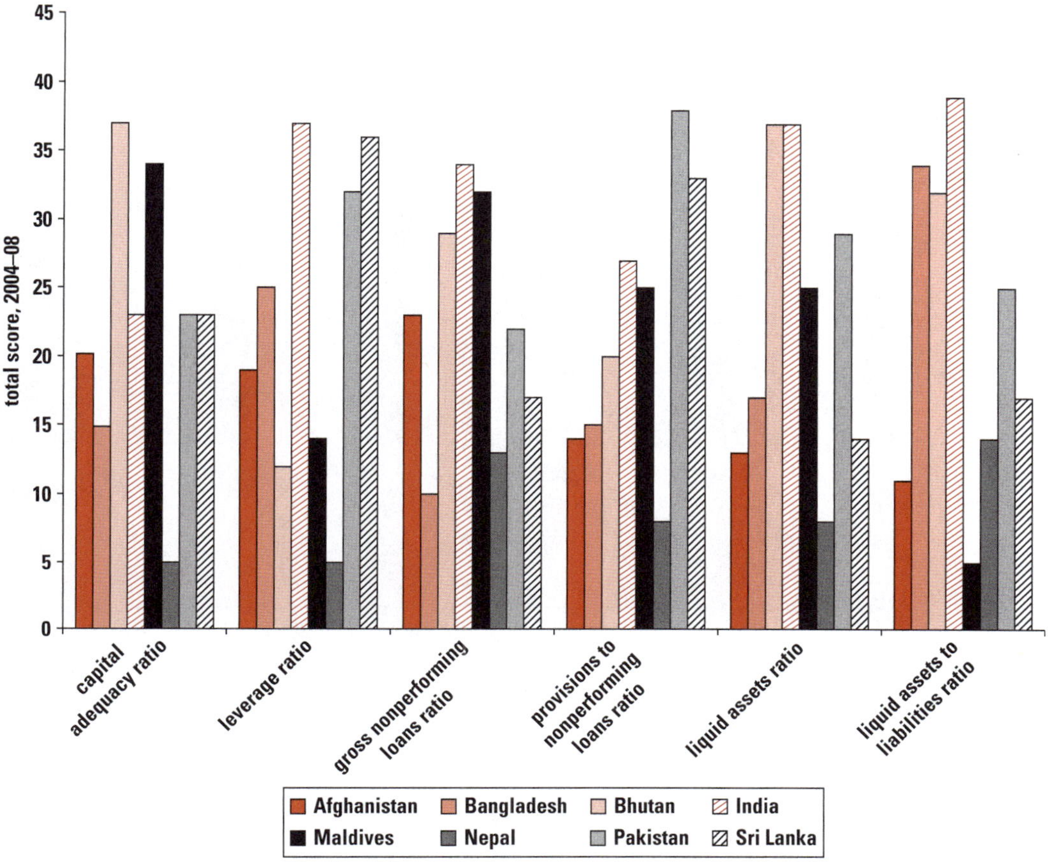

Source: Table 8.1.

follows with high worker remittances and good savings rates but needs to address the negative real deposit interest rate. Other countries have also had persistently negative interest rates. But most countries enjoy steady worker remittances, a boon during these troubled economic times.

Corporate Governance

The assessment of corporate governance mainly shows how well defined the relevant guidelines are in a country. Pakistan has the most comprehensive guidelines (figure 4.10). While all countries in the region have issued guidelines, more work is needed on many issues, such as those relating to government ownership, shareholder rights, indirect or beneficial share ownership, auditors and audit committees, accounting standards, and disclosure requirements. And although rankings may not reflect these aspects, even more important is that banks achieve more comprehensive compliance with the guidelines that have been issued and that authorities strengthen their monitoring and enforcement.

Figure 4.6 India Has the Region's Most Developed Capital Market

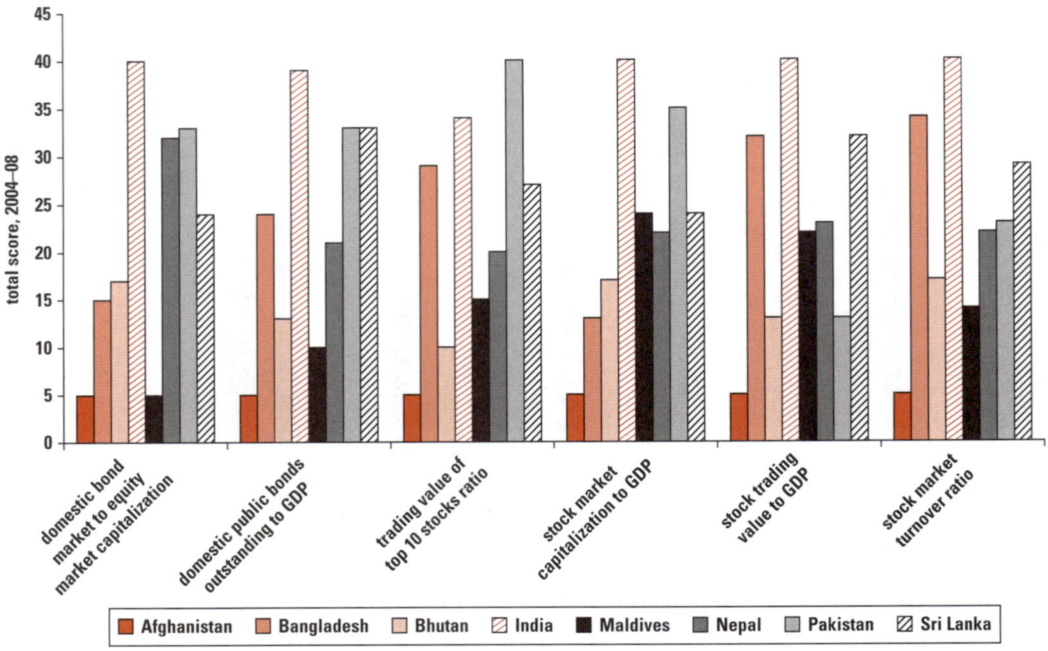

Source: Table 8.1.

Figure 4.7 India and Bangladesh Have Lower Market Concentration

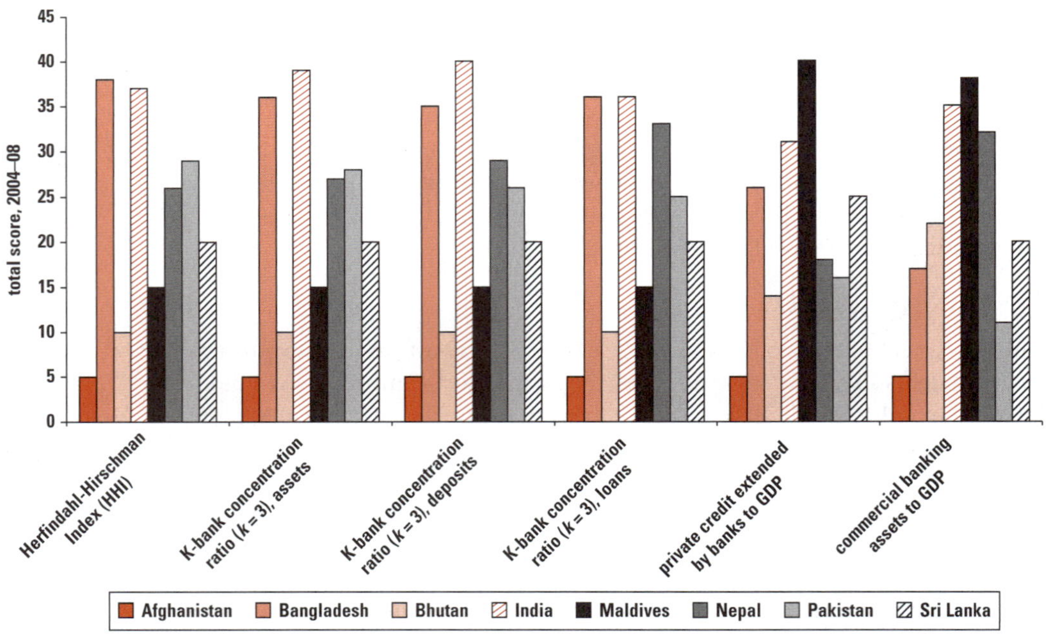

Source: Table 8.1.

Figure 4.8 Sri Lanka Shows Laudable Progress in Payment Systems Development

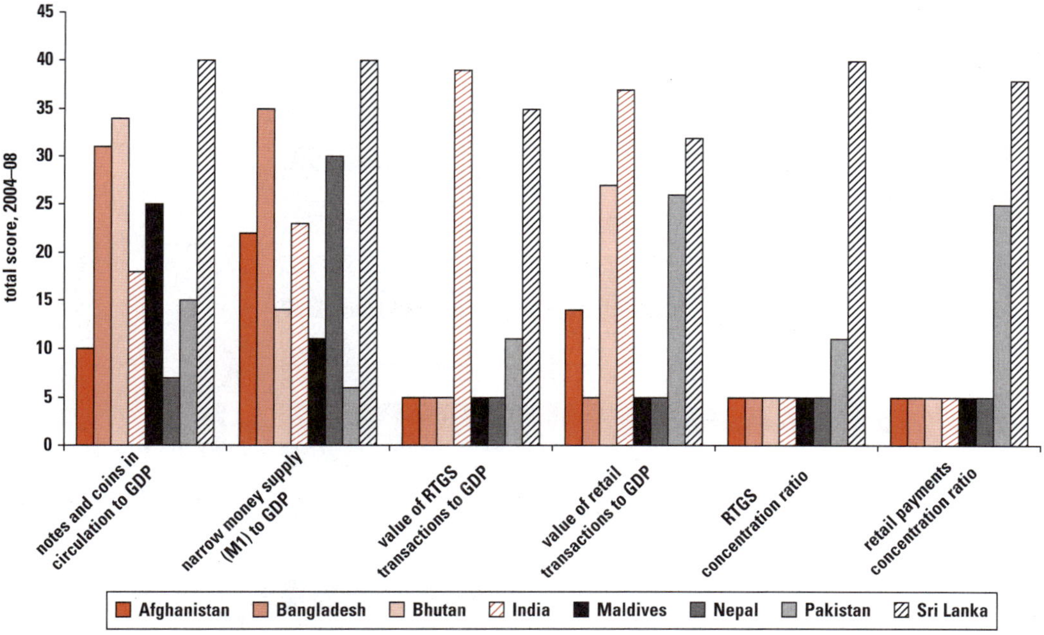

Source: Table 8.1.

Figure 4.9 India Performs Best in Savings Mobilization

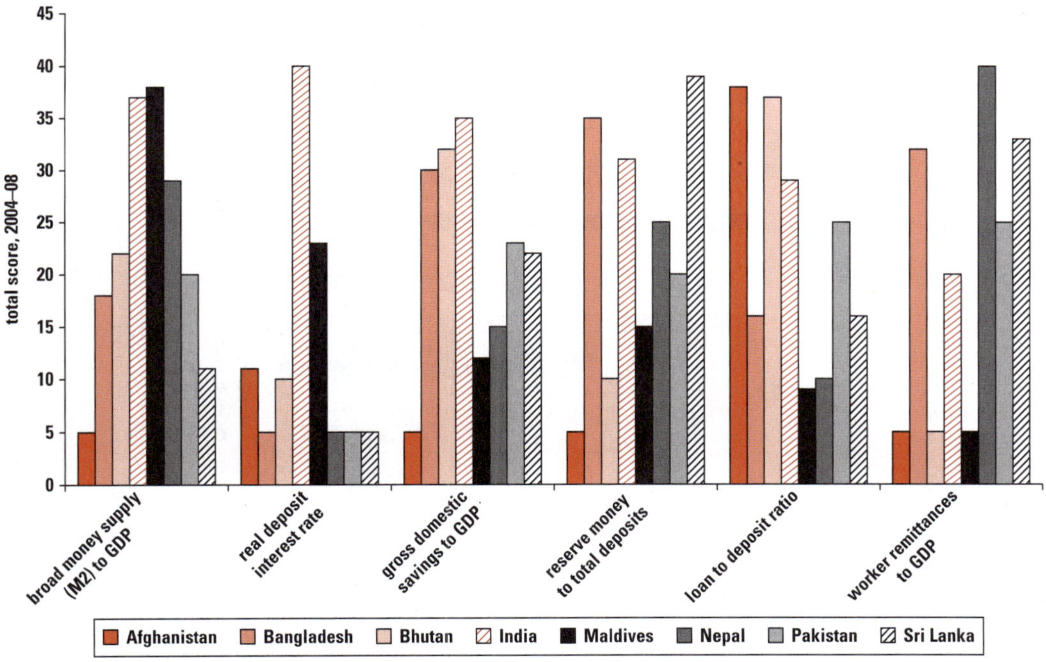

Source: Table 8.1.

Figure 4.10 Pakistan Leads in Corporate Governance

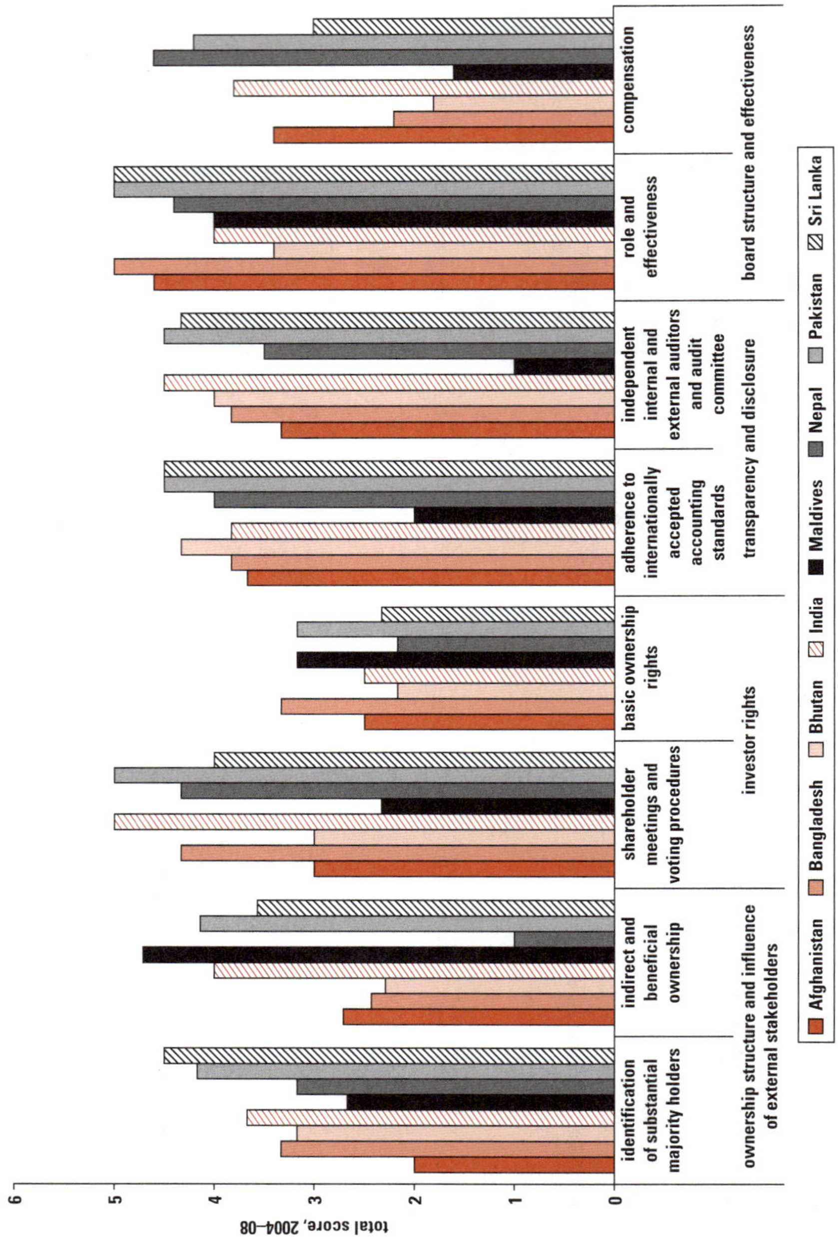

Source: Table 8.1.

Endnotes

1. As discussed in chapter 3, while Maldives scores high on access to finance, the indicators do not take into account the geographic dispersion of its population, and actual access to finance is far worse than the indicators suggest. This underscores the importance, emphasized in the introduction to this chapter, of using multiple tools to assess financial sector development.

2. While Bhutan scores high on financial stability, the ratios do not reflect its simplified capital adequacy standards and lax provisioning rules.

3. Not reflected in Nepal's market concentration ratios is that it has too many new entrants to the banking sector, which has contributed to a real estate price bubble. To curb entry, Nepal Rastra Bank has temporarily suspended the licensing of new banks.

4. Attention is drawn once again to the fact that assessment of corporate governance in this exercise is confined to reviewing whether the necessary guidelines are in place or whether the law provides for such guidelines. No attempt is made to assess compliance and enforcement, both very important aspects.

5

An International Perspective

To develop a modern, well-functioning financial system that will speed economic growth, countries need to understand international best practices, assess their own performance, and continually adapt the development effort to meet emerging challenges. Benchmarking is a useful tool in this process, making it possible to identify gaps and shortfalls in performance through comparison with other countries.

To provide benchmarks for South Asian countries, the previous edition of this report used selected high-income Organisation for Economic Co-operation and Development (OECD) member and nonmember economies: Australia; Canada; Hong Kong, China; New Zealand; Singapore; the United Kingdom; and the United States. Depending on the availability of data, that edition focused on standard-setting OECD countries and members of the SEANZA (South East Asia, New Zealand, and Australia) group. This edition expands the benchmark group. It adds France, Germany, and Italy to provide comparisons with members of the European Union. And it adds China, Japan, the Republic of Korea, Malaysia, and Thailand to strengthen the representation of high-growth Asian comparator economies.

This chapter compares the performance of South Asian countries with the benchmark ranges—from low to high—for indicators in each of the seven financial dimensions (corporate governance is not benchmarked). Because of data availability issues for the benchmark economies for 2008, the comparison uses 2007 data. (See appendix 3A for the underlying benchmark data and appendix 3B for data sources; see appendix tables A2.1–A2.8 for data for the South Asian countries and the benchmark ranges for each year in 2001–08.) The chapter also compares the performance of South Asian countries with that of individual benchmark economies, again using 2007 data.

Benchmark Comparison

Relative to the benchmark economies, South Asia performs better in some financial dimensions than in others. The region compares well on performance and efficiency, capital adequacy (under financial stability), market concentration and competitiveness, and savings mobilization. In other areas, the benchmark comparison suggests a need for further improvements—such as access to finance, nonperforming loans and provisioning (under financial stability), capital market development, and payment systems development. And while some South Asian countries come out well in the benchmark comparison, others are still at an earlier stage of development. While more work needs to be done, it must be emphasized that South Asia has made laudable progress in key areas such as financial stability and performance and efficiency.

Access to Finance

A comparison of geographic branch penetration shows that some South Asian countries had high penetration ratios in 2007—especially Maldives, with 96.70 branches per 1,000 square kilometers, and Bangladesh, with 45.52 (figure 5.1). (As explained in chapter 3 and elsewhere, however, access indicators for Maldives are skewed by the geographic dispersion of its population.) The benchmark range was from a low of 1 branch per 1,000 square kilometers to a high of 110. All South Asian countries except Afghanistan had higher geographic branch penetration than the benchmark low. In benchmark economies, the use of technology for banking activities, allowing "branchless banking," is one reason for the relatively low penetration levels.

For automated teller machines (ATMs), the benchmark range for geographic penetration was from 3 ATMs per 1,000 square kilometers to 146. Among South Asian countries, Maldives had the highest penetration ratio, with 130 ATMs per 1,000 square kilometers, followed by Sri Lanka, with 13. Thus, to compare well with the international group, South Asia needs to further improve geographic ATM penetration.

Figure 5.1 **Geographic Penetration Significant for Branches, Weak for ATMs in South Asia in 2007**

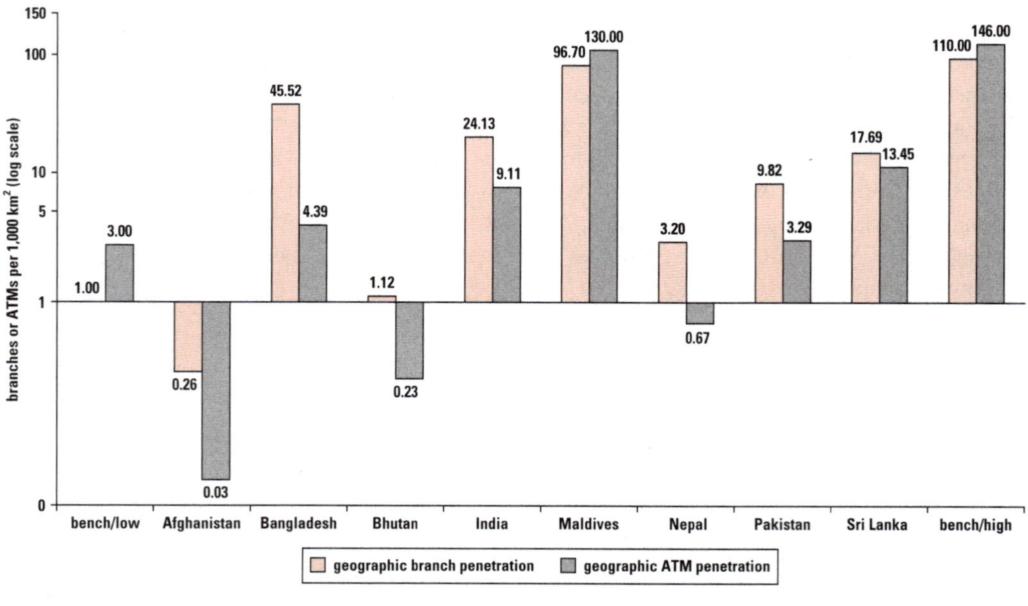

Source: Appendix tables A2.7 and A3.7.

Performance and Efficiency

South Asia compared well with the benchmark economies on performance and efficiency ratios. The benchmark range for return on assets in 2007 was from a low of 0.2 percent to a high of 1.9 percent, and all South Asian countries except Afghanistan (because of negative returns) recorded ratios that were either very close to or above the benchmark high (figure 5.2). And Maldives reported a return on assets significantly higher than the benchmark high, 6.33 percent.

Net interest margins in some South Asian countries were significantly higher than those in the benchmark economies. The benchmark range was from 0.4 percent to 3.61 percent. All South Asian ratios were higher than the benchmark low. Significantly higher ratios were reported by Afghanistan (7.45 percent), Maldives (5.41 percent), and Sri Lanka (4.54 percent).

South Asia outperformed the benchmark economies in cost management. The benchmark range for the operating cost ratio was from a low of 55.82 percent to a high of 313.18 percent. Three South Asian countries had operating cost ratios below the benchmark low: Nepal (22.62 percent), Maldives (26.83 percent), and Bhutan (49.97 percent). And the highest ratio in South Asia was just a third of the benchmark high—Afghanistan's, at 101.79 percent.

Financial Stability

South Asia showed mixed performance in financial stability. The region compared favorably on capital adequacy ratios (figure 5.3). The benchmark range

Figure 5.2 **South Asia's Performance Ratios a Good Match for the Benchmark Group's in 2007**

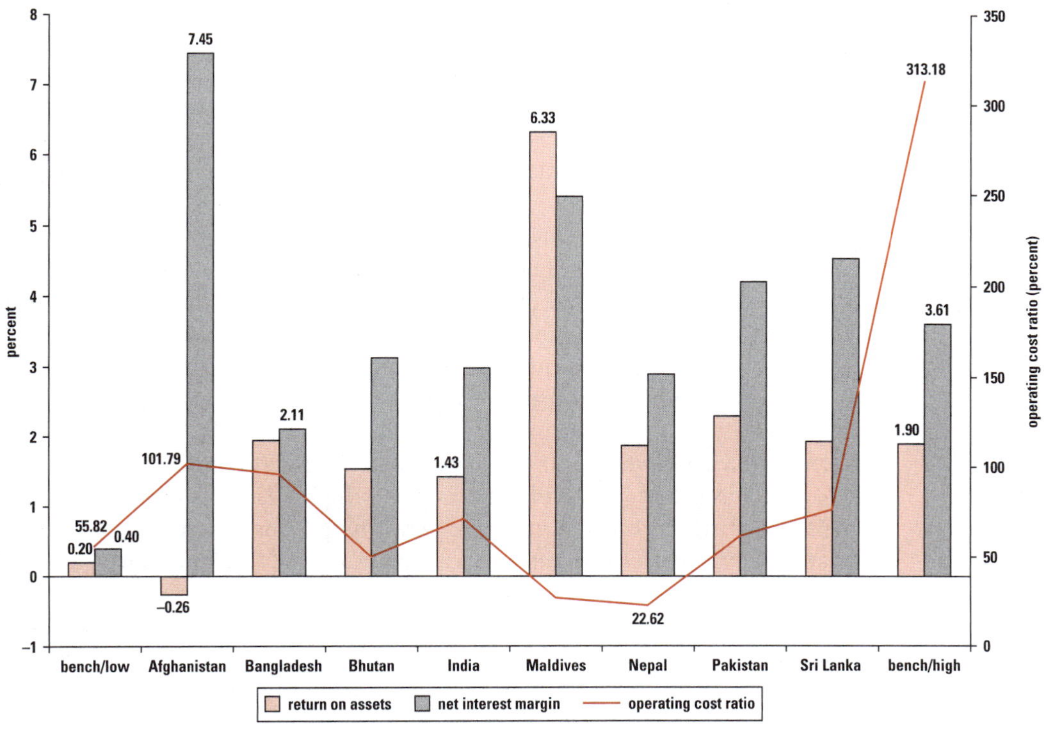

Source: Appendix tables A2.7 and A3.7.

Figure 5.3 **South Asia's Capital Adequacy Favorable in 2007, but Room to Improve Credit Quality**

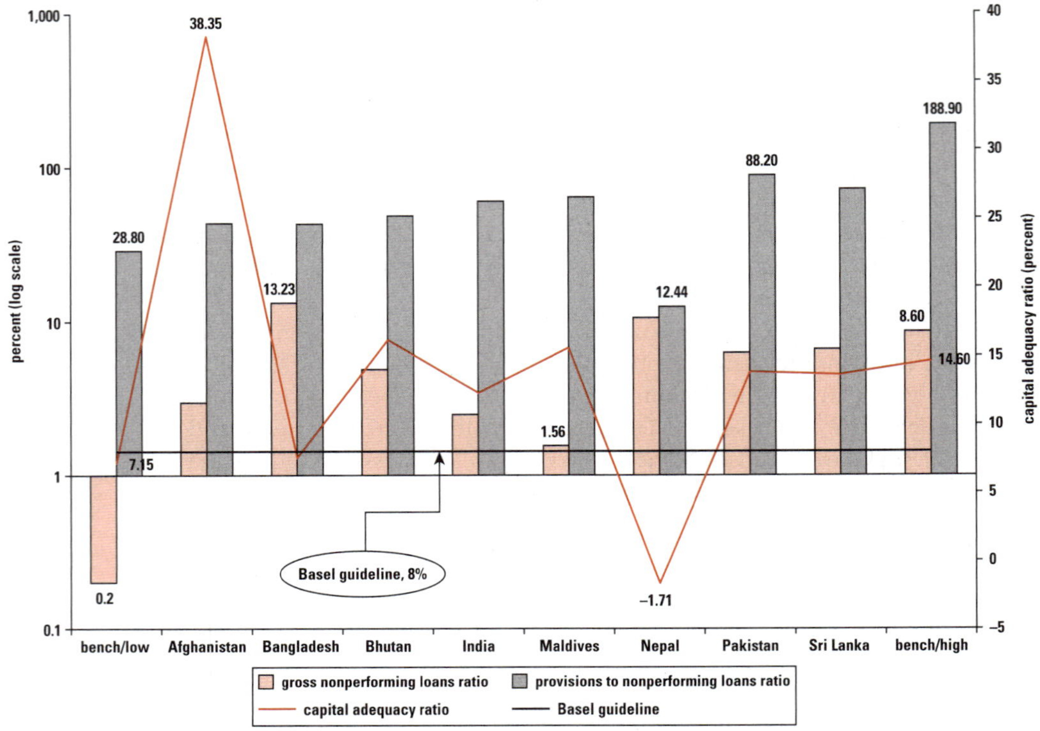

Source: Appendix tables A2.7 and A3.7.

was from 7.15 percent (below the Basel II capital adequacy limit of 8 percent) to 14.60 percent. All South Asian countries reported capital adequacy ratios above the Basel II limit except Nepal (−1.71 percent) and Bangladesh (7.52 percent). Afghanistan had a capital adequacy ratio of 38.35 percent, significantly higher than the benchmark high.

Comparing South Asian countries on the financial stability dimension is difficult because not all of them have adopted Basel II. Over time, South Asian countries will need to ensure that all banks are complying with additional capital requirements for liquidity, market, and operational risks under new guidelines proposed by the Basel Committee on Banking Supervision (2009).

But the benchmark comparison suggests that South Asian countries need to pay more attention to reducing nonperforming loans to bring the gross nonperforming loans ratio much closer to the benchmark low. The benchmark low for the ratio was 0.2 percent, and the benchmark high was 8.6 percent. Two South Asian countries recorded a gross nonperforming loans ratio above the benchmark high: Nepal (10.56 percent) and Bangladesh (13.23 percent). Maldives recorded the lowest ratio, at around 1.56 percent.

Results also suggest a need for South Asian countries to further increase provisions for nonperforming loans. In the benchmark economies provisions for nonperforming loans ranged from 28.8 percent to 188.9 percent. Among South Asian countries, Pakistan had the highest provisions ratio, at 88.20 percent. But even this did not compare well with the benchmark high, and all other ratios in the region were closer to the benchmark low. Nepal's ratio was below the benchmark low at 12.44 percent.

That being said, it should be noted that having higher provisions alone does not denote good banking practice. High provisioning could also mean that the loans are not recoverable.

Capital Market Development

The benchmark comparison shows that capital markets are relatively undeveloped in South Asia and should be made a focus of development efforts. Only India recorded capital market development ratios somewhat comparable to those of the benchmark economies. For the stock market capitalization to GDP ratio, the benchmark range was from 36.70 percent to 1,284.15 percent, while India's ratio was 83.77 percent (figure 5.4). For the stock trading value to GDP ratio, the benchmark range was from 18.68 percent to 1,033.79 percent, while India recorded a ratio of 70.33 percent, significantly higher than the benchmark low. And for the stock market turnover ratio the benchmark range was from 0.52 to 2.70, while India's ratio was 0.67.

Market Concentration and Competitiveness

Several South Asian countries had concentration ratios that were fairly competitive with those of the benchmark economies, indicating overall lower concentration in

Figure 5.4 South Asia Lagged in Capital Market Development in 2007

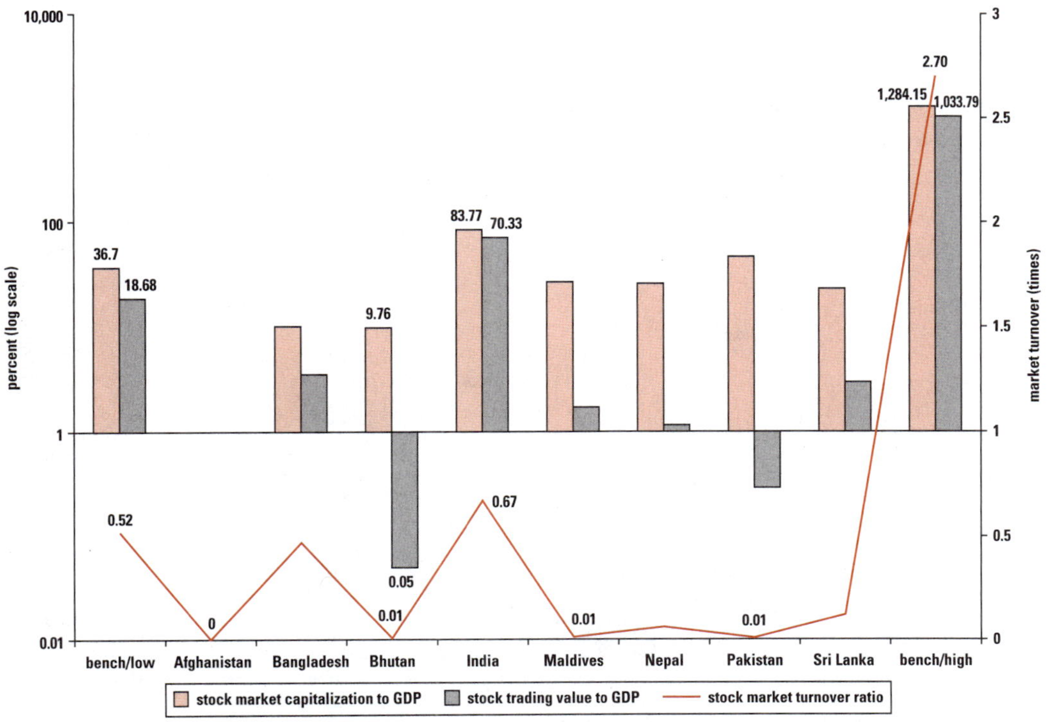

Source: Appendix tables A2.7 and A3.7.
Note: Afghanistan has no stock market, hence no data are available.

their banking markets (figure 5.5). With small banking sectors, however, Bhutan and Maldives have highly concentrated markets. Sri Lanka also has high concentration. No data were available for Afghanistan.

For the Herfindahl-Hirschman Index the range for benchmark economies was from 280.88 (classified as unconcentrated) to 2,080.86 (highly concentrated). Other than Bhutan, Maldives, and Sri Lanka, South Asian countries have markets that are unconcentrated on the basis of this measure. Bhutan has only two banks and therefore very high concentration. Sri Lanka's market is moderately concentrated, with a Herfindahl-Hirschman Index value of 1,217.18 in 2007. Results for the three-bank concentration ratios were similar.

For private credit extended by banks, most South Asian countries had lower ratios than the benchmark economies. The benchmark range was from 62.44 percent to 189.58 percent. Only Maldives had a ratio above the benchmark low, at 91.28 percent.

Payment Systems Development

The benchmark comparison on payment systems development shows mixed results in South Asia, and the overall assessment is that this is an area needing attention in most of the region's countries. India, Pakistan, and Sri Lanka reported figures comparable to those of the benchmark economies. But other South Asian countries fared poorly in the benchmark comparison because of a low level of payment systems development or lack of data.

Figure 5.5 Varied Results on Market Concentration in South Asia in 2007

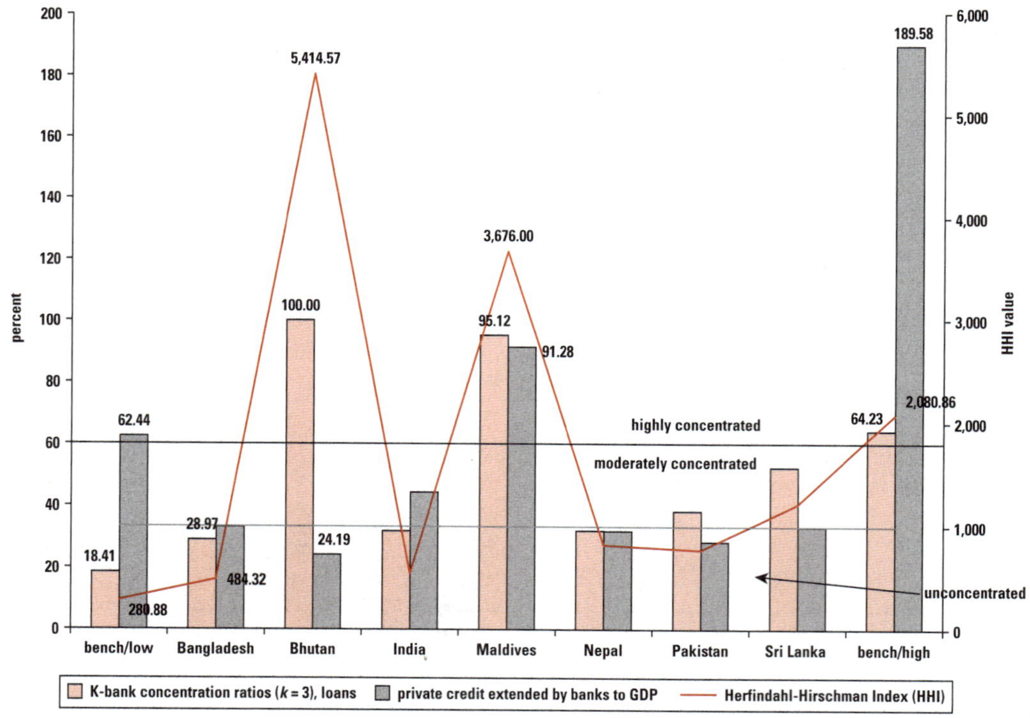

Source: Appendix tables A2.7 and A3.7.
Note: No data available for Afghanistan.

For the value of real-time gross settlement transactions to GDP ratio, the benchmark range was from 2,147 percent to 17,557 percent (figure 5.6). The highest ratio recorded for South Asia was India's 596.72 percent. For the value of retail transactions to GDP ratio, the benchmark range was from 0.57 percent to 5,067.78 percent. All reported ratios for South Asia compared well with the benchmark low, while the highest ratio for South Asia, Pakistan's 1,423 percent, was closer to the benchmark high. For the ratio of notes and coins in circulation to GDP, the benchmark range was from 1.94 percent to 31.03 percent. Most South Asian countries recorded significantly higher ratios than the benchmark low. The exception was Sri Lanka, which recorded a ratio of 4.89 percent. The relatively high ratios for South Asia reflect the higher use of currency in the region.

Savings Mobilization

South Asia compared well with the benchmark economies on savings mobilization in 2007 (figure 5.7). For the ratio of worker remittances to GDP, the benchmark range was from 0.02 percent to 1.02 percent. All reported ratios for South Asia were significantly higher than this range, indicating the importance of worker remittances in the region. Nepal had the region's highest ratio, at 13.77 percent, followed by Bangladesh with 10 percent.

Figure 5.6 Payment Systems Development in 2007: More Work to Be Done in Most of South Asia

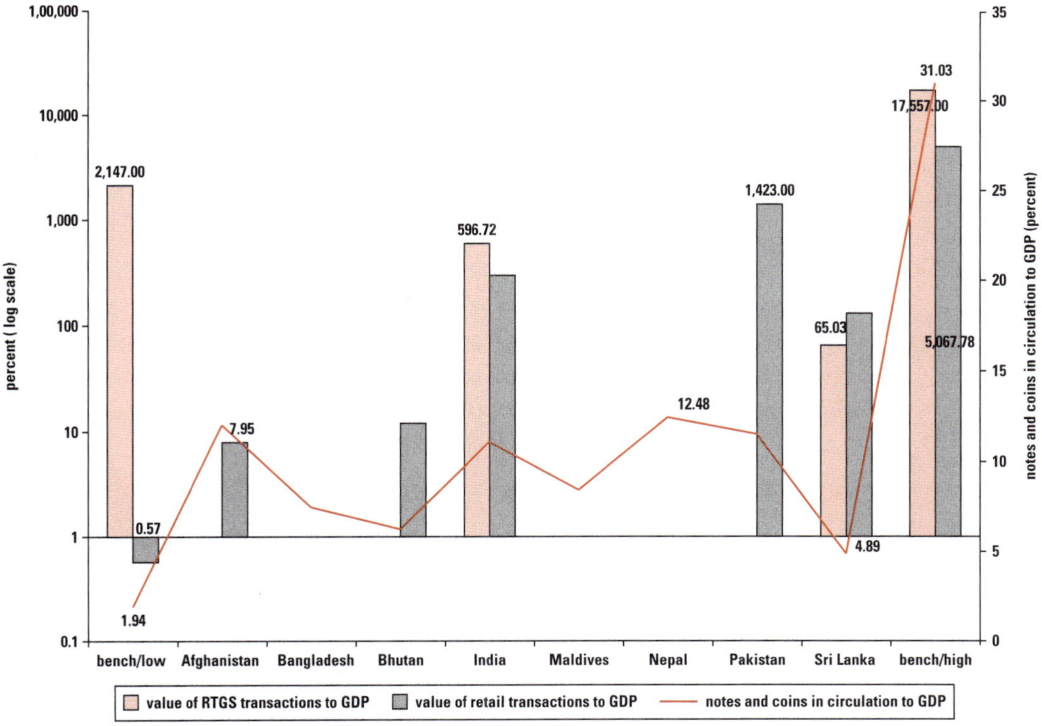

Source: Appendix tables A2.7 and A3.7.

Note: RTGS = real-time gross settlement. Afghanistan, Bangladesh, Bhutan, Maldives, and Nepal have no RTGS systems, hence no data are available. Pakistan has an RTGS system, but no data are available. Bangladesh, Maldives, and Nepal have no data available on the value of retail transactions to GDP.

Figure 5.7 Savings Mobilization Favorable in South Asia in 2007, with Room to Improve

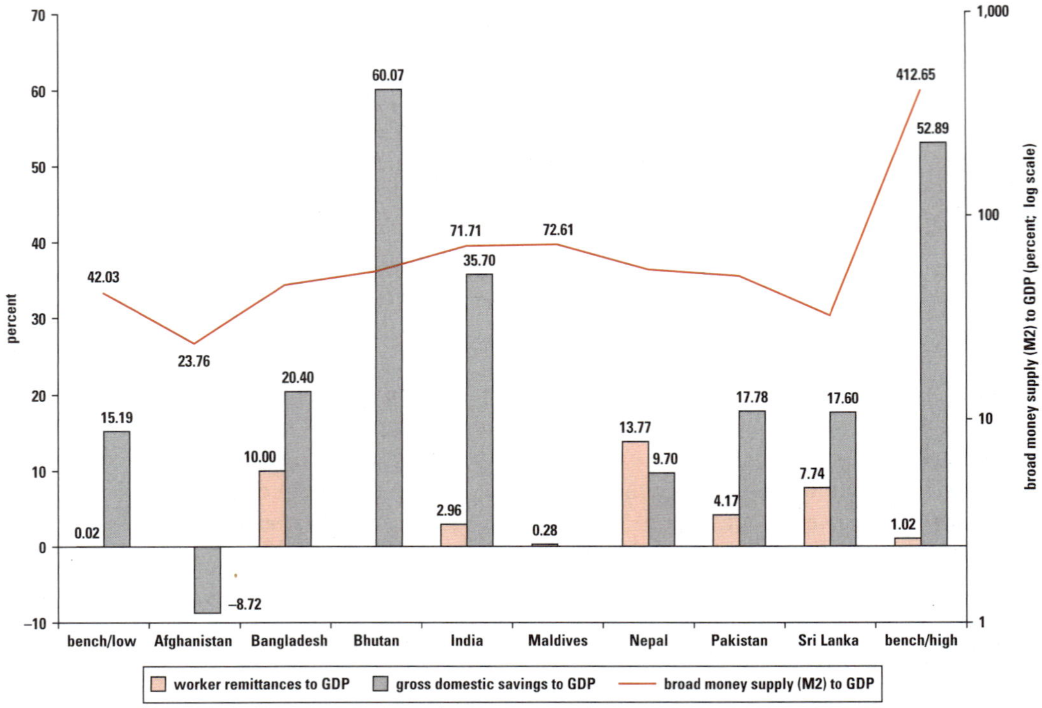

Source: Appendix tables A2.7 and A3.7.
Note: Afghanistan and Bhutan: no data on worker remittances to GDP are available. Maldives: no data on gross domestic savings to GDP are available.

Results for the gross domestic savings to GDP ratio were similar. The benchmark range was from 15.19 percent to 52.89 percent. While Afghanistan had a negative savings rate (−8.72 percent), all other rates reported for South Asian countries were highly favorable. Bhutan recorded the highest at 60.07 percent.

Results for the broad money supply to GDP ratio, which indicates the extent of financial deepening in a country, show a need to improve financial deepening and intermediation in South Asian countries. The benchmark range was from 42.03 percent to 412.65 percent. Maldives recorded the highest ratio in South Asia, at around 72.61 percent, followed by India with 71.71 percent.

Benchmark Comparison with Individual Economies

While the previous section compares the performance of South Asian countries on financial indicators against benchmark ranges, this section compares their performance on selected indicators against that of individual economies in the two benchmark groups: OECD countries (Australia, Canada, France, Germany, Italy, Japan, the Republic of Korea, New Zealand, the United Kingdom, and the United States) and a peer group in Asia (China; Hong Kong, China; Malaysia; Singapore; and Thailand). The comparison is done graphically.

Some of the comparative data are given in table 5.1. For the graphic presentation (in figures 5.8–5.14), the underlying data are available in appendix tables

Table 5.1 Financial Ratios for South Asian Countries and OECD and Asian Economies (Selected), 2007
(percent, except where otherwise specified)

		Access to finance		Performance and efficiency		Financial stability		Capital market development		Market concentration and competitiveness		Payment systems development		Savings mobilization	
	Economy	Branches per 1,000 km^2	ATMs per 1,000 km^2	Return on equity	Return on assets	Capital adequacy ratio	Gross nonperforming loans ratio	Domestic public bonds to GDP	Stock market capitalization to GDP	K-bank concentration ratio (k=3), assets	Private credit extended by banks to GDP	Notes and coins in circulation to GDP	Value of RTGS transactions to GDP	Gross domestic savings to GDP	Worker remittances to GDP
South Asian countries	Afghanistan	0.26	0.03	−1.07	−0.26	38.35	3.00	—	—	—	—	12.07	—	−8.72	—
	Bangladesh	45.52	4.39	50.94	1.95	7.52	13.23	18.78	10.07	31.58	33.11	7.50	—	20.40	10.00
	Bhutan	1.12	0.23	18.31	1.54	16.17	4.91	3.53	9.76	100.00	24.19	6.27	—	60.07	—
	India	24.13	9.11	17.31	1.43	12.28	2.50	34.71	83.77	31.12	44.30	11.13	596.72	35.70	2.96
	Maldives	96.70	130.00	49.99	6.33	15.58	1.56	4.02	26.65	92.55	91.28	8.46	—	—	0.28
	Nepal	3.20	0.67	−78.70	1.87	−1.71	10.56	13.66	25.62	35.83	31.94	12.50	—	9.70	13.77
	Pakistan	9.82	3.29	21.90	2.30	13.80	6.30	32.94	46.20	38.62	28.43	11.55	—	17.78	4.17
	Sri Lanka	17.69	13.45	25.37	1.93	13.59	6.62	29.99	23.00	51.79	33.26	4.85	65.03	17.60	7.74
Asian peer group	China	5.52	5.96	19.90	1.00	7.70	6.60	34.65	136.55	35.01	115.83	31.03	—	52.89	1.02
	Hong Kong, China	1,234.00	2,420.00	20.05	1.90	13.40	0.90	8.95	1,284.15	56.87	139.58	10.91	15,069.65	32.18	0.17
	Malaysia	—	—	16.14	1.40	13.20	6.60	38.57	180.00	32.37	105.13	8.36	5,923.89	42.20	0.97
	Singapore	487.00	1,658.00	13.40	1.40	14.00	1.80	42.21	334.17	64.11	95.72	7.14	6,546.88	51.41	—
	Thailand	6.84	—	7.30	0.30	14.60	8.60	38.52	80.19	31.99	84.10	10.34	2,147.19	34.49	0.67
OECD countries	Australia	0.68	3.32	28.10	1.60	10.30	0.20	14.46	158.00	35.60	122.81	16.58	17,557.12	26.23	0.47
	Canada	—	—	12.50	0.60	12.10	0.40	55.24	164.85	57.13	127.26	3.30	3,186.06	—	—
	France	—	—	9.88	0.31	—	2.80	54.84	164.80	57.17	—	7.18	8,658.22	20.20	0.53
	Germany	—	—	14.04	0.44	—	—	42.25	63.85	64.30	—	7.18	9,621.95	25.32	0.26
	Italy	110.40	145.65	11.40	0.76	10.90	—	84.10	50.89	66.89	—	7.18	2,749.44	21.18	0.15
	Japan	—	—	3.20	0.20	12.90	1.50	163.25	106.56	25.21	96.92	16.66	6,815.76	—	0.04
	Korea, Rep.	—	—	14.98	1.00	12.70	0.80	48.05	115.76	29.01	107.81	3.67	—	30.20	0.12
	New Zealand	4.28	8.93	16.24	1.06	7.15	—	—	36.70	55.25	149.49	1.94	5,658.53	—	0.48
	United Kingdom	—	—	8.25	0.51	—	—	33.10	141.20	39.51	189.58	3.51	9,159.75	15.19	0.30
	United States	6.96	—	10.50	1.10	12.80	1.10	47.72	144.25	40.47	62.44	5.74	8,382.42	—	0.02

Source: Appendix tables A2.7 and A3.7.
— = not available.

Figure 5.8 South Asia Showed Improving Access in 2007

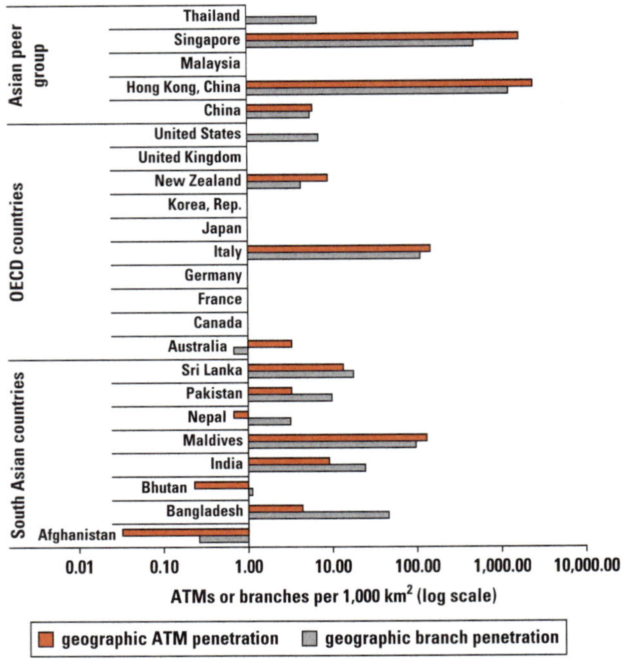

Source: Appendix tables A2.7 and A3.7.

Figure 5.9 South Asia Outperformed Comparator Group in Return on Equity in 2007

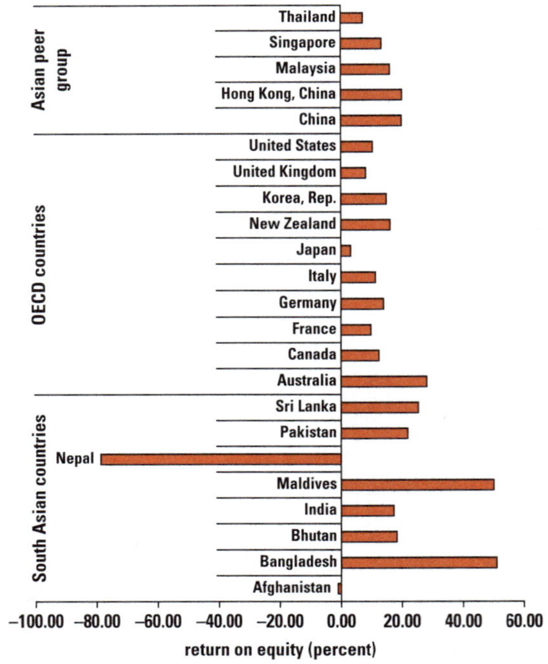

Source: Appendix tables A2.7 and A3.7.

Figure 5.10 South Asian Capital Adequacy Ratios Compared Well in 2007

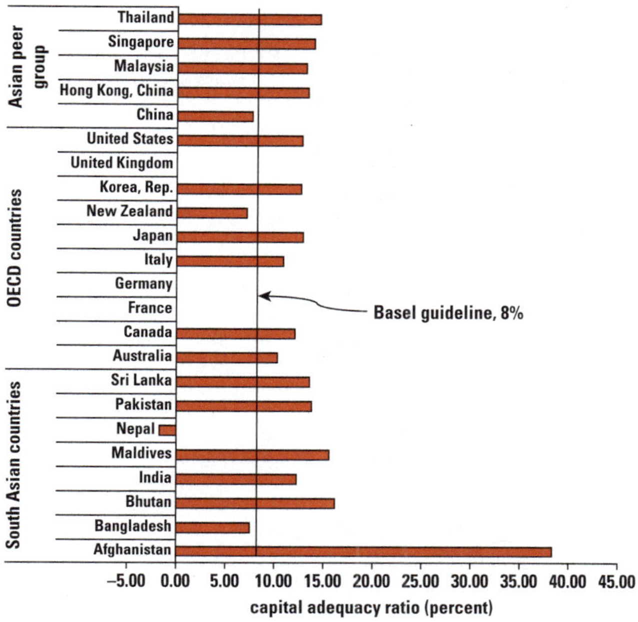

Source: Appendix tables A2.7 and A3.7.

Figure 5.11 Outstanding Public Bonds Slightly Lower in South Asia Than in Comparator Group in 2007

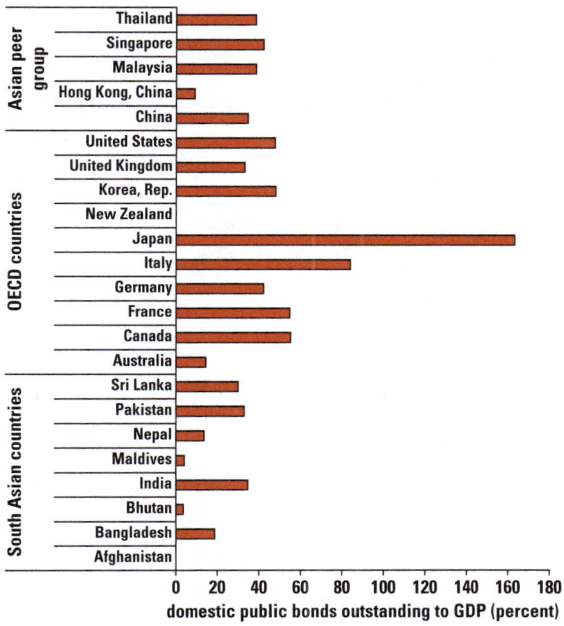

Source: Appendix tables A2.7 and A3.7.

Figure 5.12 South Asia Matched Comparator Group in Concentration of Banking Assets in 2007

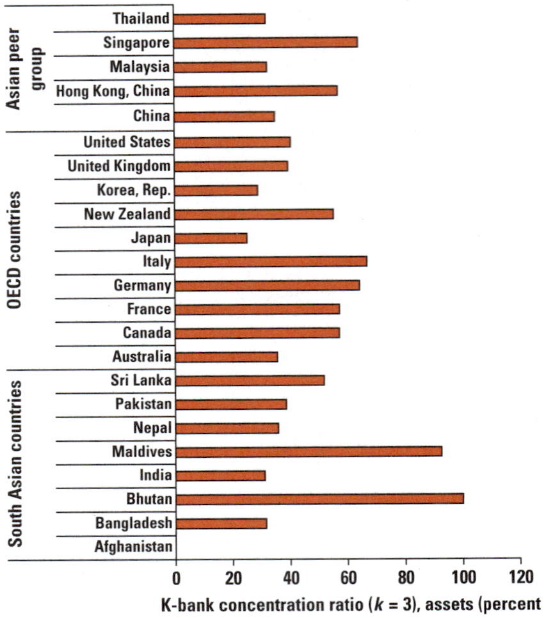

Source: Appendix tables A2.7 and A3.7.

Figure 5.13 South Asia's Narrow Money Supply to GDP Ratio High and Comparable to That in Most Benchmark Economies in 2007

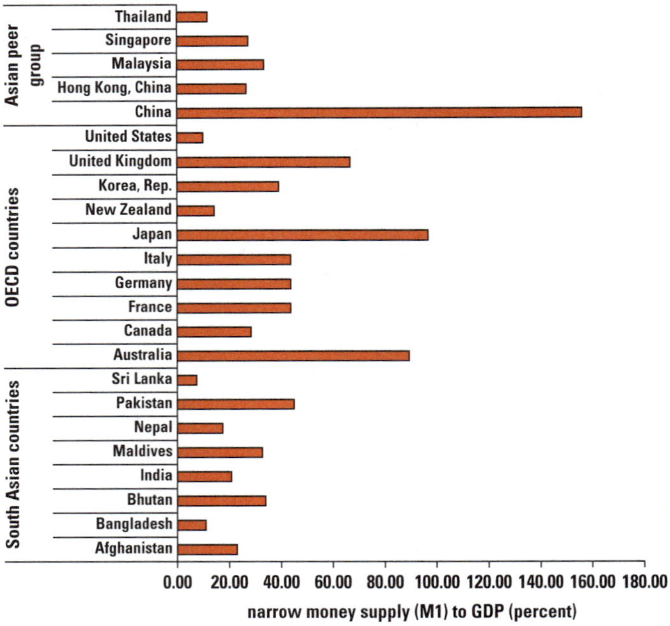

Source: Appendix tables A2.7 and A3.7.

Figure 5.14 **South Asia Strong on Worker Remittances in 2007**

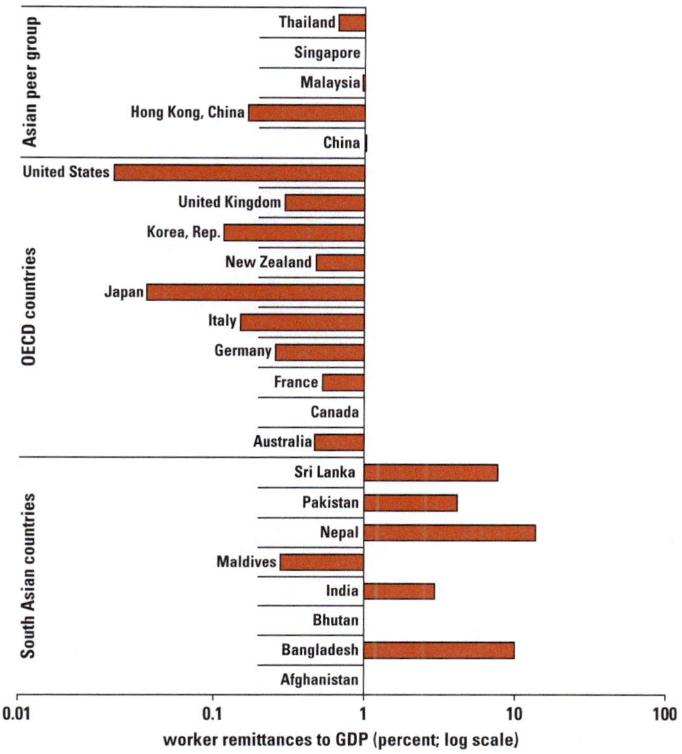

Source: Appendix tables A2.7 and A3.7.

A2.7 and A3.7). Because the data in the table and figures are analyzed in aggregate form in the previous section, there is no further discussion of the comparative performance in this section.

The comparison uses data for 2007 because more recent data were not available for the benchmark economies. Interestingly, beyond 2007 the financial performance ratios of the most advanced economies would have deteriorated. Thus, the applicability of benchmarks and best practices may be reviewed in future editions.

6

Findings and Observations

The eight economies of South Asia, from the smallest one (Afghanistan) to the largest and most dynamic (India), face both common challenges and unique ones. As they pursue lasting economic growth, top priority should be accorded to financial reforms that build stable financial systems—systems resilient to economic shocks. Financial sector development is multifaceted, encompassing such aspects as lower intermediation costs, dynamic savings mobilization, market-oriented regulatory systems, diversity of market players, expanded access to finance, better allocation of resources, greater efficiency through improved technology, and availability of innovative financial instruments. Progress should be continually monitored by the authorities and remedial action taken to ensure the desired outcomes. The analysis and findings in this report should help in this process.

In pursuing reform, South Asian countries have introduced structural changes and policy reforms, adopted new technologies, undertaken legal and regulatory reforms, developed capital adequacy frameworks, strengthened bank supervision, promoted capital market development, and developed market infrastructure and payment systems. They have also introduced corporate governance guidelines to improve transparency and accountability. The region's countries should be commended for undertaking these reforms in the face of daunting economic challenges. These reforms, still ongoing, have helped improve financial system soundness.

Analysis of the Getting Finance Indicators confirms that the region's commercial banking sectors have made progress. It also shows that much work remains—and that progress has been uneven across countries. Most countries have made improvements in such dimensions as performance and efficiency, market concentration and competitiveness, savings mobilization, and corporate governance. Greater efforts are needed in access to finance, financial stability, capital market development, and payment systems development.

In interpreting the findings in this report, readers should bear in mind the technical and practical limitations of the analysis and underlying data noted elsewhere in the report. The indicator analysis for different development dimensions should not be considered in isolation. Indicator analysis can only provide clues to the financial soundness of a banking system and thus should be considered together with qualitative analysis of other important information—such as a country's prudential regulations (and the compliance with those regulations) and the state of its economy. Still, the country analysis based on the indicators, together with the comparative analysis of prudential norms and the country rankings, can provide valuable information on both the strengths and the deficiencies of South Asian banking systems, helping the authorities focus their development efforts.

Access to Finance

To provide financial services to the poor, South Asian countries will need to improve access to commercial banking facilities. In most countries, such facilities are largely confined to urban areas. While microfinance is common in South Asia, bank finance plays a vital role, sometimes as the sole source of long-term funding in the absence of developed capital markets.

Among South Asian countries, Sri Lanka has high access as well as use ratios and these are expected to improve further with the North-East rehabilitation program started in 2009. Maldives has the highest penetration ratios, but these do not reflect the true picture because they do not account for the geographic dispersion of the population among atolls. Indeed, access to finance is a serious issue in Maldives, one that the country is addressing through a mobile banking project.

In Afghanistan, credit penetration is low because of the lack of an extensive banking network. Bhutan needs to improve access to finance to speed economic growth. Nepal finds itself in a unique situation: even with rapid growth in the number of banks, financial access in rural areas remains limited. Bangladesh, India, and Pakistan also need to improve financial access in underserved rural areas. In the benchmark group, greater use of technology has made branchless banking possible, resulting in low branch penetration levels. South Asia is also moving in this direction.

Performance and Efficiency

Performance and efficiency are one area in which South Asian banks appear to have done well. Supported by high net interest margins, both the return on assets and the return on equity steadily improved over the years. But higher spreads could mean higher risk taking, and banks could be vulnerable to interest rate risk as well as credit risk. Overall, South Asian banks had higher performance indicators and lower operating costs than those in the benchmark economies—and their profitability has steadily increased. Even so, the region's banks should focus on reducing operating costs.

Afghan banks operate with high interest spreads but low recurring earning power. Bangladesh banks need to further lower operating costs. Those in Bhutan need to work toward achieving cost as well as technological efficiency. In Maldives, return ratios are falling while operating costs are rising, a trend that needs to be managed. Driving this trend is the high concentration of bank lending in tourism and fisheries, industries affected by recent economic events.

Financial Stability

Some South Asian countries have adopted the Basel II capital adequacy framework, while others are moving toward this important milestone. And South Asian banks have generally done well in maintaining capital adequacy ratios. But rising levels of nonperforming loans and declining provisions are a matter for concern. The nonperforming loan situation will need to be monitored carefully given the economic downturn that came in the wake of the global financial crisis. This situation is expected to worsen, and if banks are unable to provide for the bad loans and manage their asset portfolios, this could threaten the stability of the region's financial systems. Compared with the benchmark economies, South Asia does well on capital adequacy ratios but appears to lag in nonperforming loans and provisioning.

India, Pakistan, and Sri Lanka have already adopted Basel II capital guidelines. Nepal and Bangladesh have been conducting parallel runs in anticipation of the adoption of Basel II. Afghanistan, Bhutan, and Maldives are using the Basel I framework, with Maldives issuing guidelines in 2009 on the use of the new capital framework. Most South Asian countries lag behind in reporting operational risks and in initiating efforts to mitigate such risks. Among the countries that have moved to Basel II, only India has started to require its banks to rate their corporate customers. In addition, countries differ in their financial reporting and accounting standards, and the region as a whole is not yet fully compliant with the International Accounting Standards.

Afghanistan reports high capital ratios and low nonperforming loans. But liquidity needs to be carefully monitored. Bangladesh is in the midst of restructuring systemically important public sector banks. The overall capital adequacy ratio remained below the regulatory requirement until 2008, and nonperforming loans and provisions need to be better managed. Recapitalization of banks would improve the stability of the banking system. In Bhutan, the growth of lending activity has reduced the capital adequacy ratio, but it is still very high. For avoidance of a credit bubble, however, the growth in loans should be monitored carefully. And lax regulatory guidelines on loan classification and provisioning should be tightened.

The Indian banking system has maintained steady capital ratios. But improving performance should enable banks to further augment the capital base. In Maldives, the capital adequacy ratio is stable, but rising levels of nonperforming loans and declining provisions are a major cause for concern. Asset quality should be improved through efforts to diversify lending and enhance credit information. In Nepal, the restructuring of ailing public sector banks has made these banks profitable for the first time. But the banks continue to have large negative returns, suggesting a need to continue the process. Another concern for Nepal is the rapid entry of new banks. Aggressive competition has led to risky lending practices, and excessive exposure to real estate has created a real estate price bubble. This represents a major risk to financial stability, since most banks lack substantial capital cushions. In most South Asian countries, the recoverability of nonperforming loans is an issue, especially for those backed by real estate. And this raises a question about whether such collateral has realizable value. India, Pakistan, and Sri Lanka have speedily passed debt recovery laws, a move that other South Asian countries would do well to follow.

In Pakistan, better regulatory guidelines and higher performance levels have ensured higher capital levels. But rising levels of nonperforming loans and declining provisions are major concerns given the economic downturn. In Sri Lanka, the capital adequacy ratio is steady and above regulatory requirements, but the banking system would benefit from capital infusions. In addition, nonperforming loans are rising with the economic slowdown and need to be watched.

South Asian regulators also need to be mindful of high statutory reserve requirements and cash reserve requirements, because these raise the cost of funds and thus have a cascading effect on the transaction chain. To support the expansion of credit, central banks should reduce such requirements over time.

Capital Market Development

Capital market development needs attention in all South Asian countries. Only India has a developed capital market. The region's stock markets tend to be small and concentrated among a few players, and its bond markets are dominated by government bonds. Pakistan and Sri Lanka have fairly developed stock markets but, like other countries in the region, lack developed corporate bond markets. Along with India, both countries experienced capital outflows after the onset of the financial crisis as investors deleveraged their portfolios. And in Pakistan, the stock market crash of 2008 slowed the development of the market, though it is showing signs of recovery. Among the region's countries, only India lists government securities on the stock exchange and benchmarks on the yield curve. Other South Asian countries would benefit from doing the same at some point, to support the development of their corporate bond markets.

Lack of a developed capital market hampers domestic investment because of the greater difficulty in obtaining long-term funding—and requires banks to include long-term lending in their portfolios. Such practices could expose banks to credit risks because of maturity mismatch issues. Thus, capital market development should be considered as a vehicle for long-term growth. All South Asian countries except India need to greatly improve their measures of capital market development to match the benchmark economies.

Market Concentration and Competitiveness

Lower concentration in banking is widely believed to foster healthy competition and thus reduce intermediary costs. Market concentration is low in all major economies of South Asia except Sri Lanka, where the top three banks account for more than 50 percent of commercial banking assets. Bangladesh and India have low market concentration in terms of assets as well as loans and deposits. But in India, as in most countries, concentration within banking segments (public sector, private sector, and foreign banks) needs to be monitored carefully. Pakistan managed to reduce concentration ratios over the eight-year period studied.

In the region's three smaller economies, concentration is high. In Afghanistan, two banks account for more than 45 percent of assets, and in Maldives three account for more than 90 percent. Bhutan has only two banks. By contrast, Nepal has a market dilution problem: too many banks competing for too few assets, resulting in an asset price bubble. Thus, too much competition can also foster unhealthy situations.

Driven by high interest margins, private credit has increased rapidly in all countries in the region. In 2008, however, the pace of growth appeared to slow somewhat as the economic slowdown began and banks started to scale back on lending operations in favor of consolidation. A rapid increase in private credit coupled with high interest margins is a cause for concern: if economic activity slows and interest rates drop, as is happening in the region today, this situation could give rise to both interest rate risk and credit risk. This issue requires immediate attention to maintain system stability. And Bhutan and Nepal need to take care to avoid asset bubbles, which would undermine the health of their financial systems.

In India's case, the rapid credit growth was backed by dynamic economic growth. The benchmark economies have higher ratios of private credit to GDP than their South Asian counterparts but, like India, also have far higher levels of economic development and growth.

Payment Systems Development

Payment systems development is another area needing greater attention in all South Asian countries. The payment system forms an integral part of the financial infrastructure, enabling timely execution of the financial transactions arising from economic activity. In addition to retail payment systems, India, Pakistan, and Sri Lanka have implemented real-time gross settlement (RTGS) systems to handle large-value, time-critical payments. The region's other countries have retail payment systems and end-of-day net settlement systems for large-value payments. Sri Lanka has also developed a strong institutional, legal, and regulatory framework to back its systemically important payment systems and established the National Payments Council as the decision-making body. Payment reforms in other countries have been focused mostly on automating the systems to increase efficiency. The benchmark economies are far ahead in payment systems development, showing that South Asia still has much work to do.

Thanks to efforts by the Payments Council of the South Asian Association for Regional Cooperation (SAARC), all SAARC countries—including Afghanistan, Bhutan, and Nepal—have now established an appropriate forum to discuss payment systems development, such as a national payments council or committee. The needs in developing payment systems differ among countries in the region. Countries such as India, Pakistan, and Sri Lanka need to strengthen their existing RTGS systems, while other countries need to introduce systems with RTGS capabilities for large-value and time-critical payments. The solutions also differ. In some countries, the most economically viable solution is to implement one integrated system (and to automate the system). All countries need to develop their retail payment infrastructure. While the limited selection of indicators may not clearly reflect the weaknesses in this area, all countries have low levels of use of electronic payment instruments such as payment cards and credit and debit transfers. The availability of such payment instruments and services is low in South Asia compared with the benchmark economies.

Savings Mobilization

Savings mobilization was already important in South Asia because its capital markets are not fully developed, and it became even more so with the impact of the global financial crisis on external capital flows into the region's countries. Higher domestic savings could sustain capital investments and help countries move away from overreliance on external capital.

All South Asian countries except Maldives enjoy steady inflows of worker remittances, a stream that has continued to flow despite the global financial crisis. In Maldives, the outflows of remittances are far greater than the inflows. Savings rates in South Asia are generally high, though persistent inflation has driven real deposit interest rates into negative territory, affecting overall savings. One area that needs greater focus is financial deepening. Most countries have fairly high broad money supply (M2) to GDP ratios, but these could be improved.

Compared with the benchmark economies, South Asian countries have fared better on worker remittances as well as domestic savings relative to GDP. But they fall short in financial deepening and real deposit interest rates. Overall, domestic savings are much more important in South Asian countries because of their lower levels of capital market development.

In Afghanistan, the low savings rate and lack of a capital market have forced the country to rely heavily on external funding. Bangladesh has high worker remittances but needs to address its negative interest rates. Bhutan has a high savings rate but needs to curb inflation so as to maintain positive interest rates. India enjoys a high savings rate, positive real interest rates, and a high level of financial deepening. Even so, India's economic growth rate and its increasing requirements for domestic investment suggest a need to further encourage domestic savings.

Maldives has not pursued a policy of savings mobilization but nevertheless has a high savings rate. Nepal has the second lowest domestic savings rate in South Asia after Afghanistan, but the highest remittance inflows relative to GDP. Pakistan has a low domestic savings rate, indicating a weak savings culture, and it is also battling high negative real interest rates resulting from persistent high inflation. In Sri Lanka, unprecedented inflation drove the real deposit interest rate to a new low. Sri Lanka also has a low savings rate, but its remittance inflows are stable. The country could further improve financial deepening.

Corporate Governance

All South Asian countries have attempted to incorporate guidelines on corporate governance into their prudential norms for banks. Some have issued comprehensive guidelines, including Pakistan, India, and, more recently, Sri Lanka. Others have issued guidelines covering different areas. But all countries need to focus more on compliance and enforcement. Government control over public sector banks is another common issue. In addition, different countries need to strengthen different areas of their regulatory guidelines.

Afghanistan recently issued fairly detailed corporate governance guidelines, but it is still too soon to comment on their effectiveness. Some issues need further attention, including minority shareholder rights, influence of external stakeholders, and disclosure requirements relating to beneficial ownership. In addition, setting up a local accounting body should be among the priorities in working toward compliance with international accounting standards.

Bangladesh has issued several guidelines covering key areas. But this process of developing comprehensive guidelines needs to be fast-tracked. There is a need to clearly define legal provisions governing beneficial ownership, minority shareholder rights, remuneration of directors, and roles and responsibilities of external and internal auditors. Full conformity with international accounting and auditing standards should be actively pursued.

Bhutan's banking regulations include requirements relating to corporate governance, but there is no corporate governance code for banks. The country's banks would benefit from improvements in provisions governing such areas as beneficial ownership, proxy voting rights, special voting rights, remuneration of directors, and disclosure requirements. Other key efforts would include building awareness on corporate governance and shareholder and investor rights, developing a code of corporate governance for banks, and streamlining accounting and auditing procedures.

India has issued comprehensive guidelines. But additional efforts are needed besides strengthening compliance and enforcement and addressing government control over public sector banks. These include harmonizing standards and codes, revising statutes and guidelines to improve transparency and consistency, and reviewing performance-based compensation mechanisms and monitoring performance levels given recent events in the international arena.

Maldives has issued a set of guidelines, though too recently to assess their effectiveness. Still, there is a need to clearly define voting procedures, minority shareholder rights, and transparency and disclosure principles, with an emphasis on accounting and auditing standards. In addition, the recently established local accounting body needs to be further strengthened and compliance with international standards pursued.

While Nepal has issued guidelines for banks, weak corporate governance in some private sector banks is a growing concern because of the intense competition and high risk taking observed in the market. Also important is to focus on broadening investor rights, increasing disclosure, strengthening board effectiveness, and improving adherence to international accounting and auditing standards.

Pakistan has issued comprehensive guidelines and developed a code of corporate governance. In addition, it has set up the Pakistan Institute of Corporate Governance to provide training and build awareness on corporate governance issues. Corporate governance of banks could be strengthened through greater transparency and disclosure, greater accountability, more disclosure on beneficial ownership, safeguards on stakeholder rights, greater clarification of board responsibilities, and greater emphasis on self-governance for institutions.

Sri Lanka has taken important steps to improve corporate governance in banking by issuing mandatory guidelines. But further work is needed to make the guidelines more comprehensive and effective. Among the areas needing review are disclosure requirements, stakeholder rights, the rights of minority shareholders, and basic ownership rights to reflect shareholders' right to vote on bank operations.

Because of lack of data as well as resource constraints, this study has not done a comparative assessment of corporate governance in the benchmark economies.

Impact of the Financial Crisis

While the global financial crisis has had little or no direct effect on South Asian countries, it has had an indirect effect in two ways. The ensuing recession in developed countries led to a slowdown in export activity and growth in South Asian economies. And the deleveraging activities of international investors led to an outflow of funds from portfolio investments and, to a lesser extent, from direct investments. For banks, these effects meant a slowing of the growth momentum and rising levels of nonperforming loans. Banks pulled back funding and became more concerned with preserving their asset portfolios than with pursuing aggressive lending, resulting in a credit crunch. While South Asia will feel the impact of the economic slowdown for the next few years, the region's banks can be expected to weather the slowdown well, thanks in part to conservative prudential guidelines established by regulatory authorities.

South Asian countries share some common features in macroeconomic indicators and financial systems, and almost all have gone through similar phases of development at different times. In that light, it is hoped that this edition provides an opportunity for the region's policy makers and regulators to assess the status of their financial systems and replicate reforms and advances where suitable.

Part II

Indicators

7

Compilation Guide for the Getting Finance Indicators for South Asia

As part of the World Bank's regional initiative to develop standardized indicators to measure the performance and soundness of the financial sector, this study uses indicators under eight categories: access to finance, performance and efficiency, financial stability, capital market development, market concentration and competitiveness, payment systems development, savings mobilization, and corporate governance.[1] Initially, these indicators are being computed only for commercial banks.

Interpretation and analysis of these indicators are likely to vary unless banking supervisors adopt a common methodology for computing them. Because most of the indicators take the form of ratios, understanding the underlying data is imperative. This guide provides common definitions, data sources, and concepts for both compilers and users of the indicators. For indicators appearing in previous editions of *Getting Finance in South Asia*, the definitions are the same as those given in the compilation guide issued for those editions.

Access to Finance

In countries seeking to develop financial markets, it is important to monitor and measure the level of access to financial services. This knowledge provides a more balanced picture of financial sector development. It also enables policy makers and regulatory authorities to better target the development efforts. Initially, access to finance is being analyzed using data relating to providers of finance (supply-side data). Both demographic and geographic market penetration is analyzed.

1. Demographic branch penetration

$$\text{Bank branches per 100,000 people} = \frac{\text{Number of bank branches}}{\text{Total population}} \times 100{,}000$$

Number of bank branches: Number of commercial bank branches in the country at year-end.
Total population: Total population at year-end.

This indicator measures the demographic penetration of the banking sector in terms of access to banks' physical outlets. Higher penetration means more branches and thus easier access.

2. Demographic ATM penetration

$$\text{ATMs per 100,000 people} = \frac{\text{Number of ATMs}}{\text{Total population}} \times 100{,}000$$

Number of ATMs: Number of automated teller machines (ATMs) of commercial banks in the country at year-end.
Total population: As defined in eq. (1) above.

This indicator also measures the demographic penetration of the banking sector in terms of access to physical outlets. Higher penetration means more ATMs and thus easier access.

3. Deposit accounts per 1,000 people

$$\text{Deposit accounts per 1,000 people} = \frac{\text{Number of deposit accounts}}{\text{Total population}} \times 1{,}000$$

Number of deposit accounts: Number of deposit accounts in commercial banks in the country at year-end.
Total population: As defined in eq. (1) above.

This indicator measures the use of banking services. Higher values mean greater use of services.

4. Loan accounts per 1,000 people

$$\text{Loan accounts per 1,000 people} = \frac{\text{Number of loan accounts}}{\text{Total population}} \times 1{,}000$$

Number of loan accounts: Number of loan accounts granted by commercial banks in the country at year-end.
Total population: As defined in eq. (1) above.

This indicator also measures the use of banking services, with higher values indicating greater use.

5. Geographic branch penetration

$$\text{Bank branches per 1,000 km}^2 = \frac{\text{Number of bank branches}}{\text{Total surface area (km}^2\text{)}} \times 1{,}000$$

Number of bank branches: As defined in eq. (1) above.
Total surface area (km^2): Total surface area of the country measured in square kilometers.

This indicator measures the geographic penetration of the banking sector in terms of access to physical outlets. Higher values mean easier geographic access to branches.

6. Geographic ATM penetration

$$\text{ATMs per 1,000 km}^2 = \frac{\text{Number of ATMs}}{\text{Total surface area (km}^2\text{)}} \times 1{,}000$$

Number of ATMs: As defined in eq. (2) above.
Total surface area (km^2): As defined in eq. (5) above.

This indicator also measures the geographic penetration of the banking sector in terms of access to physical outlets, with higher values indicating easier geographic access to ATMs.

Performance and Efficiency

Bank efficiency has become critical in an environment of increasingly competitive international markets. Thus comparative data on the efficiency of banks are important both to regulators and to banks, which can use the data to adjust their operating policies. For this study two types of efficiency are analyzed: returns efficiency and cost efficiency.

7. Return on equity (profits to period-average equity)

$$\text{Return on equity} = \frac{\text{Net income}}{\text{Average value of total equity}}$$

Net income: Net profit before tax and other extraordinary adjustments.
Average value of total equity: Can be calculated by taking the beginning- and end-period values for total capital (total equity) and finding the average.
Total capital (total equity): Also called regulatory capital funds or own funds. Defined as Tier 1 (core) capital plus Tier 2 (supplementary) capital.
Tier 1 capital: Equity capital and disclosed reserves that are freely available to meet claims against the bank. Tier 1 capital comprises paid-up shares, share premiums, retained earnings, statutory reserves, and general reserves. Goodwill should be deducted because its value may fall during crises. According to international best practice, Tier 1 capital should be at least 50 percent of total capital funds.
Tier 2 capital: Undisclosed reserves, revaluation reserves, general loan loss provisions, and hybrid instruments that combine the characteristics of debt and equity and are available to meet losses and unsecured subordinated debt. According to international best practice, Tier 2 capital should be less than or equal to Tier 1 capital, subordinated debt should not exceed 50 percent of Tier 1 capital, and loan loss provisions should not exceed 1.25 percent of total risk-weighted assets.

This ratio measures the efficiency with which a bank uses capital and, over time, the sustainability of the bank's capital position.

8. Return on assets (profits to period-average assets)

$$\text{Return on assets} = \frac{\text{Net income}}{\text{Average value of total assets}}$$

Net income: As defined in eq. (7) above.
Average value of total assets: Can be calculated by taking the beginning- and end-period values for total assets and finding the average.

This ratio measures the efficiency with which a bank uses assets.

9. Staff cost ratio

$$\text{Staff cost ratio} = \frac{\text{Personnel expenses}}{\text{Operating expenses}}$$

Personnel expenses: Total remuneration payable to employees.
Operating expenses: All expenses other than interest expenses and provisions.

This ratio measures personnel cost as a share of total operating expenses and reflects cost efficiency.

10. Operating cost ratio

$$\text{Operating cost ratio} = \frac{\text{Operating expenses}}{\text{Net interest earnings}}$$

Operating expenses: As defined in eq. (9) above.
Net interest earnings (net interest income): Interest earned less interest expenses.

This ratio measures efficiency in controlling operating expenses in relation to net interest income.

11. Net interest margin

$$\text{Net interest margin} = \frac{\text{Net interest earnings}}{\text{Average value of total assets}}$$

Net interest earnings (net interest income): As defined in eq. (10) above.
Average value of total assets: As defined in eq. (8) above.

This ratio measures the overall operating efficiency of the banking sector.

12. Recurring earning power

$$\text{Recurring earning power} = \frac{\text{Preprovision profits}}{\text{Average value of total assets}}$$

Preprovision profits: Profits before tax and loan loss provisions.
Average value of total assets: As defined in eq. (8) above.

This ratio measures the recurring earning strength and efficiency of the banking sector.

Financial Stability

Financial stability means avoiding significant disruptions to the financial system and its functions. It is key to achieving both low inflation and sustainable economic growth. While different indicators measure different aspects of financial sector stability, this study uses capital adequacy, asset quality, and liquidity ratios. The two capital adequacy ratios measure the capacity of an institution to absorb losses and thus indicate its financial strength. The asset quality and liquidity ratios measure major vulnerabilities relating to credit risk and liquidity risk.

13. Capital adequacy ratio (CAR)

$$\text{Capital adequacy ratio} = \frac{\text{Regulatory capital funds}}{\text{Risk-weighted assets}}$$

Regulatory capital funds: Also called own funds or total capital funds, as defined in eq. (7) above.

Risk-weighted assets: Each class of assets and off–balance sheet exposures is weighted using weights related to the credit risk associated with each type of assets. The standard risk weights used as international best practice (Basel I) are as follows:

- Cash, gold, and government or treasury securities, 0 percent
- Loans to government agencies, 20 percent
- Mortgage loans, 50 percent
- Others, 100 percent

The CAR assesses how well capital cushions fluctuations in earnings and supports asset growth. The ratio should be calculated on a consolidated basis. In international best practice 8 percent of total risk-weighted assets on a consolidated basis is considered adequate capital.

14. Leverage ratio

$$\text{Leverage ratio} = \frac{\text{Total equity}}{\text{Total assets}}$$

Total equity: Total capital funds as defined in eq. (7) above.

Total assets: Total assets on the balance sheet at the end of the period without risk weighting.

This ratio measures the extent to which assets are financed by funds other than own funds and thus is an indicator of capital adequacy.

15. Gross nonperforming loans ratio

$$\text{Gross nonperforming loans ratio} = \frac{\text{Gross nonperforming loans}}{\text{Total advances}}$$

Gross nonperforming loans (NPLs): Amount of NPLs before specific loan loss provisions are deducted. In accordance with prudential norms, loans are classified as nonperforming when payments of principal and interest are past due by three months.
Total advances: Gross loans and advances, including NPLs before deducting specific loan loss provisions.

This ratio is a measure of asset quality and indicates the credit quality of a bank's loan portfolio.

16. Provisions to nonperforming loans ratio

$$\text{Provisions to nonperforming loans ratio} = \frac{\text{Loan loss provisions}}{\text{Gross nonperforming loans}}$$

Loan loss provisions: Specific loan loss provisions outstanding at the end of the period.
Gross NPLs: As defined in eq. (15) above.

This ratio is a measure of asset quality and identifies the adequacy or shortfall of the specific provisions made for NPLs.

17. Liquid assets ratio

$$\text{Liquid assets ratio} = \frac{\text{Liquid assets}}{\text{Total assets}}$$

Liquid assets: Cash, demand deposits, and other financial assets that are available on demand or within three months or less.
Total assets: As defined in eq. (14) above.

This ratio measures stability. It indicates the liquidity available to meet expected and unexpected short-term demands for cash—and thus the vulnerability of the banking sector to loss of funding sources.

18. Liquid assets to liabilities ratio

$$\text{Liquid assets to liabilities ratio} = \frac{\text{Liquid assets}}{\text{Liquid liabilities}}$$

Liquid assets: As defined in eq. (17) above.
Liquid liabilities: Short-term debt liabilities and the net market value of financial derivatives positions (short term).

This ratio also measures stability. It captures the liquidity mismatch between short-term assets and liabilities and indicates the extent to which a bank can meet its short-term obligations without incurring liquidity problems.

Capital Market Development

The development of capital markets is a powerful indicator of the depth of the financial sector. By allocating funds for viable investment projects, healthy capital markets diversify the channels of financial intermediation. This study uses ratios to measure the size and structure of the stock and bond markets.

19. Domestic bond market to equity market capitalization ratio

$$\text{Domestic bond market to equity market capitalization ratio} = \frac{\text{Domestic bonds outstanding}}{\text{Equity market capitalization}}$$

Domestic bonds outstanding: Total value of outstanding domestic debt securities issued by private entities as well as public entities, at the end of the period.
Equity (stock) market capitalization: Market value of all outstanding shares calculated as share price times the number of shares outstanding at the end of the period.

This ratio gives an indication of the size and structure of the capital markets. It also reflects financial depth and diversity.

20. Domestic public bonds outstanding to GDP ratio

$$\text{Domestic public bonds outstanding to GDP ratio} = \frac{\text{Domestic public bonds outstanding}}{\text{GDP}}$$

Domestic public bonds outstanding: Total value of outstanding domestic debt securities issued by public entities.
Gross domestic product (GDP): An aggregate measure of production in the economy equal to the total value added of all residential units engaged in production, for the given period. This is the nominal GDP.

This ratio is a measure of the size of the bond market. It reflects the extent to which the public sector preempts resources that would otherwise be available to the private sector.

21. Trading value of top 10 stocks ratio

$$\text{Trading value of top 10 stocks ratio} = \frac{\text{Trading value of top 10 stocks}}{\text{Total value of shares traded}}$$

Trading value of top 10 stocks: Total value of the top 10 actively traded stocks in the stock exchange for the period under consideration, such as the financial year or calendar year.
Total value of shares traded: Total value of shares traded in the stock exchange for the period under consideration, such as the financial year or calendar year.

This ratio measures the degree of concentration of the top 10 firms in the stock market and reflects the depth of the market.

22. Stock market capitalization to GDP ratio

$$\text{Stock market capitalization to GDP ratio} = \frac{\text{Stock market capitalization}}{\text{GDP}}$$

Stock market capitalization: As defined in eq. (19) above.
GDP: As defined in eq. (20) above.

This ratio measures the importance of the stock market relative to the size of the economy.

23. Stock trading value to GDP ratio

$$\text{Stock trading value to GDP ratio} = \frac{\text{Total value of shares traded}}{\text{GDP}}$$

Total value of shares traded: As defined in eq. (21) above.
GDP: As defined in eq. (20) above.

This ratio measures the activity or liquidity in the stock market and reflects the ease of trading.

24. Stock market turnover ratio

$$\text{Stock market turnover ratio} = \frac{\text{Total value of shares traded}}{\text{Average market capitalization}}$$

Total value of shares traded: As defined in eq. (21) above.
Average market capitalization: Average of the end-period market capitalization values for the current period and the previous period.

This ratio is a measure of efficiency in the stock market.

Market Concentration and Competitiveness

The study examines the market structure of the banking sector to evaluate the banking system's proneness to instability and crisis. A high level of concentration in the banking industry, by reducing competition and increasing cost, has an adverse impact on efficiency. At the same time, a highly competitive banking sector might be more prone to crisis (because of greater fragility resulting from intense competition) than a more concentrated one.

25. Herfindahl-Hirschman Index (HHI)

$$\text{Herfindahl-Hirschman Index} = \sum_{i=1}^{n} (MS_i)^{\wedge 2}$$

HHI is calculated by squaring the market share (for assets) of each bank in the geographic banking market and summing the squares.

This ratio measures market concentration in the commercial banking sector. A high value indicates a highly concentrated sector, which may lead to a lack of competitive pressure.

26. K-bank concentration ratio, assets

$$\text{K-bank concentration ratio } (CR_k)\text{, assets} = \frac{\text{Three largest banks' total assets}}{\text{Total assets of commercial banks}}$$

(CR_k), where k = three largest banks.
Three largest banks' total assets: Calculated as the total assets of the three largest banks.
Total assets of commercial banks: Total assets of the commercial banking sector.

This ratio measures banking concentration in terms of assets.

27. K-bank concentration ratio, deposits

$$\text{K-bank concentration ratio } (CR_k)\text{, deposits} = \frac{\text{Three largest banks' total deposits}}{\text{Total deposits of commercial banks}}$$

(CR_k), where k = three largest banks.
Three largest banks' total deposits: Calculated as the total deposits of the three largest banks.
Total deposits of commercial banks: Total deposits of the commercial banking sector.

This ratio measures banking concentration in terms of deposits.

28. K-bank concentration ratio, loans

$$\text{K-bank concentration ratio } (CR_k)\text{, loans} = \frac{\text{Three largest banks' total loans}}{\text{Total loans of commercial banks}}$$

(CR_k), where k = three largest banks.
Three largest banks' total loans: Calculated as the total loans of the three largest banks.
Total loans of commercial banks: Total loans of the commercial banking sector.

This ratio measures banking concentration in terms of loans.

29. Private credit extended by banks to GDP ratio

$$\text{Private credit extended by banks to GDP ratio} = \frac{\text{Total value of private credit by commercial banks}}{\text{GDP}}$$

Total value of private credit by commercial banks: Claims on the private sector by commercial banks.
GDP: As defined in eq. (20) above.

This ratio measures the activity of banks as financial intermediaries in channeling savings to investors, relative to the size of the economy.

30. Commercial banking assets to GDP ratio

$$\text{Commercial banking assets to GDP ratio} = \frac{\text{Total commercial banking assets}}{\text{GDP}}$$

Total commercial banking assets: As defined in eq. (26) above.
GDP: As defined in eq. (20) above.

This ratio measures the importance of the commercial banking sector relative to the size of the economy.

Payment Systems Development

Safe and efficient payment systems are critical to the effective functioning of the financial system. Payment systems are the means by which funds are transferred between banks, and the most significant ones, referred to in this report as systemically important payment systems, are a major channel for the transmission of shocks across domestic and international financial systems and markets. Robust payment systems are therefore a key to maintaining and promoting financial stability. In the past few years a broad international consensus has developed on the need to strengthen payment systems by promoting internationally accepted standards and practices for their design and operation (CPSS 2001). The six indicators selected to measure the development of payment systems are standard ones used by the Committee on Payment and Settlement Systems of the Bank for International Settlements (CPSS various years).

31. Notes and coins in circulation to GDP ratio

$$\text{Notes and coins in circulation to GDP ratio} = \frac{\text{Value of notes and coins in circulation}}{\text{GDP}}$$

Notes and coins in circulation: Notes and coins (or currency) in circulation outside banks. This is the narrowest measure of money supply and is identified as a settlement medium used by nonbanks. Notes and coins represent the value of cash in circulation in the economy at the end of the year. This excludes the value of banknotes and coins kept in vaults at central banks or at banks but includes the value held by nonresidents. It also excludes commemorative coins not used for payments. When such coins are included, this should be mentioned in a footnote.

GDP: As defined in eq. (20) above.

This ratio measures the importance of cash as a means of settlement used by nonbanks relative to the size of the economy. A higher ratio means greater use of basic instruments in settlement as against more advanced methods.

32. Narrow money supply to GDP ratio

$$\text{Narrow money supply to GDP ratio} = \frac{\text{Narrow money supply (M1)}}{\text{GDP}}$$

Narrow money supply (M1): Cash in circulation and transferable deposits held by nonbanks, including nonresidents. This is also classified as a settlement medium used by nonbanks. When national definitions of narrow money supply or M1 differ from the definition here, this should be noted in a footnote.

GDP: As defined in eq. (20) above.

This ratio measures the dominance of narrow money as a means of settlement used by nonbanks relative to the size of the economy.

33. Value of RTGS transactions to GDP ratio

$$\text{Value of RTGS transactions to GDP ratio} = \frac{\text{Total annual value of RTGS transactions}}{\text{GDP}}$$

Total annual value of RTGS transactions: Total value of transactions processed through the real-time gross settlement (RTGS) system in the year.

GDP: As defined in eq. (20) above.

This ratio measures the importance of the RTGS system as an interbank fund transfer system relative to the size of the economy.

34. Value of retail transactions to GDP ratio

$$\text{Value of retail transactions to GDP ratio} = \frac{\text{Total annual value of retail transactions}}{\text{GDP}}$$

Total annual value of retail transactions: Total value of transactions (such as checks and credit clearing) processed through the retail payment system in the year.

GDP: As defined in eq. (20) above.

This ratio measures the importance of the retail payment system as an interbank fund transfer system relative to the size of the economy.

35. RTGS concentration ratio

$$\text{Retail payments concentration ratio} = \frac{\begin{array}{c}\text{Total annual value of RTGS}\\ \text{transactions of five largest participants}\end{array}}{\text{Total annual value of RTGS transactions}}$$

Total annual value of RTGS transactions of five largest participants: Market share of the five largest participants in the RTGS system, based on the total volume of transactions.
Total annual value of RTGS transactions: As defined in eq. (33) above.

This ratio measures the participation of users in the RTGS system as a fund transfer system, with high concentration denoting less participation.

36. Retail payments concentration ratio

$$\text{Retail payments concentration ratio} = \frac{\begin{array}{c}\text{Total annual value of retail}\\ \text{transactions of five largest participants}\end{array}}{\text{Total annual value of retail transactions}}$$

Total annual value of retail transactions of five largest participants: Market share of the five largest participants in the retail payment system, based on the total volume of transactions.
Total annual value of retail transactions: As defined in eq. (34) above.

This ratio measures the participation of users in the retail payment system as a fund transfer system, with high concentration denoting less participation.

Savings Mobilization

Financial systems that are more effective at pooling the savings of individuals can profoundly affect economic development. Besides having a direct effect on capital accumulation, better savings mobilization can improve resource allocation and boost technological innovation (Levine 1999). The growth of output of any economy depends on capital accumulation, which in turn requires investment and an equivalent amount of savings to match it. Two of the most important issues in development economics, and for developing countries, are how to stimulate investment and how to bring about a higher level of saving to fund the increased investment (Thirlwall 2002).

37. Broad money supply to GDP ratio

$$\text{Broad money supply to GDP ratio} = \frac{\text{Broad money (M2)}}{\text{GDP}}$$

Broad money (M2): M1 (currency and demand deposits held by the public) plus time and savings deposits held by the public with commercial banks.

GDP: As defined in eq. (20) above.

This ratio measures the impact of broad money on savings, which is the financial depth, or volume of intermediation. Financial deepening would be expected to have a positive effect on savings in the long run (Baliamoune and Chowdhury 2003).

38. Real deposit interest rate

Real deposit interest rate = Nominal (average) deposit interest rate adjusted for inflation

Real deposit interest rate: Nominal (average) deposit interest rate adjusted for inflation (or price changes). The deposit interest rate is the (average) rate paid by commercial or similar banks on demand, time, or savings deposits.

This indicator measures the effect of the real interest rate on savings mobilization. Higher real interest rates imply higher rates of return on savings, which would lead to a shift of funds to savings.

39. Gross domestic savings to GDP ratio

$$\text{Gross domestic savings to GDP ratio} = \frac{\text{Gross domestic savings}}{\text{GDP}}$$

Gross domestic savings: Calculated as GDP less final consumption expenditure (total consumption).
GDP: As defined in eq. (20) above.

This ratio measures the level of domestic savings relative to the size of the economy. Higher savings would be expected to increase the funds available for investment.

40. Reserve money to total deposits ratio

$$\text{Reserve money to total deposits ratio} = \frac{\text{Reserve money}}{\text{Total deposits}}$$

Reserve money: Currency held by the public and commercial banks, plus commercial bank and other government agency deposits held at the central bank.
Total deposits: Total deposit liabilities held by financial institutions.

This ratio is an indicator of the efficiency of financial intermediaries. A lower ratio means higher efficiency in financial intermediation, which would be expected to lead to better instruments and incentives for saving.

41. Loan to deposit ratio

$$\text{Loan to deposit ratio} = \frac{\text{Gross value of bank loans}}{\text{Total deposit liability}}$$

Gross value of bank loans: Total gross value of bank loans outstanding at the end of the period.

Total deposit liability: Total deposit liability of the banking sector at the end of the period.

This ratio indicates a bank's use of savings. The higher the ratio, the more the bank is relying on borrowed funds, which are generally costlier than most types of deposits.

42. Worker remittances to GDP ratio

$$\text{Worker remittances to GDP ratio} = \frac{\text{Worker remittances and compensation of employees}}{\text{GDP}}$$

Worker remittances: Current private transfers from migrant workers who are residents of the host country to recipients in their country of origin. Worker remittances include only transfers made by workers who have been living in the host country for more than a year, regardless of their immigration status.
Compensation of employees: Income of migrants who have lived in the host country for less than a year. Migrants' transfers are defined as the net worth of migrants who are expected to remain in the host country for more than one year and that is transferred from one country to another at the time of migration.[2]
GDP: As defined in eq. (20) above.

This ratio measures worker remittances relative to the size of the economy. Worker remittances provide an important external source of funding for most developing countries and would be expected to have a positive impact on savings.

Corporate Governance

Sound corporate governance creates an environment that promotes banking efficiency, mitigates financial risks, and increases the stability and therefore the credibility of financial institutions. Developing countries have much to gain by improving their corporate governance standards. The basic principles are the same everywhere: fairness, transparency, accountability, and responsibility. These are the minimum standards that give banks legitimacy, reduce vulnerability to financial crisis, and broaden and deepen access to capital.

Scoring performance on corporate governance is hugely challenging and must be done with care. Unlike other types of financial analysis, where quantitative measures can provide "hard" benchmarks to guide the more qualitative aspects of analysis, assessing corporate governance is a largely qualitative exercise. Because corporate governance is assessed in this study through a series of straightforward questions, no definitions or guidelines are provided here.

The questionnaire developed to assess corporate governance is based on the good governance practices outlined by the Organisation for Economic Co-operation and Development (OECD) (table 7.1). The *OECD Principles of Corporate Governance* (OECD 2004) provides the framework for the work of the World Bank Group in this area and identifies the key practical issues: the rights and equitable treatment of shareholders and other financial stakeholders, the role of nonfinancial stakeholders, disclosure and transparency, and the responsibilities of the board of directors (World Bank 2003).

Table 7.1 OECD Principles Applied in the Corporate Governance Questionnaire

Principle	Explanation
1. The rights of shareholders	A corporate governance framework should protect shareholders' rights.
2. The equitable treatment of shareholders	All shareholders, including minority and foreign shareholders, should be treated equally.
3. The role of stakeholders in corporate governance	Good corporate governance recognizes that it is in the long-term interest of the corporation to respect the rights and interests of stakeholders.
4. Disclosure and transparency	There is a need to ensure timely and accurate disclosure of all material matters relating to the corporation, including financial aspects, performance, ownership, and governance.
5. The responsibilities of the board	The board is key to the strategic guidance of the company and the effective monitoring of the management. It should be fully able to undertake its tasks and responsibilities and be fully accountable to shareholders.

Source: Enterprise Development Impact Assessment Information Service 2003.

Table 7.2 Basel Committee Principles for Sound Corporate Governance

Principle 1	Board members should be qualified for their positions, have a clear understanding of their role in corporate governance, and be able to exercise sound judgment about the affairs of the bank.
Principle 2	The board of directors should approve and oversee the bank's strategic objectives and corporate values that are communicated throughout the organization.
Principle 3	The board of directors should set and enforce clear lines of responsibility and accountability throughout the organization.
Principle 4	The board should ensure that there is appropriate oversight by senior management consistent with board policy.
Principle 5	The board and senior management should effectively utilize the work conducted by the internal audit function, external auditors, and internal control functions.
Principle 6	The board should ensure that compensation policies and practices are consistent with the bank's corporate culture, long-term objectives and strategy, and control environment.
Principle 7	The bank should be governed in a transparent manner.
Principle 8	The board and senior management should understand the bank's operational structure, including where the bank operates in jurisdictions, or through structures, that impede transparency (the "know your structure" principle).

Source: Basel Committee on Banking Supervision 2006.

Also underlying the corporate governance questionnaire is a guidance paper issued in February 2006 by the Basel Committee on Banking Supervision. The guidance paper articulates eight principles to enhance corporate governance for banking organizations and to guide the actions of the directors, managers, and supervisors of a diverse range of banks (table 7.2).

Endnotes

1. This guide does not include definitions for the corporate governance indicators, for which a separate questionnaire is used to collect the information (for more details, see the section in this chapter on corporate governance).
2. World Bank, World Development Indicators database.

8

Methodology

This report, presenting findings on the financial soundness of the commercial banking sectors of South Asian countries, is based on a unique data set. In this edition, for the first time, the data set includes all eight South Asian countries. This chapter describes the compilation of the data, the choice of indicators, and the ranking methodology.

Data Compilation

Annual data on the commercial banking sector in each of the eight countries were compiled for the eight years from 2001 to 2008. The financial data were collected using a data collection template (see appendix 2 for the results). The corporate governance data were collected using a questionnaire in which the responders were asked to provide responses to each question as well as legal references to justify those responses (see appendix 4A for the responses).

The data set is unique for two reasons. First, the data for each country were collected directly from its regulatory authorities or their published reports. Second, data comparability across the region was ensured by providing the data collectors with a compilation guide setting out definitions of the indicators and underlying concepts (see chapter 7).

Data for benchmark economies were compiled from published reports of national authorities, reputable databases of international organizations, and, where ratios were unavailable, calculations by the authors. Definitions from the compilation guide could not always be strictly followed for benchmark economies. But because the preparation of the compilation guide took into account international best practices and standards, the variations are minor. Moreover, even if definitions vary somewhat, these benchmarks provide the best available proxy for comparisons with the data collected for South Asian countries.

Choice of Indicators

To provide a holistic perspective on getting finance in South Asia and to improve the understanding of the region's financial systems, indicators were selected under eight dimensions (or categories): access to finance, performance and efficiency, financial stability, capital market development, market concentration and competitiveness, payment systems development, savings mobilization, and corporate governance.

The financial indicators are based on internationally accepted measures and reflect the structure of financial systems in South Asia, just as in the previous editions of the report. The corporate governance indicators are based primarily on the guidelines issued by the Basel Committee on Banking Supervision, which in turn rely on the principles of corporate governance published by the Organisation for Economic Co-operation and Development (OECD) (see chapter 7).

While market-based indicators such as credit ratings and market volatility would better serve macroprudential analysis, such indicators were not selected for this study. The effectiveness of these indicators depends on the quality and depth of financial markets. In most South Asian countries, these characteristics are directly affected by the ownership structure of the commercial banking sector (with government-owned or government-controlled banks accounting for a large share of banking sector assets) and by the lack of stringent public disclosure requirements (for a detailed discussion of the advantages and disadvantages of macroprudential analysis, see World Bank and IMF 2005). It was therefore concluded that microprudential indicators would be better measures of the soundness of financial sectors in South Asia.

Method for Country Rankings

The ranking of countries on the financial and corporate governance indicators is based on a simple-average ranking method. Because of the limited size of the sample, using a ranking method based on percentile averages is not warranted. Simple-average ranking also appears to be appropriate because of the lack of sufficiently detailed data to assess the impact of each indicator on financial soundness and, thus, to assign different weights to the indicators (see Djankov and others 2005).

The report presents two types of rankings—a composite ranking based on the average scores for the five years 2004–08 and annual rankings for each of those years.

Financial Indicator Scores

For each financial indicator for each year, each country is ranked relative to the others, and scores are assigned based on the ranking, with 1 assigned for the lowest ranking and 8 for the highest. The lowest score of 1 is also given for any year for which no data are available (indicated in the data tables in appendix 2 by a dash). Each country receives a different score except in instances in which no data are available for more than one country or more than one country reports the same ratio.

For the composite ranking, these scores are aggregated across the years to arrive at the score for the five-year period for each indicator—and the scores for the indicators within a dimension are added to arrive at the aggregate score for that dimension (access to finance, performance and efficiency, financial stability, capital market development, market concentration and competitiveness, payment systems development, or savings mobilization). This aggregate score is then divided by the maximum "possible" total score for the dimension. That maximum score is 240, derived by multiplying the number of indicators in the dimension (6) by the highest possible score (8), then multiplying that by the number of years (5). Dividing the aggregate score by the maximum possible total score of 240 gives the composite score for each dimension. The composite scores range from 0 to 1. (See table 8.1 for the composite scores received by each country for each dimension and table 4.1 for the ranking of countries in each dimension.)

For the annual rankings for each year, the countries are similarly ranked on the financial indicators, scores are assigned on the basis of that ranking, and the scores for the indicators within each dimension are added to arrive at the aggregate score for that dimension (see appendix 6 for annual rankings for each of the five years 2004–08).

Corporate Governance Scores

For corporate governance, each country is individually scored on the two major sections of each of the four topics on a scale from 1 (not observed) to 5 (largely observed), based on the responses to the questionnaire (see appendix 4A), the country's corporate governance guidelines, and various reports. Here again, a score of 1 is given if no data are available. Since the scores are not based on country rankings, more than one country can receive the same score for a section.

With four topics and two major sections in each, and with the highest possible score for a section being 5, the maximum "possible" score on corporate governance is 40. Because data are not available for all five years in the period (information on corporate governance was collected in 2005 and revised in 2008, with no significant changes observed), the scores cannot be aggregated over the period. Instead, the total score for 2008 is simply divided by the maximum possible score to arrive at the composite score for corporate governance (see table 8.1 for the composite scores and table 4.1 for the ranking of countries on corporate governance). For the same reason, the corporate governance score is calculated only for 2008 in the annual rankings (see appendix 6).

Financial Soundness Ranking

The composite scores for the eight categories of indicators are averaged for each country. These simple averages are then arranged from highest to lowest to identify the overall financial soundness ranking for each country, with 1 being the highest ranking and 8 the lowest (see table 4.1 for the overall ranking and appendix 6 for annual overall rankings).

Presentation of Data

For enhancement of the points made in the analysis, graphs and tables are used throughout the report. Some of the graphs are semilogarithmic, with the y axis having a logarithmic scale and the x axis a normal linear scale. The objective in using a semilogarithmic graph is to make it easier to visualize small values as well as the large values on the y axis. The regional data include numbers that range over many orders of magnitude. The range is so great that visualization of the data is almost impossible if only linear scales are used.

Table 8.1 Five-Year Average Composite Scores on the Getting Finance Indicators for South Asian Countries, 2008

Indicator	Afghanistan	Bangladesh	Bhutan	India	Maldives	Nepal	Pakistan	Sri Lanka
Access to finance								
Demographic branch penetration	5	16	29	26	40	10	19	35
Demographic ATM penetration	6	14	22	25	37	13	25	38
Deposit accounts per 1,000 people	5	21	24	30	35	10	15	40
Loan accounts per 1,000 people	5	26	19	31	33	10	16	40
Geographic branch penetration	5	35	10	30	40	15	20	25
Geographic ATM penetration	6	26	11	25	40	16	21	35
Aggregate score	**32**	**138**	**115**	**167**	**225**	**74**	**116**	**213**
Composite score (aggregate score/240)	**0.13**	**0.58**	**0.48**	**0.70**	**0.94**	**0.31**	**0.48**	**0.89**
Performance and efficiency								
Return on equity	6	29	17	18	37	12	29	27
Return on assets	8	20	14	14	40	28	33	23
Staff cost ratio	11	15	23	21	36	9	29	36
Operating cost ratio	7	8	33	21	32	40	24	15
Net interest margin	25	8	20	20	38	12	27	30
Recurring earning power	5	27	15	21	40	18	32	22
Aggregate score	**62**	**107**	**122**	**115**	**223**	**119**	**174**	**153**
Composite score (aggregate score/240)	**0.26**	**0.45**	**0.51**	**0.48**	**0.93**	**0.50**	**0.73**	**0.64**
Financial stability								
Capital adequacy ratio	19	13	37	23	34	5	23	23
Leverage ratio	19	25	12	37	14	5	32	36
Gross nonperforming loans ratio	23	10	29	34	32	13	22	17
Provisions to nonperforming loans ratio	14	15	20	27	25	8	38	33
Liquid assets ratio	13	17	37	37	25	8	29	14
Liquid assets to liabilities ratio	11	34	32	39	5	14	25	17
Aggregate score	**99**	**114**	**167**	**197**	**135**	**53**	**169**	**140**
Composite score (aggregate score/240)	**0.41**	**0.48**	**0.70**	**0.82**	**0.56**	**0.22**	**0.70**	**0.58**

Capital market development								
Domestic bond market to equity market capitalization	5	15	17	40	5	32	33	24
Domestic public bonds outstanding to GDP	5	24	13	39	10	21	33	33
Trading value of top 10 stocks ratio	5	29	10	34	15	20	40	27
Stock market capitalization to GDP	5	13	17	40	24	22	35	24
Stock trading value to GDP	5	32	13	40	22	23	13	32
Stock market turnover ratio	5	34	17	40	14	22	23	29
Aggregate score	**30**	**147**	**87**	**233**	**90**	**140**	**177**	**169**
Composite score (aggregate score/240)	**0.13**	**0.61**	**0.36**	**0.97**	**0.38**	**0.58**	**0.74**	**0.70**
Market concentration and competitiveness								
Herfindahl-Hirschman Index (HHI)	5	38	10	37	15	26	29	20
K-bank concentration ratio ($k = 3$), assets	5	36	10	39	15	27	28	20
K-bank concentration ratio ($k = 3$), deposits	5	35	10	40	15	29	26	20
K-bank concentration ratio ($k = 3$), loans	5	36	10	36	15	33	25	20
Private credit extended by banks to GDP	5	26	14	31	40	18	16	25
Commercial banking assets to GDP	5	17	22	35	38	32	11	20
Aggregate score	**30**	**188**	**76**	**218**	**138**	**165**	**135**	**125**
Composite score (aggregate score/240)	**0.13**	**0.78**	**0.32**	**0.91**	**0.58**	**0.69**	**0.56**	**0.52**
Payment systems development								
Notes and coins in circulation to GDP	10	31	34	18	25	7	15	40
Narrow money supply (M1) to GDP	22	35	14	23	11	30	6	40
Value of RTGS transactions to GDP	5	5	5	39	5	5	11	35
Value of retail transactions to GDP	14	5	27	37	5	5	26	32
RTGS concentration ratio	5	5	5	5	5	5	11	40
Retail payments concentration ratio	5	5	5	5	5	5	25	38
Aggregate score	**61**	**86**	**90**	**127**	**56**	**57**	**94**	**225**
Composite score (aggregate score/240)	**0.25**	**0.36**	**0.38**	**0.53**	**0.23**	**0.24**	**0.39**	**0.94**

(Table continues on next page)

Table 8.1 Five-Year Average Composite Scores on the Getting Finance Indicators for South Asian Countries, 2008 *(continued)*

Indicator	Afghanistan	Bangladesh	Bhutan	India	Maldives	Nepal	Pakistan	Sri Lanka
Savings mobilization								
Broad money supply (M2) to GDP	5	18	22	37	38	29	20	11
Real deposit interest rate	11	5	10	40	23	5	5	5
Gross domestic savings to GDP	5	30	32	35	12	15	23	22
Reserve money to total deposits	5	35	10	31	15	25	20	39
Loan to deposit ratio	38	16	37	29	9	10	25	16
Worker remittances to GDP	5	32	5	20	5	40	25	33
Aggregate score	**69**	**136**	**116**	**192**	**102**	**124**	**118**	**126**
Composite score (aggregate score/240)	**0.29**	**0.57**	**0.48**	**0.80**	**0.43**	**0.52**	**0.49**	**0.53**
Corporate governance								
Ownership structure and influence of external stakeholders								
Identification of substantial majority holders	2	3	3	4	3	3	4	5
Indirect and beneficial ownership	3	2	2	4	5	1	4	4
Investor rights								
Shareholder meetings and voting procedures	3	4	3	5	2	4	5	4
Basic ownership rights	3	3	2	3	3	2	3	2
Transparency and disclosure								
Adherence to internationally accepted accounting standards	4	4	4	4	2	4	5	5
Independent internal and external auditors and audit committee	3	4	4	5	1	4	5	4
Board structure and effectiveness								
Role and effectiveness	5	5	3	4	4	4	5	5
Compensation	3	2	2	4	2	5	4	3
Aggregate score	**25**	**28**	**24**	**31**	**21**	**27**	**35**	**31**
Composite score (aggregate score/40)	**0.63**	**0.71**	**0.60**	**0.78**	**0.54**	**0.68**	**0.87**	**0.78**

Source: Authors' calculations based on data from appendixes 2 and 4.
Note: See appendix 6 for annual rankings and underlying scores by dimension.

9

Major Policy Developments in the Prudential Regulations of South Asia, 2007–08

In recent years stewardship of the global financial system was crippled by banks' excessive risk taking and profit seeking; by failures in their corporate governance, due diligence, and risk management; and by gaps in regulatory and supervisory regimes (eStandards Forum 2009a). The global financial crisis to which all this led underscored the importance of prudential regulations in the stability of financial systems. Supervisory authorities in South Asia have been updating their legal and regulatory frameworks for the banking sector over the past years. These efforts have led to improvements, though progress is still needed in many areas.

This chapter summarizes major policy developments in prudential regulations in 2007 and 2008 (and, where information was available, in 2009) for each country in the region along with other policy developments and legislative actions relevant to the banking sector. Since Afghanistan, Bhutan, and Maldives are included for the first time in this edition, the chapter also includes some information for earlier years for these three countries. The information was collected from the regulatory authorities of the eight countries, their official Web sites, and other sources.[1]

Afghanistan

Prudential Regulations

Prudential regulations issued by Da Afghanistan Bank in recent years include the following.

2004

- **July:** Regulation on credit extended to related persons.

2005

- **February:** Regulation on open positions in foreign currencies.
- **February:** Regulation on enforcement.
- **February:** Regulation on corporate governance.

- **February:** Regulation on acquiring a participation that yields a qualifying holding or that increases a qualifying holding above certain threshold limits.

2006

- **March:** Regulation on capital adequacy.
- **March:** Regulation on liquidity measurement and management.
- **June:** Regulation on the responsibilities of financial institutions in the fight against money laundering and terrorist financing.
- **September:** Responsibilities of Financial Institutions under the Laws on Combating of Financing of Terrorism and Anti-Money-Laundering and Proceeds of Crime.
- **October:** Regulation on asset classifications and provisioning.
- **October:** Procurement regulation.

2008

- **February:** Regulation on prohibited and authorized activities.
- **February:** Regulation on asset risk diversification and limitations on large exposures of banking organizations (latest amendment).
- **February:** Regulation for licensing and permitting of commercial banks.
- **July:** Human Resources Regulation.

Other Policy Developments

Other policy developments relevant to the banking sector in Afghanistan in recent years include issuance of the following regulations.

2005

- **January:** Regulation on defining operating rules for the clearing and settlement of interbank payments in Afghanistan.
- **December:** Reserve requirement for monetary policy purposes: revised regulation.

2006

- **March:** Standing Facilities Regulation: Administrative Instructions.
- **June:** Regulation for the Protection of the Payment System.
- **July:** Regulation on the licensing, regulation, and supervision of depository microfinance institutions.

2007

- **February:** Capital Note Issuance and Auction Regulations.

2008

- **March:** Regulation to establish a basic framework for secondary market transactions in capital notes issued by Da Afghanistan Bank.
- **July:** Regulation on the licensing, regulation, and supervision of money service providers.
- **July:** Regulation on the licensing, regulation, and supervision of foreign exchange dealers.

2009

- **August:** Amendments to the Money Service Providers Regulation to Extend Regulatory Oversight to E-Money Institutions.

Legislation Enacted

Legislation relevant to the banking sector enacted in Afghanistan in recent years includes the following laws.

2003

- **July:** The Afghanistan Bank Law–Law of Da Afghanistan Bank.
- **July:** Law of Banking in Afghanistan.

2004

- **September:** The Law of Anti-Money-Laundering and Proceeds of Crime.

2005

- **April:** Insurance Law of 1989 (amended by Presidential Decree).

2007

- **February:** Law for Mortgage on Immovable Property in Banking Transactions (Amendment).
- **February:** Leasing Law.
- **February:** Negotiable Instruments Law.

2008

- **March:** Law for Secured Transaction on Movable Property in Banking Transactions (Amendment).
- **June:** Insurance Law (Amendment).
- **September:** Afghanistan Law on Combating the Financing of Terrorism.

Bangladesh

Prudential Regulations

Bangladesh Bank (BB) issued a range of prudential guidelines in 2007–09, including the following.

2007

- **February:** Risk weights applicable under balance sheet items: a risk weight of 20 percent for claims on AAA-rated multilateral development banks is included under "Advances (other financial institutions)."
- **February:** As per clause 5(I) of the Bank Deposit Insurance Act, 2000, risk-based premium rates (as per the guideline issued) will be applicable for all scheduled banks in the country. This instruction is effective from the half year January–June 2007.
- **March:** Guidelines were issued for compliance of financial institutions in writing off loans and leases.
- **March:** Uniform guidelines were issued for compliance of banks and financial institutions with a view to structuring and disciplining the process of mergers and amalgamations of banking companies and financial institutions.

- **March:** Guidelines were issued for financial institutions with a view to bringing discipline in loan and lease rescheduling.
- **May:** With a view to strengthening the capital base of banks and making them prepare for the implementation of the Basel II accord, banks are required to maintain a capital to risk-weighted assets ratio of 10 percent at a minimum, with core capital not less than 5 percent. This requirement was to be achieved by December 31, 2007.
- **September:** Guidelines were issued for banks' compliance regarding the appointment of consultants.
- **September:** Guidelines were issued regarding the responsibility and accountability of the board of directors, chairman of the board, and chief executive or managing director of financial institutions.
- **September:** Instructions were issued for opening and maintaining the accounts of Politically Exposed Persons by the power conferred under the Money Laundering Prevention Act, 2002 (Act No. 7 of 2002), in compliance with the United Nations Convention against Corruption and recommendation no. 6 of the Financial Action Task Force for all scheduled banks and financial institutions to follow properly.
- **November:** The paid-up capital and statutory capital of all bank companies was raised to a minimum of Tk 2 billion.

2008

- **January:** Any bank company can invest a maximum of 10 percent of its total capital in bonds or debentures of any company that are approved by the Securities and Exchange Commission.
- **February:** Credit norms for the Agricultural and Rural Credit Program were relaxed because of an uptrend in the price of agricultural inputs.
- **February:** A guideline was issued, to be followed by all resident individuals and organizations, requiring the permission of BB under section 18A of Foreign Exchange Regulation Act, 1947, before commencing business or receiving any proposal to act as an agent (as satellite channel distributor) of foreign principals.
- **March:** Policy on Capital Adequacy of Banks: Revaluation reserves against held-to-maturity securities (up to 50 percent of the revaluation reserves) were added to the components of supplementary capital. In addition, "hedging the price risk of commodity transactions" was included in short-term, self-liquidating trade-related contingencies.
- **March:** With a view to reducing the recent upward trend in the market price of powdered milk and ensuring sufficient supply of powdered milk in the market, the interest rate on import finance of powdered milk was temporarily fixed at 12 percent.
- **April:** Guidelines were issued for the compliance of financial institutions at the time of appointment of consultants.
- **April:** Banks were advised to repay loans taken under the Export Development Fund with interest by the time due or, if necessary, to submit an application before the time due for extending the time. If a bank fails to repay amounts overdue on loans by the time they are due or is unable to inform the Forex

Reserve and Treasury Management Department of BB earlier regarding its inability to do so, the principal amount with interest will be recovered by debiting the foreign currency clearing account with BB on the next working day of overdue. This instruction is in effect from May 4, 2008.

- **May:** Banking Regulation and Policy Department circular no. 10 dated November 25, 2002, was revised and some amendments were made to cover "hedging the price risk of commodity transactions."
- **June:** BB issued a circular on mainstreaming corporate social responsibility with a strategic guideline for banks and financial institutions in Bangladesh.
- **June:** A uniform açcount opening and "know your customer" profile form for all banks was introduced. All banks were asked to implement the form by December 31, 2008.
- **July:** A notification was issued by BB to the effect that it would follow the following guidelines at the time of appointment of directors to the board of a bank company from the depositors under subclause 15(5) of the Bank Company Act, 1991:

  Fit and Proper

  - The person concerned will be a depositor of the bank company. During the time of holding the post of director, he or she must continue to maintain a deposit account with the bank.
  - He or she must have at least a bachelor's degree from a recognized university.
  - Depositors who have higher educational qualifications in economics, trade, business administration, and the like, or who have professional experience in industrial business, will be given priority at the time of appointment as director.
  - He or she cannot be a director, officer, staff member, or adviser of any bank company, financial institution, insurance company, or stock exchange.
  - He or she or his or her family members cannot hold more than 1 percent of deposits or paid-up capital in aggregate of the concerned bank company.
  - He or she cannot keep any business or profit-motive relationship with the bank company except for maintaining a deposit account or holding not more than 1 percent of paid-up capital.
  - He or she cannot be involved in any activity of a political party.
  - He or she cannot be a loan, tax, or bill defaulter.
  - Fit-and-proper test criteria issued by BB from time to time will be applicable for directors appointed from depositors.

  Selection Procedure

  - The board of directors of the concerned bank company will send a proposal to BB to appoint two directors from the depositors on the basis of the fit-and-proper test criteria above.
  - The term of directors selected from the depositors will be three years.
  - Any director selected from the depositors cannot hold the post for more than two terms or six years at a time.

Others

- Directors appointed from the depositors will be in addition to the 13 directors mentioned in subclause 15(6) of the Bank Company Act, 1991.

- **August:** BB directives were issued for banks, financial institutions, insurance companies, and all money changers for compliance with the provisions contained in the Money Laundering Prevention Ordinance, 2008, and Anti-Terrorism Ordinance, 2008.
- **September:** Guidelines on recognition of eligible external credit assessment institutions (ECAIs) were issued by BB. Now, under the Standardized Approach of the Risk-Based Capital Adequacy Framework (Basel II), a credit rating is to be determined on the basis of a risk profile assessed by the ECAIs duly recognized by BB. All scheduled banks are required to nominate a recognized ECAI for their own as well as their counterparty credit rating. BB completes the recognition process when applications are obtained from interested credit rating agencies.
- **October:** As a result of an amendment to Import Policy Order 2006-2009, it was decided to make changes in Regulation 21 of Prudential Regulations for Consumer Financing, which now stands as follows: "The banks desirous of financing the purchase of used cars shall prepare uniform guidelines for determining the value of the used vehicles. However, in no case shall the bank finance cars older than 6 (six) years."

2009

- **January:** In pursuance of the objectives of monetary policy, all scheduled banks of BB have been required to maintain the cash reserve requirement at 5 percent of their total demand and time liabilities effective from October 1, 2005. Banks are also required to maintain the cash reserve requirement at the rate of 5 percent daily on a biweekly average basis, subject to the condition that the rate should not be less than 4 percent on any day. After review of the present situation of the monetary policy, it was decided that the cash reserve requirement would remain unchanged at the rate of 5 percent, with the condition that the rate should not be less than 4.5 percent on any day. This instruction is in effect from March 1, 2009.
- **January:** A draft regulation was issued to accommodate new products and instruments of payment being used in modern payment systems.
- **January:** Some instructions were given regarding revaluation on the basis of marking to market of treasury bills and bonds held by banking companies.
- **February:** A guideline was issued by BB to banks about the requirement they must meet to participate in and interface with the Automated Cheque Processing System (BACPS), as part of the Bangladesh Automated Clearing House implementation.
- **March:** A circular was issued unifying all earlier directives issued by BB regarding the imposition of a penalty interest rate for a shortfall by banks in maintaining the cash reserve requirement.
- **April:** Considering the existing inflation rate and global economic situation, the maximum rate of interest on agricultural loans, term loans and working capital for large and medium-scale industry, housing sector loans, and trade financing was fixed at 13 percent. Directives were issued to all scheduled banks.

- **April:** Guidelines were issued regarding the mapping of external credit assessment institutions and the rating with BB Rating Grade. Credit Rating Information and Services Ltd. and Credit Rating Agency of Bangladesh Ltd. have been recognized as eligible external credit assessment institutions.
- **May:** Instructions were issued referring to the previously issued circular about restrictions in respect of responsibilities and accountabilities of the board of directors and the chief executive officers of private banks.
- **June:** BB set a maximum interest rate of 13 percent for bank financing to non-bank financial institutions.
- **July:** BB released its Monetary Policy Statement on July 19 for July–December 2009. It forecast that the economy would grow at 6 percent in fiscal 2009/10 despite the global downturn that weighed on exports.[2]
- **July:** BB announced its Annual Agriculture and Rural Credit Policy FY2009/10 with the highest target ever. The loan disbursement target was set at Tk 115.13 billion, marking 22.74 percent growth over that of the previous fiscal year.
- **July:** A separate guideline was issued on "Risk Factors Relating to Islamic Mode of Investment" within the purview of guidelines on "Risk-Based Capital Adequacy (RBCA) for Banks" issued on December 31, 2008.

Other Policy Developments

Other policy developments relevant to the banking sector in Bangladesh in 2007–08 include the following.

2007

- **January:** As per the appeal of BB, the government declared a moratorium on the activities of The Oriental Bank Limited for six months effective from January 25, 2007, except for certain important activities.
- **February:** With a view to ensuring balanced and organized industrial development in the country, a decision was made to allocate a minimum 10 percent of the total funds for small and medium-size enterprises (SMEs) provided by BB for women entrepreneurs of SMEs to provide more institutional credit facilities on easy terms and conditions.
- **July:** BB undertook the Refinance Scheme for Housing to provide a refinancing facility to banks and financial institutions against loans provided to buy or build new apartments for own residential purposes.
- **August:** A decision was made to the effect that, if flood-affected farmers were loan defaulters, credit facilities would be provided to them through loan rescheduling.
- **October:** The credit facility given under the Export Development Fund was raised from US$100 million to US$150 million to facilitate the ongoing trend of expansion and development of export-oriented industry in the country.
- **October:** Policy guidelines for establishing drawing arrangements by banks in Bangladesh with exchange houses abroad were put in place from October 9, 2007.
- **December:** On the basis of a quantitative impact study conducted by BB to assess the readiness of banks for implementing the Basel II Capital Accord

(scheduled to be implemented from early 2009), an action plan/road map was finalized and approved by the competent authority and sent to banks for gearing up efforts for implementing Basel II.

2008

- **April:** To resume the banking business of The Oriental Bank Ltd. (presently ICB–Islamic Bank Limited), the moratorium order issued by the government was rescinded with effect from May 5, 2008, at the request of BB for the implementation of The Oriental Bank Ltd. (Reconstruction) Scheme, 2007.
- **May:** With a view to encouraging transactions in government securities after issuance and to establishing a more effective secondary market, it was decided to make some amendments in the guidelines regarding revaluation of treasury bills and bonds on the basis of marking to market. For this purpose, detailed revised guidelines were issued through a Department of Off-Site Supervision circular letter no. 05, dated May 26, 2008. The revised guidelines are in effect from July 1, 2008.
- **May:** BB made a decision in principle to grant permission to open SME Service Centers. Scheduled banks operating in Bangladesh were advised to apply to the Banking Regulation and Policy Department of BB to open a limited number of SME Service Centers only in areas of Bangladesh where no branches of the same bank exist at present.
- **June:** With a view to making secondary trading of government securities competitive, some amendments were made in the guidelines issued earlier regarding provision of liquidity facility to primary dealers.
- **June:** For the necessity of strengthening, encouraging, and expanding the SME sector, the funding for the Refinance Scheme for the Small Enterprise Sector was raised from Tk 3 billion to Tk 5 billion with effect from June 12, 2008.
- **July:** Credit norms for different crops were formulated by the Agricultural Credit and Special Programs Department of BB for fiscal 2008/09. Banks may increase or decrease the loan amount up to a maximum 10 percent on the basis of actual credit demand.
- **August:** With a view to encouraging export trade, it was decided to provide export subsidy and cash incentives for some export goods in fiscal 2008/09 as in preceding years. However, no subsidy or cash incentives were to be provided against export of tobacco. According to this decision, export subsidy and cash incentives were to be provided at a rate of up to 5–20 percent for different export commodities.
- **September:** In order to ensure food security by enhancing agricultural production through increasing disbursement of agricultural loans and advances, the following decisions were made:
  - All scheduled banks (including private and foreign banks) working in Bangladesh would have to participate in agricultural credit activities.
  - Every bank would fix a portion of its total loan portfolio for agricultural credit. At the beginning of the fiscal year banks would fix a realistic target and inform BB. Banks would ensure proper monitoring to achieve their annual target for agricultural lending.
  - Banks that did not fix an agricultural credit disbursement target for the fiscal year 2008/09 were to fix it immediately and subsequently inform BB.

- If BB considered the target fixed by a bank to be not realistic, BB would give direction to the bank concerned for refixing the target.
- Agricultural credit should be disbursed following an "area approach" by giving importance to the cultivation of crops based on region and type of crops, that is, which region is suitable for cultivation of a particular crop.
- Banks that do not have branches in rural areas or do not have an adequate number of branches would disburse agricultural credit through links with nongovernmental organizations.

- **September:** For effective agricultural credit operation—that is, to make agricultural credit easier and hassle free for the farmers and to ensure a continuous flow of agricultural credit at the farmer level—BB introduced the Revolving Crop Credit Limit System of three years' tenure. Under this system, the following guidelines are to be followed:
  - Farmers engaged in continuous crop production will be allowed a Revolving Crop Credit Limit System facility.
  - After realization of a previous loan (principal and interest accrued thereon), the farmer will get a further loan or renewal without redocumentation.
  - All paperwork will be simplified as much as possible.
  - Loan sanctioning power should be delegated to the branch manager.
  - Once the disbursement is made, any changes in production planning and demand for credit would require further approval from the bank.
  - The details of the new scheme, including credit limits, mortgage, and interest rate, will be determined by the bank itself.
  - Farmers will be encouraged to receive loans under this system.
  - Banks will closely monitor to ensure that the farmers are getting the facilities.
- **September:** With a view to making the foreign exchange transaction system up to date and to clarify some existing instructions, several amendments were made in the Guidelines for Foreign Exchange Transactions 1996 (vol. 1).
- **September:** With a view to liberalizing the payment system through international cards, it was decided that international cards (debit, credit, or prepaid, as the case may be) may also be issued against foreign exchange entitlements fixed by the Ministry of Finance or competent authority for official or semiofficial visits abroad by officials of the government, autonomous or semiautonomous institutions, and the like; per diem foreign exchange entitlements for private sector participants attending seminars, conferences, or workshops abroad arranged by recognized international bodies; balances held in private foreign currency accounts; personal entitlements fixed by the government of Bangladesh in each year for pilgrims intending to perform Hajj; and payment of mobile phone roaming bills.
- **October:** With a view to ensuring food security and simplifying the agricultural credit disbursement system in favor of sharecroppers, and in consideration of their important contribution to agricultural development and to the national economy, guidelines were issued that include the following:
  - Sharecroppers who are directly involved in agricultural production will be eligible for obtaining agricultural credit under these guidelines.

  - Sharecroppers shall be permanent residents of the jurisdiction under the bank branch disbursing agricultural credit.
  - Sharecroppers shall hold a national identification card or farmers' identification card.
  - The bank branch disbursing agricultural credit is responsible for identifying genuine sharecroppers.
- **October:** It was decided by the board of directors of the Asian Clearing Union that with effect from January 1, 2009, transactions among the union's member countries may also be settled in euros. Some instructions were given in this regard to be followed by authorized dealers.
- **November:** With a view to bringing dynamism to economic activities and generating employment opportunities by expanding the broadband and information technology sectors, banks were advised to finance entrepreneurs in these sectors from the SME sector.
- **December:** To comply with international best practices, make bank capital more risk sensitive, and build a banking industry that is more shock absorbent and stable, a revised regulatory capital framework, Risk-Based Capital Adequacy for Banks, in line with Basel II, was devised and sent to banks for implementation from January 2009. Along with the existing capital adequacy rules and reporting to BB, banks will start quarterly reporting as per the reporting format enclosed in the guidelines.

Legislation Enacted

Legislation relevant to the banking sector enacted in Bangladesh in 2007–08 includes the following.

2007

- **July:** Money Laundering Prevention (Amendment) Ordinance, 2007, was promulgated through the *Bangladesh Gazette* on July 30, 2007, making a partial amendment of the Money Laundering Prevention Act, 2002 (Act No. 7 of 2002).

2008

- **April:** Money Laundering Prevention Ordinance, 2008 (Ordinance No. 12 of 2008), was promulgated on April 15, 2008, repealing the Money Laundering Prevention Act, 2002 (Act No. 7 of 2002).
- **June:** Anti-Terrorism Ordinance, 2008 (Ordinance No. 28 of 2008), was promulgated on June 11, 2008, to prevent certain terrorist acts and to formulate regulations regarding effective punishment and related matters.

Bhutan

Prudential Regulations

Actions relating to prudential regulations in Bhutan in recent years include the following.

2002

- The Financial Institutions Supervision Division of the Royal Monetary Authority (RMA) issued a number of prudential regulations in 2002:
  - Regulations on Directors and Chief Executives of Financial Institutions (RMA/PR-1/2002).
  - Regulations on Related-Party Transactions (RMA/PR-2/2002).
  - Regulations on the Code of Ethics for Directors and Employees of Financial Institutions (RMA/PR-3/2002).
  - Regulations on Shares Trading (RMA/PR-4/2002).
  - Regulations on Human Resources Development Fund (RMA/PR-5/2002).
  - Regulations on Submission of Annual Accounts (RMA/PR-6/2002).
  - Regulations on Capital Requirements (RMA/PR-7/2002).
  - Regulations on Liquidity Requirements (RMA/PR-8/2002).
  - Regulations on Credit Concentration to Borrowers (RMA/PR-9/2002).
  - Regulations on Asset Classifications (RMA/PR-10/2002).
  - Regulations on Borrower Information (RMA/PR-11/2002).
  - Regulations on Revaluation and Appropriation of Reserves (RMA/PR-12/2002).
  - Regulations on Dividends and Reserves (RMA/PR-13/2002).
  - Regulations on Collateral and Others (RMA/PR-14/2002).
  - Regulations on Share Capital Ownership of Banks and Nonbank Financial Institutions (RMA/PR-15/2002).
  - Regulations on Investment in Equity (RMA/PR-16/2002).
  - Regulations on Establishment of Branches, Agencies, and Other Such Offices of Financial Institutions (RMA/PR-17/2002).
  - Regulations on Money Laundering (RMA/PR-18/2002).
  - Regulations on On-Site Examinations of Financial Institutions (RMA/PR-19/2002).
  - Reporting Requirements (RMA/PR-20/2002).
  - Guidelines for Compliance Officer (RMA/PR-21/2002).
  - Regulations on Penalty for Noncompliance (RMA/PR-22/2002).
- The RMA also issued regulations on the establishment of commercial banks in Bhutan.

2007

- Revisions to minimum capital requirements were issued.
- Revisions to provisioning rates were issued.
- **September:** Special Schemes forms were amended.

2008

- **January:** The limit on commercial bank holdings of convertible currency was set at US$10 million.
- **February:** Rupee management.
- **March:** An amendment to Section 7.2 and Section 9.4 of Prudential Regulations 2002 was issued.

- **August:** A notification was issued on the cash reserve ratio.
- **December:** Information on check-clearing operation in line with banks' year-end closing.
- The RMA gave an "in-principle approval" to two new financial service providers and one existing development finance corporation to carry out banking activities.

Pending

- Implementation of clearing hours.
- Closing of Samdruqionskhar Regional Clearing House.
- Final notice on discontinuation of non-MICR (magnetic ink character recognition) checks.
- Reassignment of bank branches under Samdrupjongkhar Regional Clearing House to different regional clearing houses.
- **September 2009:** The Credit Information Bureau was launched.

Other Policy Developments

Other policy developments relevant to the banking sector in Bhutan include the following.

- The RMA issued licensing regulations for the establishment of an insurance business in Bhutan.

2007

- **March:** The National Pension and Provident Fund formally came under the purview of the RMA.
- **March:** The RMA was appointed the implementing agency for the activity "Strengthening the Financial Sector through Information Technology Investments" under the World Bank Private Sector Development Project.
- In line with the objective of promoting the development of the financial sector in the country, the RMA granted approval to Bhutan National Bank Limited to open branches in Wangdue and Bumthang.

2008

- The RMA issued Note Refund Rule 2008.

2009

- **August:** The RMA licensed Bhutan Insurance Limited to engage in the general insurance business.
- The RMA granted approval to Bhutan Development Finance Corporation to open branches in Dorokha and Nganglam.
- The RMA granted approval to Royal Insurance Corporation of Bhutan to open an extension office at Lobeysa, Punakha.
- Drafting of rules and regulations for the Credit Information Bureau.

Legislation Enacted or Pending

Legislation relevant to the banking sector enacted or pending in Bhutan includes the following.

Enacted

- The Royal Monetary Authority of Bhutan Act, 1982.
- Financial Institutions Act of Bhutan, 1992.
- Foreign Exchange Regulations of Bhutan, 1997.
- Bankruptcy Act of the Kingdom of Bhutan, 1999.
- Movable and Immovable Property Act of the Kingdom of Bhutan, 1999: An act relating to loans, mortgages, and other security interests in movable and immovable property.
- Royal Monetary Authority Bylaws, 2000.
- The Negotiable Instruments Act of the Kingdom of Bhutan, 2000.
- The Evidence Act of Bhutan, 2005.

Pending

- Financial Services Act, in draft form to be passed by the National Assembly.
- Proposed Bylaws for the Bhutan Electronic Clearing House, under development.

India

Prudential Regulations

The Reserve Bank of India (RBI) issued many circulars in 2007–09. The following are actions relating to some of the most important ones.

2007

- **February:** The RBI advised banks to formulate an appropriate plan of action on corporate social responsibility with the aim of raising the level of awareness and focusing the attention of banks on the issue; and to start nonfinancial reporting along with their annual accounts, which will be used to audit their initiatives toward corporate social responsibility. Such reporting will cover the work done by banks toward the social, economic, and environmental betterment of society.
- **March:** The RBI issued detailed guidelines stipulating, among other things, that floating provisions can be used only for contingencies under extraordinary circumstances for making specific provisions in impaired accounts. Such extraordinary circumstances were illustrated in the guidelines.
- **April:** Comprehensive guidelines on derivatives were issued to all scheduled commercial banks.
- **April:** The definition of micro, small, and medium-size enterprises engaged in manufacturing or production and providing or rendering of services was modified, and the new definition was required to be implemented by banks along with other policy measures, with immediate effect.
- **April:** The cash reserve ratio was increased by 50 basis points of net demand and time liabilities in two stages to 6.25 percent and 6.50 percent, respectively, effective from the fortnights beginning April 14, 2007, and April 28, 2007. However, the effective cash reserve ratio maintained by scheduled commercial banks on total demand and time liabilities was not to be less than 3.0 percent,

as stipulated under the RBI Act, 1934. With effect from the fortnight beginning April 14, 2007, scheduled commercial banks were to be paid interest at the rate of 0.50 percent per annum on eligible cash balances maintained with the RBI under the cash reserve ratio requirement.

- **April:** The RBI, after due consultation with market players and on the basis of feedback received on its second draft, issued guidelines for implementation of the new capital adequacy framework.
- **April:** Guidelines were issued to streamline the accounting for amortization of the premium for banks' "held to maturity" securities.
- **May:** A modification was made to risk weights for housing loans against the mortgage of residential housing properties and banks' investments in mortgage-backed securities that were backed by housing loans.
- **May:** Guidelines on the purchase and sale of nonperforming assets were issued.
- **June:** Draft guidelines on restructuring or rescheduling of dues were issued to all scheduled commercial banks (excluding regional rural banks and local area banks).
- **June:** Guidelines on stress testing were issued.
- **July:** A master circular was issued on prudential norms for classification, valuation, and operation of investment portfolios by banks.
- **August:** Final guidelines on prudential norms for off–balance sheet exposures of banks were issued to all scheduled commercial banks.
- **August:** Directives were issued covering the framework for the trading of currency futures in recognized exchanges.
- **October:** Commercial banks were allowed a wider choice of instruments for raising Tier 1 and Upper Tier 2 capital by issuing preference shares such as perpetual noncumulative, perpetual cumulative, redeemable noncumulative, and redeemable cumulative preference shares, subject to guidelines.
- **October:** Operating guidelines for banks relating to mobile banking transactions were issued to all scheduled commercial banks.
- **October:** Following a review of the liquidity situation, the cash reserve ratio of scheduled commercial banks was increased by 50 basis points to 7.5 percent of their net demand and time liabilities with effect from the fortnight beginning November 10, 2007.
- **October:** Guidelines on the asset and liability management system were amended.
- **October:** Guidelines on the purchase and sale of nonperforming assets were issued.
- **November:** The RBI laid out specific "fit and proper" criteria to be fulfilled by the persons elected as directors on the boards of nationalized banks under the provisions of Section 9(3)(i) of Banking Companies (Acquisition and Transfer of Undertakings) Act, 1970/80.
- **November:** To contain the equity funding risk that banks face (in instances where promoters bring in equity funds proportionate to the debt financing by banks), banks were advised to have a clear policy on the debt-equity ratio. Banks were also advised to ensure that the infusion of equity funds by promoters was such that the stipulated level of debt-equity ratio was maintained

at all times. Further, they were advised to adopt funding sequences so that the possibility of equity funding by banks was obviated.

- **December:** To encourage banks to increase the flow of credit to the infrastructure sector, the RBI permitted banks to invest in unrated bonds of companies engaged in infrastructure activities; such investments should be within the ceiling of 10 percent for unlisted nonstatutory liquidity ratio securities.
- **December:** The Payment and Settlement Systems Act, 2007, was notified.

2008

- **January:** All education loans were classified as nonconsumer credit for the purpose of capital adequacy norms. Accordingly, the risk weight applicable to education loans would be 100 percent and 75 percent under the Basel I and Basel II frameworks, respectively.
- **February:** The RBI issued revised Know Your Customer, Anti-Money-Laundering, and Combating Financing of Terrorism guidelines to banks.
- **March:** With effect from April 1, 2008, all payment transactions of Rs 1 crore (Rs 10 million) and above between RBI-regulated entities such as banks, primary dealers, and nonbanking financial companies were required to be routed through electronic payment mechanisms. Furthermore, all payments of Rs 1 crore and above in RBI-regulated markets, such as the money market, government securities market, and foreign exchange market, would also be routed through electronic payment mechanisms with effect from April 1, 2008.
- **March:** Effective March 31, 2008, amendments to the capital adequacy framework were announced with respect to innovative perpetual debt instruments, banks' aggregate investment in all types of instruments, and changes in risk weights on direct loan, credit, and overdraft exposure to state governments, investment in state government securities, and claims guaranteed by state governments.
- **March:** Banks were mandated to provide cost-free access to automated teller machines (ATMs) installed anywhere in the country to noncustomers effective April 1, 2009.
- **March:** With the objective of ensuring that banks have adequate capital to support all the risks in their business as well as encouraging them to develop and use better risk management techniques for monitoring and managing their risks, the RBI issued guidelines providing only broad principles to be followed by banks in developing their internal capital adequacy assessment process. The banks are advised to develop and put in place, with the approval of their board, an internal capital adequacy assessment process commensurate with their size, level of complexity, risk profile, and scope of operations.
- **April:** The cash reserve ratio was increased in two stages of 25 basis points each, to 7.75 percent with effect from the fortnight beginning April 26, 2008, and to 8.00 percent with effect from the fortnight beginning May 10, 2008.
- **April:** The cash reserve ratio was increased by 25 basis points to 8.25 percent with effect from the fortnight beginning May 24, 2008.
- **May:** The RBI issued guidelines on the treatment of banks' investments in subsidiaries or associates and of the subsidiaries' or associates' investments in parent banks in the context of the Basel I and Basel II frameworks.

- **May:** The risk weight for claims secured by residential property was changed.
- **June:** The cash reserve ratio was increased by 50 basis points in two stages, to 8.5 percent and 8.75 percent, with effect from the fortnights beginning July 5, 2008, and July 19, 2008, respectively.
- **June:** The repurchase (repo) rate was increased by 25 basis points to 8.0 percent with effect from June 12, 2008.
- **June:** The repo rate was increased by 50 basis points to 8.5 percent with effect from June 25, 2008.
- **June:** The threshold for mandatory routing through electronic payment systems of all payment transactions between RBI-regulated entities in RBI-regulated markets was reduced to Rs 10 lakh (Rs 1 million) with effect from August 1, 2008.
- **July:** The cash reserve ratio was increased by 25 basis points to 9.0 percent with effect from the fortnight beginning August 30, 2008.
- **July:** The repo rate was increased by 50 basis points to 9.0 percent effective from July 30, 2008.
- **August:** Prudential guidelines on restructuring of advances by banks were issued.
- **August:** The RBI issued guidelines on accounting for off–balance sheet credit exposures arising on account of interest rate and foreign exchange derivative transactions and gold, using the "current exposure method."
- **August:** The Payment and Settlement Systems Act, 2007 came into effect.
- **September:** Guidelines were issued on the asset classification status of overdue payments in respect of derivative transactions and restructuring of derivative contracts.
- **September:** The cash reserve ratio was reduced by 150 basis points to 7.5 percent with effect from the fortnight beginning October 11, 2008.
- **September:** The cash reserve ratio was further reduced by 100 basis points to 6.50 percent with effect from the fortnight beginning October 11, 2008.
- **September:** The repo rate was cut by 100 basis points to 8.0 percent with effect from October 20, 2008.
- **October:** The RBI issued guidelines permitting the applicability of the principle of borrower-wise asset classification to be confined to only the overdues arising from forward contracts and plain-vanilla swaps and options. The classification of all other assets of such clients will, however, continue to be governed by the extant income recognition and asset classification norms.
- **November:** Prudential norms (provisioning norms and risk weights) were amended as a countercyclical measure.
- **November:** Prudential guidelines on restructuring of advances by banks were issued.
- **November:** The statutory liquidity ratio was reduced by 100 basis points to 24.0 percent of net demand and time liabilities, with effect from the fortnight beginning November 8, 2008.
- **November:** The cash reserve ratio was reduced by 100 basis points, by 50 basis points to 6.0 percent and a further 50 basis points to 5.5 percent, with effect from the fortnights beginning October 25, 2008, and November 8, 2008, respectively.

- **November:** The repo rate was cut by 50 basis points to 7.5 percent with effect from November 3, 2008.
- **December:** The repo rate was cut by 100 basis points to 6.5 percent, and the reverse repo rate by 100 basis points to 5.0 percent, with effect from December 8, 2008.

2009

- **January:** The repo rate was cut by 100 basis points to 5.5 percent, and the reverse repo rate by 100 basis points to 4.0 percent, with effect from January 2, 2009.
- **January:** The cash reserve ratio was further reduced by 50 basis points to 5.0 percent with effect from the fortnight beginning January 17, 2009.
- **February:** Prudential guidelines on restructuring advances by banks were issued.
- **March:** The repo rate was cut by 50 basis points to 5.0 percent, and the reverse repo rate by 50 basis points to 3.5 percent, with effect from March 24, 2009.
- **April:** The repo rate was cut by 25 basis points to 4.75 percent, and the reverse repo rate by 25 basis points to 3.25 percent, with effect from April 21, 2009.
- **May:** Revised guidelines were issued to banks to address credit risk exposures to the central counterparties on account of derivatives trading and securities financing transactions.
- **May:** To avoid significant systemic implications and impeding the development of a genuine corporate debt market, banks were advised not to provide guarantees or equivalent commitments for issuance of bonds or debt instruments on behalf of corporate entities with respect to nonconvertible debentures or any debt instrument issued by such entities.
- **June:** The RBI issued guidelines on additional provisions for nonperforming assets at higher than prescribed rates; excess provisions on the sale of nonperforming assets; and provisions for diminution of the fair value of restructured advances, with respect to both standard assets and nonperforming assets.
- **July:** The RBI reiterated the need for all participants to have necessary backup sites for their critical payment systems that interact with the systems at its data centers and to participate in the disaster recovery drills as and when requested by the RBI.
- **August:** RBI guidelines permit banks to continue to have the choice between deducting their existing floating provisions from gross nonperforming assets to arrive at net nonperforming assets or using such floating provisions as part of Tier 2 capital subject to the overall ceiling of 1.25 percent of total risk-weighted assets.
- **September:** Guidelines were issued on the classification of exposures as commercial real estate exposures.

Other Policy Developments

Other policy developments relevant to the banking sector in India in 2007–09 include the following.

2007

- **June:** With a view to providing greater flexibility to residents with overseas direct investments (in equity and loans), banks are permitted to allow the cancellation of forward contracts entered into by residents for overseas direct investments (in equity and loans) for hedging the exchange risk. Further, 50 percent of the canceled contracts may be allowed to be rebooked.

- **October:** As part of anti-money-laundering guidelines, limits for payments in cash by foreign visitors and nonresident Indians were raised from US$2,000 to US$3,000. Further, to establish a relationship with a business entity, the PAN (permanent account number) card issued by income tax authorities is permitted to be accepted as a suitable identification document.

2008

- **February:** The check truncation system was implemented as a pilot project with the 10 banks in the National Capital Region.
- **June:** The government of India issued a set of clarifications relating to the Agricultural Debt Waiver and Debt Relief Scheme, 2008, in response to operational queries received from lending institutions.
- **July:** Operating guidelines for banks relating to mobile banking transactions in India were issued.
- **July:** All the member banks of the New Delhi Bankers' Clearing House were required to participate in the check truncation system in the National Capital Region.
- **September:** On the basis of recommendations made by a working group and feedback received, the criteria for participation in the national payment systems—real-time gross settlement (RTGS) and national electronic fund transfer (NEFT) systems—were finalized. The financial strength of an institution would be the guiding parameter for participation in national payment systems. The RTGS and NEFT systems would continue to be regulated by membership regulations, business guidelines, or procedural guidelines, which are binding on the participating members. The norms for access criteria prescribe only the standards for entry to and exit from national payment systems.
- **October:** Operating guidelines for banks relating to mobile banking transactions in India were modified.
- **December:** Draft regulatory guidelines for securitization and reconstruction companies were issued.
- **November:** Draft guidelines were issued on uniform accounting for repo and reverse repo transactions.
- **December:** Draft revised reporting procedures for foreign direct investments were issued.

2009

- **January:** Draft guidelines were issued for the issuance and operation of prepaid payment instruments in India.
- **February:** A model scheme for financial literacy and credit counseling centers supported or proposed to be supported by banks should be formulated. Banks can either individually or with pooled resources create such centers to provide credit and technological counseling to farmers to make them aware of their rights and responsibilities.
- **February:** A draft schedule was issued for the introduction of advanced approaches under the Basel II framework in India.

- **April:** The RBI mandated that member banks set up a maker-checker facility for RTGS during data entry. Further, all transactions through the RTGS system are to be digitally signed and encrypted, and banks were advised to use adequate checks and balances to maintain the two-tier security system inherent in the architecture of RTGS.
- **April:** The RBI advised banks to provide a customer receiving RTGS credit with the name of the remitter in his or her account statements or passbook. Similarly, the bank customer sending an RTGS remittance shall be provided with the name of the beneficiary in his or her account statements or passbook.
- **May:** Draft guidelines on stripping and reconstitution of government securities were issued for public comment.
- **June:** The RBI reiterated that banks and financial institutions are to ensure strict compliance with the provisions of the Credit Information Companies (Regulation) Act, 2005, which provides access to own credit reports.
- **July:** The RBI permitted cash withdrawals at point-of-sale terminals. To start with, this facility will be available for all debit cards issued in India, up to Rs 1,000 per day.
- **August:** The government of India extended the last date for payment of 75 percent of the overdue portion by the "other farmer" under the Agricultural Debt Waiver and Debt Relief Scheme, 2008, by six months, that is, up to December 31, 2009.
- **August:** In a relaxation of the mandatory instructions issued in March 2008, banks were permitted to levy service charges on noncustomers for cash withdrawals of Rs 10,000 or above on any day or if the number of transactions exceed five in a month, effective October 15, 2009.
- **August:** The RBI issued updated and consolidated instructions and directives to banks with respect to providing credit facilities to minority communities.
- **August:** Directions relating to the framework for trading of interest rate futures in recognized exchanges were issued in consultation with the Securities and Exchange Board of India, to take effect from August 28, 2009.
- **September:** The RBI permitted banks to issue subordinated debt as Tier 2 capital with call and step-up options subject to certain terms and conditions.

Legislation Enacted or Pending

Legislation relevant to the banking sector enacted or pending in India in 2007–09 includes the following.

2007

- **January:** The Banking Regulation (Amendment) Act, 2007.
- **April:** Foreign Exchange Management Act (FEMA), 1999 Current Account Transaction Rules—Amendment.
- **May:** The Securities Contracts (Regulation) Amendment Act, 2007.
- **June:** The State Bank of India (Amendment) Ordinance, 2007 (effected amendments to State Bank of India Act, 1955).
- **July:** The State Bank of India (Subsidiary Banks Laws) Amendment Act, 2007.
- **December:** Payment and Settlement Systems Act, 2007.

2008

- **December:** The Information Technology (Amendment) Act, 2008, dealing with interception of messages from mobile phones, computers, and other communication devices; blocking of Web sites in the interest of national security; measures to tackle cybercrime (fraud, phishing, terrorism, pornography); and the setting up of a cyber appellate tribunal.

2009

- **January:** Limited Liability Partnership (LLP) Act, 2008 (formation and regulation).
- **February:** The Prevention of Money Laundering (Amendment) Act, 2009, to bring certain financial institutions, such as full-fledged money changers, money transfer service providers like Western Union, and international payment gateways including Visa and MasterCard, within the reporting regime of the act. The act incorporates provisions to combat financing of terrorism and introduces a new category of offenses that have cross-border implications.

Pending

- The Micro Financial Sector (Development and Regulations) Bill, 2007 (presented to Lok Sabha).

Maldives

Prudential Regulations

The following are among the prudential regulations issued by the Maldives Monetary Authority (MMA) since 1995.

1995

- **June:** Banks are free to set interest rates on loans and deposits denominated in U.S. dollars.
- **June:** Banks are free to set interest rates on loans and advances denominated in rufiyaa provided that the rate does not exceed 20 percent per annum.

1996

- **December:** Banks must obtain prior approval from the MMA for all payments and profit repatriation to their head offices overseas.

1998

- **January:** The MMA issued Regulations for Banks and Financial Institutions (Amended).

1999

- **September:** Guidelines were issued on consumer protection in electronic fund transfers.

2001

- **August:** Banks are free to set interest rates on rufiyaa deposits.

2006

- **March:** Banks are required to formulate and adopt written policies and procedures to prevent money laundering and financing of terrorism; provide adequate staff training for effective prevention, detection, and control of possible money laundering or terrorism financing activities; accurately identify all customers and unusual and suspicious transactions; maintain customer information; appoint a compliance officer; and report all transactions that indicate possible money laundering or attempts to conceal the true identity of customers or ownership of assets to the MMA.

- **June:** The minimum reserve requirement for commercial banks was reduced to 25 percent (from 30 percent) based on the average demand and time liabilities in both rufiyaa and foreign currency. The first 15 percent of minimum reserve deposits earn no interest. Reserve requirements must be satisfied in the same currency as the underlying deposit liabilities.
- **June:** Rufiyaa balances in excess of 15 percent earn interest at 2.5 percent per annum.
- **September:** The MMA is the issuing and paying agent for treasury bills issued by the government. Banks and public enterprises may purchase such treasury bills. Treasury bills are issued at maturities of 28 days and 91 days, and interest rates (as of July 2009) are 6.0 percent for 28 days and 6.25 percent for 91 days. Treasury bills are denominated in rufiyaa, sold at a discount to par, and carry no coupon.
- **November:** A repurchase facility was introduced to replace the "Lombard Facility" as a mechanism for providing short-term rufiyaa liquidity to commercial banks. Terms are one to seven days, and the repo rate is set at a margin above the one-month treasury bill rate.

2009

- Issued in May 2009 were the following prudential regulations:
  - No. 01–2009: Capital Adequacy.
  - No. 02–2009: Single-Borrower and Large Exposure Limits.
  - No. 03–2009: Limits on Loans to Related Persons.
  - No. 04–2009: Transactions with Related Persons.
  - No. 05–2009: Asset Classification and Provisioning.
  - No. 06–2009: Interbank Exposures.
  - No. 07–2009: External Audits.
  - No. 08–2009: Publication and Disclosure.
  - No. 09–2009: Fit-and-Proper Requirements.
  - No. 10–2009: Corporate Governance.

Other Policy Developments

Other policy developments relevant to the banking sector in Maldives include the issuance of the following regulations.

- **March 1987:** Monetary regulations.
- **March 1987:** Regulations outlining arrangements for money changers.
- **September 1995:** Regulation for the replacement of damaged banknotes (amendment).
- **May 2002:** Regulations for finance leasing companies and finance leasing transactions.
- **September 2004:** Insurance industry regulations.

Legislation Enacted or Pending

Legislation relevant to the banking sector enacted or pending in Maldives includes the following.

Enacted

- **May 1981:** Maldives Monetary Authority Act, Law 6/81 (amended by Law No. 3/2007).
- **June 1985:** Law 9/85, under which banks operating in Maldives are required to pay a profit tax of 25 percent of net profits.
- **December 1993:** Mortgage Act 9/93.
- **December 1995:** Negotiable Instruments Act 16/95.
- **January 2006:** Maldives Securities Act 2/2006.

Pending

- Bill amending the Evidence Act (work in progress).
- Bill amending the Negotiable Instruments Act (proposal stage).
- Bill amending the Mortgage Act (proposal stage).
- Banking Bill (drafted).
- Bankruptcy Bill (proposal stage).
- Central Security Depository Bill (drafted).
- Trust Bill (drafted).

Nepal

Prudential Regulations

Nepal Rastra Bank (NRB) issued the following circulars in 2007–08.

2007

- **January:** Circular 19: Reopening Branches and Counters.
- **February:** Circular 20: Loans against Guarantee and Counterguarantee.
- **February:** Circular 21: Preoperational Expenditure Restriction on Deposit and Credit.
- **February:** Circular 22: Action against Willful Defaulters.
- **March:** Circular 23: Lending for Initial Public Offering (IPO) Application.
- **March:** Circular 24: Compulsory Lending to Deprived Sector.
- **April:** Circular 25: Minimum Paid-Up Capital.
- **April:** Circular 26: Prize-Based Deposit Scheme.
- **May:** Circular 27: Credit Purchase, Repurchase, and Takeover.
- **June:** Circular 28: Business, Capital Plan.
- **June:** Circular 29: Core Capital Ratio.
- **June:** Circular 30: Forms of Credit Information and Blacklisting.
- **July:** Circular 01: Priority Sector Lending Phased Out, Deprived Sector Lending Continued.
- **July:** Circular 02: Microcredit, Credit Purchase, Prize Deposit.
- **July:** Circular 03: Export Refinancing Rate, 11 Percent Capital Adequacy Ratio.

- **July:** Circular 04: Punishing Defaulters.
- **August:** Circular 05: Seizure of Passport.
- **August:** Circular 06: Withdrawal Legal Actions Deposit-Lockers.
- **August:** Circular 07: Parallel Implementation of Capital Adequacy.
- **August:** Circular 08: Recordings of Interest and Principal.
- **August:** Circular 09: Account of Royal Family Members Frozen.
- **September:** Circular 10: Recognizing Interest Incomes.
- **September:** Circular 11: Preparation of Long-Form Audit Report.
- **September:** Circular 12: Audit Report by External Auditor.
- **October:** Circular 13: Margin Lending up to 50 Percent of the Average Value of the Closing Price of the Shares for the Last 90 Days.
- **October:** Circular 14: Promoters' Shares Cross-Holding.
- **October:** Circular 15: Single Obligator Limit to Hydropower.
- **October:** Circular 16: Cash Reserve Requirement.
- **November:** Circular 17: Promoters' Shares Tradable on Nepal Stock Exchange (NEPSE).
- **November:** Circular 18: Promoters' Shares Tradable on NEPSE.
- **December:** Circular 19: Business, Capital Plan.
- **December:** Circular 20: Prohibition of TRO.
- **December:** Circular 21: Lending against Guarantee of Microfinance Institutions 0 Risk Weight.
- **December:** Circular 22: Suspension of Margin Lending.

2008

- **January:** Circular 23: Margin Lending, 50 Percent, 180 Days, 25 Percent.
- **January:** Circular 24: Divest Promoters' Shareholding to 51 Percent.
- **January:** Circular 25: G & S Loan, Insurance Agent, Software.
- **January:** Circular 26: Interest Rate for Trust Receipt Loans and Loans against Fixed Deposit Receipts.
- **February:** Circular 27: No Deprived Sector Lending via Agricultural Development Bank Nepal.
- **February:** Circular 28: Writing Off of Bad Debts.
- **February:** Circular 29: Board of Directors Chairman Only on Board; Loans against Fixed Deposit Receipts.
- **March:** Circular 30: Deprived Sector Loans, up to 25 Percent in Real Estate, No IPO Loan.
- **March:** Circular 31: Statutory Liquidity Facility to Commercial Banks Extended to 75 Percent.
- **April:** Circular 32: Cash Reserve Requirement for Constituent Assembly Election.
- **April:** Circular 33: Ownership Transfer of 1 Percent or Less of Promoters' Share without Prior Permission of NRB.
- **April:** Circular 34: Mandatory Forms for Branch Expansion.
- **April:** Circular 35: Capital Adequacy Ratio Every Time, Penalty for Exc Borrow.

- **April:** Circular 36: Capital Adequacy Ratio at Every Time from 2065 Kartik 1 (October–November 2008).
- **May:** Circular 37: "D," Invest in Promoters' Shares but Others Not.
- **June:** Circular 38: Delay in Repayment of Interest and Principal due to CA.
- **June:** Circular 39: Cash Reserve Requirement due to Republic Declaration.
- **July:** Circular 01: Clarification of Promoter Group Shares.
- **August:** Circular 02: Statistics: "D" Class.
- **August:** Circular 03: Option-Linked Scheme, Capital Structure.
- **August:** Circular 04: Lending against Coupon Securities.
- **August:** Circular 05: IPO within Two Years.
- **August:** Circular 06: New Account Opening.
- **July:** Circular 07: Updated Capital Adequacy Framework.
- **September:** Circular 08: Domestic SWIFT Transactions.
- **September:** Circular 09: Electronic Payment.
- **September:** Circular 10: Application for Merger and Upgrade.
- **September:** Circular 11: Clarification on Power Purchase Agreement in Circular no. 15-064 65.
- **September:** Circular 12: Amendment in SWIFT Timing.
- **September:** Circular 13: Excess Shareholding, Bank Guarantee, Low-Cost Housing, Microcredit.
- **October:** Circular 14: Monetary Policy Provision.
- **October:** Circular 15: Cash Reserve Requirement.
- **October:** Circular 16: Cross-Holding.
- **October:** Circular 17: Deprived Sector—Hospitals.
- **November:** Circular 18: Upgrading, Merger Policy—New.
- **November:** Circular 19: Amendment in Trust Receipt Loans.
- **November:** Circular 20: Right Share and Banking Documentation.
- **December:** Circular 21: Amendment in Right Share (Circ.14).
- **December:** Circular 22: Amendment in Circ. 35-64-65 and Interbank.
- **December:** Circular 23: Margin Lending, Amortization, Loans against Fixed Deposit Receipts, Borrowing.
- **December:** Circular 24: Productwise Credit Information.

Other Policy Developments

Other policy developments relevant to the banking sector in Nepal include issuance of the following by NRB.

2007

- NRB Document Destruction Bylaws, 2007.

2008

- Notice of expression of interest for the management team of Rastriya Banijya Bank Ltd., issued in February 2008.
- NRB Auction Directives, 2008.
- NRB Expenditure Management Bylaws, 2008.

Forthcoming in 2009

- NRB Note Printing and Coin Minting Directives, 2009.
- NRB Authority Delegation Bylaws, 2009.

Legislation Enacted

Legislation relevant to the banking sector enacted in Nepal in 2007–08 includes the following.

2007

- Banking Offense and Punishment Act, 2064 (2007).

2008

- Asset (Money) Laundering Prevention Act, 2008.
- Bank and Financial Institutions' Prompt Corrective Action Bylaws, 2008.

Pakistan

Prudential Regulations

The following circulars and circular letters were issued by the State Bank of Pakistan's (SBP) Banking Inspection (On-Site) Department, Banking Policy and Regulations Department, Banking Surveillance Department, Islamic Banking Department, Offsite Supervision and Enforcement Department, and Payment Systems Department (PSD):

2007

- **January:** Maintenance of Cash Reserve Requirement and Statutory Liquidity Requirement.
- **January:** Refund of Charges on Failed Transactions (PSD circular letter).
- **February:** Minimum Capital Requirements for Banks and Development Finance Institutions (DFIs) (circular letter).
- **March:** Revised Prudential Regulations for Microfinance Banks.
- **March:** Prudential Regulations for Corporate and SME Financing Amendment in the Definition of "Subordinated Loan" (circular letter).
- **March:** Prudential Regulation M-1: Opening of Accounts (circular letter).
- **March:** Minimum Capital Requirements: Implementation of Basel II.
- **March:** Salient Features of Products and Services (Islamic banking circular letter).
- **March:** Fit-and-Proper Criteria for Shari'ah Advisors (Islamic banking circular letter).
- **March:** Data Based on Annual Audited Accounts (Islamic banking circular letter).
- **April:** Deduction of Withholding Tax on Cash Withdrawal.
- **April:** Amendments in Regulation G-1 of Prudential Regulations.
- **April:** Fit-and-Proper Test.
- **April:** Prudential Regulations for Consumer Financing: Withdrawal of 10 Percent Limit for Housing Finance, Regulation R-17 (circular letter).
- **April:** Policy Framework in Banks and DFIs.

- **April:** Panel of Auditors, under Section 35(1) of the Banking Companies Ordinance, 1962 (2) (circular letter).
- **May:** Panel of Auditors, under Section 35(1) of the Banking Companies Ordinance, 1962 (circular letter).
- **May:** Submission of Returns to Islamic Banking Department (Islamic banking circular letter).
- **June:** Master Circular on Security Standards for Enhancement of Security of the Lockers.
- **June:** Writing Off of Irrecoverable Loans and Advances.
- **June:** Amendment in Prudential Regulations for Corporate and Commercial Banking (circular letter).
- **June:** Prudential Regulation R-5 (circular letter).
- **July:** Establishment of Financial Monitoring Unit.
- **July:** Combating Counterfeiting of Currency.
- **July:** Guidelines on Outsourcing Arrangements.
- **July:** Guidelines for Issuance of Depositary Receipts.
- **July:** Financing Facilities by State Bank: Enhancement in Repo Rate from 9.5 Percent to 10.0 Percent.
- **July:** Prudential Regulation M-1: Obtaining Computerized National Identity Card from All Bank and DFI Customers and Clients (circular letter).
- **July:** Statutory Liquidity and Cash Reserve Requirement (circular letter).
- **July:** Islamic Financial Accounting Standard-1 Murabaha (Islamic banking circular letter).
- **July:** Implementation of Countrywide Netting of Clearing Results (RTGS circular).
- **August:** Pricing of Lending Products and Loan Documentation.
- **August:** Branch Licensing Policy, Amendment.
- **August:** Amendment in Prudential Regulations for Corporate and Commercial Banking (circular letter).
- **August:** Maintenance of Cash Reserve Requirement.
- **August:** Statutory Liquidity and Cash Reserve Requirements.
- **August:** Panel of Auditors, under Section 35(1) of the Banking Companies Ordinance, 1962 (circular letter).
- **August:** Maintenance of Cash Reserve Requirement (circular letter).
- **August:** Minimum Capital Requirements for Banks and DFIs: Revised Regulatory Capital Framework under Basel II (circular letter).
- **August:** Directive under Section 41 of Banking Companies Ordinance, 1962 (Islamic banking circular letter).
- **August:** Fit-and-Proper Criteria for Shari'ah Advisors (Islamic banking circular letter).
- **August:** Settlement of Intra- and Inter-Switch ATM Transactions by Karachi Office of SBP-BSC (Banking Services Corporation) (PSD circular).
- **September:** Surrendering of Unclaimed Foreign Currency Deposits and Funds of Unclaimed Foreign Currency Instruments by Banks to the SBP under Section 31 of Banking Companies Ordinance, 1962.

- **September:** National Disaster Management Programme (circular letter).
- **September:** Prudential Regulation M-1: Opening of Accounts (circular letter).
- **September:** Amendment in Prudential Regulations (circular letter).
- **September:** Clarification in Prudential Regulations for Corporate and Commercial Banking (circular letter).
- **September:** Revaluation Surplus/Deficit.
- **September:** Guidelines for Islamic Microfinance Business (Islamic banking circular letter).
- **September:** Operational Guidelines on ATMs (PSD circular).
- **October:** Revised Branch Licensing Policy.
- **October:** Amendments in Prudential Regulations: Provisioning for Loans and Advances.
- **October:** Guidelines on Internal Credit Risk Rating Systems in Banks and DFIs.
- **October:** Submission of Returns to Islamic Banking Department (Islamic banking circular letter).
- **November:** Minimum Capital Requirements: Implementation of Basel II (circular letter).
- **November:** Information about Islamic Banking Windows (Islamic banking circular letter).
- **November:** Declaration of Weightages and Profit Sharing Ratios (Islamic banking circular letter).
- **December:** Prudential Regulation M-1: Obtaining Copies of Computerized National Identity Card from All Bank and DFI Customers and Clients (circular letter).
- **December:** Cash Reserve Requirement for Deposits Raised under FE Circular 25 of 1998.
- **December:** Compliance of Prudential Regulations on Classification and Provisioning (circular letter).
- **December:** Panel of Auditors, under Section 35(1) of the Banking Companies Ordinance, 1962 (circular letter).

2008

- **January:** Financing Facilities by State Bank: Enhancement in Repo Rate from 10.0 Percent to 10.5 Percent.
- **January:** Minimum Capital Requirements: Implementation of Basel II.
- **January:** Statutory Liquidity and Cash Reserve Requirements.
- **January:** Maintenance of Cash Reserve Requirements.
- **January:** Risk Management Guidelines for Islamic Banking Institutions (Islamic banking circular letter).
- **January:** Guidelines for Retained/Disabled Cards on ATMs (PSD circular).
- **February:** Statutory Liquidity and Cash Reserve Requirements.
- **February:** Minimum Capital Requirements: Implementation of Basel II.
- **February:** Panel of Auditors, under Section 35(1) of the Banking Companies Ordinance, 1962 (circular letter).
- **February:** Submission of Information regarding Sukuk Issued in Pakistan (Islamic banking circular letter).

- **March:** Withdrawal of Instructions for Reporting of Classified Advances and Written-Off Loans.
- **March:** Branchless Banking Regulations for Financial Institutions.
- **March:** Guidelines on Internal Controls.
- **March:** Prudential Regulation No. 4: Minimum Capital Requirements.
- **March:** Instructions and Guidelines for Shari'ah Compliance in Islamic Banking Institutions (Islamic banking circular letter).
- **April:** Regulations for Continuous Funding System (CFS MK II) Financing.
- **April:** Prudential Regulation M-1: Obtaining Computerized National Identity Card from All Bank and DFI Customers and Clients (circular letter).
- **April:** Prudential Regulation M-5: Suspicious Transactions (circular letter).
- **April:** Section 86 of the Insurance Ordinance 2000 (circular letter).
- **April:** Cash Reserve Requirements against FE-25 Deposits Maintained by Islamic Banks and Islamic Banking Branches.
- **April:** Minimum Capital Requirements: Implementation of Basel II (circular letter).
- **May:** Deposit of Sponsor Shares in Blocked Account with Central Depository Company of Pakistan.
- **May:** Financing Facilities by State Bank: Enhancement in Repo Rate from 10.50 Percent to 12 Percent.
- **May:** Minimum Margin Restriction on Import Letters of Credit.
- **May:** Minimum Rate of Return on Savings/PLS (Profit-Loss Sharing) Saving Deposit.
- **May:** Regulations for Continuous Funding System (CFS MK II) Financing (circular letter).
- **May:** Minimum Capital Requirements: Implementation of Basel II.
- **May:** Cash Reserve and Statutory Liquidity Requirements (2).
- **May:** Upward Revision in Penalties for Misreporting and Late Submission of Returns.
- **June:** On-Line Banking (circular letter).
- **June:** Prudential Regulation R-5 (circular letter).
- **June:** Minimum Margin Restriction on Import Letters of Credit (circular letter).
- **June:** Pledge of Third-Party Share against Financing to Brokers (circular letter).
- **June:** Minimum Margin Restriction on Import Letters of Credit (circular letter).
- **June:** Prudential Regulation M-1: Obtaining Computerized National Identity Card from All Bank and DFI Customers and Clients (circular letter).
- **June:** Statutory Liquidity Requirement (2).
- **June:** Cash Reserve Requirements for Deposits Raised under FE Circular 25 of 1998 (2).
- **June:** Minimum Capital Requirements: Implementation of Basel II.
- **June:** Internal Credit Rating System: Obligor and Facility Ratings (circular letter).

- **July:** Financing Facilities by the SBP: Enhancement in Repo Rate from 12 Percent to 13 Percent.
- **July:** Panel of Auditors, under Section 35(1) of Banking Companies Ordinance, 1962 (circular letter).
- **August:** Amendment in Regulation G-1 of Prudential Regulations.
- **August:** Amendment in Revised Prudential Regulation for Microfinance Banks.
- **August:** Imposition of 100 Percent Letter of Credit Margin on Nonessential and Luxury Items.
- **August:** Discriminating Consumer Finance Practices (circular letter).
- **August:** Guidelines on Internal Capital Adequacy Assessment Process.
- **August:** Statutory Liquidity Requirements.
- **September:** Amendment in Regulation R-8, Para. 4 of Prudential Regulations for SME Financing (circular letter).
- **September:** Minimum Margin Restriction on Import Letters of Credit (circular letter).
- **September:** Minimum Capital Requirements for Banks and DFIs.
- **September:** Panel of Auditors, under Section 35(1) of Banking Companies Ordinance, 1962 (circular letter).
- **September:** Fit-and-Proper Criteria for Shari'ah Advisors (Islamic banking circular letter).
- **October:** Imposition of Minimum Balance Requirements for the Account Holders in Earthquake-Affected Areas (circular letter).
- **October:** Amendment in Regulation O-3 of Prudential Regulations for Corporate and Commercial Banking (circular letter).
- **October:** Exposure against Shares (circular letter).
- **October:** Customer Facilitation Centers to Reduce Concerns and Grievances of Depositors and Borrowers (circular letter).
- **October:** Cash Reserve and Statutory Liquidity Requirements (4).
- **October:** Government of Pakistan Ijara Sukuk.
- **October:** Held-to-Maturity Securities.
- **October:** Statutory Liquidity Requirements.
- **October:** Liquidity Management.
- **October:** Liquidity Management-Advances to Deposit Ratio.
- **November:** Fair Debt Collection Guidelines.
- **November:** Financing Facilities by the SBP: Enhancement in Repo Rate from 13 Percent to 15 Percent.
- **November:** Minimum Margin Restriction on Import Letters of Credit (circular letter).
- **November:** Pricing of Lending Products and Loan Documentation (circular letter).
- **November:** Minimum Margin Restriction on Import Letters of Credit (circular letter).
- **November:** Cash Reserve Requirements.

- **November:** Minimum Capital Requirements for Banks and DFIs.
- **November:** Minimum Capital Requirements: Implementation of Basel II (circular letter).
- **November:** Instructions and Guidelines for Shari'ah Compliance in Islamic Banking Institutions (Islamic banking circular letter).
- **December:** Financing Facilities by Banks and DFIs to Microfinance Banks and Microfinance Institutions.
- **December:** Prudential Regulation M-1: Obtaining Computerized National Identity Card from All Bank and DFI Customers and Clients (circular letter).
- **December:** Statutory Liquidity Requirements.
- **December:** Revaluation Surplus/Deficit (circular letter).
- **December:** Questionnaires for Self-Assessment—Institutional Risk Assessment Framework.

2009

- **January:** Amendment in Prudential Regulations for Corporate and Commercial Banking.
- **January:** Minimum Capital Requirement: Implementation of Basel II.
- **January:** Amendments in Prudential Regulations: Provisioning for Loans and Advances.
- **January:** Internal Credit Rating System: Obligor and Facility Ratings (circular letter).
- **January:** Revaluation Surplus/Deficit (circular letter).
- **January:** Implementation of Islamic Financial Accounting Standard for Ijarah (IFAS 2) (Islamic banking circular letter).
- **January:** Discontinuation of Hard-Copy Submission of Quarterly Report of Condition (circular letter).
- **January:** Operational Guidelines for Credit Card Business in Pakistan (PSD circular).
- **February:** Margin Restrictions for Financing against the Security of Sugar Stock (Both Raw and Refined).
- **February:** Amendment in Prudential Regulation for Corporate and Commercial Banking (R-3).
- **February:** Amendments in Prudential Regulations for Consumer Financing.
- **February:** Statutory Liquidity Requirements.
- **February:** Revaluation Surplus/Deficit.
- **February:** Guidelines on Internal Controls.
- **March:** Policy for Opening of Overseas Offices and Establishment of a Subsidiary Banking Company Outside Pakistan.
- **March:** Regulation R-5: Prudential Regulations for Corporate and Commercial Banking.
- **March:** Prudential Regulations for Corporate and Commercial Banking, M-1 and M-2 (circular letter).
- **April:** Financing Facilities by the SBP: Reduction in Repo Rate from 15 Percent to 14 Percent.

- **April:** Amendment in Prudential Regulation G-1 (circular letter).
- **April:** Amendment of Para. 5(vi) of Guidelines on Commercial Paper (circular letter).
- **April:** Minimum Capital Requirements for Banks and DFIs.
- **April:** Submission of Returns to Islamic Banking Department: Revision of Monthly Statement of Position (Islamic banking circular letter).
- **May:** Banking Facilities for Internally Displaced Persons.
- **May:** Deposit of Sponsor Shares in Blocked Account with Central Depository Company of Pakistan.
- **May:** Amendments in Microfinance Credit Guarantee Facility.
- **May:** Panel of Auditors, under Section 35(1) of the Banking Companies Ordinance, 1962 (circular letter).
- **June:** Pension Disbursement through Banks.
- **June:** Minimum Margin Restriction on Import Letters of Credit.
- **June:** Internal Credit Rating System: Obligator and Facility Ratings (circular letter).
- **June:** Revision of Capital Adequacy Requirement for Islamic Banking Branches (Islamic banking circular letter).
- **July:** Margin Restrictions for Financing against the Security of Sugar Stock (Both Raw and Refined).
- **July:** Prudential Regulation M-1: Obtaining Computerized National Identity Card from All Bank and DFI Customers and Clients (circular letter).
- **July:** Amendments in Microfinance Credit Guarantee Facility (circular letter).
- **July:** Panel of Auditors, under Section 35(1) of the Banking Companies Ordinance, 1962 (circular letter).
- **August:** Remuneration of Directors and Chairman: Prudential Regulations G-1.
- **August:** Revaluation Surplus/Deficit.
- **August:** Panel of Auditors, under Section 35(1) of the Banking Companies Ordinance, 1962 (circular letter).
- **August:** Payment and Settlement of Home Remittance Transactions under Pakistan Remittance Initiative (PSD circular).

Other Policy Developments

Other policy developments relevant to the banking sector in Pakistan in 2007–08 include the following.

2007

- The SBP launched its first comprehensive financial stability review.
- The SBP rolled out its microfinance outreach strategy, providing a comprehensive road map for the development of microfinance in Pakistan.
- **February:** A detailed survey to assess the level of preparedness for Basel II was conducted.

2008

- **February:** A separate Financial Stability Department was established in the Monetary Policy and Research Cluster of the SBP.

- **June:** A SAARCFINANCE seminar on Basel II was held in Islamabad.
- **July:** The real-time gross settlement system—Pakistan Real Time Interbank Settlement Mechanism (PRISM), which has real-time interface with Globus—started live operations.
- **August:** The definition of time and demand liabilities was revised to exclude deposits with tenor of less than one year from time liabilities and to include the same in demand liabilities.
- The SBP initiated a reform process in the exchange companies sector with a view to bringing better market discipline.

Legislation Enacted or Pending

Several legislative actions relevant to the banking sector were taken in Pakistan in 2007, and several others are under way.

2007

- Finance Bill 2007.
- Anti-Money-Laundering Ordinance, 2007.
- Payment Systems and Electronic Fund Transfers Act, 2007.

Pending

- Banking Act 2009 (an act to repeal and, with certain modifications, to consolidate and reenact the Banking Companies Ordinance, 1962), draft stage.
- Banking Companies (Amendment) Act, 2008 (to amend the Banking Companies Ordinance, 1962), draft stage.
- Deposit Protection Fund Act, 2008, draft stage.

Sri Lanka

Prudential Regulations

Among the prudential guidelines issued by the Central Bank of Sri Lanka (CBSL) in 2007–08 are the following.

2007

- **January:** Banking Act Direction No. 1 of 2007: Ownership of Issued Capital Carrying Voting Rights.
- **January:** Customer Due Diligence: "Know Your Customer" Procedures.
- **January:** Investment in Rupee-Denominated Treasury Bonds by Foreign Investors.
- **January:** Foreign Currency Fixed Deposit Accounts for Dual Citizenship Applicants: Operating Instructions.
- **January:** Amendment to LankaSettle System Rules, August 2003.
- **January:** Central Bank of Sri Lanka Wide Area Network (CBSLNet)–Based Application to Record Overnight Customer Repo Repositioning Transactions Involving Government Securities.
- **March:** Resident Guest Scheme, Special Accounts: Operating Instructions.
- **March:** Krushi Navodaya Loan Scheme.
- **April:** Light a Million Candles Campaign.

- **April:** Poverty Alleviation Microfinance Project (Revolving Fund) Loan Scheme.
- **May:** Compliance with the Reporting Requirements under the Financial Transactions Reporting Act, No. 6 of 2006.
- **May:** Financial Transactions Reporting Act, No. 6 of 2006 (FTRA): Know Your Customer and Customer Due Diligence Rules Prescribed in Terms of Section 2(3) of the FTRA.
- **June:** Mandatory Reporting Requirement: Electronic Fund Transfers.
- **June:** Issuance of Foreign Currency Notes to Sri Lankans Traveling Abroad.
- **June:** Permission for Third-Party Foreign Exchange Deposits in Nonresident Foreign Currency Accounts.
- **July:** Matale Regional Economic Advancement Project Revolving Fund.
- **August:** Compliance with Know Your Customer and Customer Due Diligence Rules for New Customers and Existing Customers: State of Readiness.
- **September:** Amendments to LankaSettle System Rules Issued in August 2003 (2).
- **September:** Central Bank of Sri Lanka Wide Area Network (CBSLNet)–Based Application to Record Customer Repositioning Transactions Involving Government Securities.
- **October:** Construction Sector Development Project to Assist the Construction and Public Works Relating to Post-Tsunami Reconstruction.
- **November:** General Direction on the Participating Institutions' Service Norms and Standard Times for Accepting Check Deposits from Customers and Crediting Check Proceeds to Customers' Accounts under the Check Imaging and Truncation System.
- **November:** Banking Act Direction No. 7 of 2007: Maximum Amount of Accommodation.
- **December:** Banking Act Direction No. 11 of 2007: Corporate Governance for Licensed Commercial Banks in Sri Lanka.
- **December:** Investment in Rupee-Denominated Treasury Bonds by Foreign Investors (Increase of the Holding Limits of Foreign Investors in Rupee-Denominated Treasury Bonds from 5 Percent to 10 Percent).
- **December:** Construction Sector Development Project to Assist the Construction and Public Works Relating to Post-Tsunami Reconstruction (Amendment).

2008

- **January:** Enhancement of Minimum Capital Requirement of Banks.
- **February:** Reverse Repurchase Facility.
- **March:** Operating Instructions on Issuing Central Bank Securities in Scripless Form under Open-Market Operations of the CBSL.
- **April:** Agro Livestock Development Loan Scheme.
- **May:** Enhancing Lending to Agriculture Sector.
- **May:** Banking Act Direction No. 3 of 2008: Classification of Loans and Advances, Income Recognition, and Provisioning.
- **May:** Establishment of Bank Branches.

- **May:** Operating Instructions on Long-Term Repo Transactions under the Auction System.
- **May:** Investment in Treasury Bills by Foreign Investors.
- **May:** Compliance with the Rules on Customer Due Diligence for Financial Institutions.
- **June:** Foreign Investment Deposit Accounts.
- **June:** Compliance with the Reporting Requirements under the Financial Transactions Reporting Act, No. 6 of 2006.
- **July:** Nonresident Blocked Accounts.
- **July:** Sale of Foreign Exchange to Emigrants.
- **August:** Banking Act Direction No. 5 of 2008: Amendments to Directions on Corporate Governance for Licensed Commercial Banks in Sri Lanka.
- **August:** Permitting Licensed Commercial Banks to Trade in the International Sovereign Bonds Issued in 2007 by the Government of Sri Lanka.
- **August:** Definition of Liquid Assets under Section 86 of Banking Act No. 30 of 1988 as Amended by Banking (Amendment) Act No. 33 of 1995.
- **August:** Amendment to the LankaSettle System Rules Issued in August 2003: Introduction of Personal Computer–Based Payment and Securities Settlement System (PC-Based System).
- **September:** Banking Act, Order No. 1 of 2008: Banking (Off-Shore Banking Business Scheme) Order Designated Foreign Currencies (Addition of New Zealand Dollar as a Designated Currency for Foreign Exchange Transactions).
- **September:** Recommendation of Interest Subsidy under New Comprehensive Rural Credit Scheme, 2008/09 Maha.
- **September:** Banking Act Determination No. 1 of 2008: Annual License Fees of Licensed Commercial Banks.
- **October:** Banking Act Direction No. 7 of 2008: Amendments to Directions on Corporate Governance for Licensed Commercial Banks in Sri Lanka.
- **October:** Use of Banking System by Institutions and Persons Not Authorized to Accept Deposits.
- **October:** Reserve Requirements.
- **October:** Reverse Repurchase Facility (2).
- **October:** Forward Sales and Purchases of Foreign Exchange.
- **October:** Imports on Documents Against Acceptance Terms.
- **October:** Margin Requirements against Letters of Credit.
- **October:** Prepayment of Import Bills.
- **November:** Regulations Made under the Public Security Ordinance Proscription of Tamil Rehabilitation Organisation.
- **November:** Misleading and Unethical Advertisements.
- **November:** Imports on Documents against Acceptance Terms.
- **November:** Imports of Motor Vehicles on Documents Against Acceptance Terms.
- **November:** Reserve Requirements.
- **November:** Margin Requirements against Letters of Credit (2).
- **November:** Margin Requirements for Imports Made on Advance Payment Terms (2).

- **December:** Margin Requirements against Letters of Credit.
- **December:** Imports on Documents against Acceptance Terms.
- **December:** Imports of Motor Vehicles on Documents against Acceptance Terms.
- **December:** Margin Requirements for Imports Made on Advance Payment Terms.
- **December:** Banking Act Direction No. 9 of 2008: Amendments to Directions on Classification of Loans and Advances, Income Recognition, and Provisioning for Licensed Commercial Banks in Sri Lanka.

Other Policy Developments

Other policy developments relevant to the banking sector in Sri Lanka in the past three years include the following.

2007

- **January:** Road Map: Monetary and Financial Sector Policies for 2007 and Beyond was released by the CBSL.
- **January:** The Foreign Currency Fixed Deposit Accounts scheme was introduced for ex–Sri Lankans and Sri Lankans living abroad, who would apply for dual citizenship status, in domestic banking units.
- **February:** The Inter-Regulatory Institutions Council was established to promote coordination among regulators in the financial sector.
- **February:** The CBSL's wide area network (CBSLNet)–based application to record small-value customer overnight repo repositioning transactions was implemented.
- **March:** Two foreign currency account schemes, the Resident Guest Foreign Currency Account and the Resident Guest Rupee Current Account, were introduced for foreigners who obtain visas under the Resident Guest Scheme.
- **June:** A consultative paper on the implementation of the new capital adequacy framework, Basel II, was issued to banks for their comments, before the issuing of directions to banks.
- **August:** Assets and liabilities of Pramuka Savings and Development Bank were vested in a new state bank called Sri Lanka Savings Bank Ltd.
- **October:** The first international sovereign bond of Sri Lanka, amounting to US$500 million, was issued.

2008

- **January:** *Road Map: Monetary and Financial Sector Policies for 2008 and Beyond* was released by the CBSL.
- **January:** Commercial banks were required to apply the Standardized Approach for credit risk, Standardized Measurement Method for market risk, and the Basic Indicator Approach for operational risk under Basel II.
- **March:** Sri Lanka Savings Bank Ltd. commenced its operations.
- **May:** The road map for full implementation of International Accounting Standards by January 1, 2011, was issued, requiring banks to comply fully with the standards from 2011, with a parallel run commencing June 2008.

- **May:** Foreign investment in treasury bills was permitted to nonresident Sri Lankans, citizens of foreign states, corporate bodies incorporated outside Sri Lanka, and foreign institutional investors not exceeding 10 percent of the outstanding treasury bill stock.
- **June:** A scheme, the Special Foreign Investment Deposit Account, both in foreign currency and in rupees, was introduced to mobilize funds from citizens of foreign states, investors and corporate bodies incorporated outside Sri Lanka, Sri Lankan citizens residing outside Sri Lanka, and foreign institutional investors.
- **August:** The system rules of LankaSettle were amended to introduce a personal computer–based payment and securities settlement system as an alternative settlement system to be used in the event of a prolonged, unrecoverable LankaSettle application event.
- **October:** Draft guidelines on integrated risk management were issued to the banking industry for its comments and suggestions.
- **October:** Draft guidelines on outsourcing activities of banks were issued in consultation with the banking industry to improve the risk management processes of banks.
- **October:** A circular was issued to all institutions participating in the check imaging and truncation system, stipulating deadlines (March 31, 2009, for Western Province and June 30, 2009, for all other provinces) for migrating to the system in which the check images captured at the collecting bank are to be submitted on a compact disc, as an interim arrangement before moving toward direct connectivity allowing the check images and information to be transmitted online to LankaClear.
- **October:** The CBSL reduced the statutory reserve ratio by 75 basis points from 10.00 percent to 9.25 percent.
- **October:** The shutdown time for the RTGS system was advanced by 15 minutes as a result of system upgrades and improvements. Accordingly, effective from November 3, 2008, the shutdown time for the RTGS system is 5:00 p.m.
- **November:** The CBSL reduced the statutory reserve ratio by 150 basis points from 9.25 percent to 7.75 percent.
- **December:** The Asian Clearing Union Agreement and Procedure Rules were amended, permitting member countries to process transactions either in U.S. dollars or in euros within the Asian Clearing Union mechanism with effect from January 1, 2009.
- **December:** Bank of Ceylon was appointed by the CBSL to carry on the business of Seylan Bank under a new board of directors appointed by Bank of Ceylon.
- **December:** Finance Companies (Corporate Governance, Amendment) Direction No. 4 of 2008 was issued.

2009

- Implementation of an integrated risk management framework for banks:
  - Issuing guidelines on compilation of maturity gap analysis and introducing regulatory limits on negative mismatches in the asset and liability maturity profiles.

   - Initiating draft guidelines on Pillar II of Basel II.
   - Fully implementing Part IX (Sections 72 to 76) of the Banking Act on Abandoned Property.
   - Formulating a framework for consolidated supervision.
   - Introducing a model to rate banks to identify risks and provide early warning signals.
   - Continuing the work on preparing the banking industry to adopt the new accounting standards on financial instruments (SLAS 44 and 45).
- The master repo agreement, which can be commonly used by primary dealers and licensed commercial banks, was implemented in January 2009.
- The rupee-denominated treasury bill and treasury bond market was opened up to the Sri Lankan diaspora and migrant workforce in January 2009.
- Implementing the first stage of the primary dealer diversification program. Directions issued in November 2009 and effective from December 2009 allow primary dealers to diversify their activities.

Legislation Enacted

Legislation relevant to the banking sector enacted in Sri Lanka in 2007–08 includes the following.

2007

- **April:** Debits Tax (Amendment) Act, No. 12 of 2007: An act to amend the Debits Tax Act, No. 16 of 2002.
- **April:** Finance (Amendment) Act, No. 13 of 2007: An act to amend the Finance Act, No. 11 of 2006; Finance Act, No. 5 of 2005; and Finance Act, No. 11 of 2002.
- **July:** Computer Crime Act, No. 24 of 2007: An act to provide for the identification of computer crime and to provide the procedure for the investigation and prevention of such crimes; and to provide for matters connected therewith and incidental thereto.
- **July:** Regulation of Insurance Industry (Amendment) Act, No. 27 of 2007: An act to amend the Regulation of Insurance Industry Act, No. 43 of 2000.
- **July:** National Insurance Trust Fund (Amendment) Act, No. 28 of 2007: An act to amend the National Insurance Trust Fund Act, No. 28 of 2006.
- **August:** Finance Leasing (Amendment) Act, No. 33 of 2007: An act to amend the Finance Leasing Act, No. 56 of 2000 (to enable specialized leasing companies to mobilize funds from the public by issuing debt securities, thus broadening their funding sources).

2008

- **February:** Finance (Amendment) Act, No. 7 of 2008: An act to amend the Finance Act, No. 5 of 2005. The Finance Act, No. 11 of 2004 is amended in Part II (Imposition of Cellular Mobile Telephone Subscribers' Levy).
- **February:** Stamp Duty (Special Provisions) (Amendment) Act, No. 10 of 2008: An act to amend the Stamp Duty (Special Provisions) Act, No. 12 of 2006.

- **February:** Economic Service Charge (Amendment) Act, No. 11 of 2008: An act to amend the Economic Service Charge Act, No. 13 of 2006.
- **February:** Regional Infrastructure Development Levy (Amendment) Act, No. 12 of 2008: An act to amend the Regional Infrastructure Development Levy Act, No. 51 of 2006.
- **February:** Value Added Tax (Amendment) Act, No. 15 of 2008: An act to amend the Value Added Tax Act, No. 14 of 2002.
- **December:** Pradeshiya Sanwardana Bank Act, No. 41 of 2008: An act to provide for the establishment of the Pradeshiya Sanwardana Bank and for the absorption of the assets, liabilities, contracts, employees, etc., of the development banks established under the Regional Development Banks Act, No. 6 of 1997 and to provide for matters connected therewith or incidental thereto.
- **December:** Credit Information Bureau of Sri Lanka (Amendment) Act, No. 42 of 2008: An act to amend the Credit Information Bureau of Sri Lanka Act, No. 18 of 1990.

Endnotes

1. Indian Banks' Association 2006a, 2006b, 2006c, 2008a, 2008b, 2008c; RBI 2006a, 2006b, 2007a, 2007b, 2008a, 2008b, *Annual Report* (various years).
2. The fiscal year for the Bangladesh government is from July 1 to June 30.

Special Feature

Managing the Impact of the Global Financial Crisis and Economic Slowdown

Navigating the global financial storm appears daunting from whatever viewpoint one chooses to look at it. The World Bank, in a February 2009 press release (2009), outlined some of the devastating effects that the financial crisis could have on the poor and most vulnerable. According to World Bank estimates for 2009, lower economic growth rates will trap an extra 53 million in poverty (living on less than $2 a day). The sharp slowdown in growth also threatens achievement of the Millennium Development Goals, including reducing infant mortality. If the crisis persists, preliminary estimates for 2009–15 show, an average 200,000–400,000 more children a year may die.

South Asian countries, home to more than half the world's poorest people, already face the challenging dual task of developing their economies while eradicating poverty. According to the World Bank's income group classification in 2008, Bhutan, India, Maldives, Pakistan, and Sri Lanka are lower-middle-income countries, while Afghanistan, Bangladesh, and Nepal are low-income countries.[1] With 1.59 billion people, South Asia accounts for around 24 percent of world population but a mere 2.50 percent of world GDP. Worker remittances are the largest source of external funding for the region, which accounted for 14 percent of global inflows of remittances in 2007. These remittances amounted to 3.85 percent of regional GDP, ahead of official development assistance (0.72 percent) and foreign direct investment (2.07 percent).[2]

A recent World Bank study (Cord and others 2009) confirms the potential vulnerability of South Asian countries. According to its estimates, almost 40 percent of developing countries are highly exposed to the poverty effects of the crisis (facing both decelerating growth rates and high poverty levels), while another 56 percent are moderately exposed (facing either decelerating growth or high poverty levels). Among the South Asian economies, Afghanistan, Bangladesh, Bhutan, India, and Pakistan are categorized as having high exposure, Sri Lanka as facing decelerating growth, and Nepal as facing high poverty levels. (Maldives is excluded from the categorization, either because of lack of data or because it has a population of less than 0.5 million.)

These background facts underscore the importance of examining the impact of the financial crisis and the ensuing economic slowdown in South Asia as well as the region's response. The following discussion is aimed at both providing insight into how South Asian countries are coping with the crisis and shedding light on remedial actions they could take to mitigate its impact.

An Overview

By mid-2008, the global financial crisis had triggered a slump in demand from the United States and the Euro Area. That in turn caused a sharp fall in terms of trade (export prices relative to import prices) for emerging markets. Private capital flows to emerging markets came to a sudden stop as a result of a massive retreat by investors after the collapse in September 2008 of Lehman Brothers, a major U.S. investment banking firm. External financing dried up even for developing countries with solid economies.

The global community took swift action to try to prevent the adverse effects of the financial crisis from spreading worldwide (box 1). The International Monetary Fund and other multilateral institutions have made new commitments to countries affected by the crisis. Besides financial support, every international financial institution also provides important research and analytical support, technical and policy advice, and other assistance. For private capital flows, the Group of Twenty meeting in April 2009 marked a turning point, with even foreign direct investment now resuming.

The belief was that South Asia would not be seriously affected by the ongoing global financial crisis. The region's banking systems had little exposure to complex financial instruments and had not resorted to the excessively risky practices of the more sophisticated banking systems of developed countries. But because of financial and economic integration with the rest of the world, South Asia did not escape unscathed and has felt the impact of the second-round effects of the crisis.

The global financial crisis hit at a time that South Asia was already reeling from the effects of severe terms-of-trade shock. The substantial terms-of-trade losses have been reflected in a slowdown of growth, a worsening of macroeconomic balances, and huge inflationary pressures. Countries have responded by partially adjusting domestic fuel prices, cutting development spending, and tightening monetary policy. But the global financial crisis is likely to worsen those trends, particularly on the growth and balance of payments front. The second-round effects of the crisis have had an adverse impact on South Asian exports and hurt income from remittances. Smaller inflows of foreign capital and harder terms have reduced domestic investment. These effects will undermine growth prospects in the region.

South Asia's financial sectors are broadly resilient thanks to past financial sector reforms, capital controls that help insulate these economies from the risk of a financial crisis transmitted from abroad, and only partial integration with the rest of the world. But the risks for individual countries vary substantially because of considerable differences in macroeconomic performance, financial sector health, and exposure to foreign capital markets.

The Crisis and South Asian Economies

The degree of economic impact from the financial crisis varies from country to country in South Asia. Maldives, with capital and current accounts fully open, has been affected more severely than India, Pakistan, and Sri Lanka, where there

Box 1 Crisis Response by Multilateral Institutions and Major Bilateral Donors

In response to the global financial crisis, the Group of Twenty leaders, at their April 2009 summit meeting, decided to add US$1.1 trillion in resources for the international financial institutions—US$750 billion for the International Monetary Fund (IMF), US$250 billion to boost global trade, and US$100 billion for multilateral development banks. The United States increased its quota in the IMF by 4.5 billion special drawing rights (US$7.69 billion) and provided loans to the IMF of up to an additional 75 billion special drawing rights (US$116.01 billion) (Nanto 2009).

The IMF aims to triple its total resources allocated to combating the crisis to US$750 billion. In addition to ongoing development programs, the World Bank is prepared to commit up to US$100 billion in 2009–10, including by tripling investment in safety nets and social protection to US$12 billion and by setting up a US$55 billion infrastructure platform.

The African Development Bank Group, facing an unprecedented increase in requests from its members, has responded accordingly. Its financing in 2009 was expected to total US$15 billion, more than three times the projections under its medium-term strategy.[a] The Inter-American Development Bank plans to accelerate loans to finance projects and enhance social programs and expected to approve up to US$12 billion in 2009, a record level and up from about US$10 billion in 2008. The bank is also setting up a quick-disbursing US$6 billion liquidity facility—the Liquidity Program for Growth Sustainability—to help Latin American and Caribbean economies sustain growth (ADB 2009b).

The European Bank for Reconstruction and Development increased its planned investment in 2009 to €8 billion (around US$12 billion) and is setting up a corporate support facility (€250 million, or US$367 million) and recapitalizing sound banks. It is also collaborating with the World Bank to commit up to €24.5 billion (US$36 billion) to the banking sector.[b]

In February 2009, the finance ministers of the Association of Southeast Asian Nations plus China, Japan, and the Republic of Korea agreed to expand the Multilateralised Chiang Mai Initiative from the initially agreed level of US$80 billion to US$120 billion. (The initiative, a currency swap arrangement, was created to manage regional short-term liquidity problems and facilitate the work of other international financial arrangements and organizations.) The Asian Development Bank (ADB) expects to increase its crisis-related lending by more than US$10 billion in 2009–10. In addition, the ADB established the US$3 billion Countercyclical Support Facility to provide short-term, fast-disbursing loans. And to help ease the severe resource constraints faced by low-income countries, the ADB approved additional liquidity of US$400 million for those eligible to borrow on concessional terms from the Asian Development Fund.[c]

a. African Development Bank Group, "Financial Crisis," http://www.afdb.org/en/topics-sectors/topics/financial-crisis/.
b. European Bank for Reconstruction and Development, "EBRD Responds to the Global Financial Crisis," http://www.ebrd.com/new/fin_crisis.htm.
c. ADB, "The Global Economic Crisis," http://www.adb.org/Economic-Crisis/default.asp.

are some restrictions in place. But these economies, because of the openness of their real sector, remain very vulnerable to global economic slowdown—through lower export earnings due to weakening consumer demand in developed economies and tight external financing due to global deleveraging activities.

Economic Impact

The terms-of-trade shocks already affecting South Asia before the onset of the financial crisis stemmed from high oil and commodity prices. In 2003–08 they led to losses ranging from 8 percent of GDP for Bangladesh to 34 percent for Maldives (World Bank 2008b). The regional average current account balance dropped from −1.7 percent of GDP in 2007 to −3.1 percent in 2008, indicating export income losses (figure 1, panels a and b). The current account balance remained negative in 2009, at an estimated −1.7 percent, and is projected at −2.2 percent in 2010. Bhutan, Bangladesh, and Nepal managed to maintain surplus balances—Bhutan thanks to stable hydropower exports to India, and Bangladesh and Nepal thanks to large inflows of remittances. In the absence of trade surpluses and with no certainty of achieving higher growth in remittances, however, these countries may be unable to maintain their current account surpluses in the future.

International reserves deteriorated, with the ratio of reserves to imports declining sharply for all major economies in the region (figure 1, panel c). Recent inflows of external capital have improved the reserve situation for some countries, such as Pakistan and Sri Lanka, while India has benefited from valuation gains. Bhutan has the strongest import cover among the South Asian countries, followed by India.

Fiscal deficits increased further between 2007 and 2008 (figure 1, panel d). India, Maldives, and Pakistan registered the sharpest increases, though the main reasons for the deterioration varied. In India, the main cause was tax reductions and domestic spending increases to stimulate growth. In Maldives, it was a loss of revenue from tourism. And in Pakistan it was a rise in domestic debt servicing costs. In light of the need for higher domestic spending to counter economic slowdown, managing the fiscal deficits will be a major challenge for South Asian countries.

As a result of these adverse conditions, growth decelerated during the period. The regional growth rate fell from 8.6 percent in 2007 to 6.9 percent in 2008 and an estimated 5.6 percent in 2009. In 2010, however, GDP growth is projected to recover to around 6.4 percent, mainly because of the resilience of the Indian economy (figure 1, panel e). India, the third largest economy in Asia, had annual growth averaging 9 percent in 2005–07. But its growth rate slipped to 6.7 percent in 2008 and an estimated 6 percent in 2009, though it is projected to rise to 7 percent in 2010. While uncertainties in external demand and international market conditions mean that it remains too early to predict the sustainability of such growth, the projected turnaround is still an important sign of an anticipated recovery.

Other indicators also provide signals about whether South Asia is on track toward a sustainable recovery. One such indicator is the inflation rate. South Asian countries have been battling rising inflation, with significant increases in 2008. Four economies recorded double-digit inflation—Afghanistan 26.8 percent, Maldives 11.9 percent, Pakistan 12 percent, and Sri Lanka 22.6 percent—mainly as a result of high food and fuel prices. India posted inflation of 8.4 percent in 2008. But except for Nepal and Pakistan, the region's countries managed to curtail inflation in 2009 (figure 2, panel a). A drop in fuel prices was a major factor in this. For South Asia as a whole, inflation averaged around 9.6 percent in 2008 and an estimated 4.7 percent in 2009 and is projected at 4.9 percent in 2010.

Since policy effects may take longer to manifest as a result of the economic downturn, maintaining a good balance between inflation and policy measures is imperative. If high inflation were to continue, fiscal stimulus packages, tax cuts, and other expansionary policy measures needed to boost production and move toward economic recovery may not provide the desired effects. While price indexes are not necessarily comparable across South Asian countries, the changes clearly indicate the inflationary trends in the countries—and the trends are positive.[3]

Figure 1 **Twin Deficits Have Led to a Deceleration of Growth**

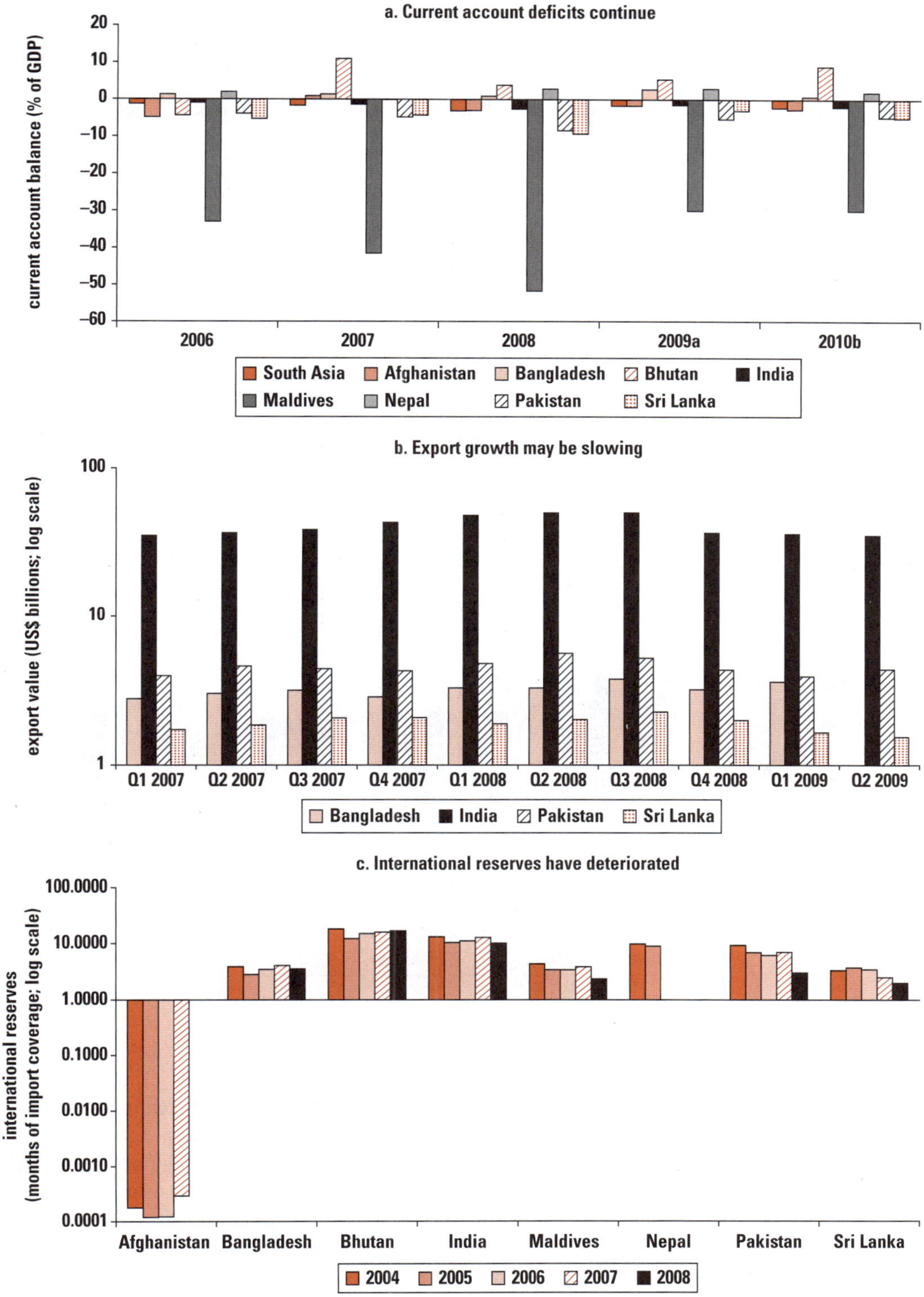

(Figure continues on next page)

Figure 1 **Twin Deficits Have Led to a Deceleration of Growth** *(continued)*

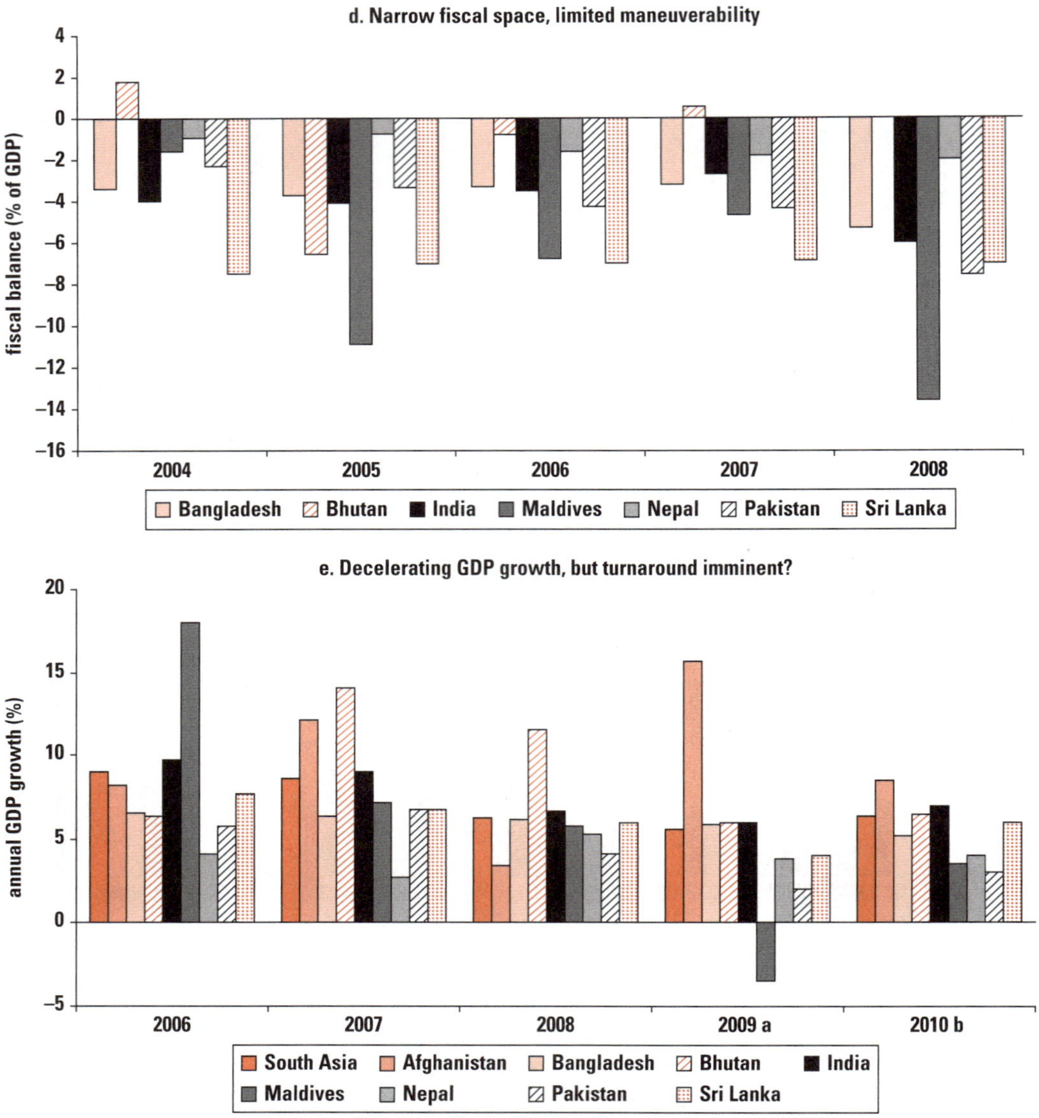

Source: ADB 2009a.
Note: a = estimated; b = projected.

Another favorable factor is the relative constancy of worker remittances, which are among the main stable sources of funding for most South Asian countries. Remittance flows showed a steady trend through 2008 (figure 2, panel b), though they were estimated to drop in 2009 and are projected to drop again in 2010. But South Asian governments and central banks have taken measures to ensure that there is no significant reduction in remittance flows. In Sri Lanka, for example, the government offers tax holidays for those who remit their earnings into the country, while the banks offer higher interest rates on foreign currency deposits, provide remittance-related products such as housing finance and education

Figure 2 **Recovery Is Expected**

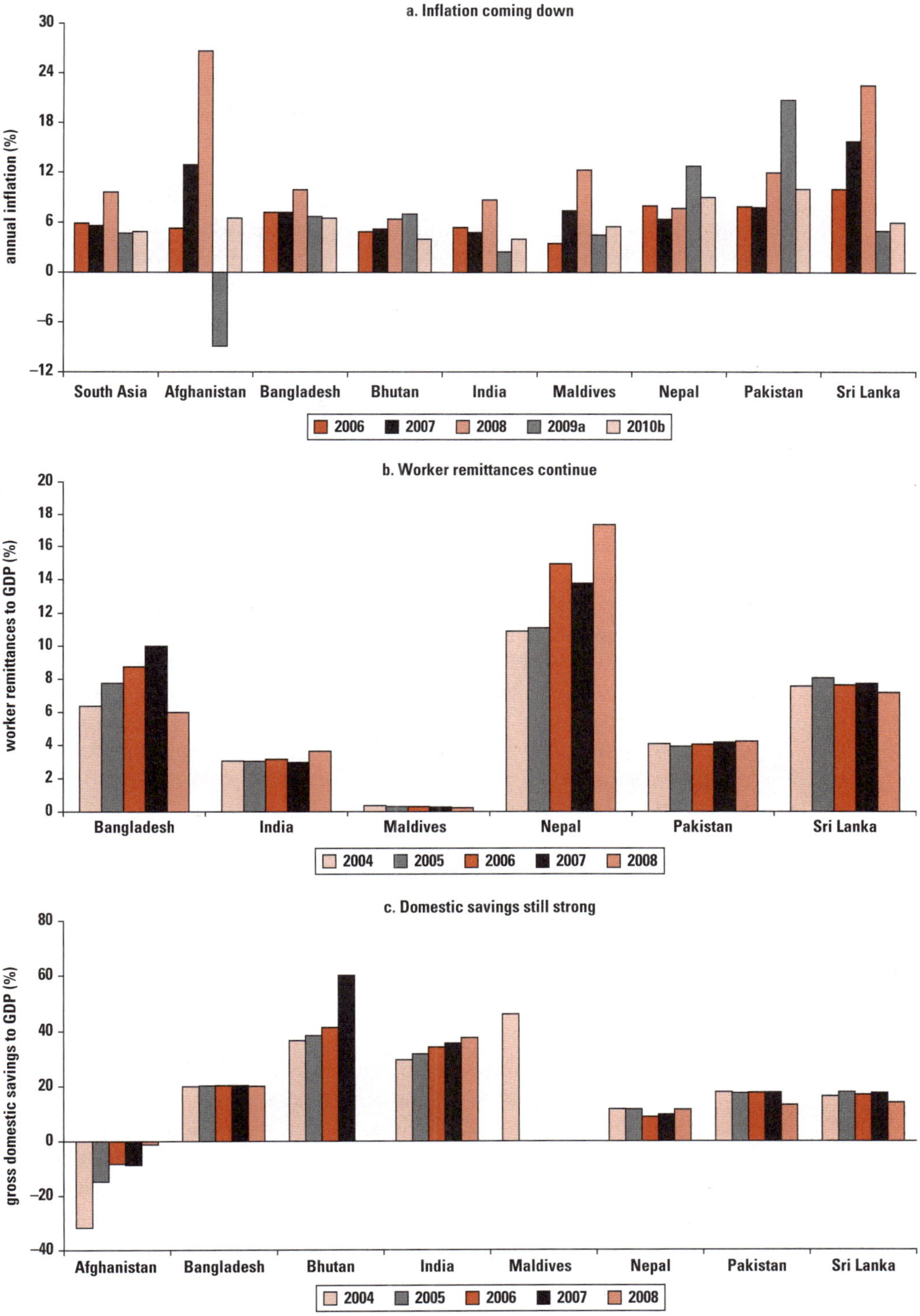

Sources: ADB 2009a (for inflation data); appendix 2 (for worker remittances and domestic savings).
Note: a = estimated; b = projected. Data on domestic savings to GDP not available for Maldives, 2005–08.

loans, market dedicated bonds to attract savings from the diaspora, and open branches and exchange houses in countries that are large sources of remittances. Developed countries are also making important efforts to facilitate remittance flows to developing countries. For example, the G-8 (Group of Eight) remittance group has been working on the "5 x 5 initiative," an effort aimed at reducing the cost of remittance transfers by 5 percent over five years with a view to mitigating the impact of a potential 10–15 percent decline in remittances in 2008–10 due to the world financial crisis.

The significant positive savings rates in almost all countries in the region would also facilitate the recovery process (figure 2, panel c). South Asia's strong savings culture and reliable remittance patterns could help bridge the savings-investments gap to sustain economic growth. This is especially important as a precursor to moving away from overreliance on external funding.

Policy Responses and Challenges

To counter the economic slowdown, South Asian countries have adopted both monetary and fiscal policy measures. Despite large fiscal deficits and considerable public debt that limit the fiscal space to maneuver, Bangladesh, India, and Sri Lanka have introduced fiscal stimulus packages (table 1). These stimulus measures are aimed at boosting production and exports, strengthening agriculture and other critical sectors, developing infrastructure and social safety nets, and promoting domestic demand. Other measures taken by the region's countries include easing policy rates, reducing cash reserve requirements, introducing targeted lending, and relaxing loan restructuring and provisioning requirements.

While the indicators appear to support the expectation of a modest economic recovery in 2010, significant challenges clearly lie ahead for these diverse economies trying to navigate toward sustainable growth. Common challenges include keeping inflationary pressures low, maintaining a flexible fiscal policy (at least in the short term) while managing already large fiscal deficits, attracting much-needed external financing, and boosting export income.

Beyond these common challenges are country-specific ones. In several countries, the financial crisis has had minimal impact—Afghanistan, Bangladesh, Bhutan, and Nepal. For Afghanistan, the challenges at this stage are primarily security related. Bangladesh and Nepal both need to focus on controlling inflation and improving export growth. Bhutan needs to diversify its export avenues. The rest of the countries in the region—India, Maldives, Pakistan, and Sri Lanka—have been affected by the crisis to some extent. India's economy shows sign of recovery, though managing inflation, maintaining fiscal balance, and attracting external capital are issues that still need attention. Maldives needs to battle the twin deficits—fiscal and current account—as well as improve its reserve position. Pakistan needs to focus on such issues as inflation, diversified export growth, and adherence to its stabilization program. And Sri Lanka needs to focus on attracting external capital while maintaining fiscal balance.

The Crisis and South Asian Banking Sectors

South Asian banking systems, with limited exposure to complex financial instruments and failed financial institutions, had little to do with the subprime mortgage crisis. But because of both economic and financial integration with the rest

Table 1 Salient Features of Fiscal Stimulus Packages Introduced by South Asian Countries

Stimulus package	Features
Bangladesh	
Fiscal spending of Tk 34.24 billion (US$500 million, 0.6% of GDP) announced in April 2009, to be expanded to 0.8% of GDP in the 2010 budget	– Expenditure on cash subsidies to exporters (Tk 4.5 billion) – Expenditure on agriculture (Tk 15 billion) – Expenditure on power sector (Tk 6 billion) – Expenditure on agricultural loans (Tk 5 billion) – Expenditure on social security (Tk 3.74 billion)
India	
Three stimulus packages announced, in December 2008, January 2009, and February 2009, with total fiscal spending of Rs 186,000 crore (US$39 billion, 3.5% of GDP)	– Support extended to exports, textile sector, infrastructure, housing, and small and medium-size enterprises – Spending increased on public projects to create employment and public assets – Prices cut for gasoline (by Rs 5 per liter) and diesel (Rs 3) – Interest rates on loans for infrastructure and exports lowered – Excise duties on all manufactured goods (except petroleum products) cut by 4% – India Infrastructure Finance Company Limited permitted to raise funds to provide refinancing to public sector banks in the infrastructure sector – External commercial borrowings policy liberalized to increase lending to borrowers in the infrastructure sector – Countervailing duty and special countervailing duty reimposed on cement imports – Service tax cut across the board from 12% to 10% – Excise duty reduced by 2% for items currently attracting 10%
Sri Lanka	
Package to support export sectors through spending of SL Rs 16 billion (US$141 million, 0.4% GDP) announced in December 2008, and another of SL Rs 8 billion (US$70 million, 0.2% of GDP) in May 2009	– Incentives for the agricultural and industrial export sectors (tea, textiles, tourism, leather, rubber), including fertilizer subsidy and 5% export incentive – Reduction in fuel prices – Waiver on 15% electricity surcharge
Pakistan	
No new fiscal spending introduced because of huge fiscal deficit, but efforts made to reprioritize expenditures in 2008/09, so as to increase spending on social safety nets	– Benazir Income Support Program launched with a budget of PRs 34 billion (0.3% of GDP), to help poor families through monthly cash benefits – Increase in Private Sector Development Program spending (up to 62% of previous year's program budget) introduced in 2010 budget

Sources: ESCAP 2009; official sources.

of the world, all regional banking systems suffered to varying degrees from the adverse effects of the global deleveraging and contraction in the real sector. Liquidity and credit markets tightened as inflows of external capital declined and outflows of capital (such as portfolio investment) increased. And the level of nonperforming loans rose as a result of the real sector slowdown. But regulatory measures taken by banking supervisory authorities and the financial sector reforms already under way in most of the region's countries appear to have helped the banking systems remain resilient. The dominance of local banks in all major banking systems in the region also helped limit the effects of the crisis. Getting Finance Indicators on banking soundness and performance over the five-year period 2004–08 can help in understanding the environment of the South Asian commercial banking sector and regional trends in banking practices. (For detailed time-series analysis and financial soundness rankings for each country, see part I.)

Impact on Banking

Private credit extended by banks showed a generally increasing trend over the 2004–08 period (figure 3, panel a). In 2008, however, the ratio dropped slightly in Nepal, Pakistan, and Sri Lanka, largely because banks adopted overly cautious lending policies toward import- and export-related businesses in response to the decline in demand for exports. The rising levels of nonperforming loans were also a factor for banks. Credit extended by banks averaged around 36 percent of GDP over the period in most South Asian countries. The exception was Maldives, where the five-year average was 71 percent and the 2008 ratio a high 100.84 percent, pointing to a disproportionate reliance on bank credit that should be viewed with caution.

Private credit growth appeared to slow in 2009 as the economic slowdown led to lower demand. In Maldives and Pakistan, however, heavy government borrowing appears to have crowded out private credit, also a cause for concern. This development is due in part to banks choosing the easy option of investing in relatively risk-free assets such as treasury bonds and treasury bills.

Liquidity appeared to tighten during 2004–08. While the liquid assets ratio for the region's countries averaged 29 percent over the five-year period, it dropped to 24 percent in 2008 (figure 3, panel b). Liquidity was tight in Nepal, where liquid assets averaged 11 percent of total assets, and in Sri Lanka, where the average was 20 percent. Tightening liquidity was also evident from the steadily increasing loan to deposit ratios (figure 3, panel c). Rising loan to deposit ratios mean increasing liquidity stress for the banking system and thus increasing liquidity risk. The loan to deposit ratio for the region averaged around 72 percent over the five-year period. Maldives had the highest ratio, averaging 101.71 percent over the five years and reaching 133.41 percent in 2008. These ratios suggest that banks could face liquidity constraints in the near future and possible credit risks as the economic slowdown affects the real sector.

In 2009, loan to deposit ratios generally fell, although in Nepal the ratio rose as a result of growth in real estate lending. Most countries appear to have managed liquidity tightness through the easing of policy rates, the cash reserve ratio, and the statutory liquidity ratio.

In this environment of slowing credit growth and tight liquidity, it is important to look at the performance and stability of the commercial banking sector. On the performance side, the return on assets generally improved across the region over the five-year period (figure 4, panel a). In Maldives and Pakistan, the return on assets dropped in 2008, but these two countries still posted higher average returns over the period than the rest of the region. While the regional average over the five-year period was around 2.25 percent, Maldives posted an average of 5.43 percent, the region's highest. In 2008, the return on assets in Maldives fell to 4.53 percent.

Figure 3 **Challenges to Manage**

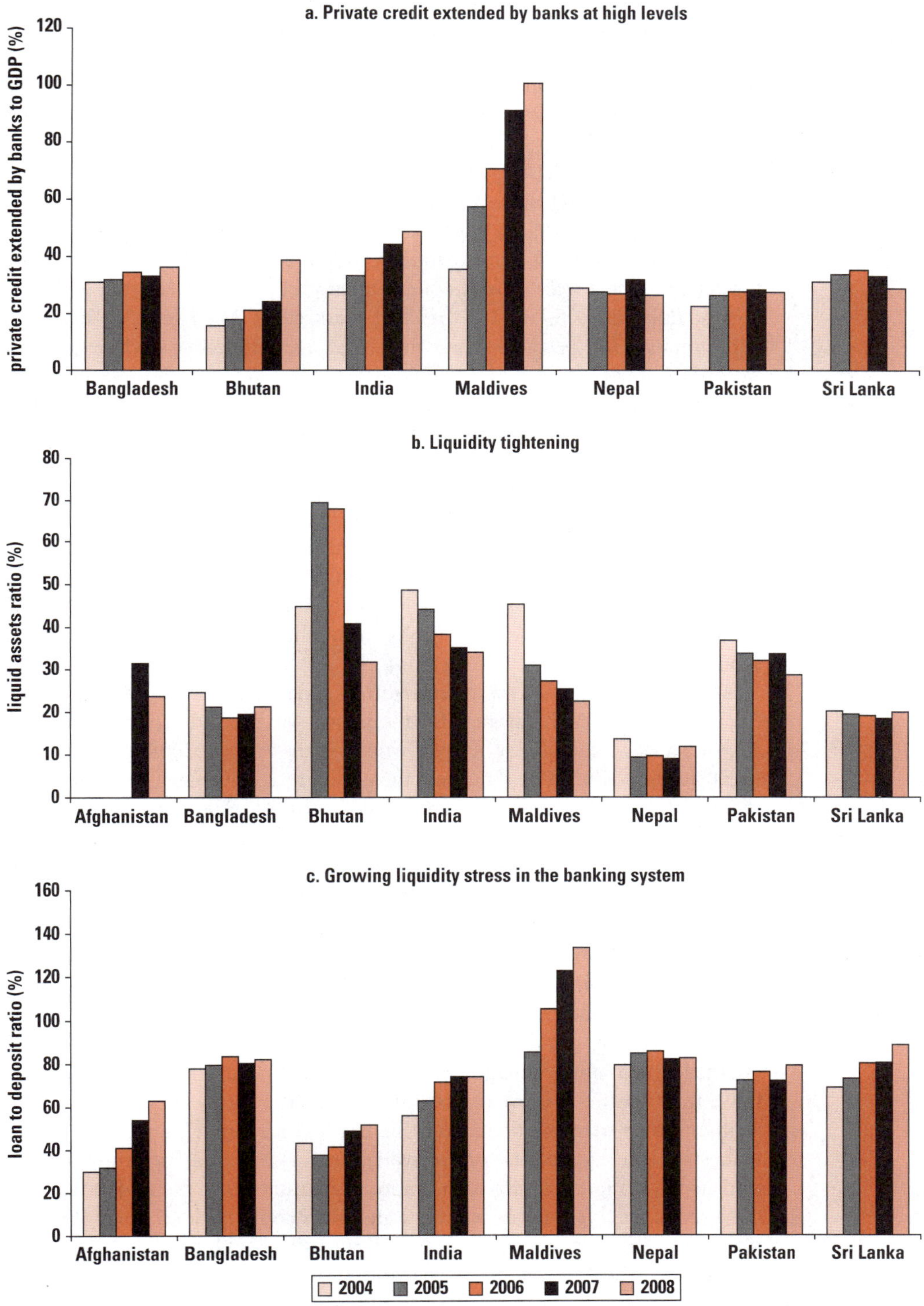

Source: Appendix 2.
Note: Liquid assets ratio data are not available for Afghanistan, 2004–06.

Banks in South Asia continue to enjoy high interest rate spreads. The net interest margin averaged nearly 4 percent over the period, with Afghanistan posting the highest in 2008 at 7.12 percent (figure 4, panel b). Even with central banks cutting policy rates in 2009, banks are unlikely to reduce interest rates significantly and, thus, will continue to earn high margins. Given these recent trends in returns and interest rate spreads, it appears unlikely that the performance levels of South Asian banking systems will be severely affected.

On the stability side, all South Asian countries except Nepal maintained capital adequacy levels well above the statutory requirements (figure 4, panel c). After years of being saddled with negative equity, the Nepalese banking sector managed to post a positive capital adequacy ratio in 2008; at 4.04 percent, however, the 2008 ratio was well below the statutory requirement. Afghanistan posted the highest ratio in 2008, at 31.77 percent, followed by Maldives (21.01 percent) and Bhutan (13.93 percent). These three countries still follow the Basel I Capital Accord, however, with the result that risk weights are not adjusted for market and operational risks. Sri Lanka moved to Basel II by 2008, and India (all local banks) by 2009. These two countries therefore have lower capital ratios, because of the additional capital charge for market risk, but they also have more stable performance on capital adequacy. Bangladesh, Nepal, and Pakistan planned to do a parallel run of both accords until 2010.

Conditions were conducive to a further decline in capital adequacy in 2009. For most countries with dominant state banks, this may be a concern—because the lack of fiscal space during these times could hamper government recapitalization efforts. Even for nonstate banks recapitalization will be a problem during economic slowdown.

The region's average gross nonperforming loans ratio fell over the five years (figure 4, panel d). The average for the period was around 6.29 percent. While Afghanistan had the lowest nonperforming loans ratio in 2008, at 0.9 percent, India steadily reduced its ratio over the period to 2.25 percent. By contrast, the ratio in Maldives jumped from 1.56 percent in 2007 to 8.90 percent in 2008. The ratio also rose in several other countries in the region.

The provisions to nonperforming loans ratio was high in all countries except Nepal (figure 4, panel e). In Nepal, the five-year average for the ratio was 10.30 percent, and the 2008 ratio was 8.16 percent. The regional average over the five years was 52.62 percent. In Maldives, provisions dropped from 63.94 percent of gross nonperforming loans in 2007 to 14.02 percent in 2008. All other countries except Afghanistan and Bangladesh also registered a decline in provisions from the previous year.

The levels of nonperforming loans and provisions need to be watched carefully. In 2009 the level of nonperforming loans rose in all countries except Afghanistan, where the financial crisis has had no impact, and Nepal, where real estate lending, because of the availability of collateral, has led to a reduction in the nonperforming loans ratio. The situation in Nepal is a concern, however, since fluctuations in real estate prices could lead to higher exposures for banks. The recovery of loans and advances backed by real estate collateral has been a critical problem in Nepal and Maldives as a result of archaic mortgage and property laws and the lack of special debt recovery provisions and commercial courts.

Figure 4 **Returns and Capital Levels Fair, But Nonperforming Loans Need Watching**

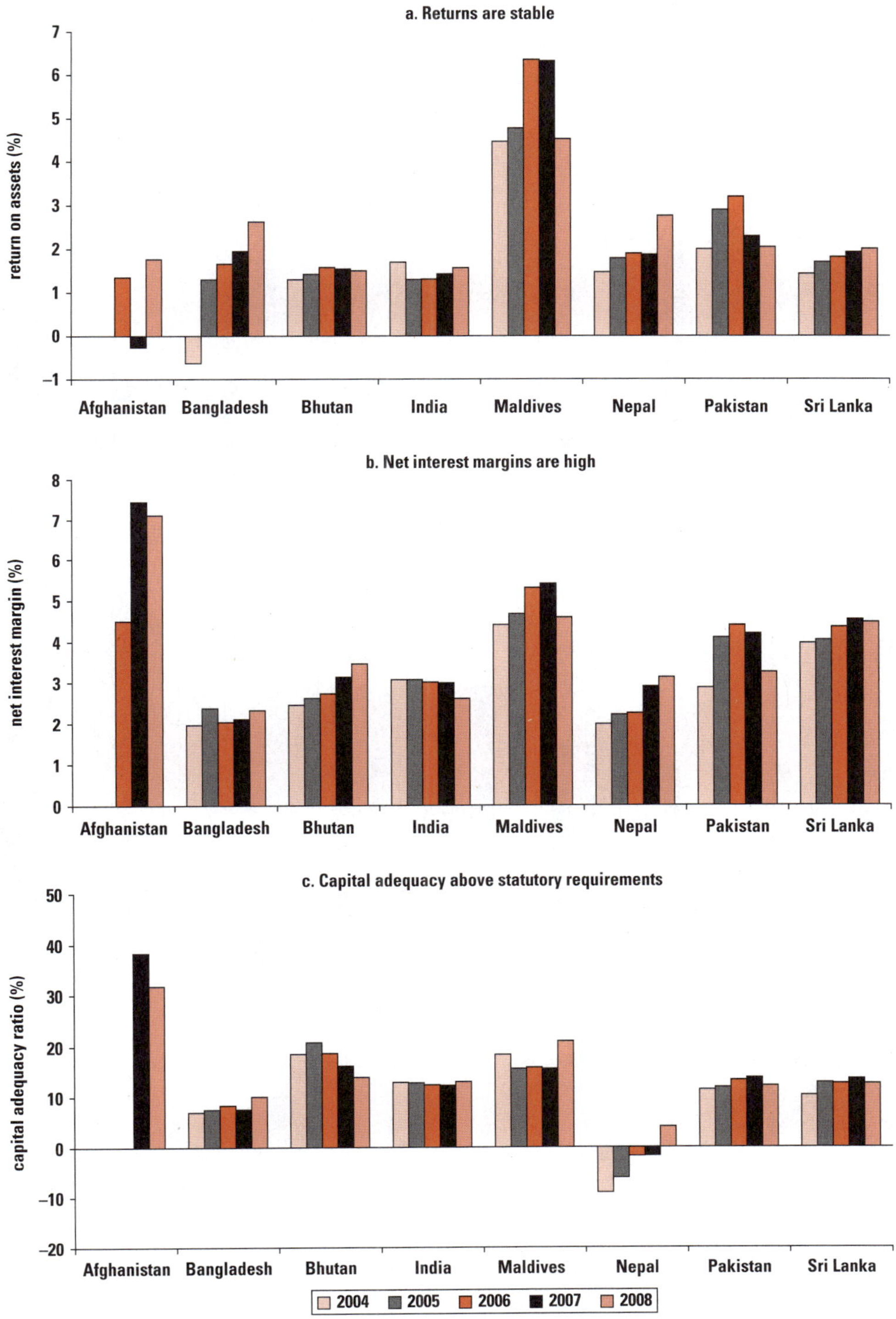

(Figure continues on next page)

Figure 4 **Returns and Capital Levels Fair, But Nonperforming Loans Need Watching** *(continued)*

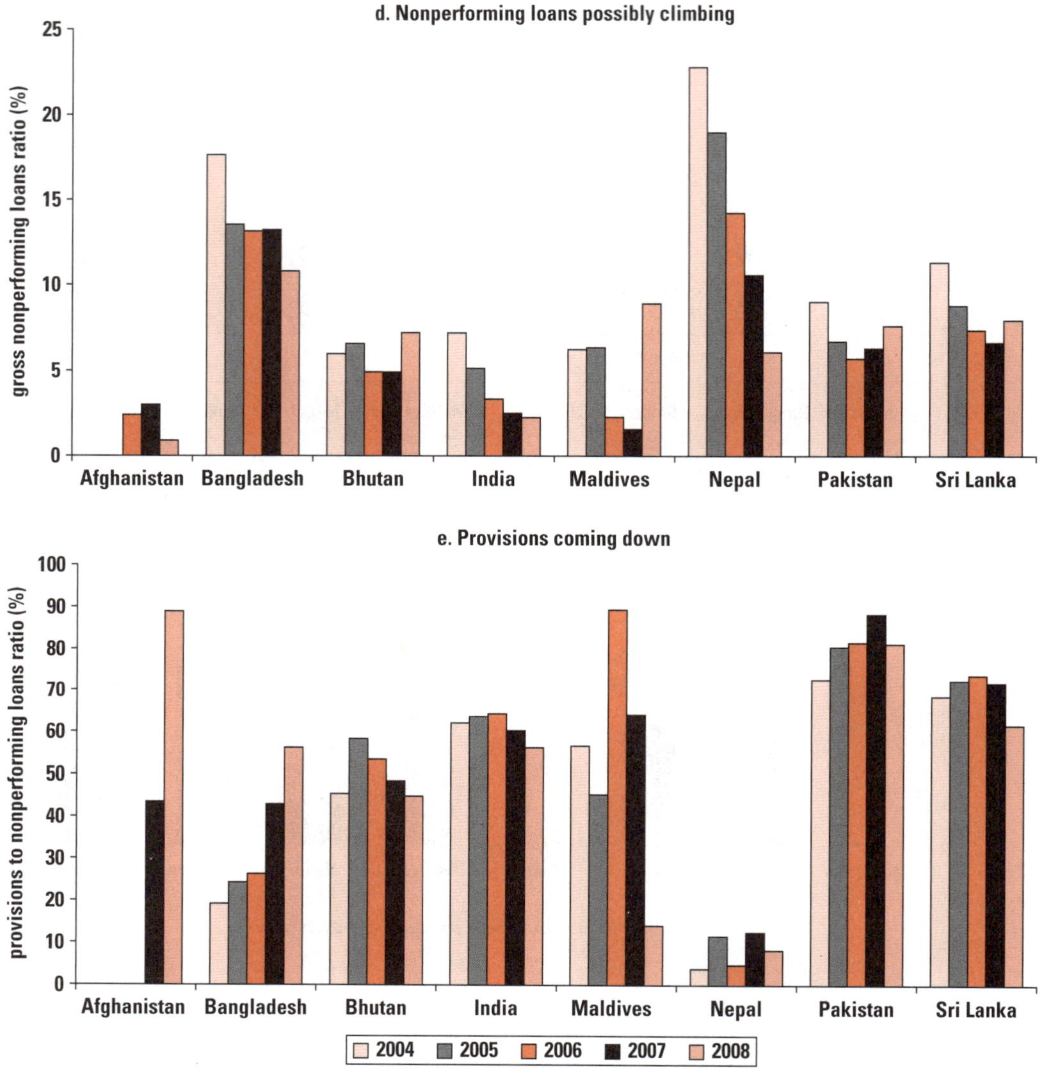

Source: Appendix 2.
Note: For Afghanistan, return on assets data for 2004–05 and capital adequacy ratio data for 2004–06 are unavailable.

If the economic recovery is weak, nonperforming loans may increase further. It may therefore be prudent to assume that the nonperforming loan position will not improve significantly in the near term.

Policy Responses and Challenges

Just as the impact of the crisis on the banking sector has varied among countries in the region, so have the policy responses. On the monetary policy side, most countries have resorted to rate cuts and reductions in the statutory liquidity and cash reserve ratios to manage liquidity. India has introduced special refinance facilities. Bangladesh has imposed a lending rate ceiling and has also introduced targeted lending by commercial banks. While capital infusions are difficult for most countries at this stage, India has recapitalized some of the state banks. The World Bank has extended a US$2 billion loan to India for this purpose, to help ensure that banks can maintain credit growth, support social banking and employment growth, and help strengthen the economic recovery ahead. The loan is part of a US$4.3 billion loan program to support India's economic stimulus and infrastructure investments. Most countries have engaged in regulatory forbearance, such as relaxing risk weights and loan restructuring and provisioning requirements, with the aim of boosting banks' returns and capital positions. India has restructured part of the loan portfolio. In addition to responses such as these, the regulatory reforms and capacity-building programs taking place in most countries may also have helped.

Regulatory authorities appear to have responded swiftly and aggressively to contain the crisis and avert an erosion of public confidence in the banking system. As the impact of the financial crisis and the ensuing economic slowdown continues to evolve, regulators need to identify gaps in the regulatory and supervisory systems and take remedial actions as well as to continue adjusting actions taken so far to restore financial stability and improve crisis preparedness. This points to a need to pursue development programs, such as implementing the Basel II Capital Accord, improving prudential regulation and supervision systems, strengthening corporate governance, and restructuring and recapitalizing banks.

While the banking systems in South Asia have so far weathered the second-round effects of the global financial and economic meltdown better than those in some other regions, each of the region's countries will have to overcome challenges in the continuing recovery process. For most countries, the real sector slowdown and global deleveraging will pose challenges in credit quality and funding. Other issues needing careful attention by all countries include ensuring adequate capitalization, managing the risk environment, and minimizing delinquent loans. In addition to these common challenges, Afghanistan and Bhutan need to address many development issues in their banking systems (see the discussions in chapter 3). Maldives and Pakistan need to be concerned about heavy government borrowing through the commercial banks, which is crowding out private sector credit. Nepal needs to monitor real estate lending, which could lead to further deterioration in the nonperforming loans position. Bangladesh needs to improve banks' capital position to maintain stability while remaining mindful of the additional capital charges needed for market and operational risk when it adopts Basel II. And India and Sri Lanka need to further manage the transition to Basel II by strengthening banks' capital cushions.

Beyond such operational issues, South Asian countries also need to focus on deposit insurance. Today, only Bangladesh and India have explicit deposit insurance schemes in place. While no country in the region experienced a loss of confidence in the banking system as a result of the global financial crisis, having a deposit insurance scheme is nevertheless important to help maintain confidence in the system. Such schemes will not address the root cause of an erosion in confidence. But they may help stall bank runs and restore confidence, as shown by events in the United States during the financial crisis. Having a deposit insurance scheme can also lead to moral hazard. But during a crisis, restoring public confidence is of prime importance to the stability of the banking system.

Another critical focus is credit for the real sector. Economic deceleration would affect all industries and could further reduce output. This impact on the real economy could be exacerbated by the financial squeeze that might ensue with a reduction in remittance receipts and in foreign direct investment and other financing options as a result of deleveraging activities by developed country investors. Thus, in addition to the other reforms discussed, South Asian countries need to take all necessary steps to ensure the availability of credit and liquidity to the real sector so that economic activity can continue unabated. Even more important is that South Asian economies and banking sectors strive not only for strong and stable growth but also for a more inclusive growth that minimizes inequalities.

Endnotes

1. The World Bank classifies economies based on their per capita gross national income (GNI), calculated using the Atlas method. For the 2008 classification a GNI of US$975 or less is low income, and a GNI of US$976–3,855, lower middle income (for more details and the entire classification, see http://go.worldbank.org/K2CKM78CC0).
2. World Bank, World Development Indicators database.
3. Inflation figures may vary as a result of differences in methods and in the goods and services included in the basket of commodities used for measuring inflation. For example, India uses wholesale price indexes for measuring inflation, while Pakistan, Sri Lanka, and others use retail price indexes. In addition, some countries have removed price increases due to the unprecedentedly high oil prices in 2007/08 from their price indexes and publish data on core inflation rather than point-to-point or average inflation.

Appendixes

Appendix 1. Prudential Regulations in South Asian Countries, End of 2008

Table A1.1 Capital Adequacy Requirements for Banks

Afghanistan	Bangladesh	Bhutan	India	Maldives	Nepal	Pakistan	Sri Lanka
Capital adequacy requirement (as % of risk-weighted assets)							
12	10	10	9	12 (from 2009; 8 earlier)	10	10	10
Tier 1 capital (as % of risk-weighted assets)							
6	5	5	6 (by March 2010)	6 (from 2009; 4 earlier)	6	5 (since the sum of Tier 2 and 3 capital cannot exceed Tier 1 capital)	5
Minimum paid-up capital requirement							
Af 500 million (US$10 million) (Incumbent banks are given 5 years to comply.)	For mainstream commercial banks: minimum capital requirement of Tk 400 crore (Tk 4 billion or US$59 million), of which minimum paid-up capital must be Tk 200 crore (Tk 2 billion or US$29.5 million), with any capital shortfall to be met by August 2011 For Islamic banks: minimum paid-up capital requirement of Tk 100 crore (Tk 1 billion or US$14.5 million)	Nu 300 million (US$6.25 million)	Rs 300 crore (Rs 3 billion or US$62.5 million)	Rf 150 million (US$11.7 million) A minimum leverage ratio of 5% is added to provide a basic "tangible net worth" threshold of safety.	NRs 2 billion (US$26 million)	PRs 6 billion (US$72.5 million) by the end of December 2009 (up from PRs 5 billion in 2008)	SL Rs 2.5 billion (US$21.8 million)

Source: National prudential regulations for commercial banks.

Table A1.2 Tier 1, Tier 2, and Tier 3 Capital Composition

Afghanistan	Bangladesh	Bhutan	India	Maldives	Nepal	Pakistan	Sri Lanka
Tier 1 capital composition							
Paid-in capital such as: - Common equity shares and their related surplus - Noncumulative, perpetual preferred shares - Such other instruments as may be approved by Da Afghanistan Bank (DAB) - Retained profit or loss for previous years - Legal reserves - Other reserves set aside for after-tax profit - Losses of current year (if any) *Deductions* - Goodwill - Intangible assets - Future tax benefits - Equity investments, to be deducted from a bank's regulatory (total) capital	- Paid-up capital - Nonrepayable share premium - Statutory reserves - General reserves - Retained earnings - Minority interest in subsidiaries - Noncumulative irredeemable preference shares - Dividend equalization account	- Paid-up capital - General reserves (statutory reserves) - Share premium account - Retained earnings (free reserve) *Deductions* - Loss for the current year	- Paid-up capital - Statutory reserves - Other disclosed free reserves - Capital reserves representing any surplus arising from sale proceeds of assets - Specified innovative perpetual debt instruments (limited to 15% of previous year's Tier 1 capital) - Specified perpetual noncumulative preference shares - Any other type of instruments as specified by the Reserve Bank of India (RBI) *Deductions* - Equity investments in subsidiaries - Intangible assets and current or brought-forward losses - Deferred tax assets	- Permanent shareholders' equity (issued and fully paid-up ordinary shares and noncumulative perpetual preference shares) - Disclosed reserves (additional paid-in share premium plus undistributed profits) - Minority interests in equity of consolidated subsidiaries *Deductions* - Goodwill and other intangible assets - Loan loss provisions (both general and specific)	- Paid-up capital - Share premium - Nonredeemable preference shares - Proposed bonus equity shares - Statutory general reserves - Retained earnings - Unaudited current year's cumulative profit, after provisions (including staff bonuses and taxes) - Capital redemption reserves created in lieu of redeemable instruments - Capital adjustment reserves - Dividend equalization reserves - Any other type of reserves as notified by Nepal Rastra Bank (NRB) *Deductions* - Goodwill - Miscellaneous expenditure as specified - Investments in equity licensed by NRB	- Paid-up capital or capital deposited with the State Bank of Pakistan (SBP) (for foreign banks) - Share premium account - Reserve for bonus shares - General reserves - Unappropriated or unremitted profits (net of losses, if any) *Deductions* - Goodwill - Intangible assets - Shortfall in provisions required against classified assets - Deficit on account of revaluation of investments held in "available for sale" category	- Paid-up ordinary shares or assigned capital - Noncumulative or nonredeemable preference shares - Share premium - Statutory reserve fund - Retained profits or losses - General and other reserves - Gains or losses after tax from sale of fixed and long-term investments - Unpublished current year's profits or losses - Minority interests - Perpetual debt capital instruments *Deductions* - Goodwill - Net deferred tax - Other intangible assets - Employee advances to share ownership plans - Dues to or from head office and branches (foreign banks) - 50% of investments in unconsolidated banking and financial subsidiary companies

(Table continues on next page)

Table A1.2 Tier 1, Tier 2, and Tier 3 Capital Composition *(continued)*

Afghanistan	Bangladesh	Bhutan	India	Maldives	Nepal	Pakistan	Sri Lanka
				- All other asset revaluation reserves - Future income tax benefits - Losses carried forward - Encumbered assets	- All investments in equity of institutions with financial interest - Investments in equity in excess of prescribed limits - Investments arising from underwriting agreements - Reciprocal cross-holding of bank capital designed to inflate capital, not disposed of within 1 year of commitment - Any other as stipulated by NRB		- 50% of investments in capital of other banks and financial institutions
Tier 2 capital composition							
- Ordinary preferred shares - Term preferred shares - Term debt instruments fully subordinated to the rights of depositors - Hybrid debt-equity instruments (unsecured and fully paid up) - Debt instruments mandated to be convertible into common shares, which are unsecured and fully paid in	- General provisions (1% of unclassified loans)[a] - Asset revaluation reserves - All other preference shares - Perpetual subordinated debt - Exchange equalization account - Revaluation reserves of held-to-maturity securities (up to 50% of revaluation reserves)	- Capital reserve - Fixed assets revaluation reserve - Exchange fluctuation reserve - Investment fluctuation reserve - Research and development fund - General provisions (not exceeding 1.25% of total risk-weighted assets) - Subordinated term debts with a minimum original maturity of at least 5 years (must be fully paid or repayment must not be guaranteed)	- Undisclosed reserves - Cumulative perpetual preference shares (fully paid up and no redemption rights) - Revaluation reserves on premises and marketable securities (discounted by 55%) - Excess provisions toward depreciation on investments - General provisions and loss reserves (up to a maximum of 1.25% of risk-weighted assets)	- Year-to-date earnings (or losses) - Undisclosed reserves - Asset revaluation reserves (if allowed by the Maldives Monetary Authority [MMA] and consistent with applicable accounting standards) - General loan loss provisions (limited to 1.25% of risk-weighted assets)	- Cumulative or redeemable preference shares with maturity of more than 5 years - General loan loss provisions (subject to a maximum of 1.25% of total risk-weighted assets) - Exchange equalization reserve - Investments adjustment reserve - Assets revaluation reserve (only up to 2% of total Tier 2 capital, inclusive of this reserve) - Hybrid capital instruments	- General provisions or reserves for loan losses (subject to a maximum of 1.25% of total risk-weighted assets) - Exchange translation reserves - 50% of revaluation reserves on fixed assets only - Undisclosed reserves - Subordinated debt (up to 50% of Tier 1 capital) *For capital adequacy purposes, supplementary capital is limited to 50% of core capital.*	- Approved revaluation reserves (50%) - General provisions (subject to a maximum of 1.25% of total risk-weighted assets) - Hybrid capital instruments - Approved subordinated term debt (50%) - Minority interests arising from preference shares issued by subsidiaries *Deductions* - 50% of investments in unconsolidated banking and financial subsidiary companies - 50% of investments in capital of other banks and financial institutions

- General reserves for loan losses up to a maximum of 1.25% of risk-weighted assets at any one time - Revaluation reserves of fixed assets, available-for-sale investments, and cash flow hedges and other assets - Profits of current year (if any) *In the calculation of regulatory capital, supplementary capital is limited to 100% of core capital.*		- Profit for current year *In the calculation of regulatory capital, Tier 2 capital is limited to 100% of core capital. And subordinated debt shall not exceed 50% of Tier 1 capital.*	- Hybrid capital instruments - Subordinated debt (up to 50% of Tier 1 capital) - Investment fluctuation reserves - Innovative perpetual debt instruments (in excess of 15% of Tier 1 capital) - Any other type of instruments specified by the RBI *Total Tier 2 capital is limited to 100% of Tier 1 capital.*	- Subordinated term debt (limited to 50% of Tier 1 capital) - Hybrid debt-equity capital instruments (unsecured, subordinated, and fully paid up) *Total Tier 2 capital is limited to 100% of Tier 1 capital.*	- Subordinated term debt fully paid up with maturity of more than 5 years (limited to 50% of Tier 1 capital) - Other reserves as specified by NRB *Total Tier 2 capital is limited to 100% of Tier 1 capital.*		*Total Tier 2 capital is limited to 100% of Tier 1 capital.*
Tier 3 capital composition							
			Capital issued solely to meet the market risk capital charge in accordance with the criteria laid down (for primary dealers)			Short-term subordinated debt; will be used solely for the purpose of meeting a proportion of the capital requirements for market risks	Short-term subordinated debt; may be used for the sole purpose of meeting a proportion of the capital requirements for market risk

Source: National prudential regulations for commercial banks.

a. Except for housing and small and medium-size enterprise loans (2%) and consumer credit and special mention loans (5%).

Table A1.3 Basel I Risk Weights in Use and Basel II Status

Afghanistan	Bangladesh	Bhutan	India[a]	Maldives	Nepal[a]	Pakistan[a]	Sri Lanka[a]
Basel I risk weights in use for computing capital charges							
0% weight - Cash - Bank balances and claims in category A countries - Precious metal in vault - Current accounts and obligations in DAB - Loans with cash collateral *20% weight* - Loans and direct claims - Claims with maturity of more than 1 year supported by collateral or securities issued, offered by Category A countries - Loans supported by collateral of multilateral lending institutions - Cash in process of collection	*0% weight* - Cash in hand (local banks, Bangladesh Bank [BB], public OFIs [other financial institutions]) - Money at call (local banks, public OFIs) - Foreign currency in hand, in banks abroad, in BB, and in wage earners' accounts - Import and inland bills (Ministry of Food, government) - Advances (Ministry of Food, President and Prime Minister's Office, parliament, autonomous and semiautonomous bodies) - Investments (treasury bills, government savings certificates and other securities, prize and income tax bonds) - Head office and interbranch adjustments	*0% weight* - Cash in hand - Precious metals - Balances with the Royal Monetary Authority (RMA) (current deposits and cash reserve requirements) - Bills issued by the RMA - Bills and bonds issued or guaranteed by the government - Reserves repurchased by the RMA - Loans and overdrafts secured by cash deposits with banks in Bhutan - Claims and guarantees with remaining maturity of less than 1 year issued by governments or central banks of Zone A countries *20% weight* - Claims on financial institutions in Bhutan - Claims on financial institutions incorporated in Zone A countries	*0% weight* - Cash at bank and branches abroad - Gold and bullion - Balances with the RBI - Treasury bills and bonds - Central bank securities - Loans and advances against cash, deposits, and gold - Loans and advances against government guarantees or securities - Loans and advances guaranteed by the central bank *2.5% weight* - Other government securities and securities guaranteed by the government *20% weight* - Staff loans secured by provident fund balances	*0% weight* - Cash at bank and in transit - Claims and balances with the MMA - Claims on, or guaranteed or fully secured by, securities issued by the government of Maldives - Claims on central governments and central banks denominated in national currency and funded in that currency - Other claims on OECD central governments and central banks - Claims collateralized by securities of, or guaranteed by, OECD central governments - Claims fully secured by cash or pledged deposits in same bank *20% weight* - Claims on multilateral development banks and claims guaranteed or collateralized by securities issued by such banks	*0% weight* - Cash at bank - Balances with NRB - Treasury bills and bonds - Central bank securities - Other government securities or securities guaranteed by the government - Loans and advances against cash, deposits, and gold - Loans and advances against government guarantees or securities - Loans and advances guaranteed by the central bank - Staff loans secured by provident fund balances *20% weight* - Claims guaranteed by OECD central governments or central banks	*0% weight* - Cash at bank - Gold and bullion - Balances with the SBP - Treasury bills and bonds - Central bank securities - Other government securities and securities guaranteed by the government - Loans and advances against cash, deposits, and gold - Loans and advances against government guarantees or securities - Loans and advances guaranteed by the central bank - Staff loans secured by provident fund balances - Claims guaranteed by OECD central governments or central banks - Claims guaranteed by non-OECD central governments or central banks *20% weight* - Claims guaranteed by commercial banks (maturity up to 1 year)	*0% weight* - Cash at bank and branches abroad - Gold and bullion - Balances with the Central Bank of Sri Lanka (CBSL) - Treasury bills and bonds - Central bank securities - Other government securities and securities guaranteed by the government - Loans and advances against cash, deposits, and gold - Loans and advances against government guarantees or securities - Loans and advances guaranteed by the central bank - Staff loans secured by provident fund balances - Gold and gold jewelry against advances *10% weight* - Claims guaranteed by OECD central governments or central banks

3–50% weight - Loans with residential mortgages as collateral, not past due for 30 days - Loans to builders to finance real estate construction where property is presold or leased with finances assigned to the bank - Other approved assets *100% weight* - All loans to private debtors - Premises, plant and equipment, other fixed assets, and other real estate owned as a result of foreclosures or defaults - Real estate held for investment - Any other assets	- Other assets as specified - Off–balance sheet commitments with residual maturity of less than 1 year that can be revoked at any time *20% weight* - Balances and money at call with private OFIs - Foreign investments in OECD countries - Import and inland bills (autonomous and semiautonomous bodies, OFIs, banks, local authorities) - Advances (government autonomous and semiautonomous bodies; public OFIs; AAA-rated multilateral development banks, banks, and local authorities) - Investments (autonomous and semiautonomous bodies, OFIs, banks, local authorities, negotiable CDs)	- Claims and guarantees with maturity of more than 1 year issued by governments or central banks of Zone A countries - Claims and guarantees with maturity of less than 1 year issued by governments or central banks of Zone B countries *50% weight* - Claims and guarantees with maturity of more than 1 year issued by governments or central banks of Zone B countries - Claims with maturity of less than 1 year on financial institutions incorporated in Zone B countries, including deposits in India *100% weight* - Equity investments (net of specific provisions) - Investments in real estate (net of specific provisions) - Term loans and overdrafts (net of specific and general provisions)	- Claims guaranteed by OECD central governments or central banks - Claims guaranteed by non-OECD central governments or central banks - Claims guaranteed by commercial banks (maturity up to 1 year) - Claims and loans guaranteed by banks incorporated in OECD countries - Balances with banks abroad - Balances with local banks - Balances with foreign currency banking units *50% weight* - Loans fully secured by primary mortgages on residential property *75% weight* - Balances with other financial institutions *100% weight* - Other loans and advances - Fixed assets	- Claims and loans guaranteed by banks incorporated in OECD countries - Claims and loans guaranteed by domestic banks incorporated in non-OECD countries with residual maturity of less than 1 year - Claims and loans guaranteed by non-domestic OECD public sector entities, excluding the central government (with prior approval of the MMA) - Cash items in process of collection (domestic and foreign) *50% weight* - Loans fully secured by first-priority mortgages on residential property - Claims and loans guaranteed by local government authorities of Maldives - Claims on public enterprises if approved by the MMA *100% weight* - Claims on the private sector	- Claims guaranteed by non-OECD central governments or central banks - Claims guaranteed by commercial banks (maturity up to 1 year) - Claims and loans guaranteed by banks incorporated in OECD countries - Balances with branches abroad - Balances with banks abroad - Balances with local banks - Balances with foreign currency banking units - Cash in process of collection *100% weight* - Loans fully secured by primary mortgages on residential property - Other loans and advances - Fixed assets - Other assets - Other investments	- Claims and loans guaranteed by banks incorporated in OECD countries - Balances with branches abroad - Balances with banks abroad - Balances with local banks - Balances with foreign currency banking units *0–50% weight* - Loans and advances on enterprises owned and controlled by the government *50% weight* - Loans fully secured by primary mortgages on residential property *100% weight* - Other loans and advances - Other investments - Fixed assets - Other assets	- Balances with foreign currency banking units *20% weight* - Claims guaranteed by non-OECD central governments or central banks - Claims guaranteed by commercial banks (maturity up to 1 year) - Claims and loans guaranteed by banks incorporated in OECD countries - Balances with banks abroad - Balances with local banks - Cash in process of collection *50% weight* - Claims guaranteed by Sri Lanka Export Credit Insurance Corporation (SLECIC) - Loans granted for housing purposes and fully secured by primary mortgages on residential property *100% weight* - Other loans and advances - Other investments - Fixed assets

(Table continues on next page)

Table A1.3 Basel I Risk Weights in Use and Basel II Status *(continued)*

Afghanistan	Bangladesh	Bhutan	India[a]	Maldives	Nepal[a]	Pakistan[a]	Sri Lanka[a]
	- Other assets (letters of credit of government, contingent assets for other banks, claims guaranteed by AAA-rated multilateral development banks) - Off–balance sheet self-liquidating trade-related contingencies *50% weight* - Foreign currencies held for bilateral trade credits - Export and other foreign bills - Foreign investments in non-OECD countries - Import and inland bills (nonfinancial public enterprises) - Advances (OFIs, nonfinancial public enterprises) - Investments (OFIs, nonfinancial public enterprises)	- Claims with maturity of more than 1 year on financial institutions incorporated in Zone B countries (including India) - Fixed assets - Other assets - Off–balance sheet items (net of margin money)	- Other assets *102.5% weight* - Other investments *125% weight* - Gold and gold jewelry less than 10% of total advances	- Claims and loans guaranteed by domestic commercial banks and other banks incorporated outside the OECD with residual maturity of more than 1 year - Claims on central governments outside the OECD (unless denominated or funded in national currency) - Claims on public sector entities not listed above - Claims on commercial companies owned by public sector entities - Premises, plant and equipment, and other fixed assets - Real estate owned and other investments (including nonconsolidated investment participations in other companies) - Capital instruments issued by other banks (unless deducted from capital) - All other assets, excluding those deducted from capital			- Other assets - Fixed deposits with finance companies - Loans against fixed deposits with finance companies

	- Other assets - Other off–balance sheet items - Fixed assets and valuation adjustments - Off–balance sheet transaction-related contingent items - All note issuance facilities and revolving under-writing facilities with maturity of more than 1 year *100% weight* - Import and inland bills (private sector) - Advances (private sector) - Investments (private sector) - Other assets not specified in any other category - Off–balance sheet direct credit substitutes, sale and repurchase agreements, forward assets purchased, and placements of forward deposits						

(Table continues on next page)

Table A1.3 **Basel I Risk Weights in Use and Basel II Status** *(continued)*

Afghanistan	Bangladesh	Bhutan	India[a]	Maldives	Nepal[a]	Pakistan[a]	Sri Lanka[a]
Status of Basel II implementation							
Not yet implemented	Moving toward implementation since 2009. Both Basel I and II are allowed for capital adequacy purposes. Banks are to use Basel II from 2010. Initially, banks are to use the Standardized Approach to calculate capital requirements for credit risk, the Standardized (Rule Based) Approach to calculate those for market risk, and the Basic Indicator Approach to calculate those for operational risk. Guidelines for recognition of eligible external credit assessment institutions have been issued.	Not yet implemented	Foreign banks operating in India and Indian banks with operations outside India have migrated to the Basel II framework since March 2008. All other commercial banks (except local area banks and regional rural banks) migrated to the new framework by March 2009. Parallel runs are reviewed on a quarterly basis. All commercial banks in India (excluding local area banks and regional rural banks) are required to adopt the Standardized Approach for credit risk and the Basic Indicator Approach for operational	Not yet implemented New guidelines issued in 2009 allow banks to apply the new methods for computing Basel II capital requirements in a manner prescribed by the MMA. Initially, banks are to use the Standardized Approach and the Basic Indicator Approach to establish capital requirements (Pillar I), but in no event will a bank be allowed to have a leverage capital ratio less than 5.0%. The adequacy of a bank's capital will remain subject to supervisory review (Pillar II) and market discipline (Pillar III), and higher capital levels may be required, depending on the bank's risk profile and activities.	Banks were to conduct parallel runs of Basel I and II in the 2007/08 financial year, with the new capital adequacy framework made compulsory from 2008/09.[b] New guidelines called for using: - A simplified standardized approach for credit risk - A basic indicator approach for operational risk - An indigenous net open exchange model for market risk	All banks were required to adopt the Standardized Approach for credit and market risk and the Basic Indicator or Standardized Approach for operational risk beginning January 1, 2008. Banks were advised to adopt a parallel run of two years for the Internal Ratings–Based Approach starting January 1, 2008. Adoption of the Foundation or Advanced Internal Ratings–Based Approach for credit risk and the Internal Models Approach for market risk is subject to the prior written approval of the SBP. While the requirement to use the Standardized Approach for reporting capital adequacy took effect on January 1, 2008, banks were also required to continue to submit	The CBSL adopted the Basel II capital adequacy standards for all licensed banks effective from January 2008. Accordingly, all banks are required, in computing capital charges for capital adequacy purposes, to follow the Standardized Approach for credit risk, the Standardized Measurement Approach for market risk, and the Basic Indicator Approach for operational risk.

			risk. Banks are to continue to apply the Standardized Duration Approach for computing capital requirements for market risk. Banks need RBI approval to migrate to the Internal Ratings–Based Approach for credit risk and the Standardized Approach or Advanced Measurement Approach for operational risk.			their calculations based on Basel I until the SBP issues instructions to stop doing so.	

Source: National prudential regulations for commercial banks.

a. Risk weights shown for India, Nepal, Pakistan, and Sri Lanka were or are being phased out with the switch to Basel II.

b. The financial year for banks in Nepal is from mid-July to mid-July.

Table A1.4 Asset Quality: Loan Classification Criteria

Afghanistan	Bangladesh	Bhutan	India	Maldives	Nepal	Pakistan	Sri Lanka
- *Standard:* a performing asset, being repaid in accordance with the contract - *Watch:* 31–60 days past due (most favorable classification; could be lower based on subjective criteria) - *Substandard:* 61–90 days past due (most favorable classification; could be lower based on subjective criteria) - *Doubtful:* 91–180 days past due (most favorable classification; could be lower based on subjective criteria) - *Loss:* 181 days or more past due A loan secured by collateral is classified as follows: a. The portion of the outstanding balance that is equal to or greater than the market value of the collateral (as determined	- *Standard:* all unclassified loans other than special mention accounts - *Special mention accounts:* continuous credit, demand loans, or term loans remaining overdue for 90 days or more *Continuous loans* - *Past due/overdue* if not repaid or renewed by the fixed expiration date - *Substandard* if past due/overdue for 6–9 months - *Doubtful* if past due/overdue for 9–12 months - *Bad debt* if past due/overdue for more than 12 months *Demand loans* - *Past due/overdue* if not repaid or rescheduled by the fixed expiration date	- *Standard:* a performing asset, being repaid in accordance with the contract - *Watch:* 31–90 days overdue - *Substandard:* 91–360 days past due - *Doubtful:* 360–720 days past due - *Loss:* 720 days or more past due Provisions on credit extensions (such as overdrafts, working capital advances, and credit cards) that do not have preestablished repayment schedules shall be allocated as follows: - Credit facilities on which no repayments have been received for 91–360 days shall be	Loans are nonperforming if past due for 90 days or more. Classifications are as follows. - *Standard:* principal amount not past due for up to 3 months - *Substandard:* past due for up to 12 months - *Doubtful:* remained in substandard category for 12 months - *Loss:* identified as a loss by the auditors, regulators, or bank and not written off fully Classification of assets to be done taking into account the degree of well-defined credit weaknesses and the extent of dependence on collateral security for realization of amounts due.	Loans are past due if unpaid for 30 days or more. Classifications are as follows. - *Pass/standard:* 0–60 days past due - *Special mention:* 61–90 days past due - *Substandard:* 91–180 days past due - *Doubtful:* 181–360 days past due - *Loss:* 360 or more days past due Classification criteria go beyond simply the number of days past due and now take into account qualitative factors such as repayment capacity, adverse financial trends, deteriorating financial conditions, and the like.	Loans and advances are classified as nonperforming if unpaid for 30 days or more. Classifications are as follows. - *Pass:* not past due or past due for up to 3 months - *Substandard:* past due for 3–6 months - *Doubtful:* past due for 6–12 months - *Loss:* past due for more than 1 year	Loans are classified by the period for which mark-up/interest or principal is overdue: - *Substandard* if by 90 days or more - *Doubtful* if by 180 days or more - *Loss* if by 1 year or more (or, for trade bills, such as import/export or inland bills, if not paid or adjusted for 180 days or more) Besides the time-based criteria, subjective evaluation of the performing and nonperforming credit portfolio shall be made for risk assessment. And where considered necessary, any account, including the performing account, will be classified, and the	Loans are nonperforming if past due for 90 days or more. Classifications are as follows. *Special mention* - Overdrafts: 90–180 days - Installment credit: 3–6 installments unpaid - Credit cards: 90–120 days - Other credit: 90–180 days *Substandard* - Overdrafts: 180–360 days - Installment credit: 6–12 installments unpaid - Credit cards: 120–180 days - Other credit: 180–360 days *Doubtful* - Overdrafts: 360–540 days - Installment credit: 12–18 installments unpaid - Credit cards: 180–240 days - Other credit: 360–540 days

in accordance with International Valuation Standards and International Accounting Standards) is classified in the category that is one category higher than the combination of objective and subjective criteria would imply. b. The remaining portion of the outstanding balance, if any, is classified in the category consistent with the combination of objective and subjective criteria used for that category. c. If all or a portion of the outstanding balance is fully secured by readily marketable collateral, that portion may be classified as standard, and the remaining portion is classified in the category consistent with the combination of objective and subjective criteria used for that category.	- *Substandard* if unpaid for 6–9 months - *Doubtful* if unpaid for 9–12 months - *Bad debt/loss* if unpaid for 12 months or more *Fixed-term loans repayable within 5 years* - *Substandard* if installments in default for more than 6 months - *Doubtful* if for more than 12 months - *Loss* if for more than 18 months *Fixed-term loans repayable in more than 5 years* - *Substandard* if installments in default for more than 12 months - *Doubtful* if for more than 18 months - *Loss* if for more than 24 months *Short-term agricultural and micro credits* - *Irregular* if not repaid by the due date as stipulated in the loan agreement - *Substandard* if loan remains irregular beyond 12 months	classified substandard, requiring 20% provisioning. - Credit facilities with no repayments for more than 360 days, or whose term has expired, shall be classified as a loss and require 100% provisioning. Loans could also be classified under the above categories (even if the specified period has not elapsed) subject to other conditions specified in the regulations.				category of classification determined on time-based criteria shall be further downgraded.	*Loss* - Overdrafts: more than 540 days - Installment credit: more than 18 installments unpaid - Credit cards: more than 240 days - Other credit: more than 540 days Classification is based on potential risks as well as period risks: banks shall classify performing loans as nonperforming where full recoverability in accordance with the agreed terms is in doubt because of circumstances affecting repayment capacity.

(Table continues on next page)

Table A1.4 Asset Quality: Loan Classification Criteria *(continued)*

Afghanistan	Bangladesh	Bhutan	India	Maldives	Nepal	Pakistan	Sri Lanka
	- *Doubtful* if loan remains irregular beyond 36 months - *Bad debt* if loan remains irregular beyond 60 months If any uncertainty or doubt arises with respect to recovery of any continuous, demand, or fixed-term loan, the loan will have to be classified on the basis of a qualitative judgment on whether or not it is classifiable on the basis of objective criteria.						

Source: National prudential regulations for commercial banks.

Table A1.5 Asset Quality: Provisioning Requirements for Different Loan Classifications

Afghanistan	Bangladesh	Bhutan	India	Maldives	Nepal	Pakistan	Sri Lanka
- *Standard:* 0% - *Watch:* 5% - Substandard*:* 25% - *Doubtful:* 50% - *Loss:* immediate charge-off against the reserve for losses For the standard category, general loss reserves are encouraged on loans to nonfinancial institutions and other clients. For other categories, specific loan loss reserves are required in the indicated percentages, as a minimum.	*Standard* - Loans other than consumer finance loans and special mention accounts: 1% general provisions - Housing finance and loans to professionals under consumer finance: 2% general provisions - Other unclassified consumer finance loans as well as special mention accounts after netting of interest in suspense: 5% general provisions *Continuous, demand, and fixed-term loans* - *Substandard:* 20% - *Doubtful:* 50% - *Bad/loss:* 100% *Short-term agricultural and microcredit loans*	- *Standard:* 1.5% general provisions - *Watch:* 1.5% general provisions - *Substandard:* 20% (30% for sectors with highest exposures) - *Doubtful:* 50% (60% for sectors with highest exposures) - *Loss:* 100% Provisions against credit exposures secured by risk-free collateral shall be maintained in an amount being the net difference between the principal amount and the value of the risk-free collateral. For this purpose precious metals, cash deposits in banks, and securities issued by the RMA or by the government of Bhutan shall be deemed to be risk-free collateral.	*Standard* - Agricultural and small and medium-size enterprise loans: 0.25% general provisions - All other loans and advances: 0.40% general provisions *Substandard* 10% general provisions (unsecured exposures attract additional 10%) *Doubtful* a. 100% to the extent not covered by security's realizable value; and b. An additional amount for the period for which the loan remains doubtful: 20% (of security value) if up to 1 year, 30% if 1–3 years, 100% if more than 3 years.	- *Pass/standard:* 1% general provisions - *Special mention:* 5% general provisions - *Substandard:* 25% specific provisions - *Doubtful:* 50% specific provisions - *Loss:* 100% specific provisions Netting of collateral is allowed only for the doubtful and loss classifications. Group pooling of provisions is allowed for small loans.	- *Standard:* 1% (for priority sector, 0.25% if insured) - *Substandard:* 25% (for priority sector, 6.25% if insured) - *Doubtful:* 50% (for priority sector, 12.5%) - *Loss:* 100% (for priority sector, 25% if insured) An additional 20% provision is required for unsecured loans with only personal or corporate guarantees. Provisioning is done on the outstanding amount.	- *Standard:* 0% except for consumer loans (5% if unsecured; 1.5% if secured) - *Substandard:* 25% - *Doubtful:* 50% - *Loss:* 100% Provisioning is made on gross loans net of liquid assets realizable and 30% of the forced sale value of pledged security. For the loss category, the benefit of forced sale value (FSV) against nonperforming loans shall not be available after 3 years from the date of classification of the loan or advance. Classified loans and advances guaranteed by the government do not require provisioning.	*General provisions* - *Performing assets:* 1% - *Special mention accounts* (net of interest in suspense): 1% General provisions are not necessary for loans secured by cash, gold, or government securities. *Specific provisions* - *Substandard:* 25% for credit card debt; 20% for others - *Doubtful:* 50% - *Loss:* 100% Specific provisioning is made on gross loans net of realizable security value and interest suspended. A haircut[a] is applied to the value of collateral depending on the period remaining in the loss category.

(Table continues on next page)

Table A1.5 Asset Quality: Provisioning Requirements for Different Loan Classifications *(continued)*

Afghanistan	Bangladesh	Bhutan	India	Maldives	Nepal	Pakistan	Sri Lanka
	- *All except bad/loss* (standard, substandard, doubtful): 5% - *Bad/loss:* 100% *Off–balance sheet assets* (general provisions) - Effective December 31, 2007, 0.5% - Effective December 31, 2008, 1% Provisioning made after deducting the interest in suspense and the value of eligible securities (at 50% of the market value of the securities).		*Loss* - To be written off - If not written off, 100% Except for doubtful assets, provisioning is done as a percentage of the gross loan amount. The RBI has comprehensive provisioning rules for leased assets and all other types of advances as well.			The SBP withdrew the FSV benefit for determining provisioning requirements to create a cushion in the balance sheet of banks. In 2009 the SBP partially allowed the FSV benefit (up to 30%) for pledged stock as well as residential and commercial properties. Furthermore, at the end of 2007 the SBP no longer allowed banks to reduce provisions for loans collateralized by illiquid assets. But banks continued to be able to reduce provisions on loans collateralized by liquid assets, including listed securities.	

Source: National prudential regulations for commercial banks.

a. Haircut = The percentage by which an asset's market value is reduced for the purpose of calculating capital requirement, margin, and collateral levels.

Table A1.6 Income Recognition

Afghanistan	Bangladesh	Bhutan	India	Maldives	Nepal	Pakistan	Sri Lanka
Income on loans and advances is recognized on an accrual basis. Banks must suspend the accrual of interest on all interest-earning assets for which principal or interest payments have been past due for periods exceeding 90 days. The loan is then placed on nonaccrual status, and interest income is recognized only upon payment in cash. The only exception to this rule is when such an asset is both well secured and in the process of collection. When an asset is placed on nonaccrual status, all accrued but unpaid interest must be	Income on loans and advances is recognized on an accrual basis. For nonperforming loans, based on the record of recovery, income is recognized on a cash basis. Income on substandard and doubtful loans can be charged to the loan account. The interest charged cannot be transferred to the income account, however, but must be maintained in an interest-in-suspense account (also referred to as an interest suspense account).	Income on loans and advances is recognized on an accrual basis. Interest accrued on a credit exposure that is classified as nonperforming shall not be recognized as income, but shall be suspended and booked in a valuation reserve designated as an interest-in-suspense account. Thereafter, any payments received against the credit exposure must be first applied toward interest arrears, and the remaining balance, if any, toward the principal.	Income on loans and advances is recognized on an accrual basis. For nonperforming loans, based on the record of recovery, income is not recognized on an accrual basis but is booked only on actual realization. Banks, using their own discretion, can debit interest to a nonperforming asset account, crediting the interest to an interest-in-suspense account, or maintain only a record of such interest in pro forma accounts.	Income on loans and advances is recognized on an accrual basis. A loan or advance will be placed on nonaccrual status: - If it is maintained on a cash basis because of deterioration in the borrower's financial condition or ability to pay - If full payment of principal and interest is not expected - Or if it is nonperforming, unless it is both well secured and in the process of collection	Interest accruals on loans and advances shall be recognized on a cash basis. Interest accrued but not received must be debited to the accrued interest account on the asset side of the balance sheet and credited to the interest-in-suspense account on the liability side.	Following the new rules of the Securities and Exchange Commission (SEC) permitting companies to delay recognition of any losses on securities (available for sale) in their income statements until end-December 2009, the SBP has allowed banks the option to follow instructions issued by the SEC on recognition of impairment on their capital position, but encouraged early recognition in income statements. Income on loans and advances is	All interest accrued from the date an advance is classified as nonperforming shall forthwith be suspended and credited to an interest-in-suspense account. Interest on nonperforming loans is recognized as income only on a cash basis. At the time of classifying credit facilities as nonperforming, a bank shall reverse the accrued interest and credit it to an interest-in-suspense

(Table continues on next page)

Table A1.6 Income Recognition *(continued)*

Afghanistan	Bangladesh	Bhutan	India	Maldives	Nepal	Pakistan	Sri Lanka
reversed through a debit to interest income and a credit to accrued interest.	As soon as any loan is classified as bad debt, the charging of interest on that loan will cease. Regulations do not specify whether the interest income accrued but not received on loans that have subsequently become nonperforming has to be reversed or clawed back or provided for.		If any advance becomes nonperforming, the interest accrued and credited to the income account in the previous year should be reversed or provided for, if the interest is not realized. This applies to government-guaranteed accounts as well.	All interest that is accrued but not collected and still carried on the books shall be written off by the end of the calendar quarter in which the loan is, or should have been, placed on nonaccrual status, but in no event later than 90 days after being transferred to nonaccrual status.		recognized on an accrual basis. For nonperforming loans, unrealized mark-up/interest is to be put in a suspense account and not to be credited to the income account except when realized in cash. Unrealized mark-up/interest already credited to the income account is to be reversed and kept in the suspense (memorandum) account.	account. The reversal of unearned income identified after the close of a financial year could be accounted for in the financial year in which the advances were identified as nonperforming.

Source: National prudential regulations for commercial banks.

Table A1.7 Write-Off Policy

Afghanistan	Bangladesh	Bhutan	India	Maldives	Nepal	Pakistan	Sri Lanka
Assets classified as a loss are to be immediately charged off against the reserve for losses. An asset classified as a loss is considered not collectible and of such little value that its continuance as a bankable asset is not warranted. A loss classification does not mean that the asset has absolutely no recovery or salvage value, but that deferring the write-off of this basically worthless asset is not practical or desirable even though partial recovery may be effected in the future.	At any time banks may write off without delay loans classified as bad/loss for the previous 5 years and for which 100% provision has already been made. Banks may write off loans by debiting their current year's income account where 100% provision is not found adequate for writing off such loans.	No guidelines have been issued.	Banks should either make full provision in accordance with the guidelines or write off nonperforming assets and claim tax benefits as applicable, in consultation with their auditors or tax consultants. Banks may write off advances at the head office level even though they are outstanding in the branch books. But provisions need to be made in accordance with the classification assigned to the accounts.	Any asset past due for 360 days or more shall be classified as a loss and written off at the end of the current calendar quarter but not later than 90 days after first being identified as a loss. The write-off may be deferred, but only if the loan is well secured, legal action has commenced, and the time to realize the collateral is less than 1 year. Guarantees must be honored within 90 days of being called to preclude a loss classification.	NRB has issued no specific prudential guidelines on the write-off of nonperforming loans. But it has instructed banks to have their write-off policy approved by NRB through their board.	Bad or irrecoverable loans may be written off by banks with the express approval of their board of directors or their nominated or designated authority or committee. Before allowance of a loan write-off, all liquid assets held under lien and pledged goods should be realized and appropriated toward the reduction of the outstanding amount and should be legally cleared by the bank's legal counsel.	The CBSL has issued no specific prudential guidelines on the write-off of nonperforming loans. Banks can write off loss advances at their own discretion.

Source: National prudential regulations for commercial banks.

Table A1.8 Exposure Limits

Afghanistan	Bangladesh	Bhutan	India	Maldives	Nepal	Pakistan	Sri Lanka
No bank is permitted to grant credit to a single obligor or group of related obligors if, as a result of that action, the exposure to that obligor or group exceeds 15% of regulatory capital or increases the amount by which the exposure already exceeds 15% of regulatory capital. The corresponding limit for an Afghan branch of a foreign bank is 4% of the total assets of the branch. In calculating compliance with this limit, exposures to each obligor in a group of related obligors are aggregated and considered as an exposure to a single obligor. When the aggregation is	Effective April 9, 2005, a bank cannot lend to an individual or organization or to a group in excess of 35% of its total capital (previously, 50% of capital), and the funded portion of the approved loan should not be more than 15% of the bank's total capital. For large loans (more than 10% of capital), the ceiling depends on the bank's nonperforming loans ratio. If the ratio is less than 5%, large loans can go up to 56% of the bank's capital funds. If the ratio is 5–10%, the ceiling is 52%. For 10–15%, it is 48%. For 15–20%, it is 44%. And for more than 20%, it is 40%.	No financial institution shall extend credit (funded and nonfunded) to a single borrower exceeding 30% of its capital funds (*single borrower* includes individuals; spouse and dependents; entities with common financial or business interests, such as partnerships, enterprises, companies, and subsidiaries; and a group of companies with common ownership). An exposure may exceed the limit by another 10% if the additional credit exposure is for infrastructure. Exclusions include the following: - Interbank exposures of less than 1 year	The exposure limit is 15% of capital funds for a single borrower and 40% for a group. Individual exposure may exceed the norm by 5%, and group exposure by an additional 10%, if the excess is for infrastructure projects such as power, telecoms, roads, or ports. In exceptional circumstances these limits can be increased by another 5%. This limit includes both funded and nonfunded credit limits, underwriting, and similar commitments. With effect from May 29, 2008, the exposure limit for a single borrower has been raised to 25% of capital funds for oil companies that have been issued oil bonds	The basic single-borrower limit is 15% of capital, but exceptions allow loans of up to 30% to one borrower under specific "low-risk" circumstances. Groups of closely related borrowers are limited to 40% of capital. An aggregate limit of 500% is established for large exposures (defined as 10% or more of capital). The basic limit for loans to "insiders" is 15% of capital (the same as for non-insiders), but insider loans must be fully secured. The requirement for security is waived if the total loans to an insider	A bank may grant a single borrower or group of related borrowers fund-based advances up to 25% of its core capital and non-fund-based off–balance sheet facilities up to 50% of its core capital fund. From the 2010/11 financial year, the total limit (funded and nonfunded) is to be within 25%.[a] Exposures secured by cash, national savings bonds, and first-class international bank guarantees are exempt from single-obligator limits. For hydropower, a total of 50% of core capital is allowed.	The single-borrower limit is 30% of the bank's capital, subject to a cap of 20% for cash credit. (For foreign banks, it is 30% of the bank's assigned capital, subject to a cap of 20% of capital for cash credit or PRs 12 million, whichever is higher.) The group limit is 50% of the bank's capital, subject to a cap of 35% for cash credit. Unsecured loans are limited to PRs 500,000 per person. (For small and medium-size enterprises, the limit is PRs 3 million.) The maximum exposure to a single small or medium-size enterprise is PRs 75 million.	For a single company, public corporation, firm, association of persons, or individual, the lending limit for banks is 30% of capital funds. The limit is 33% in aggregate for an individual, his close relations, and a company or firm in which he has a substantial interest, or for a company and one or more of its subsidiaries, associates, or one that has a substantial interest in it. The aggregate of all loans exceeding 15% of capital funds shall not exceed 55% of the total advances of the bank, except in the case of loans granted to

performed, each individual credit is counted.	Loans against shares are limited to 5% of total liabilities. For listed shares, up to 40% of the market value can be granted as loans, or Tk 10 million per borrower.	- Exposures fully covered by cash collateral - Exposures covered by government guarantees - Exposures to governments and central banks Aggregate borrowing of a bank's 10 largest borrowers should not exceed 30% of its total loan portfolio. The total of the bank's large advances shall not exceed 8 times its capital funds. For such purposes, amounts are specified for each sector.	(which do not have statutory liquidity ratio status) by the government of India.[b] In addition, banks may in exceptional circumstances consider enhancement of the exposure to such oil companies up to another 5% of capital funds. These limits are not applicable to existing or additional credit facilities (including funding of interest and irregularities) granted to weak or sick industrial units under rehabilitation packages. In addition to the above, there are exposure limits for other types of facilities.	are less than 2% of capital. The aggregate of all loans to all insiders is capped at 50% of capital.		The maximum unsecured credit card loan per person is PRs 500,000. The maximum per-party limit for housing finance is PRs 10 million. Advances against a bank's own shares, toward floating of shares, against non-listed shares, and the like are prohibited. Exposure against shares of a listed company shall be restricted to 30% of their current market value.	certain state-owned entities, entities engaged to undertake large infrastructure projects, and the like.

Source: National prudential regulations for commercial banks.

a. The financial year for banks in Nepal is from mid-July to mid-July.

b. A statutory liquidity ratio status makes a bond more attractive, since under statutory liquidity requirements the RBI requires banks to invest 24% of the deposits in government-approved securities.

Table A1.9 Directed Lending Guidelines

Afghanistan	Bangladesh	Bhutan	India	Maldives	Nepal	Pakistan	Sri Lanka
No guidelines have been issued	Locally incorporated banks are required to allocate credit through directed lending programs to certain economic sectors (such as agriculture) as directed by the government or BB. But specific targets or amounts have not been made public (for fiscal 2009/10 the disbursement target for agriculture is Tk 115 billion).[a] In view of the global economic situation, effective April 2009 BB has capped at 13% the interest rate on loans to various sectors, including productive sectors such as agriculture; housing sector loans; and bank loans to nonbank financial institutions.	No guidelines have been issued.	All domestic banks must make 40% of their net loans to the priority sector (of which 18% is to go to agriculture and 10% to the "weaker sections"), and 1% of the previous year's total advances are given under the Differential Rate of Interest scheme. Foreign banks must make 32% of their loans to the sector, of which loans to small enterprises should not be less than 10% and export credit not less than 12% of net bank credit (there is no target for agriculture). The priority sector broadly covers agriculture, small-scale industry, and other activities such	No guidelines have been issued	The minimum percentage of total credit to be invested in the priority sector was phased out according to a timetable, from 7% for fiscal 2002/03 to 6% for 2003/04, 4% for 2004/05, and 2% for 2005/06 and 2006/07.[b] From fiscal 2007/08 this program of priority sector lending is not compulsory. From fiscal 2007/08 the portfolio of deprived sector lending of licensed A- and B-class banks and financial institutions must be at least 3% and 1%, respectively, of their total outstanding loans and advances (loans outstanding for the previous 6 months, including bills purchase	The SBP has issued comprehensive guidelines on priority sector lending, such as prudential regulations for agricultural financing and the like. The agricultural lending target for fiscal 2007/08 was PRs 200 billion.[c] The SBP is phasing out these directed lending programs, however. To help improve credit to rural projects, and to improve access to finance in rural areas, the SBP has mandated that banks establish 20% of their new branches in rural areas.	All banks were required to ensure that at least 10% of their lending was directed to agriculture by the end of 2009. For this purpose, agriculture is defined as the cultivation, processing, and purchasing of tea, rubber, coconut, paddy, and minor export crops; livestock and dairy farming; fisheries; minor food crops; horticulture; forestry; beekeeping; and the like; as well as the processing of products for value addition for export purposes.

			as small business, retail trade, small transport operators, professional and self-employed persons, housing, education loans, microcredit, and the like. The RBI has also issued directives to banks on providing credit facilities to minority communities.		and discount). For this purpose, the deprived class has been defined as people having low incomes, mainly socially backward women, scheduled castes, dalits, marginal and small farmers, artisans, laborers, landless families, and people who are blind, deaf, or handicapped. The loans that were provided, up to the limit set by NRB, to microenterprises that generate self-employment and were established to improve the economic and social conditions of deprived people are also accounted as deprived sector lending.		

Source: National prudential regulations for commercial banks.
a. The fiscal year for the Bangladesh government is from July 1 to June 30.
b. The fiscal year for the Nepalese government is from mid-July to mid-July.
c. The fiscal year for the Pakistan government is from July 1 to June 30.

Table A1.10 Liquidity Requirements

Afghanistan	Bangladesh	Bhutan	India	Maldives	Nepal	Pakistan	Sri Lanka
Statutory liquidity requirements							
Quick liquidity ratio: high-liquid assets must be at least 20% of volatile liabilities. (Volatile liabilities include demand deposits of banks, deposits of other financial institutions, borrowings under securities repurchase agreements, short-term borrowings from banks, and other short-term borrowings.) *Broad liquidity ratio:* liquid assets must be at least 15% of the sum of attracted funds and designated off–balance sheet items.	18% of demand and time liabilities for mainstream commercial banks, 10% for Islamic banks	20% of total liabilities, excluding capital fund and liabilities to the RMA (from July 2009)	24% of net demand and time liabilities	With effect from June 1, 2006, the minimum reserve requirement for commercial banks was reduced from 30% to 25% of the average rufiyaa and foreign currency demand and time liabilities, excluding interbank liabilities and letter of credit margin deposits. Balances of the minimum reserve local currency deposits in excess of 15% bear an interest rate of 2.5% a year. With effect from December 30, 2008, foreign currency deposits in	In 2009, after a decade and a half NRB reintroduced a statutory liquidity requirement to contain inflation and fuel growth. The requirement rose from 6% of total deposits in the second quarter to 8% by the end of the fourth quarter.	15% of time and demand liabilities	20% of all liabilities (excluding contingent liabilities), less liabilities to shareholders and the CBSL, for the domestic banking unit in Sri Lanka rupees and for the offshore banking unit in U.S. dollars, for each month

				excess of 15% of the minimum reserve bear an interest rate of 0.25% a year. The reserve requirement for rufiyaa must be met in the form of rufiyaa deposits, while for foreign currency, U.S. dollar deposits are required.			
Cash reserve requirements							
At least 8% of customer deposits, held in a special, blocked current account at the central bank	5% of total demand and time liabilities on a biweekly average basis, on the condition that the cash reserve ratio should not be less than 4.5% on any day. (This is counted toward the statutory liquidity requirement.)	17% of total liabilities (from September 2008)	5% (from 2009; 8.25% in August 2008)	No cash reserve requirements established	5.5% of total deposit liabilities (based on the average of the deposits of 2 weeks back), to be held with NRB	5% of time and demand liabilities on a weekly average basis, subject to a daily minimum of 4%	Statutory reserve ratio of 7% of deposits with the CBSL (from February 2009)

Source: National prudential regulations for commercial banks.

Table A1.11 Debt Restructuring Policy

Afghanistan	Bangladesh	Bhutan	India	Maldives	Nepal	Pakistan	Sri Lanka
No specific policy on troubled debt restructuring; banks are to follow International Accounting Standards and International Financial Reporting Standards.	Borrowers can be rescheduled as performing, according to BB rules, if they pay a set fee (10% of the outstanding debt for the first rescheduling). The fee is treated as income for the bank, and any specific provisions that it has made are reversed. Restructuring is considered after defined cash payments: - For the first time, 15% of overdue installments or 10% of the total outstanding, whichever is less - For the second time, 30% and 20% - After 2 times, 50% and 30%	A restructuring facility may be granted only for credit exposures that have been regular and are affected by genuine unforeseen financial constraints. Before the loan can be rescheduled, financial institutions must reassess the borrower's financial position and make a full credit evaluation of the borrower's financial condition and prospects for repayment, to avoid "evergreening" of the loan. In this regard, financial institutions are permitted to reschedule a loan only once in 2 years and not more than 3 times during the term of the loan.	Banks can restructure assets classified as standard, substandard, or doubtful. No account can be restructured unless financial viability and certainty of repayment are established. Upon restructuring: - A standard asset should be reclassified as substandard. - Nonperforming assets would continue to have the same classification. - Such nonperforming assets are eligible for upgrading to standard after satisfactory performance for a period specified by the bank.	A restructured loan includes any new loan to repay or replace any loan that is overdue, rescheduled, rolled over, or otherwise modified because of deterioration in the borrower's financial condition or an inability to repay the loan according to the original terms. A bank shall document the basis for restructuring a loan. If all overdue interest is paid by the borrower in cash at the time of restructuring, the restructured loan shall be classified substandard. After payments have been made according to	Banks may reschedule or restructure nonperforming assets upon receipt of a written action plan from the borrower with payment of at least 25% of the total accrued interest up to the date of rescheduling or restructuring. Loan rescheduling or restructuring that results in an improvement in classification to the least-risk category (pass) is not prohibited. But such a rescheduled loan shall require provisioning of at least 12.5%. If the loan is priority sector credit, the provisioning is 3.125% (one-fourth of the 12.5%). Rescheduled or restructured loans cannot be reclassified in the pass	The rescheduling or restructuring of nonperforming assets shall not change the asset classification unless the terms and conditions of the rescheduling or restructuring have been fully met for at least 1 year (excluding the grace period, if any) from the date of the rescheduling or restructuring and at least 10% of the outstanding amount has been recovered in cash. Further, the unrealized mark-up on such loans (declassified after rescheduling or restructuring) shall not be taken (credited) to the income account unless at least 50% of the amount has been realized in cash. But this will not affect the declassification of this account if all other criteria are met.	For rescheduled credit facilities, when rescheduling occurs before an account is classified as nonperforming, the rescheduled account shall be classified as nonperforming when, in the aggregate, the period of time the account is in arrears before rescheduling (if any) and after rescheduling is 3 months or more (for loans repayable in monthly installments, when 3 installments have not been paid; and for loans payable quarterly or semiannually, loans with bullet payments, and credit cards, when amounts due are not paid for 90 days from the due date). Banks shall reclassify nonperforming loans as performing if

	For rescheduling of demand or continuous loans, a down payment is required, with the rate based on the amount outstanding: - Up to Tk 1 crore (Tk 10 million), 15% - Tk 1–5 crore (Tk 10–50 million), 10% (not less than Tk 15 lakh [Tk 15 million]) - Tk 5 crore (Tk 50 million) and above, 5% (not less than Tk 50 million) Borrowers with rescheduled loans will get any new facilities subject to conditions specified by BB. For restructuring of large loans, a separate scheme exists.			the restructured loan terms for a period of at least 6 months, the loan may be reclassified using the criteria specified. If a loan is restructured but all overdue interest is not paid by the borrower in cash at the time of restructuring, the loan shall be classified according to the criteria specified.	category until the terms of the restructured loan have been observed for 2 years; that is, loss provisions cannot be written back and distributed.		interest and principal in arrears are paid by the borrower in relation to classified nonperforming loans. A nonperforming advance that has been rescheduled would be eligible to be upgraded to the performing category only after satisfactory performance for a period the length of which depends on the category of the nonperforming loan: - For special mention, a period of 90 days after the date on which the first payment of interest or principal falls due, whichever is earlier, under the rescheduled terms - For substandard, a period of 180 days - For loss, a period of 360 days

Source: National prudential regulations for commercial banks.

Appendix 2. Getting Finance Indicators for South Asia, by Country and Year, 2001–08

Table A2.1 Getting Finance Indicators for South Asian Countries, 2001

Indicator	Afghanistan	Bangladesh	Bhutan	India	Maldives	Nepal	Pakistan	Sri Lanka	Benchmark
Access to finance									
Demographic branch penetration (branches per 100,000 people)	—	4.83	3.58	6.42	6.29	2.09	4.88	6.03	5–69
Demographic ATM penetration (ATMs per 100,000 people)	—	0.10	—	—	2.96	0.05	—	2.55	43–115
Deposit accounts per 1,000 people	—	231.97	—	416.77	397.13	111.59	195.84	939.32	976–1,671
Loan accounts per 1,000 people	—	56.56	18.75	50.99	—	19.07	16.04	256.88	248–513
Geographic branch penetration (branches per 1,000 km^2)	—	42.50	0.54	22.18	56.70	3.29	8.77	11.68	1–159
Geographic ATM penetration (ATMs per 1,000 km^2)	—	0.91	—	—	26.70	0.08	—	4.93	1–378
Performance and efficiency									
Return on equity (%)	—	17.12	19.03	13.80	43.72	–93.62	12.20	20.57	4.42–32.80
Return on assets (%)	—	0.74	1.23	0.90	5.59	–3.04	0.60	0.84	0.20–1.47
Staff cost ratio (%)	—	44.75	55.04	68.10	33.96	194.25	52.58	46.21	14.87–46.31
Operating cost ratio (%)	—	236.78	40.14	92.33	40.99	35.87	90.91	118.66	49.86–294.02
Net interest margin (%)	—	1.66	1.63	2.98	5.06	1.76	3.24	3.30	0.64–3.55
Recurring earning power (%)	—	1.70	1.76	1.60	5.90	0.86	1.17	1.64	0.10–2.29
Financial stability									
Capital adequacy ratio (%)	—	7.02	14.83	11.40	24.00	4.00	11.30	8.59	10.40–18.20[a]
Leverage ratio (times)	—	4.17	0.07	19.12	0.14	3.27	4.58	3.90	4.11–15.01
Gross nonperforming loans ratio (%)	—	31.49	8.80	11.40	9.89	29.31	19.60	19.57	0.60–29.80
Provisions to nonperforming loans ratio (%)	—	25.36	38.72	49.70	24.95	30.59	53.20	44.43	25.40–128.80
Liquid assets ratio (%)	—	30.03	47.46	48.20	47.90	22.10	39.90	22.80	7.42–44.39
Liquid assets to liabilities ratio (%)	—	122.90	136.39	260.00	—	47.88	56.25	26.30	2.83–42.20
Capital market development									
Domestic bond market to equity market capitalization (%)	—	663.50	16.98	117.85	—	129.55	537.75	659.05	8.90–256.86
Domestic public bonds outstanding to GDP (%)	—	16.17	2.18	26.80	—	14.50	38.90	16.28	8.83–95.34

Trading value of top 10 stocks ratio (%)	—	59.16	100.00	72.90	—	83.13	22.52	54.37	6.04–61.90
Stock market capitalization to GDP (%)	—	2.57	12.86	29.40	—	11.76	8.06	8.81	35.58–350.02
Stock trading value to GDP (%)	—	1.28	0.34	112.00	—	0.59	0.02	0.99	16.21–290.00
Stock market turnover ratio (times)	—	0.50	0.03	2.13	—	0.05	0.12	0.13	0.34–2.21
Market concentration and competitiveness									
Herfindahl-Hirschman Index (HHI)	—	944.90	5,774.98	784.67	3,347.00	1563.48	1,091.80	1,650.62	427.10–1,658.53[b]
K-bank concentration ratio ($k = 3$), assets (%)	—	47.38	100.00	33.80	91.69	58.02	50.30	63.09	27.04–79.45
K-bank concentration ratio ($k = 3$), deposits (%)	—	50.55	100.00	33.98	91.95	51.73	53.23	62.02	23.53–60.18
K-bank concentration ratio ($k = 3$), loans (%)	—	45.76	100.00	33.04	94.12	52.06	50.86	65.16	22.28–66.30
Private credit extended by banks to GDP (%)	—	24.33	10.61	21.50	23.57	26.95	17.82	28.19	42.00–157.85
Commercial banking assets to GDP (%)	—	50.35	58.67	61.90	50.92	63.83	43.61	56.80	44.90–174.28
Payment systems development									
Notes and coins in circulation to GDP (%)	—	5.47	7.03	9.90	7.40	11.90	10.20	5.44	1.98–28.97
Narrow money supply (M1) to GDP (%)	—	9.53	21.55	17.07	21.23	15.99	20.32	8.68	11.29–110.57
Value of real-time gross settlement transactions to GDP (%)	n.a.	n.a.	n.a.	n.a.	n.a.	n.a.	n.a.	n.a.	1,381.00–14,835.00
Value of retail transactions to GDP (%)	—	—	—	514.34	—	—	—	289.85	0.62–1,432.30
RTGS concentration ratio (%)	n.a.	n.a.	n.a.	n.a.	n.a.	n.a.	n.a.	n.a.	38.70–84.00
Retail payments concentration ratio (%)	—	—	100.00	—	—	—	—	85.70	22.50–83.60
Savings mobilization									
Broad money supply (M2) to GDP (%)	—	36.10	47.18	58.58	43.04	48.57	39.20	32.03	48.81–286.09
Real deposit interest rate (%)	—	3.95	4.10	3.35	3.24	2.40	1.38	–3.42	—
Gross domestic savings to GDP (%)	—	18.16	33.95	23.70	44.93	11.70	16.28	15.80	15.11–41.84
Reserve money to total deposits (%)	—	26.43	58.84	29.37	62.90	38.90	48.67	21.69	—
Loan to deposit ratio (%)	—	84.17	26.18	53.13	61.92	74.80	63.54	79.01	—
Worker remittances to GDP (%)	—	5.26	—	3.09	0.32	10.69	2.14	7.34	0.03–1.98

Sources: South Asian central banks, securities and exchange commissions and boards, and stock exchanges; Indian Banks' Association 2006a, 2006b, 2006c, 2008a, 2008b, 2008c; RBI 2006a, 2006b, 2007a, 2007b, 2008a, 2008b, *Annual Report* (various years); World Bank, World Development Indicators database, 2006b; International Monetary Fund (IMF), International Financial Statistics database, World Economic Outlook database; Asian Development Bank (ADB), statistical database; CPSS 2004; Ratha and Xu 2008.

Note: All benchmark indicators are for selected high-income OECD member countries and nonmember Asian economies (Australia; Canada; China; France; Germany; Hong Kong, China; Italy; Japan; the Republic of Korea; Malaysia; New Zealand; Singapore; Thailand; the United Kingdom; and the United States).

a. Basel guideline: not less than 8 percent of risk-weighted assets.

b. Accepted norms for HHI: less than 1,000, banking industry is unconcentrated; 1,000–1,800, moderately concentrated; more than 1,800, highly concentrated.

ATM = automated teller machine, — = not available, n.a. = not applicable.

Table A2.2 Getting Finance Indicators for South Asian Countries, 2002

Indicator	Afghanistan	Bangladesh	Bhutan	India	Maldives	Nepal	Pakistan	Sri Lanka	Benchmark
Access to finance									
Demographic branch penetration (branches per 100,000 people)	—	4.74	3.49	6.33	6.66	1.85	4.73	6.70	5–65
Demographic ATM penetration (ATMs per 100,000 people)	—	0.14	—	—	3.70	0.06	—	3.27	37–128
Deposit accounts per 1,000 people	—	234.75	—	420.84	456.03	123.21	194.87	989.94	976–1,671
Loan accounts per 1,000 people	—	57.14	21.24	53.93	—	14.92	14.93	257.66	248–513
Geographic branch penetration (branches per 1,000 km^2)	—	42.26	0.54	22.26	60.00	2.96	8.72	13.17	1–149
Geographic ATM penetration (ATMs per 1,000 km^2)	—	1.22	—	—	33.30	0.10	—	6.43	2–371
Performance and efficiency									
Return on equity (%)	—	12.40	17.03	17.30	25.77	–96.16	27.50	25.71	2.90–25.51
Return on assets (%)	—	0.54	1.19	1.10	3.42	–3.37	1.50	1.11	0.10–1.50
Staff cost ratio (%)	—	66.53	56.88	64.70	35.46	185.00	50.75	47.62	16.39–47.27
Operating cost ratio (%)	—	187.63	46.11	85.38	51.83	59.78	85.81	99.80	53.39–238.96
Net interest margin (%)	—	1.04	2.02	2.66	3.69	0.92	3.10	3.78	0.84–3.55
Recurring earning power (%)	—	1.50	1.70	2.00	4.27	0.21	2.00	2.07	0.17–2.39
Financial stability									
Capital adequacy ratio (%)	—	7.60	13.94	12.00	23.13	–7.25	12.60	10.35	9.60–16.90[a]
Leverage ratio (times)	—	4.34	0.06	15.69	0.12	3.71	4.11	4.71	1.21–14.64
Gross nonperforming loans ratio (%)	—	28.10	7.23	10.40	10.01	30.41	17.70	19.09	0.70–26.00
Provisions to nonperforming loans ratio (%)	—	25.3	43.62	53.40	27.59	29.98	58.20	50.38	24.50–123.70
Liquid assets ratio (%)	—	25.84	40.52	47.40	50.29	18.16	48.10	18.80	7.07–37.74
Liquid assets to liabilities ratio (%)	—	121.46	96.34	250.00	—	41.33	68.95	21.70	2.99–39.60
Capital market development									
Domestic bond market to equity market capitalization (%)	—	735.42	14.53	118.92	—	212.14	278.47	585.08	10.06–347.68
Domestic public bonds outstanding to GDP (%)	—	17.53	1.89	29.80	—	17.40	37.80	21.94	9.33–123.46
Trading value of top10 stocks ratio (%)	—	51.64	100.00	62.93	90.75	81.89	21.89	57.70	9.84–78.70

Stock market capitalization to GDP (%)	—	2.61	13.03	27.40	9.48	8.54	9.15	10.28	31.85–304.85
Stock trading value to GDP (%)	—	1.28	0.15	36.00	0.07	0.38	0.15	1.91	12.47–244.23
Stock market turnover ratio (times)	—	0.49	0.01	0.88	0.001	0.04	0.90	0.21	0.27–2.91
Market concentration and competitiveness									
Herfindahl-Hirschman Index (HHI)	—	886.66	5,795.97	741.50	3,216.00	1,574.76	1,052.12	1,528.39	332.36–1,869.49[b]
K-bank concentration ratio (*k* = 3), assets (%)	—	45.77	100.00	33.67	89.82	58.68	49.71	60.88	30.03–75.23
K-bank concentration ratio (*k* = 3), deposits (%)	—	47.55	100.00	33.26	89.67	49.62	51.76	62.43	22.38–71.59
K-bank concentration ratio (*k* = 3), loans (%)	—	43.22	100.00	31.92	93.61	49.34	47.00	60.02	21.16–62.38
Private credit extended by banks to GDP (%)	—	26.32	11.38	23.80	25.56	27.21	18.04	28.09	42.30–154.98
Commercial banking assets to GDP (%)	—	52.78	62.67	67.30	59.50	67.69	47.72	54.51	45.23–172.93
Payment systems development									
Notes and coins in circulation to GDP (%)	—	5.62	6.24	10.23	6.95	13.20	10.95	5.58	1.97–29.25
Narrow money supply (M1) to GDP (%)	—	9.79	27.04	17.43	22.64	16.79	22.52	8.81	11.89–119.99
Value of RTGS transactions to GDP (%)	n.a.	n.a.	n.a.	n.a.	n.a.	n.a.	n.a.	n.a.	1,231.00–14,139.00
Value of retail transactions to GDP (%)	—	—	8.49	528.88	—	—	—	241.89	0.56–3,484.43
RTGS concentration ratio (%)	n.a.	n.a.	n.a.	n.a.	n.a.	n.a.	n.a.	n.a.	37.70–84.00
Retail payments concentration ratio (%)	—	—	100.00	—	—	—	—	85.40	31.50–81.90
Savings mobilization									
Broad money supply (M2) to GDP (%)	—	37.92	52.52	62.22	47.99	48.75	42.97	32.26	41.08–282.88
Real deposit interest rate (%)	—	1.91	4.50	2.60	0.33	1.50	–0.08	–2.13	—
Gross domestic savings to GDP (%)	–5.31	18.63	36.40	23.50	46.35	9.50	18.43	14.40	14.00–42.03
Reserve money to total deposits (%)	—	23.75	51.83	28.46	61.01	43.00	45.00	22.05	—
Loan to deposit ratio (%)	—	83.31	29.68	53.45	57.99	78.50	56.83	70.93	—
Worker remittances to GDP (%)	—	5.90	—	3.27	0.31	10.35	4.76	7.78	0.03–2.14

Sources: South Asian central banks, securities and exchange commissions and boards, and stock exchanges; Indian Banks' Association 2006a, 2006b, 2006c, 2008a, 2008b, 2008c; RBI 2006a,2006b, 2007a, 2007b, 2008a, 2008b, *Annual Report* (various years); World Bank, World Development Indicators database, 2006b; IMF, International Financial Statistics database, World Economic Outlook database; ADB, statistical database; CPSS 2004; Ratha and Xu 2008.

Note: All benchmark indicators are for selected high-income OECD member countries and nonmember Asian economies (Australia; Canada; China; France; Germany; Hong Kong, China; Italy; Japan; the Republic of Korea; Malaysia; New Zealand; Singapore; Thailand; the United Kingdom; and the United States).

a. Basel guideline: not less than 8 percent of risk-weighted assets.

b. Accepted norms for HHI: less than 1,000, banking industry is unconcentrated; 1,000–1,800, moderately concentrated; more than 1,800, highly concentrated.

— = not available.

n.a. = not applicable.

Table A2.3 Getting Finance Indicators for South Asian Countries, 2003

Indicator	Afghanistan	Bangladesh	Bhutan	India	Maldives	Nepal	Pakistan	Sri Lanka	Benchmark
Access to finance									
Demographic branch penetration (branches per 100,000 people)	—	4.67	5.86	6.25	7.77	1.85	4.61	6.85	5–65
Demographic ATM penetration (ATMs per 100,000 people)	—	0.14	0.27	—	3.70	0.08	0.37	3.69	37–139
Deposit accounts per 1,000 people	—	234.60	202.02	418.67	518.48	102.43	190.55	1,000.53	976–1,671
Loan accounts per 1,000 people	—	56.87	24.55	55.84	45.90	12.96	18.86	279.15	248–513
Geographic branch penetration (branches per 1,000 km^2)	—	42.25	1.12	22.41	70.00	3.04	8.66	13.63	1–139
Geographic ATM penetration (ATMs per 1,000 km^2)	—	1.26	0.05	—	33.30	0.14	0.69	7.34	2–364
Performance and efficiency									
Return on equity (%)	—	12.39	17.98	21.00	30.63	–22.33	33.70	26.33	3.40–65.02
Return on assets (%)	—	0.59	1.24	1.50	3.73	–0.85	2.10	1.36	0.20–1.90
Staff cost ratio (%)	—	64.53	50.12	62.10	39.29	306.16	51.48	49.58	18.89–45.76
Operating cost ratio (%)	—	161.86	44.30	80.71	46.29	40.14	83.20	94.02	49.20–200.73
Net interest margin (%)	—	1.09	2.18	2.85	4.12	1.58	2.98	4.16	0.98–3.37
Recurring earning power (%)	—	1.68	1.76	2.50	4.65	–0.01	2.57	2.58	0.14–2.30
Financial stability									
Capital adequacy ratio (%)	—	8.42	19.93	12.70	23.44	–11.74	11.10	10.31	10.00–17.90[a]
Leverage ratio (times)	—	4.77	0.09	15.87	0.12	3.87	5.03	5.53	0.75–15.39
Gross nonperforming loans ratio (%)	—	22.13	7.78	8.80	10.10	28.80	13.70	16.36	0.30–20.40
Provisions to nonperforming loans ratio (%)	—	18.35	40.67	52.40	41.06	7.55	64.80	58.74	25.50–140.40
Liquid assets ratio (%)	—	24.67	38.18	48.70	53.71	12.49	46.10	17.30	7.59–37.31
Liquid assets to liabilities ratio (%)	—	127.19	94.20	260.00	—	27.03	63.44	20.00	2.46–36.66
Capital market development									
Domestic bond market to equity market capitalization (%)	—	435.22	37.61	72.77	—	240.19	186.41	389.76	6.46–339.42
Domestic public bonds outstanding to GDP (%)	—	16.73	4.52	31.60	—	18.50	36.70	27.43	9.94–137.88
Trading value of top10 stocks ratio (%)	—	51.55	100.00	55.42	74.90	58.35	19.18	60.83	11.90–74.00
Stock market capitalization to GDP (%)	—	2.43	12.03	22.50	11.34	8.05	15.31	14.92	31.26–382.10

Stock trading value to GDP (%)	—	1.02	0.07	37.70	0.08	0.13	0.13	4.18	13.17–214.19
Stock market turnover ratio (times)	—	0.42	0.01	1.08	0.001	0.02	0.54	0.35	0.37–1.50
Market concentration and competitiveness									
Herfindahl-Hirschman Index (HHI)	—	702.04	5,676.65	734.59	3,154.00	1,468.53	976.81	1,455.81	341.51–1,864.85[b]
K-bank concentration ratio ($k = 3$), assets (%)	—	38.33	100.00	33.49	87.33	56.67	47.47	58.19	29.64–72.31
K-bank concentration ratio ($k = 3$), deposits (%)	—	43.27	100.00	32.76	87.64	46.80	48.93	60.89	22.70–73.60
K-bank concentration ratio ($k = 3$), loans (%)	—	39.57	100.00	31.60	90.96	44.64	43.58	56.81	16.79–64.12
Private credit extended by banks to GDP (%)	—	29.42	13.40	25.90	25.37	27.80	19.46	29.50	43.11–153.39
Commercial banking assets to GDP (%)	—	53.84	59.09	68.80	57.90	69.84	50.10	56.06	45.80–172.10
Payment systems development									
Notes and coins in circulation to GDP (%)	11.83	5.75	6.13	10.73	7.05	12.50	11.64	5.42	1.98–30.39
Narrow money supply (M1) to GDP (%)	—	10.13	23.04	18.04	23.34	17.02	26.03	8.87	12.15–129.45
Value of RTGS transactions to GDP (%)	n.a.	n.a.	n.a.	n.a.	n.a.	n.a.	n.a.	61.12	1,321.00–13,653.00
Value of retail transactions to GDP (%)	—	—	9.48	548.87	—	—	—	215.16	0.54–3,603.61
RTGS concentration ratio (%)	n.a.	n.a.	n.a.	n.a.	n.a.	n.a.	n.a.	47.60	38.80–83.00
Retail payments concentration ratio (%)	—	—	100.00	—	—	—	—	84.90	20.00–81.10
Savings mobilization									
Broad money supply (M2) to GDP (%)	—	38.96	47.12	66.73	50.86	49.96	46.48	31.87	40.68–308.83
Real deposit interest rate (%)	—	–0.18	2.40	–0.30	1.79	–0.50	–1.45	–1.03	—
Gross domestic savings to GDP (%)	–35.77	19.53	35.63	26.40	49.11	8.60	20.56	16.00	13.50–43.55
Reserve money to total deposits (%)	—	22.98	66.69	26.78	51.11	39.90	44.04	21.72	—
Loan to deposit ratio (%)	—	80.53	31.94	56.93	53.09	80.10	58.83	69.56	—
Worker remittances to GDP (%)	—	5.97	—	4.09	0.29	11.01	4.69	7.75	0.03–1.25

Sources: South Asian central banks, securities and exchange commissions and boards, and stock exchanges; Indian Banks' Association 2006a, 2006b, 2006c, 2008a, 2008b, 2008c; RBI 2006a, 2006b, 2007a, 2007b, 2008a, 2008b, *Annual Report* (various years); World Bank, World Development Indicators database, 2006b; IMF, International Financial Statistics database, World Economic Outlook database; ADB, statistical database; CPSS 2004; Ratha and Xu 2008.

Note: All benchmark indicators are for selected high-income OECD member countries and nonmember Asian economies (Australia; Canada; China; France; Germany; Hong Kong, China; Italy; Japan; the Republic of Korea; Malaysia; New Zealand; Singapore; Thailand; the United Kingdom; and the United States).

a. Basel guideline: not less than 8 percent of risk-weighted assets.

b. Accepted norms for HHI: less than 1,000, banking industry is unconcentrated; 1,000–1,800, moderately concentrated; more than 1,800, highly concentrated.

— = not available.

n.a. = not applicable.

Table A2.4 Getting Finance Indicators for South Asian Countries, 2004

Indicator	Afghanistan	Bangladesh	Bhutan	India	Maldives	Nepal	Pakistan	Sri Lanka	Benchmark
Access to finance									
Demographic branch penetration (branches per 100,000 people)	0.14	4.67	5.71	6.26	8.15	1.71	4.64	7.06	5–66
Demographic ATM penetration (ATMs per 100,000 people)	0.01	0.17	0.27	—	3.70	0.11	0.52	4.16	38–152
Deposit accounts per 1,000 people	—	233.63	206.65	426.11	603.14	115.88	180.28	1,023.58	976–1,671
Loan accounts per 1,000 people	—	60.24	25.61	61.88	56.12	11.97	24.51	304.11	248–513
Geographic branch penetration (branches per 1,000 km^2)	0.07	42.71	1.12	22.57	73.30	2.87	8.84	14.20	1–133
Geographic ATM penetration (ATMs per 1,000 km^2)	0.003	1.55	0.05	—	33.30	0.18	0.99	8.37	2–361
Performance and efficiency									
Return on equity (%)	—	−13.39	14.19	23.00	36.98	−46.42	29.00	25.62	1.90–22.80
Return on assets (%)	—	−0.63	1.30	1.70	4.47	1.47	2.00	1.43	0.20–1.70
Staff cost ratio (%)	—	66.24	52.91	60.17	40.70	181.18	51.97	46.98	22.44–56.30
Operating cost ratio (%)	—	141.89	39.61	77.05	49.45	31.93	83.62	95.66	59.57–172.59
Net interest margin (%)	—	1.97	2.46	3.07	4.42	1.99	2.87	3.97	1.01–3.12
Recurring earning power (%)	—	1.86	2.08	2.90	5.27	1.81	2.26	2.33	0.61–1.97
Financial stability									
Capital adequacy ratio (%)	—	7.41	18.52	12.90	18.38	−9.07	11.40	10.29	10.40–16.10[a]
Leverage ratio (times)	0.38	4.16	0.10	15.77	0.12	−3.00	6.45	5.63	0.68–15.18
Gross nonperforming loans ratio (%)	—	17.63	5.98	7.20	6.24	22.77	9.00	11.29	0.20–12.80
Provisions to nonperforming loans ratio (%)	—	19.15	45.38	62.00	56.59	3.82	72.40	68.29	29.90–182.90
Liquid assets ratio (%)	—	23.50	44.89	48.70	45.40	13.61	37.00	20.30	7.50–34.98
Liquid assets to liabilities ratio (%)	—	121.94	116.79	260.00	—	27.30	51.88	23.10	2.47–29.42
Capital market development									
Domestic bond market to equity market capitalization (%)	—	239.99	42.30	64.33	—	204.93	108.60	299.80	5.58–299.09
Domestic public bonds outstanding to GDP (%)	—	16.57	5.63	33.40	—	17.30	33.00	31.70	9.67–148.43
Trading value of top 10 stocks ratio (%)	—	46.67	99.90	44.86	87.13	86.25	16.01	42.92	11.90–75.60
Stock market capitalization to GDP (%)	—	4.28	13.30	41.90	16.06	8.72	24.07	18.83	23.18–486.34
Stock trading value to GDP (%)	—	0.74	0.34	57.80	0.25	0.45	0.19	2.92	15.45–269.33
Stock market turnover ratio (times)	—	0.23	0.03	1.10	0.002	0.06	0.50	0.18	0.40–1.82

Market concentration and competitiveness									
Herfindahl-Hirschman Index (HHI)	—	724.09	5,552.71	677.93	3,328.00	1,245.62	903.97	1,377.33	247.12–1,449.90[b]
K-bank concentration ratio ($k = 3$), assets (%)	—	39.33	100.00	33.17	85.66	52.88	43.95	55.68	21.16–64.96
K-bank concentration ratio ($k = 3$), deposits (%)	—	40.31	100.00	31.29	85.47	44.00	45.55	58.25	18.25–61.90
K-bank concentration ratio ($k = 3$), loans (%)	—	36.54	100.00	30.97	89.63	42.14	42.56	53.28	16.79–50.45
Private credit extended by banks to GDP (%)	—	30.96	15.77	27.50	35.57	28.95	22.59	31.26	44.00–147.61
Commercial banking assets to GDP (%)	4.84	51.82	61.77	71.20	67.16	71.55	52.07	56.92	46.22–166.75
Payment systems development									
Notes and coins in circulation to GDP (%)	14.06	6.10	6.41	10.89	7.67	12.60	11.62	5.54	1.96–30.01
Narrow money supply (M1) to GDP (%)	18.67	10.63	24.92	18.57	24.92	17.51	27.33	9.01	13.24–75.85
Value of RTGS transactions to GDP (%)	n.a.	n.a.	n.a.	0.07	n.a.	n.a.	n.a.	61.51	1,133.00–14,931.00
Value of retail transactions to GDP (%)	—	—	12.05	420.18	—	—	—	153.89	0.54–3,914.02
RTGS concentration ratio (%)	n.a.	n.a.	n.a.	—	n.a.	n.a.	n.a.	39.42	44.70–81.78
Retail payments concentration ratio (%)	—	—	100.00	—	—	—	—	71.85	19.00–82.50
Savings mobilization									
Broad money supply (M2) to GDP (%)	19.09	40.85	51.36	67.15	60.21	51.66	48.42	32.90	39.15–353.91
Real deposit interest rate (%)	—	–0.86	0.30	0.83	0.72	–0.50	–6.15	–3.69	—
Gross domestic savings to GDP (%)	–31.76	20.01	36.71	29.70	46.15	11.70	17.92	16.40	13.67–47.10
Reserve money to total deposits (%)	297.43	21.56	56.19	25.97	48.28	40.60	43.28	21.57	—
Loan to deposit ratio (%)	30.00	77.87	43.19	55.95	62.04	79.30	68.02	68.93	—
Worker remittances to GDP (%)	—	6.38	—	3.05	0.37	10.92	4.08	7.57	0.02–1.01

Sources: South Asian central banks, securities and exchange commissions and boards, and stock exchanges; Indian Banks' Association 2006a, 2006b,2006c, 2008a, 2008b, 2008c; RBI 2006a, 2006b, 2007a, 2007b, 2008a, 2008b, *Annual Report* (various years); World Bank, World Development Indicators database, 2006b; IMF, International Financial Statistics database, World Economic Outlook database; ADB, statistical database; CPSS 2004; Ratha and Xu 2008.

Note: All benchmark indicators are for selected high-income OECD member countries and nonmember Asian economies (Australia; Canada; China; France; Germany; Hong Kong, China; Italy; Japan; the Republic of Korea; Malaysia; New Zealand; Singapore; Thailand; the United Kingdom; and the United States).

a. Basel guideline: not less than 8 percent of risk-weighted assets.

b. Accepted norms for HHI: less than 1,000, banking industry is unconcentrated; 1,000–1,800, moderately concentrated; more than 1,800, highly concentrated.

— = not available.

n.a. = not applicable.

Table A2.5 Getting Finance Indicators for South Asian Countries, 2005

Indicator	Afghanistan	Bangladesh	Bhutan	India	Maldives	Nepal	Pakistan	Sri Lanka	Benchmark
Access to finance									
Demographic branch penetration (branches per 100,000 people)	0.22	4.64	6.77	6.33	8.15	1.67	4.82	7.20	5–66
Demographic ATM penetration (ATMs per 100,000 people)	0.02	0.20	0.31	1.63	3.70	0.24	0.67	4.50	16–158
Deposit accounts per 1,000 people	—	237.32	269.28	432.11	703.60	113.58	173.15	1,066.24	976–1,671
Loan accounts per 1,000 people	—	60.45	29.61	71.42	115.96	11.30	30.57	344.17	248–513
Geographic branch penetration (branches per 1,000 km^2)	0.10	43.41	1.12	22.99	73.30	2.87	9.22	14.64	1–129
Geographic ATM penetration (ATMs per 1,000 km^2)	0.01	1.84	0.05	5.93	33.30	0.41	1.29	9.15	3–437
Performance and efficiency									
Return on equity (%)	1.72	28.63	15.02	16.90	40.76	–45.87	36.90	27.01	9.20–25.30
Return on assets (%)	0.73	1.30	1.42	1.30	4.78	1.79	2.90	1.70	0.30–1.80
Staff cost ratio (%)	—	65.00	57.13	58.29	37.54	135.35	50.73	44.53	23.00–52.71
Operating cost ratio (%)	—	107.91	40.96	74.32	43.49	28.55	57.73	87.70	65.19–185.82
Net interest margin (%)	—	2.38	2.62	3.07	4.68	2.22	4.11	4.05	0.71–3.13
Recurring earning power (%)	—	2.36	2.02	2.40	5.76	2.33	3.35	2.26	0.57–2.06
Financial stability									
Capital adequacy ratio (%)	—	7.65	20.81	12.80	15.57	–6.07	11.90	12.84	2.50–15.80[a]
Leverage ratio (times)	0.45	4.42	0.89	14.20	0.12	–4.65	7.64	6.93	3.76–15.25
Gross nonperforming loans ratio (%)	—	13.55	6.57	5.13	6.35	18.94	6.70	8.76	0.20–9.80
Provisions to nonperforming loans ratio (%)	—	24.31	58.25	63.50	45.20	11.49	80.40	72.05	31.20–203.00
Liquid assets ratio (%)	—	20.61	69.54	44.20	30.97	9.33	33.90	19.60	7.30–36.59
Liquid assets to liabilities ratio (%)	—	104.60	179.44	220.00	—	20.34	52.77	22.10	2.47–25.90
Capital market development									
Domestic bond market to equity market capitalization (%)	—	259.28	40.72	50.46	—	142.69	73.94	216.69	4.95–274.27
Domestic public bonds outstanding to GDP (%)	—	16.75	4.99	33.00	—	16.40	30.90	31.77	10.07–145.19
Trading value of top 10 stocks ratio (%)	—	41.89	100.00	41.66	87.60	83.96	20.48	43.10	15.88–76.40
Stock market capitalization to GDP (%)	—	6.06	12.25	52.70	14.05	10.49	30.59	24.69	17.91–499.21
Stock trading value to GDP (%)	—	2.03	0.06	53.30	0.35	0.77	0.11	4.84	16.92–294.85
Stock market turnover ratio (times)	—	0.41	0.01	0.75	0.002	0.09	0.22	0.24	0.28–2.19

Market concentration and competitiveness									
Herfindahl-Hirschman Index (HHI)	—	679.31	5,501.59	642.38	3,335.00	1,019.21	805.61	1,279.44	307.66–2,561.91[b]
K-bank concentration ratio ($k = 3$), assets (%)	—	37.05	100.00	32.02	88.56	45.87	40.35	53.02	21.30–69.34
K-bank concentration ratio ($k = 3$), deposits (%)	—	37.72	100.00	31.09	88.39	41.73	41.49	56.30	19.93–53.53
K-bank concentration ratio ($k = 3$), loans (%)	—	36.46	100.00	30.84	93.19	37.28	41.96	50.44	18.39–50.48
Private credit extended by banks to GDP (%)	—	31.87	17.96	33.30	57.42	27.57	26.34	33.87	47.84–160.48
Commercial banking assets to GDP (%)	5.95	54.93	60.52	73.00	90.85	70.25	53.89	61.79	46.50–167.76
Payment systems development									
Notes and coins in circulation to GDP (%)	13.26	6.72	6.59	11.02	9.20	12.50	11.26	5.40	1.97–30.42
Narrow money supply (M1) to GDP (%)	18.82	11.51	24.6	19.27	31.61	17.00	27.77	9.41	11.23–135.82
Value of RTGS transactions to GDP (%)	n.a.	n.a.	n.a.	130.55	n.a.	n.a.	n.a.	57.41	1,489.00–13,857.00
Value of retail transactions to GDP (%)	—	—	10.58	339.28	—	—	—	151.82	0.54–4,174.21
RTGS concentration ratio (%)	n.a.	n.a.	n.a.	—	n.a.	n.a.	n.a.	49.70	48.10–79.00
Retail payments concentration ratio (%)	—	—	100.00	—	—	—	—	71.73	17.00–81.90
Savings mobilization									
Broad money supply (M2) to GDP (%)	20.05	43.46	24.60	68.37	69.66	50.97	49.26	33.55	40.90–378.23
Real deposit interest rate (%)	—	−0.49	−0.80	1.05	0.96	−1.10	−6.51	−4.80	—
Gross domestic savings to GDP (%)	−14.79	20.25	38.50	31.80	—	11.60	17.48	17.90	13.73–49.60
Reserve money to total deposits (%)	207.30	23.00	72.12	26.17	45.06	38.50	39.94	20.93	—
Loan to deposit ratio (%)	31.87	79.52	37.52	62.79	85.32	84.80	72.31	73.10	—
Worker remittances to GDP (%)	—	7.76	—	3.03	0.31	11.12	3.92	8.06	0.02–0.93

Sources: South Asian central banks, securities and exchange commissions and boards, and stock exchanges; Indian Banks' Association 2006a, 2006b, 2006c, 2008a,2008b, 2008c; RBI 2006a,2006b, 2007a, 2007b, 2008a, 2008b, *Annual Report* (various years); World Bank, World Development Indicators database, 2006b; IMF, International Financial Statistics database, World Economic Outlook database; ADB, statistical database; CPSS 2004; Ratha and Xu 2008.

Note: All benchmark indicators are for selected high-income OECD member countries and nonmember Asian economies (Australia; Canada; China; France; Germany; Hong Kong, China; Italy; Japan; the Republic of Korea; Malaysia; New Zealand; Singapore; Thailand; the United Kingdom; and the United States).

a. Basel guideline: not less than 8 percent of risk-weighted assets.

b. Accepted norms for HHI: less than 1,000, banking industry is unconcentrated; 1,000–1,800, moderately concentrated; more than 1,800, highly concentrated.

— = not available.

n.a. = not applicable.

Table A2.6 Getting Finance Indicators for South Asian Countries, 2006

Indicator	Afghanistan	Bangladesh	Bhutan	India	Maldives	Nepal	Pakistan	Sri Lanka	Benchmark
Access to finance									
Demographic branch penetration (branches per 100,000 people)	0.41	4.73	6.65	6.37	9.03	1.73	4.96	7.69	5–65
Demographic ATM penetration (ATMs per 100,000 people)	0.06	0.29	0.31	1.93	5.02	0.28	1.25	5.67	39–167
Deposit accounts per 1,000 people	—	255.23	287.77	442.87	730.77	110.40	171.14	1,117.82	976–1,671
Loan accounts per 1,000 people	—	61.11	33.04	78.00	123.14	10.83	31.78	364.22	248–513
Geographic branch penetration (branches per 1,000 km^2)	0.19	44.53	1.12	23.46	90.00	2.97	9.67	15.81	1–119
Geographic ATM penetration (ATMs per 1,000 km^2)	0.03	2.71	0.05	7.11	50.00	0.48	2.44	11.65	3–366
Performance and efficiency									
Return on equity (%)	3.71	44.26	18.24	17.00	53.51	–43.30	34.90	25.44	7.50–27.00
Return on assets (%)	1.35	1.66	1.58	1.31	6.36	1.90	3.20	1.82	0.30–1.80
Staff cost ratio (%)	—	61.39	63.95	56.90	47.30	114.32	52.14	42.65	25.51–51.91
Operating cost ratio (%)	97.13	100.48	44.09	75.65	30.60	25.55	55.66	84.44	62.65–226.32
Net interest margin (%)	4.51	2.04	2.73	3.01	5.31	2.26	4.41	4.37	0.63–3.30
Recurring earning power (%)	0.61	2.59	1.58	2.20	7.01	2.39	3.66	2.03	0.58–2.03
Financial stability									
Capital adequacy ratio (%)	—	8.33	18.69	12.40	15.85	–1.75	13.33	12.67	4.90–15.40[a]
Leverage ratio (times)	0.31	5.33	0.09	12.59	0.12	–4.14	8.94	13.61	3.23–14.37
Gross nonperforming loans ratio (%)	2.40	13.15	4.92	3.33	2.28	14.22	5.70	7.35	0.20–8.50
Provisions to nonperforming loans ratio (%)	—	26.33	53.46	64.20	89.31	4.72	81.50	73.42	28.10–204.50
Liquid assets ratio (%)	—	18.67	68.04	38.40	27.28	9.70	32.20	19.26	8.31–38.73
Liquid assets to liabilities ratio (%)	—	116.27	158.94	180.00	—	19.07	55.13	22.17	1.82–26.62
Capital market development									
Domestic bond market to equity market capitalization (%)	—	316.64	39.21	39.77	—	92.96	71.20	136.68	2.97–250.87
Domestic public bonds outstanding to GDP (%)	—	17.13	4.50	29.60	3.10	14.10	27.46	31.62	9.49–154.47
Trading value of top 10 stocks ratio (%)	—	39.68	99.86	31.36	88.32	66.50	20.02	57.13	14.46–82.10

Stock market capitalization to GDP (%)	—	5.41	11.47	82.60	8.20	15.19	35.87	29.80	43.13–903.56
Stock trading value to GDP (%)	—	1.11	0.09	67.60	0.16	0.54	0.03	3.75	21.41–438.57
Stock market turnover ratio (times)	—	0.20	0.01	0.64	0.002	0.04	0.06	0.15	0.36–2.21
Market concentration and competitiveness									
Herfindahl-Hirschman Index (HHI)	—	596.86	5,388.02	599.43	3,467.00	949.86	784.01	1,255.02	296.88–2,414.97[b]
K-bank concentration ratio (k = 3), assets (%)	—	33.70	100.00	31.97	90.90	43.58	38.96	52.66	30.98–72.25
K-bank concentration ratio (k = 3), deposits (%)	—	35.29	100.00	30.74	89.28	38.16	40.04	55.73	26.32–58.58
K-bank concentration ratio (k = 3), loans (%)	—	34.00	100.00	32.15	95.48	30.30	39.67	52.56	24.26–56.93
Private credit extended by banks to GDP (%)	—	34.45	21.21	39.40	70.64	26.98	27.73	35.45	59.91–193.60
Commercial banking assets to GDP (%)	7.95	55.43	66.46	78.90	106.28	67.32	53.96	63.61	46.50–167.76
Payment systems development									
Notes and coins in circulation to GDP (%)	11.87	6.92	6.83	11.04	9.11	12.80	11.47	5.35	1.95–30.85
Narrow money supply (M1) to GDP (%)	19.84	12.07	31.03	20.23	31.64	17.29	41.41	8.84	10.52–143.61
Value of RTGS transactions to GDP (%)	n.a.	n.a.	n.a.	326.80	n.a.	n.a.	n.a.	60.55	1,828.00–15,326.00
Value of retail transactions to GDP (%)	3.41	—	10.23	324.95	—	—	1,256.00	145.55	0.55–4,541.88
RTGS concentration ratio (%)	n.a.	n.a.	n.a.	—	n.a.	n.a.	n.a.	43.99	45.30–80.00
Retail payments concentration ratio (%)	—	—	100.00	—	—	—	77.00	71.14	17.00–82.20
Savings mobilization									
Broad money supply (M2) to GDP (%)	20.14	44.76	60.10	69.71	68.81	53.03	48.19	33.80	45.35–393.80
Real deposit interest rate (%)	–1.49	–0.37	–0.50	0.45	0.23	–4.50	–4.26	–2.40	—
Gross domestic savings to GDP (%)	–8.32	20.35	41.39	34.30	—	8.90	17.70	17.00	13.80–52.41
Reserve money to total deposits (%)	151.49	24.09	58.18	24.33	43.97	38.20	42.64	21.39	—
Loan to deposit ratio (%)	41.12	83.54	41.39	71.46	105.12	85.80	76.19	80.27	—
Worker remittances to GDP (%)	—	8.74	—	3.15	0.31	14.94	4.04	7.64	0.02–0.99

Sources: South Asian central banks, securities and exchange commissions and boards, and stock exchanges; Indian Banks' Association 2006a, 2006b, 2006c, 2008a, 2008b, 2008c; RBI 2006a, 2006b, 2007a, 2007b, 2008a, 2008b, *Annual Report* (various years); World Bank, World Development Indicators database, 2006b; IMF, International Financial Statistics database, World Economic Outlook database; ADB, statistical database; CPSS 2004; Ratha and Xu 2008.

Note: All benchmark indicators are for selected high-income OECD member countries and nonmember Asian economies (Australia; Canada; China; France; Germany; Hong Kong, China; Italy; Japan; the Republic of Korea; Malaysia; New Zealand; Singapore; Thailand; the United Kingdom; and the United States).

a. Basel guideline: not less than 8 percent of risk-weighted assets.

b. Accepted norms for HHI: less than 1,000, banking industry is unconcentrated; 1,000–1,800, moderately concentrated; more than 1,800, highly concentrated.

— = not available.

n.a. = not applicable.

Table A2.7 Getting Finance Indicators for South Asian Countries, 2007

Indicator	Afghanistan	Bangladesh	Bhutan	India	Maldives	Nepal	Pakistan	Sri Lanka	Benchmark
Access to finance									
Demographic branch penetration (branches per 100,000 people)	0.57	4.78	6.53	6.35	9.70	1.78	4.94	8.56	5–56
Demographic ATM penetration (ATMs per 100,000 people)	0.07	0.46	1.37	2.40	13.04	0.37	1.66	4.50	35–122
Deposit accounts per 1,000 people	—	252.93	306.65	459.52	852.56	105.42	153.98	1,356.03	976–1,671
Loan accounts per 1,000 people	—	60.99	34.98	83.59	138.40	26.35	31.10	270.81	248–513
Geographic branch penetration (branches per 1,000 km^2)	0.26	45.52	1.12	24.13	96.70	3.20	9.82	17.69	1–110
Geographic ATM penetration (ATMs per 1,000 km^2)	0.03	4.39	0.23	9.11	130.00	0.67	3.29	13.45	3–146
Performance and efficiency									
Return on equity (%)	–1.07	50.94	18.31	17.31	49.99	–78.70	21.90	25.37	3.20–28.10
Return on assets (%)	–0.26	1.95	1.54	1.43	6.33	1.87	2.30	1.93	0.20–1.90
Staff cost ratio (%)	—	61.69	44.83	54.54	49.47	159.57	48.68	42.91	23.47–54.63
Operating cost ratio (%)	101.79	95.92	49.97	71.05	26.83	22.62	61.54	76.41	55.82–313.18
Net interest margin (%)	7.45	2.11	3.13	2.99	5.41	2.90	4.21	4.54	0.40–3.61
Recurring earning power (%)	–2.51	3.01	2.19	2.10	6.43	2.16	3.49	2.35	0.49–1.94
Financial stability									
Capital adequacy ratio (%)	38.35	7.52	16.17	12.28	15.58	–1.71	13.80	13.59	7.15–14.60[a]
Leverage ratio (times)	0.21	4.45	0.08	11.69	0.13	–0.01	9.35	12.71	3.10–10.08
Gross nonperforming loans ratio (%)	3.00	13.23	4.91	2.50	1.56	10.56	6.30	6.62	0.20–8.60
Provisions to nonperforming loans ratio (%)	43.49	42.91	48.40	60.20	63.94	12.44	88.20	71.51	28.80–188.90
Liquid assets ratio (%)	31.43	19.51	40.86	35.21	25.44	8.99	33.82	18.55	8.91–38.48
Liquid assets to liabilities ratio (%)	32.00	150.01	79.07	144.56	—	17.34	57.07	21.54	2.21–32.02
Capital market development									
Domestic bond market to equity market capitalization (%)	—	—	36.17	48.48	—	53.30	67.50	164.85	1.94–285.33
Domestic public bonds outstanding to GDP (%)	—	18.78	3.53	34.71	4.02	13.66	32.94	29.99	8.95–163.25
Trading value of top 10 stocks ratio (%)	—	44.12	100.00	25.25	98.20	60.37	8.93	58.28	12.50–74.10

Stock market capitalization to GDP (%)	—	10.07	9.76	83.77	26.65	25.62	46.20	23.00	36.70–1,284.15
Stock trading value to GDP (%)	—	3.49	0.05	70.33	1.70	1.15	0.29	2.93	18.68–1,033.79
Stock market turnover ratio (times)	—	0.47	0.01	0.67	0.01	0.06	0.01	0.12	0.52–2.70
Market concentration and competitiveness									
Herfindahl-Hirschman Index (HHI)	—	484.32	5,414.57	541.35	3,676.00	821.85	773.50	1,217.18	280.88–2,080.86[b]
K-bank concentration ratio (*k* = 3), assets (%)	—	31.58	100.00	31.12	92.55	35.83	38.62	51.79	25.21–66.89
K-bank concentration ratio (*k* = 3), deposits (%)	—	34.00	100.00	30.00	89.96	35.95	39.12	54.43	24.98–67.29
K-bank concentration ratio (*k* = 3), loans (%)	—	28.97	100.00	31.90	95.12	32.06	38.31	52.39	18.41–64.23
Private credit extended by banks to GDP (%)	—	33.11	24.19	44.30	91.28	31.94	28.43	33.26	62.44–189.58
Commercial banking assets to GDP (%)	11.21	58.71	58.04	83.89	135.81	67.48	57.83	58.55	138.67–376.27
Payment systems development									
Notes and coins in circulation to GDP (%)	12.07	7.50	6.27	11.13	8.46	12.50	11.55	4.85	1.94–31.03
Narrow money supply (M1) to GDP (%)	22.94	11.00	33.92	20.79	32.65	17.45	45.03	7.46	10.05–156.02
Value of RTGS transactions to GDP (%)	n.a.	n.a.	n.a.	596.72	n.a.	n.a.	n.a.	65.03	2,147–17,557
Value of retail transactions to GDP (%)	7.95	—	12.08	297.92	—	—	1,423.00	130.68	0.57–5,067.78
RTGS concentration ratio (%)	n.a.	n.a.	n.a.	—	n.a.	n.a.	n.a.	48.35	50.70–80.00
Retail payments concentration ratio (%)	—	—	100.00	—	—	—	80.00	69.79	16.00–83.60
Savings mobilization									
Broad money supply (M2) to GDP (%)	23.76	46.00	53.70	71.71	73.91	54.40	50.52	32.10	42.03–412.65
Real deposit interest rate (%)	1.20	–3.16	–0.70	1.88	–0.40	–2.90	–3.47	–5.49	—
Gross domestic savings to GDP (%)	–8.72	20.40	60.07	35.70	—	9.70	17.78	17.60	15.19–52.89
Reserve money to total deposits (%)	111.68	23.93	50.90	23.64	43.93	35.70	40.31	20.23	—
Loan to deposit ratio (%)	54.06	80.28	48.80	73.94	122.64	82.10	72.11	80.53	—
Worker remittances to GDP (%)	—	10.00	—	2.96	0.28	13.77	4.17	7.74	0.02–1.02

Sources: South Asian central banks, securities and exchange commissions and boards, and stock exchanges; Indian Banks' Association 2006a, 2006b, 2006c, 2008a, 2008b, 2008c; RBI 2006a, 2006b, 2007a, 2007b, 2008a, 2008b, *Annual Report* (various years); World Bank, World Development Indicators database, 2006b; IMF, International Financial Statistics database, World Economic Outlook database; ADB, statistical database; CPSS 2004; CBSL, *Annual Report*, 2008; Ratha and Xu 2008; Securities and Exchange Commission of Sri Lanka 2009.

Note: All benchmark indicators are for selected high-income OECD member countries and nonmember Asian economies (Australia; Canada; China; France; Germany; Hong Kong, China; Italy; Japan; the Republic of Korea; Malaysia; New Zealand; Singapore; Thailand; the United Kingdom; and the United States).

a. Basel guideline: not less than 8 percent of risk-weighted assets.

b. Accepted norms for HHI: less than 1,000, banking industry is unconcentrated; 1,000–1,800, moderately concentrated; more than 1,800, highly concentrated.

— = not available.

n.a. = not applicable.

Table A2.8 Getting Finance Indicators for South Asian Countries, 2008

Indicator	Afghanistan	Bangladesh	Bhutan	India	Maldives	Nepal	Pakistan	Sri Lanka	Benchmark
Access to finance									
Demographic branch penetration (branches per 100,000 people)	0.61	4.84	6.71	6.60	10.37	2.05	5.35	8.84	5–56
Demographic ATM penetration (ATMs per 100,000 people)	0.09	0.63	2.09	3.28	13.04	0.73	2.04	5.67	35–122
Deposit accounts per 1,000 people	26.79	255.77	325.39	467.35	965.02	106.73	154.93	1,304.31	976–1,671
Loan accounts per 1,000 people	1.30	68.65	42.82	89.03	141.97	24.64	30.75	240.37	248–513
Geographic branch penetration (branches per 1,000 km^2)	0.28	46.70	1.17	25.49	103.30	3.78	10.77	18.28	1–110
Geographic ATM penetration (ATMs per 1,000 km^2)	0.04	6.10	0.36	12.68	130.00	1.34	4.11	15.00	3–146
Performance and efficiency									
Return on equity (%)	8.93	48.35	17.08	17.34	30.36	503.55[a]	19.30	27.64	3.20–28.10
Return on assets (%)	1.77	2.63	1.50	1.57	4.53	2.77	2.05	2.01	0.20–1.90
Staff cost ratio (%)	36.00	61.12	60.73	51.55	33.64	172.89	49.64	42.74	23.47–54.63
Operating cost ratio (%)	83.87	88.87	31.76	76.03	36.30	21.56	66.82	76.82	55.82–313.18
Net interest margin (%)	7.12	2.33	3.46	2.61	4.60	3.13	3.26	4.48	0.40–3.61
Recurring earning power (%)	0.51	3.43	2.18	2.15	5.28	2.34	2.49	2.40	0.49–1.94
Financial stability									
Capital adequacy ratio (%)	31.77	10.06	13.93	13.01	21.01	4.04	12.20	12.62	7.15–14.60[b]
Leverage ratio (times)	0.19	6.21	0.08	10.63	0.16	0.02	9.23	13.15	3.10–10.08
Gross nonperforming loans ratio (%)	0.90	10.79	7.21	2.25	8.90	6.08	7.60	7.92	0.20–8.60
Provisions to nonperforming loans ratio (%)	88.93	56.15	44.79	56.18	14.02	8.16	81.10	61.41	28.80–188.90
Liquid assets ratio (%)	23.80	21.31	31.74	34.12	22.60	11.80	28.74	20.11	8.91–38.48
Liquid assets to liabilities ratio (%)	29.00	132.60	61.92	146.23	—	20.58	50.79	23.46	2.21–32.02
Capital market development									
Domestic bond market to equity market capitalization (%)	—	—	23.89	40.25	—	48.19	93.55	332.22	1.94–285.33
Domestic public bonds outstanding to GDP (%)	—	18.42	3.14	36.24	4.51	13.55	33.13	29.07	8.95–163.25
Trading value of top 10 stocks ratio (%)	—	39.83	100.00	26.78	99.35	92.48	6.81	67.30	12.50–74.10

Stock market capitalization to GDP (%)	—	19.26	13.14	106.05	20.60	28.12	36.05	11.08	36.70–1,284.15
Stock trading value to GDP (%)	—	6.07	0.06	108.86	3.19	1.68	0.14	2.50	18.68–1,033.79
Stock market turnover ratio (times)	—	0.33	0.01	1.13	0.01	0.07	0.004	0.17	0.52–2.70
Market concentration and competitiveness									
Herfindahl-Hirschman Index (HHI)	—	500.56	5,077.44	535.63	3,648.00	712.01	741.00	1,198.75	280.88–2,080.86[c]
K-bank concentration ratio (*k* =3), assets (%)	—	30.28	100.00	30.52	92.50	35.26	37.83	51.06	25.21–66.89
K-bank concentration ratio (*k* = 3), deposits (%)	—	30.66	100.00	28.56	91.11	30.98	38.89	54.48	24.98–67.29
K-bank concentration ratio (*k* = 3), loans (%)	—	25.90	100.00	30.52	94.60	26.22	38.63	49.43	18.41–64.23
Private credit extended by banks to GDP (%)	—	36.30	38.82	48.78	100.8	26.44	27.56	28.94	62.44–189.58
Commercial banking assets to GDP (%)	14.3	57.04	63.74	91.80	143.14	69.05	51.38	53.39	138.67–376.27
Payment systems development									
Notes and coins in circulation to GDP (%)	10.97	7.54	6.46	11.17	9.37	12.20	11.05	4.22	1.94–31.03
Narrow money supply (M1) to GDP (%)	21.38	12.00	25.54	21.06	37.75	18.80	39.73	6.29	10.05–156.02
Value of RTGS transactions to GDP (%)	n.a.	n.a.	n.a.	1,024.69	n.a.	n.a.	389.75	67.11	2,147.00–17,557.00
Value of retail transactions to GDP (%)	4.91	—	13.08	306.13	—	—	1,444.00	116.29	0.57–5,067.78
RTGS concentration ratio (%)	n.a.	n.a.	n.a.	—	n.a.	n.a.	32.39	45.42	50.70–80.00
Retail payments concentration ratio (%)	—	—	100.00	—	—	—	79.00	69.27	16.00–83.60
Savings mobilization									
Broad money supply (M2) to GDP (%)	22.18	49.00	45.75	76.45	76.51	60.35	45.31	29.07	42.03–412.65
Real deposit interest rate (%)	–4.17	–1.58	–3.60	1.05	–0.65	–3.50	–12.63	–10.97	—
Gross domestic savings to GDP (%)	–1.18	20.10	—	37.70	—	11.50	13.25	14.13	15.19–52.89
Reserve money to total deposits (%)	98.77	23.62	61.42	24.62	44.67	34.30	41.62	19.03	—
Loan to deposit ratio (%)	62.99	82.12	51.69	73.88	133.41	82.60	79.23	88.78	—
Worker remittances to GDP (%)	—	6.00	—	3.64	0.24	17.38	4.24	7.20	0.02–1.02

Sources: South Asian central banks, securities and exchange commissions and boards, and stock exchanges; Indian Banks' Association 2006a, 2006b, 2006c, 2008a, 2008b, 2008c; RBI 2006a, 2006b, 2007a, 2007b, 2008a, 2008b, *Annual Report* (various years); World Bank, World Development Indicators database, 2006b; IMF, International Financial Statistics database, World Economic Outlook database; ADB, statistical database, 2009c; CPSS 2004; CBSL, *Annual Report,* 2008; Ratha and Xu 2008; Securities and Exchange Commission of Sri Lanka 2009.

Note: All benchmark indicators are for selected high-income OECD member countries and nonmember Asian economies (Australia; Canada; China; France; Germany; Hong Kong, China; Italy; Japan; the Republic of Korea; Malaysia; New Zealand; Singapore; Thailand; the United Kingdom; and the United States).

a. An unusually high ratio due to negative equity at the beginning of the year turned positive during the year, making average equity for the year much smaller than year-end equity.

b. Basel guideline: not less than 8 percent of risk-weighted assets.

c. Accepted norms for HHI: less than 1,000, banking industry is unconcentrated; 1,000–1,800, moderately concentrated; more than 1,800, highly concentrated.

— = not available.

n.a. = not applicable.

Table A2.9 Getting Finance Indicators for Afghanistan, 2001–08

Indicator	2001	2002	2003	2004	2005	2006	2007	2008	Benchmark
Access to finance									
Demographic branch penetration (branches per 100,000 people)	—	—	—	0.14	0.22	0.41	0.57	0.61	5–69
Demographic ATM penetration (ATMs per 100,000 people)	—	—	—	0.01	0.02	0.06	0.07	0.09	16–167
Deposit accounts per 1,000 people	—	—	—	—	—	—	—	26.79	976–1,671
Loan accounts per 1,000 people	—	—	—	—	—	—	—	1.30	248–513
Geographic branch penetration (branches per 1,000 km^2)	—	—	—	0.07	0.10	0.19	0.26	0.28	1–159
Geographic ATM penetration (ATMs per 1,000 km^2)	—	—	—	0.003	0.01	0.03	0.03	0.04	1–437
Performance and efficiency									
Return on equity (%)	—	—	—	—	1.72	3.71	–1.07	8.93	1.90–65.02
Return on assets (%)	—	—	—	—	0.73	1.35	–0.26	1.77	0.10–1.90
Staff cost ratio (%)	—	—	—	—	—	—	—	36.00	14.87–56.30
Operating cost ratio (%)	—	—	—	—	—	97.13	101.79	83.87	49.20–313.18
Net interest margin (%)	—	—	—	—	—	4.51	7.45	7.12	0.40–3.61
Recurring earning power (%)	—	—	—	—	—	0.61	–2.51	0.51	0.10–2.39
Financial stability									
Capital adequacy ratio (%)	—	—	—	—	—	—	38.35	31.77	2.50–18.20[a]
Leverage ratio (times)	—	—	—	0.38	0.45	0.31	0.21	0.19	0.68–15.39
Gross nonperforming loans ratio (%)	—	—	—	—	—	2.40	3.00	0.90	0.20–29.80
Provisions to nonperforming loans ratio (%)	—	—	—	—	—	—	43.49	88.93	24.50–204.50
Liquid assets ratio (%)	—	—	—	—	—	—	31.43	23.80	7.07–44.39
Liquid assets to liabilities ratio (%)	—	—	—	—	—	—	32.00	29.00	1.82–42.20
Capital market development									
Domestic bond market to equity market capitalization (%)	—	—	—	—	—	—	—	—	1.94–347.68
Domestic public bonds outstanding to GDP (%)	—	—	—	—	—	—	—	—	8.83–163.25
Trading value of top 10 stocks ratio (%)	—	—	—	—	—	—	—	—	6.04–82.10

Stock market capitalization to GDP (%)	—	—	—	—	—	—	—	—	17.91–1,284.15
Stock trading value to GDP (%)	—	—	—	—	—	—	—	—	12.47–1,033.79
Stock market turnover ratio (times)	—	—	—	—	—	—	—	—	0.27–2.91
Market concentration and competitiveness									
Herfindahl-Hirschman Index (HHI)	—	—	—	—	—	—	—	—	247.12–2,561.91[b]
K-bank concentration ratio (k = 3), assets (%)	—	—	—	—	—	—	—	—	21.16–79.45
K-bank concentration ratio (k = 3), deposits (%)	—	—	—	—	—	—	—	—	18.25–73.60
K-bank concentration ratio (k = 3), loans (%)	—	—	—	—	—	—	—	—	16.79–66.30
Private credit extended by banks to GDP (%)	—	—	—	—	—	—	—	—	42.00–193.60
Commercial banking assets to GDP (%)	—	—	—	4.84	5.95	7.95	11.21	14.30	44.90–376.27
Payment systems development									
Notes and coins in circulation to GDP (%)	—	—	11.83	14.06	13.26	11.87	12.07	10.97	1.94–31.03
Narrow money supply (M1) to GDP (%)	—	—	—	18.67	18.82	19.84	22.94	21.38	10.05–156.02
Value of RTGS transactions to GDP (%)	n.a.	n.a.	n.a.	n.a.	n.a.	n.a.	n.a.	n.a.	1,133.00–17,557.00
Value of retail transactions to GDP (%)	—	—	—	—	—	3.41	7.95	4.91	0.54–5,067.78
RTGS concentration ratio (%)	n.a.	n.a.	n.a.	n.a.	n.a.	n.a.	n.a.	n.a.	37.70–84.00
Retail payments concentration ratio (%)	—	—	—	—	—	—	—	—	16.00–83.60
Savings mobilization									
Broad money supply (M2) to GDP (%)	—	—	—	19.09	20.05	20.14	23.76	22.18	39.15–412.65
Real deposit interest rate (%)	—	—	—	—	—	−1.49	1.20	−4.17	—
Gross domestic savings to GDP (%)	—	−5.31	−35.77	−31.76	−14.79	−8.32	−8.72	−1.18	13.50–52.89
Reserve money to total deposits (%)	—	—	—	297.43	207.30	151.49	111.68	98.77	—
Loan to deposit ratio (%)	—	—	—	30.00	31.87	41.12	54.06	62.99	—
Worker remittances to GDP (%)	—	—	—	—	—	—	—	—	0.02–2.14

Sources: Da Afghanistan Bank; World Bank, World Development Indicators database (gross domestic savings to GDP for 2001); IMF, World Economic Outlook database (GDP for 2004–08).

Note: All benchmark indicators are for selected high-income OECD member countries and nonmember Asian economies (Australia; Canada; China; France; Germany; Hong Kong, China; Italy; Japan; the Republic of Korea; Malaysia; New Zealand; Singapore; Thailand; the United Kingdom; and the United States).

a. Basel guideline: not less than 8 percent of risk-weighted assets.

b. Accepted norms for HHI: less than 1,000, banking industry is unconcentrated; 1,000–1,800, moderately concentrated; more than 1,800, highly concentrated.

— = not available.

n.a. = not applicable.

Table A2.10 Getting Finance Indicators for Bangladesh, 2001–08

Indicator	2001	2002	2003	2004	2005	2006	2007	2008	Benchmark
Access to finance									
Demographic branch penetration (branches per 100,000 people)	4.83	4.74	4.67	4.67	4.64	4.73	4.78	4.84	5–69
Demographic ATM penetration (ATMs per 100,000 people)	0.10	0.14	0.14	0.17	0.20	0.29	0.46	0.63	16–167
Deposit accounts per 1,000 people	231.97	234.75	234.60	233.63	237.32	255.23	252.93	255.77	976–1,671
Loan accounts per 1,000 people	56.56	57.14	56.87	60.24	60.45	61.11	60.99	68.65	248–513
Geographic branch penetration (branches per 1,000 km^2)	42.50	42.26	42.25	42.71	43.41	44.53	45.52	46.70	1–159
Geographic ATM penetration (ATMs per 1,000 km^2)	0.91	1.22	1.26	1.55	1.84	2.71	4.39	6.10	1–437
Performance and efficiency									
Return on equity (%)	17.12	12.40	12.39	–13.39	28.63	44.26	50.94	48.35	1.90–65.02
Return on assets (%)	0.74	0.54	0.59	–0.63	1.30	1.66	1.95	2.63	0.10–1.90
Staff cost ratio (%)	44.75	66.53	64.53	66.24	65.00	61.39	61.69	61.12	14.87–56.30
Operating cost ratio (%)	236.78	187.63	161.86	141.89	107.91	100.48	95.92	88.87	49.20–313.18
Net interest margin (%)	1.66	1.04	1.09	1.97	2.38	2.04	2.11	2.33	0.40–3.61
Recurring earning power (%)	1.70	1.50	1.68	1.86	2.36	2.59	3.01	3.43	0.10–2.39
Financial stability									
Capital adequacy ratio (%)	7.02	7.60	8.42	7.41	7.65	8.33	7.52	10.06	2.50–18.20[a]
Leverage ratio (times)	4.17	4.34	4.77	4.16	4.42	5.33	4.45	6.21	0.68–15.39
Gross nonperforming loans ratio (%)	31.49	28.10	22.13	17.63	13.55	13.15	13.23	10.79	0.20–29.80
Provisions to nonperforming loans ratio (%)	25.36	25.30	18.35	19.15	24.31	26.33	42.91	56.15	24.50–204.50
Liquid assets ratio (%)	30.03	25.84	24.67	23.50	20.61	18.67	19.51	21.31	7.07–44.39
Liquid assets to liabilities ratio (%)	122.90	121.46	127.19	121.94	104.60	116.27	150.01	132.60	1.82–42.20
Capital market development									
Domestic bond market to equity market capitalization (%)	663.50	735.42	435.22	239.99	259.28	316.64	—	—	1.94–347.68
Domestic public bonds outstanding to GDP (%)	16.17	17.53	16.73	16.57	16.75	17.13	18.78	18.42	8.83–163.25
Trading value of top 10 stocks ratio (%)	59.16	51.64	51.55	46.67	41.89	39.68	44.12	39.83	6.04–82.10

Stock market capitalization to GDP (%)	2.57	2.61	2.43	4.28	6.06	5.41	10.07	19.26	17.91–1,284.15
Stock trading value to GDP (%)	1.28	1.28	1.02	0.74	2.03	1.11	3.49	6.07	12.47–1,033.79
Stock market turnover ratio (times)	0.50	0.49	0.42	0.23	0.41	0.20	0.47	0.33	0.27–2.91
Market concentration and competitiveness									
Herfindahl-Hirschman Index (HHI)	944.90	886.66	702.04	724.09	679.31	596.86	484.32	500.56	247.12–2,561.91[b]
K-bank concentration ratio ($k = 3$), assets (%)	47.38	45.77	38.33	39.33	37.05	33.70	31.58	30.28	21.16–79.45
K-bank concentration ratio ($k = 3$), deposits (%)	50.55	47.55	43.27	40.31	37.72	35.29	34.00	30.66	18.25–73.60
K-bank concentration ratio ($k = 3$), loans (%)	45.76	43.22	39.57	36.54	36.46	34.00	28.97	25.90	16.79–66.30
Private credit extended by banks to GDP (%)	24.33	26.32	29.42	30.96	31.87	34.45	33.11	36.30	42.00–193.60
Commercial banking assets to GDP (%)	50.35	52.78	53.84	51.82	54.93	55.43	58.71	57.04	44.90–376.27
Payment systems development									
Notes and coins in circulation to GDP (%)	5.47	5.62	5.75	6.10	6.72	6.92	7.50	7.54	1.94–31.03
Narrow money supply (M1) to GDP (%)	9.53	9.79	10.13	10.63	11.51	12.07	11.00	12.00	10.05–156.02
Value of RTGS transactions to GDP (%)	n.a.	n.a.	n.a.	n.a.	n.a.	n.a.	n.a.	n.a.	1,133.00–17,557.00
Value of retail transactions to GDP (%)	—	—	—	—	—	—	—	—	0.54–5,067.78
RTGS concentration ratio (%)	n.a.	n.a.	n.a.	n.a.	n.a.	n.a.	n.a.	n.a.	37.70–84.00
Retail payments concentration ratio (%)	—	—	—	—	—	—	—	—	16.00–83.60
Savings mobilization									
Broad money supply (M2) to GDP (%)	36.10	37.92	38.96	40.85	43.46	44.76	46.00	49.00	39.15–412.65
Real deposit interest rate (%)	3.95	1.91	–0.18	–0.86	–0.49	–0.37	–3.16	–1.58	—
Gross domestic savings to GDP (%)	18.16	18.63	19.53	20.01	20.25	20.35	20.40	20.10	13.50–52.89
Reserve money to total deposits (%)	26.43	23.75	22.98	21.56	23.00	24.09	23.93	23.62	—
Loan to deposit ratio (%)	84.17	83.31	80.53	77.87	79.52	83.54	80.28	82.12	—
Worker remittances to GDP (%)	5.26	5.90	5.97	6.38	7.76	8.74	10.00	6.00	0.02–2.14

Sources: Bangladesh Bank; World Bank, World Development Indicators database; IMF, World Economic Outlook database (stock market capitalization to GDP for 2001); World Bank 2006b (private credit extended by banks to GDP for 2001 and 2002); ADB, statistical database (inflation data for real deposit interest rate for 2001–08).

Note: All benchmark indicators are for selected high-income OECD member countries and nonmember Asian economies (Australia; Canada; China; France; Germany; Hong Kong, China; Italy; Japan; the Republic of Korea; Malaysia; New Zealand; Singapore; Thailand; the United Kingdom; and the United States).

a. Basel guideline: not less than 8 percent of risk-weighted assets.

b. Accepted norms for HHI: less than 1,000, banking industry is unconcentrated; 1,000–1,800, moderately concentrated; more than 1,800, highly concentrated.

— = not available.

n.a. = not applicable.

Table A2.11 Getting Finance Indicators for Bhutan, 2001–08

Indicator	2001	2002	2003	2004	2005	2006	2007	2008	Benchmark
Access to finance									
Demographic branch penetration (branches per 100,000 people)	3.58	3.49	5.86	5.71	6.77	6.65	6.53	6.71	5–69
Demographic ATM penetration (ATMs per 100,000 people)	—	—	0.27	0.27	0.31	0.31	1.37	2.09	16–167
Deposit accounts per 1,000 people	—	—	202.02	206.65	269.28	287.77	306.65	325.39	976–1,671
Loan accounts per 1,000 people	18.75	21.24	24.55	25.61	29.61	33.04	34.98	42.82	248–513
Geographic branch penetration (branches per 1,000 km^2)	0.54	0.54	1.12	1.12	1.12	1.12	1.12	1.17	1–159
Geographic ATM penetration (ATMs per 1,000 km^2)	—	—	0.05	0.05	0.05	0.05	0.23	0.36	1–437
Performance and efficiency									
Return on equity (%)	19.03	17.03	17.98	14.19	15.02	18.24	18.31	17.08	1.90–65.02
Return on assets (%)	1.23	1.19	1.24	1.30	1.42	1.58	1.54	1.50	0.10–1.90
Staff cost ratio (%)	55.04	56.88	50.12	52.91	57.13	63.95	44.83	60.73	14.87–56.30
Operating cost ratio (%)	40.14	46.11	44.30	39.61	40.96	44.09	49.97	31.76	49.20–313.18
Net interest margin (%)	1.63	2.02	2.18	2.46	2.62	2.73	3.13	3.46	0.40–3.61
Recurring earning power (%)	1.76	1.70	1.76	2.08	2.02	1.58	2.19	2.18	0.10–2.39
Financial stability									
Capital adequacy ratio (%)	14.83	13.94	19.93	18.52	20.81	18.69	16.17	13.93	2.50–18.20[a]
Leverage ratio (times)	0.07	0.06	0.09	0.10	0.89	0.09	0.08	0.08	0.68–15.39
Gross nonperforming loans ratio (%)	8.80	7.23	7.78	5.98	6.57	4.92	4.91	7.21	0.20–29.80
Provisions to nonperforming loans ratio (%)	38.72	43.62	40.67	45.38	58.25	53.46	48.40	44.79	24.50–204.50
Liquid assets ratio (%)	47.46	40.52	38.18	44.89	69.54	68.04	40.86	31.74	7.07–44.39
Liquid assets to liabilities ratio (%)	136.39	96.34	94.20	116.79	179.44	158.94	79.07	61.92	1.82–42.20
Capital market development									
Domestic bond market to equity market capitalization (%)	16.98	14.53	37.61	42.30	40.72	39.21	36.17	23.89	1.94–347.68
Domestic public bonds outstanding to GDP (%)	2.18	1.89	4.52	5.63	4.99	4.50	3.53	3.14	8.83–163.25
Trading value of top 10 stocks ratio (%)	100.00	100.00	100.00	99.90	100.00	99.86	100.00	100.00	6.04–82.10

Stock market capitalization to GDP (%)	12.86	13.03	12.03	13.30	12.25	11.47	9.76	13.14	17.91–1,284.15
Stock trading value to GDP (%)	0.34	0.15	0.07	0.34	0.06	0.09	0.05	0.06	12.47–1,033.79
Stock market turnover ratio (times)	0.03	0.01	0.01	0.03	0.01	0.01	0.01	0.01	0.27–2.91
Market concentration and competitiveness									
Herfindahl-Hirschman Index (HHI)	5,774.98	5,795.97	5,676.65	5,552.71	5,501.59	5,388.02	5,414.57	5,077.44	247.12–2,561.91[b]
K-bank concentration ratio ($k = 3$), assets (%)	100.00	100.00	100.00	100.00	100.00	100.00	100.00	100.00	21.16–79.45
K-bank concentration ratio ($k = 3$), deposits (%)	100.00	100.00	100.00	100.00	100.00	100.00	100.00	100.00	18.25–73.60
K-bank concentration ratio ($k = 3$), loans (%)	100.00	100.00	100.00	100.00	100.00	100.00	100.00	100.00	16.79–66.30
Private credit extended by banks to GDP (%)	10.61	11.38	13.40	15.77	17.96	21.21	24.19	38.82	42.00–193.60
Commercial banking assets to GDP (%)	58.67	62.67	59.09	61.77	60.52	66.46	58.04	63.74	44.90–376.27
Payment systems development									
Notes and coins in circulation to GDP (%)	7.03	6.24	6.13	6.41	6.59	6.83	6.27	6.46	1.94–31.03
Narrow money supply (M1) to GDP (%)	21.55	27.04	23.04	24.92	24.60	31.03	33.92	25.54	10.05–156.02
Value of RTGS transactions to GDP (%)	n.a.	n.a.	n.a.	n.a.	n.a.	n.a.	n.a.	n.a.	1,133.00–17,557.00
Value of retail transactions to GDP (%)	—	8.49	9.48	12.05	10.58	10.23	12.08	13.08	0.54–5,067.78
RTGS concentration ratio (%)	n.a.	n.a.	n.a.	n.a.	n.a.	n.a.	n.a.	n.a.	37.70–84.00
Retail payments concentration ratio (%)	100.00	100.00	100.00	100.00	100.00	100.00	100.00	100.00	16.00–83.60
Savings mobilization									
Broad money supply (M2) to GDP (%)	47.18	52.52	47.12	51.36	24.60	60.10	53.70	45.75	39.15–412.65
Real deposit interest rate (%)	4.10	4.50	2.40	0.30	–0.80	–0.50	–0.70	–3.60	—
Gross domestic savings to GDP (%)	33.95	36.40	35.63	36.71	38.50	41.39	60.07	—	13.50–52.89
Reserve money to total deposits (%)	58.84	51.83	66.69	56.19	72.12	58.18	50.90	61.42	—
Loan to deposit ratio (%)	26.18	29.68	31.94	43.19	37.52	41.39	49.00	51.69	—
Worker remittances to GDP (%)	—	—	—	—	—	—	—	—	0.02–2.14

Sources: Royal Monetary Authority of Bhutan; World Bank, World Development Indicators database (GDP for 2001 and 2002 to calculate private credit extended by banks to GDP, notes and coins in circulation to GDP, narrow money supply to GDP, broad money supply to GDP, real deposit interest rate, and gross domestic savings to GDP); IMF, International Financial Statistics database (private credit extended by banks, and broad money supply to GDP for 2001 and 2002); ADB, statistical database (inflation data for real deposit interest rate).

Note: All benchmark indicators are for selected high-income OECD member countries and nonmember Asian economies (Australia; Canada; China; France; Germany; Hong Kong, China; Italy; Japan; the Republic of Korea; Malaysia; New Zealand; Singapore; Thailand; the United Kingdom; and the United States).

a. Basel guideline: not less than 8 percent of risk-weighted assets.

b. Accepted norms for HHI: less than 1,000, banking industry is unconcentrated; 1,000–1,800, moderately concentrated; more than 1,800, highly concentrated.

— = not available.

n.a. = not applicable.

Table A2.12 Getting Finance Indicators for India, 2001–08

Indicator	2001	2002	2003	2004	2005	2006	2007	2008	Benchmark
Access to finance									
Demographic branch penetration (branches per 100,000 people)	6.42	6.33	6.25	6.26	6.33	6.37	6.35	6.60	5–69
Demographic ATM penetration (ATMs per 100,000 people)	—	—	—	—	1.63	1.93	2.40	3.28	16–167
Deposit accounts per 1,000 people	416.77	420.84	418.67	426.11	432.11	442.87	459.52	467.35	976–1,671
Loan accounts per 1,000 people	50.99	53.93	55.84	61.88	71.42	78.00	83.59	89.03	248–513
Geographic branch penetration (branches per 1,000 km^2)	22.18	22.26	22.41	22.57	22.99	23.46	24.13	25.49	1–159
Geographic ATM penetration (ATMs per 1,000 km^2)	—	—	—	—	5.93	7.11	9.11	12.68	1–437
Performance and efficiency									
Return on equity (%)	13.80	17.30	21.00	23.00	16.90	17.00	17.31	17.34	1.90–65.02
Return on assets (%)	0.90	1.10	1.50	1.70	1.30	1.31	1.43	1.57	0.10–1.90
Staff cost ratio (%)	68.10	64.70	62.10	60.17	58.29	56.90	54.54	51.55	14.87–56.30
Operating cost ratio (%)	92.33	85.38	80.71	77.05	74.32	75.65	71.05	76.03	49.20–313.18
Net interest margin (%)	2.98	2.66	2.85	3.07	3.07	3.01	2.99	2.61	0.40–3.61
Recurring earning power (%)	1.60	2.00	2.50	2.90	2.40	2.20	2.10	2.15	0.10–2.39
Financial stability									
Capital adequacy ratio (%)	11.40	12.00	12.70	12.90	12.80	12.40	12.28	13.01	2.50–18.20[a]
Leverage ratio (times)	19.12	15.69	15.87	15.77	14.20	12.59	11.69	10.63	0.68–15.39
Gross nonperforming loans ratio (%)	11.40	10.40	8.80	7.20	5.13	3.33	2.50	2.25	0.20–29.80
Provisions to nonperforming loans ratio (%)	49.70	53.40	52.40	62.00	63.50	64.20	60.20	56.18	24.50–204.50
Liquid assets ratio (%)	48.20	47.40	48.70	48.70	44.20	38.40	35.21	34.12	7.07–44.39
Liquid assets to liabilities ratio (%)	260.00	250.00	260.00	260.00	220.00	180.00	144.56	146.23	1.82–42.20
Capital market development									
Domestic bond market to equity market capitalization (%)	117.85	118.92	72.77	64.33	50.46	39.77	48.48	40.25	1.94–347.68
Domestic public bonds outstanding to GDP (%)	26.80	29.80	31.60	33.40	33.00	29.60	34.71	36.24	8.83–163.25
Trading value of top 10 stocks ratio (%)	72.90	62.93	55.42	44.86	41.66	31.36	25.25	26.78	6.04–82.10

Stock market capitalization to GDP (%)	29.40	27.40	22.50	41.90	52.70	82.60	83.77	106.05	17.91–1,284.15
Stock trading value to GDP (%)	112.00	36.00	37.70	57.80	53.30	67.60	70.33	108.86	12.47–1,033.79
Stock market turnover ratio (times)	2.13	0.88	1.08	1.10	0.75	0.64	0.67	1.13	0.27–2.91
Market concentration and competitiveness									
Herfindahl-Hirschman Index (HHI)	784.67	741.50	734.59	677.93	642.38	599.43	541.35	535.63	247.12–2,561.91[b]
K-bank concentration ratio ($k = 3$), assets (%)	33.80	33.67	33.49	33.17	32.02	31.97	31.12	30.52	21.16–79.45
K-bank concentration ratio ($k = 3$), deposits (%)	33.98	33.26	32.76	31.29	31.09	30.74	30.00	28.56	18.25–73.60
K-bank concentration ratio ($k = 3$), loans (%)	33.04	31.92	31.60	30.97	30.84	32.15	31.90	30.52	16.79–66.30
Private credit extended by banks to GDP (%)	21.50	23.80	25.90	27.50	33.30	39.40	44.30	48.78	42.00–193.60
Commercial banking assets to GDP (%)	61.90	67.30	68.80	71.20	73.00	78.90	83.89	91.80	44.90–376.27
Payment systems development									
Notes and coins in circulation to GDP (%)	9.90	10.23	10.73	10.89	11.02	11.04	11.13	11.17	1.94–31.03
Narrow money supply (M1) to GDP (%)	17.07	17.43	18.04	18.57	19.27	20.23	20.79	21.06	10.05–156.02
Value of RTGS transactions to GDP (%)	n.a.	n.a.	n.a.	0.07	130.55	326.80	596.72	1024.69	1,133.00–17,557.00
Value of retail transactions to GDP (%)	514.34	528.88	548.87	420.18	339.28	324.95	297.92	306.10	0.54–5,067.78
RTGS concentration ratio (%)	n.a.	n.a.	n.a.	—	—	—	—	—	37.70–84.00
Retail payments concentration ratio (%)	—	—	—	—	—	—	—	—	16.00–83.60
Savings mobilization									
Broad money supply (M2) to GDP (%)	58.58	62.22	66.73	67.15	68.37	69.71	71.71	76.45	39.15–412.65
Real deposit interest rate (%)	3.35	2.60	–0.30	0.83	1.05	0.45	1.88	1.05	—
Gross domestic savings to GDP (%)	23.70	23.50	26.40	29.70	31.80	34.30	35.70	37.70	13.50–52.89
Reserve money to total deposits (%)	29.37	28.46	26.78	25.97	26.17	24.33	23.64	24.62	—
Loan to deposit ratio (%)	53.13	53.45	56.93	55.95	62.79	71.46	73.94	73.88	—
Worker remittances to GDP (%)	3.09	3.27	4.09	3.05	3.03	3.15	2.96	3.64	0.02–2.14

Sources: Indian Banks' Association 2006a, 2006b, 2006c, 2008a, 2008b, 2008c; RBI 2006a, 2006b, 2007a, 2007b, 2008a, 2008b, *Annual Report* (various years); Ratha and Xu 2008.

Note: All benchmark indicators are for selected high-income OECD member countries and nonmember Asian economies (Australia; Canada; China; France; Germany; Hong Kong, China; Italy; Japan; the Republic of Korea; Malaysia; New Zealand; Singapore; Thailand; the United Kingdom; and the United States).

a. Basel guideline: not less than 8 percent of risk-weighted assets.

b. Accepted norms for HHI: less than 1,000, banking industry is unconcentrated; 1,000–1,800, moderately concentrated; more than 1,800, highly concentrated.

— = not available.

n.a. = not applicable.

Table A2.13 Getting Finance Indicators for Maldives, 2001–08

Indicator	2001	2002	2003	2004	2005	2006	2007	2008	Benchmark
Access to finance									
Demographic branch penetration (branches per 100,000 people)	6.29	6.66	7.77	8.15	8.15	9.03	9.70	10.37	5–69
Demographic ATM penetration (ATMs per 100,000 people)	2.96	3.70	3.70	3.70	3.70	5.02	13.04	13.04	16–167
Deposit accounts per 1,000 people	397.13	456.03	518.48	603.14	703.60	730.77	852.56	965.02	976–1,671
Loan accounts per 1,000 people	—	—	45.90	56.12	115.96	123.14	138.40	141.97	248–513
Geographic branch penetration (branches per 1,000 km^2)	56.70	60.00	70.00	73.30	73.30	90.00	96.70	103.30	1–159
Geographic ATM penetration (ATMs per 1,000 km^2)	26.70	33.30	33.30	33.30	33.30	50.00	130.00	130.00	1–437
Performance and efficiency									
Return on equity (%)	43.72	25.77	30.63	36.98	40.76	53.51	49.99	30.36	1.90–65.02
Return on assets (%)	5.59	3.42	3.73	4.47	4.78	6.36	6.33	4.53	0.10–1.90
Staff cost ratio (%)	33.96	35.46	39.29	40.70	37.54	47.30	49.47	33.64	14.87–56.30
Operating cost ratio (%)	40.99	51.83	46.29	49.45	43.49	30.60	26.83	36.30	49.20–313.18
Net interest margin (%)	5.06	3.69	4.12	4.42	4.68	5.31	5.41	4.60	0.40–3.61
Recurring earning power (%)	5.90	4.27	4.65	5.27	5.76	7.01	6.43	5.28	0.10–2.39
Financial stability									
Capital adequacy ratio (%)	24.00	23.13	23.44	18.38	15.57	15.85	15.58	21.01	2.50–18.20[a]
Leverage ratio (times)	0.14	0.12	0.12	0.12	0.12	0.12	0.13	0.16	0.68–15.39
Gross nonperforming loans ratio (%)	9.89	10.01	10.10	6.24	6.35	2.28	1.56	8.90	0.20–29.80
Provisions to nonperforming loans ratio (%)	24.95	27.59	41.06	56.59	45.20	89.31	63.94	14.02	24.50–204.50
Liquid assets ratio (%)	47.90	50.29	53.71	45.40	30.97	27.28	25.44	22.60	7.07–44.39
Liquid assets to liabilities ratio (%)	—	—	—	—	—	—	—	—	1.82–42.20
Capital market development									
Domestic bond market to equity market capitalization (%)	—	—	—	—	—	—	—	—	1.94–347.68
Domestic public bonds outstanding to GDP (%)	—	—	—	—	—	3.10	4.02	4.51	8.83–163.25
Trading value of top 10 stocks ratio (%)	—	90.75	74.90	87.13	87.60	88.32	98.20	99.35	6.04–82.10

Stock market capitalization to GDP (%)	—	9.48	11.34	16.06	14.05	8.20	26.65	20.60	17.91–1,284.15
Stock trading value to GDP (%)	—	0.07	0.08	0.25	0.35	0.16	1.70	3.19	12.47–1,033.79
Stock market turnover ratio (times)	—	0.001	0.001	0.002	0.002	0.002	0.010	0.014	0.27–2.91
Market concentration and competitiveness									
Herfindahl-Hirschman Index (HHI)	3,347.00	3,216.00	3,154.00	3,328.00	3,335.00	3,467.00	3,676.00	3,648.00	247.12–2,561.91[b]
K-bank concentration ratio ($k = 3$), assets (%)	91.69	89.82	87.33	85.66	88.56	90.90	92.55	92.50	21.16–79.45
K-bank concentration ratio ($k = 3$), deposits (%)	91.95	89.67	87.64	85.47	88.39	89.28	89.96	91.11	18.25–73.60
K-bank concentration ratio ($k = 3$), loans (%)	94.12	93.61	90.96	89.63	93.19	95.48	95.12	94.60	16.79–66.30
Private credit extended by banks to GDP (%)	23.57	25.56	25.37	35.57	57.42	70.64	91.28	100.84	42.00–193.60
Commercial banking assets to GDP (%)	50.92	59.50	57.90	67.16	90.85	106.28	135.81	143.14	44.90–376.27
Payment systems development									
Notes and coins in circulation to GDP (%)	7.40	6.95	7.05	7.67	9.20	9.11	8.46	9.37	1.94–31.03
Narrow money supply (M1) to GDP (%)	21.23	22.64	23.34	24.92	31.61	31.64	32.65	37.75	10.05–156.02
Value of RTGS transactions to GDP (%)	n.a.	n.a.	n.a.	n.a.	n.a.	n.a.	n.a.	n.a.	1,133.00–17,557.00
Value of retail transactions to GDP (%)	—	—	—	—	—	—	—	—	0.54–5,067.78
RTGS concentration ratio (%)	n.a.	n.a.	n.a.	n.a.	n.a.	n.a.	n.a.	n.a.	37.70–84.00
Retail payments concentration ratio (%)	—	—	—	—	—	—	—	—	16.00–83.60
Savings mobilization									
Broad money supply (M2) to GDP (%)	43.04	47.99	50.86	60.21	69.66	68.81	73.91	76.51	39.15–412.65
Real deposit interest rate (%)	3.24	0.33	1.79	0.72	0.96	0.23	–0.40	–0.65	—
Gross domestic savings to GDP (%)	44.93	46.35	49.11	46.15	—	—	—	—	13.50–52.89
Reserve money to total deposits (%)	62.90	61.01	51.11	48.28	45.06	43.97	43.93	44.67	—
Loan to deposit ratio (%)	61.92	57.99	53.09	62.04	85.32	105.12	122.64	133.41	—
Worker remittances to GDP (%)	0.32	0.31	0.29	0.37	0.31	0.31	0.28	0.24	0.02–2.14

Sources: Maldives Monetary Authority; World Bank, World Development Indicators database (gross domestic savings to GDP for 2001–04, worker remittances to GDP for 2001–08).

Note: All benchmark indicators are for selected high-income OECD member countries and nonmember Asian economies (Australia; Canada; China; France; Germany; Hong Kong, China; Italy; Japan; the Republic of Korea; Malaysia; New Zealand; Singapore; Thailand; the United Kingdom; and the United States).

a. Basel guideline: not less than 8 percent of risk-weighted assets.

b. Accepted norms for HHI: less than 1,000, banking industry is unconcentrated; 1,000–1,800, moderately concentrated; more than 1,800, highly concentrated.

— = not available.

n.a. = not applicable.

Table A2.14 Getting Finance Indicators for Nepal, 2001–08

Indicator	2001	2002	2003	2004	2005	2006	2007	2008	Benchmark
Access to finance									
Demographic branch penetration (branches per 100,000 people)	2.09	1.85	1.85	1.71	1.67	1.73	1.78	2.05	5–69
Demographic ATM penetration (ATMs per 100,000 people)	0.05	0.06	0.08	0.11	0.24	0.28	0.37	0.73	16–167
Deposit accounts per 1,000 people	111.59	123.21	102.43	115.88	113.58	110.40	105.42	106.73	976–1,671
Loan accounts per 1,000 people	19.07	14.92	12.96	11.97	11.30	10.83	26.35	24.64	248–513
Geographic branch penetration (branches per 1,000 km^2)	3.29	2.96	3.04	2.87	2.87	2.97	3.20	3.78	1–159
Geographic ATM penetration (ATMs per 1,000 km^2)	0.08	0.10	0.14	0.18	0.41	0.48	0.67	1.34	1–437
Performance and efficiency									
Return on equity (%)	–93.62	–96.16	–22.33	–46.42	–45.87	–43.30	–78.70	503.55[a]	1.90–65.02
Return on assets (%)	–3.04	–3.37	–0.85	1.47	1.79	1.90	1.87	2.77	0.10–1.90
Staff cost ratio (%)	194.25	185.00	306.16	181.18	135.35	114.32	159.57	172.89	14.87–56.30
Operating cost ratio (%)	35.87	59.78	40.14	31.93	28.55	25.55	22.62	21.56	49.20–313.18
Net interest margin (%)	1.76	0.92	1.58	1.99	2.22	2.26	2.90	3.13	0.40–3.61
Recurring earning power (%)	0.86	0.21	–0.01	1.81	2.33	2.39	2.16	2.34	0.10–2.39
Financial stability									
Capital adequacy ratio (%)	4.00	–7.25	–11.74	–9.07	–6.07	–1.75	–1.71	4.04	2.50–18.20[b]
Leverage ratio (times)	3.27	3.71	3.87	–3.00	–4.65	–4.14	–0.01	0.02	0.68–15.39
Gross nonperforming loans ratio (%)	29.31	30.41	28.80	22.77	18.94	14.22	10.56	6.08	0.20–29.80
Provisions to nonperforming loans ratio (%)	30.59	29.98	7.55	3.82	11.49	4.72	12.44	8.16	24.50–204.50
Liquid assets ratio (%)	22.10	18.16	12.49	13.61	9.33	9.70	8.99	11.80	7.07–44.39
Liquid assets to liabilities ratio (%)	47.88	41.33	27.03	27.30	20.34	19.07	17.34	20.58	1.82–42.20
Capital market development									
Domestic bond market to equity market capitalization (%)	129.55	212.14	240.19	204.93	142.69	92.96	53.30	48.19	1.94–347.68
Domestic public bonds outstanding to GDP (%)	14.50	17.40	18.50	17.30	16.40	14.10	13.66	13.55	8.83–163.25
Trading value of top 10 stocks ratio (%)	83.13	81.89	58.35	86.25	83.96	66.50	60.37	92.48	6.04–82.10

Stock market capitalization to GDP (%)	11.76	8.54	8.05	8.72	10.49	15.19	25.62	28.12	17.91–1,284.15
Stock trading value to GDP (%)	0.59	0.38	0.13	0.45	0.77	0.54	1.15	1.68	12.47–1,033.79
Stock market turnover ratio (times)	0.05	0.04	0.02	0.06	0.09	0.04	0.06	0.07	0.27–2.91
Market concentration and competitiveness									
Herfindahl-Hirschman Index (HHI)	1,563.48	1,574.76	1,468.53	1,245.62	1,019.21	949.86	821.85	712.01	247.12–2,561.91[c]
K-bank concentration ratio (*k* = 3), assets (%)	58.02	58.68	56.67	52.88	45.87	43.58	35.83	35.26	21.16–79.45
K-bank concentration ratio (*k* = 3), deposits (%)	51.73	49.62	46.80	44.00	41.73	38.16	35.95	30.98	18.25–73.60
K-bank concentration ratio (*k* = 3), loans (%)	52.06	49.34	44.64	42.14	37.28	30.30	32.06	26.22	16.79–66.30
Private credit extended by banks to GDP (%)	26.95	27.21	27.80	28.95	27.57	26.98	31.94	26.44	42.00–193.60
Commercial banking assets to GDP (%)	63.83	67.69	69.84	71.55	70.25	67.32	67.48	69.05	44.90–376.27
Payment systems development									
Notes and coins in circulation to GDP (%)	11.90	13.20	12.50	12.60	12.50	12.80	12.50	12.20	1.94–31.03
Narrow money supply (M1) to GDP (%)	15.99	16.79	17.02	17.51	17.00	17.29	17.45	18.80	10.05–156.02
Value of RTGS transactions to GDP (%)	n.a.	n.a.	n.a.	n.a.	n.a.	n.a.	n.a.	n.a.	1,133.00–17,557.00
Value of retail transactions to GDP (%)	—	—	—	—	—	—	—	—	0.54–5,067.78
RTGS concentration ratio (%)	n.a.	n.a.	n.a.	n.a.	n.a.	n.a.	n.a.	n.a.	37.70–84.00
Retail payments concentration ratio (%)	—	—	—	—	—	—	—	—	16.00–83.60
Savings mobilization									
Broad money supply (M2) to GDP (%)	48.57	48.75	49.96	51.66	50.97	53.03	54.40	60.35	39.15–412.65
Real deposit interest rate (%)	2.40	1.50	−0.50	−0.50	−1.10	−4.50	−2.90	−3.50	—
Gross domestic savings to GDP (%)	11.70	9.50	8.60	11.70	11.60	8.90	9.70	11.50	13.50–52.89
Reserve money to total deposits (%)	38.90	43.00	39.90	40.60	38.50	38.20	35.70	34.30	—
Loan to deposit ratio (%)	74.80	78.50	80.10	79.30	84.80	85.80	82.10	82.60	—
Worker remittances to GDP (%)	10.69	10.35	11.01	10.92	11.12	14.94	13.77	17.38	0.02–2.14

Source: Nepal Rastra Bank.

Note: All benchmark indicators are for selected high-income OECD member countries and nonmember Asian economies (Australia; Canada; China; France; Germany; Hong Kong, China; Italy; Japan; the Republic of Korea; Malaysia; New Zealand; Singapore; Thailand; the United Kingdom; and the United States).

a. An unusually high ratio due to negative equity at the beginning of the year turned positive during the year, making average equity for the year much smaller than year-end equity.

b. Basel guideline: not less than 8 percent of risk-weighted assets.

c. Accepted norms for HHI: less than 1,000, banking industry is unconcentrated; 1,000–1,800, moderately concentrated; more than 1,800, highly concentrated.

— = not available.

n.a. = not applicable.

Table A2.15 Getting Finance Indicators for Pakistan, 2001–08

Indicator	2001	2002	2003	2004	2005	2006	2007	2008	Benchmark
Access to finance									
Demographic branch penetration (branches per 100,000 people)	4.88	4.73	4.61	4.64	4.82	4.96	4.94	5.35	5–69
Demographic ATM penetration (ATMs per 100,000 people)	—	—	0.37	0.52	0.67	1.25	1.66	2.04	16–167
Deposit accounts per 1,000 people	195.84	194.87	190.55	180.28	173.15	171.14	153.98	154.93	976–1,671
Loan accounts per 1,000 people	16.04	14.93	18.86	24.51	30.57	31.78	31.10	30.75	248–513
Geographic branch penetration (branches per 1,000 km^2)	8.77	8.72	8.66	8.84	9.22	9.67	9.82	10.77	1–159
Geographic ATM penetration (ATMs per 1,000 km^2)	—	—	0.69	0.99	1.29	2.44	3.29	4.11	1–437
Performance and efficiency									
Return on equity (%)	12.20	27.50	33.70	29.00	36.90	34.90	21.90	19.30	1.90–65.02
Return on assets (%)	0.60	1.50	2.10	2.00	2.90	3.20	2.30	2.05	0.10–1.90
Staff cost ratio (%)	52.58	50.75	51.48	51.97	50.73	52.14	48.68	49.64	14.87–56.30
Operating cost ratio (%)	90.91	85.81	83.20	83.62	57.73	55.66	61.54	66.82	49.20–313.18
Net interest margin (%)	3.24	3.10	2.98	2.87	4.11	4.41	4.21	3.26	0.40–3.61
Recurring earning power (%)	1.17	2.00	2.57	2.26	3.35	3.66	3.49	2.49	0.10–2.39
Financial stability									
Capital adequacy ratio (%)	11.30	12.60	11.10	11.40	11.90	13.33	13.80	12.20	2.50–18.20[a]
Leverage ratio (times)	4.58	4.11	5.03	6.45	7.64	8.94	9.35	9.23	0.68–15.39
Gross nonperforming loans ratio (%)	19.60	17.70	13.70	9.00	6.70	5.70	6.30	7.60	0.20–29.80
Provisions to nonperforming loans ratio (%)	53.20	58.20	64.80	72.40	80.40	81.50	88.20	81.10	24.50–204.50
Liquid assets ratio (%)	39.90	48.10	46.10	37.00	33.90	32.20	33.82	28.74	7.07–44.39
Liquid assets to liabilities ratio (%)	56.25	68.95	63.44	51.88	52.77	55.13	57.07	50.79	1.82–42.20
Capital market development									
Domestic bond market to equity market capitalization (%)	537.75	278.47	186.41	108.60	73.94	71.20	67.50	93.55	1.94–347.68
Domestic public bonds outstanding to GDP (%)	38.90	37.80	36.70	33.00	30.90	27.46	32.94	33.13	8.83–163.25
Trading value of top 10 stocks ratio (%)	22.52	21.89	19.18	16.01	20.48	20.02	8.93	6.81	6.04–82.10

Stock market capitalization to GDP (%)	8.06	9.15	15.31	24.07	30.59	35.87	46.20	36.05	17.91–1,284.15
Stock trading value to GDP (%)	0.02	0.15	0.13	0.19	0.11	0.03	0.29	0.14	12.47–1,033.79
Stock market turnover ratio (times)	0.12	0.90	0.54	0.50	0.22	0.06	0.01	0.004	0.27–2.91
Market concentration and competitiveness									
Herfindahl-Hirschman Index (HHI)	1,091.80	1,052.12	976.81	903.97	805.61	784.01	773.50	741.00	247.12–2,561.91[b]
K-bank concentration ratio ($k = 3$), assets (%)	50.30	49.71	47.47	43.95	40.35	38.96	38.62	37.83	21.16–79.45
K-bank concentration ratio ($k = 3$), deposits (%)	53.23	51.76	48.93	45.55	41.49	40.04	39.12	38.89	18.25–73.60
K-bank concentration ratio ($k = 3$), loans (%)	50.86	47.00	43.58	42.56	41.96	39.67	38.31	38.63	16.79–66.30
Private credit extended by banks to GDP (%)	17.82	18.04	19.46	22.59	26.34	27.73	28.43	27.56	42.00–193.60
Commercial banking assets to GDP (%)	43.61	47.72	50.10	52.07	53.89	53.96	57.83	51.38	44.90–376.27
Payment systems development									
Notes and coins in circulation to GDP (%)	10.20	10.95	11.64	11.62	11.26	11.47	11.55	11.05	1.94–31.03
Narrow money supply (M1) to GDP (%)	20.32	22.52	26.03	27.33	27.77	41.41	45.03	39.73	10.05–156.02
Value of RTGS transactions to GDP (%)	n.a.	n.a.	n.a.	n.a.	n.a.	n.a.	n.a.	389.75	1,133.00–17,557.00
Value of retail transactions to GDP (%)	—	—	—	—	—	1,256.00	1,423.00	1,444.00	0.54–5,067.78
RTGS concentration ratio (%)	n.a.	n.a.	n.a.	n.a.	n.a.	n.a.	n.a.	32.39	37.70–84.00
Retail payments concentration ratio (%)	—	—	—	—	—	77.00	80.00	79.00	16.00–83.60
Savings mobilization									
Broad money supply (M2) to GDP (%)	39.20	42.97	46.48	48.42	49.26	48.19	50.52	45.31	39.15–412.65
Real deposit interest rate (%)	1.38	−0.08	−1.45	−6.15	−6.51	−4.26	−3.47	−12.63	—
Gross domestic savings to GDP (%)	16.28	18.43	20.56	17.92	17.48	17.70	17.78	13.25	13.50–52.89
Reserve money to total deposits (%)	48.67	45.00	44.04	43.28	39.94	42.64	40.31	41.62	—
Loan to deposit ratio (%)	63.54	56.83	58.83	68.02	72.31	76.19	72.11	79.23	—
Worker remittances to GDP (%)	2.14	4.76	4.69	4.08	3.92	4.04	4.17	4.24	0.02–2.14

Source: State Bank of Pakistan.

Note: All benchmark indicators are for selected high-income OECD member countries and nonmember Asian economies (Australia; Canada; China; France; Germany; Hong Kong, China; Italy; Japan; the Republic of Korea; Malaysia; New Zealand; Singapore; Thailand; the United Kingdom; and the United States).

a. Basel guideline: not less than 8 percent of risk-weighted assets.

b. Accepted norms for HHI: less than 1,000, banking industry is unconcentrated; 1,000–1,800, moderately concentrated; more than 1,800, highly concentrated.

— = not available.

n.a. = not applicable.

Table A2.16 Getting Finance Indicators for Sri Lanka, 2001–08

Indicator	2001	2002	2003	2004	2005	2006	2007	2008	Benchmark
Access to finance									
Demographic branch penetration (branches per 100,000 people)	6.03	6.70	6.85	7.06	7.20	7.69	8.56	8.84	5–69
Demographic ATM penetration (ATMs per 100,000 people)	2.55	3.27	3.69	4.16	4.50	5.67	4.50	5.67	16–167
Deposit accounts per 1,000 people	939.32	989.94	1,000.53	1,023.58	1,066.24	1,117.82	1,356.03	1,304.31	976–1,671
Loan accounts per 1,000 people	256.88	257.66	279.15	304.11	344.17	364.22	270.81	240.37	248–513
Geographic branch penetration (branches per 1,000 km^2)	11.68	13.17	13.63	14.20	14.64	15.81	17.69	18.28	1–159
Geographic ATM penetration (ATMs per 1,000 km^2)	4.93	6.43	7.34	8.37	9.15	11.65	13.45	15.00	1–437
Performance and efficiency									
Return on equity (%)	20.57	25.71	26.33	25.62	27.01	25.44	25.37	27.64	1.90–65.02
Return on assets (%)	0.84	1.11	1.36	1.43	1.70	1.82	1.93	2.01	0.10–1.90
Staff cost ratio (%)	46.21	47.62	49.58	46.98	44.53	42.65	42.91	42.74	14.87–56.30
Operating cost ratio (%)	118.66	99.80	94.02	95.66	87.70	84.44	76.41	76.82	49.20–313.18
Net interest margin (%)	3.30	3.78	4.16	3.97	4.05	4.37	4.54	4.48	0.40–3.61
Recurring earning power (%)	1.64	2.07	2.58	2.33	2.26	2.03	2.35	2.40	0.10–2.39
Financial stability									
Capital adequacy ratio (%)	8.59	10.35	10.31	10.29	12.84	12.67	13.59	12.62	2.50–18.20[a]
Leverage ratio (times)	3.90	4.71	5.53	5.63	6.93	13.61	12.71	13.15	0.68–15.39
Gross nonperforming loans ratio (%)	19.57	19.09	16.36	11.29	8.76	7.35	6.62	7.92	0.20–29.80
Provisions to nonperforming loans ratio (%)	44.43	50.38	58.74	68.29	72.05	73.42	71.51	61.41	24.50–204.50
Liquid assets ratio (%)	22.80	18.80	17.30	20.30	19.60	19.26	18.55	20.11	7.07–44.39
Liquid assets to liabilities ratio (%)	26.30	21.70	20.00	23.10	22.10	22.17	21.54	23.46	1.82–42.20
Capital market development									
Domestic bond market to equity market capitalization (%)	659.05	585.08	389.76	299.80	216.69	136.68	164.85	332.22	1.94–347.68
Domestic public bonds outstanding to GDP (%)	16.28	21.94	27.43	31.70	31.77	31.62	29.99	29.07	8.83–163.25
Trading value of top 10 stocks ratio (%)	54.37	57.70	60.83	42.92	43.10	57.13	58.28	67.30	6.04–82.10

Stock market capitalization to GDP (%)	8.81	10.28	14.92	18.83	24.69	29.80	23.00	11.08	17.91–1,284.15
Stock trading value to GDP (%)	0.99	1.91	4.18	2.92	4.84	3.75	2.93	2.50	12.47–1,033.79
Stock market turnover ratio (times)	0.13	0.21	0.35	0.18	0.24	0.15	0.12	0.17	0.27–2.91
Market concentration and competitiveness									
Herfindahl-Hirschman Index (HHI)	1,650.62	1,528.39	1,455.81	1,377.33	1,279.44	1,255.02	1,217.18	1,198.75	247.12–2,561.91[b]
K-bank concentration ratio ($k = 3$), assets (%)	63.09	60.88	58.19	55.68	53.02	52.66	51.79	51.06	21.16–79.45
K-bank concentration ratio ($k = 3$), deposits (%)	62.02	62.43	60.89	58.25	56.30	55.73	54.43	54.48	18.25–73.60
K-bank concentration ratio ($k = 3$), loans (%)	65.16	60.02	56.81	53.28	50.44	52.56	52.39	49.43	16.79–66.30
Private credit extended by banks to GDP (%)	28.19	28.09	29.50	31.26	33.87	35.45	33.26	28.94	42.00–193.60
Commercial banking assets to GDP (%)	56.80	54.51	56.06	56.92	61.79	63.61	58.55	53.39	44.90–376.27
Payment systems development									
Notes and coins in circulation to GDP (%)	5.44	5.58	5.42	5.54	5.40	5.35	4.85	4.22	1.94–31.03
Narrow money supply (M1) to GDP (%)	8.68	8.81	8.87	9.01	9.41	8.84	7.46	6.29	10.05–156.02
Value of RTGS transactions to GDP (%)	n.a.	n.a.	61.12	61.51	57.41	60.55	65.03	67.11	1,133.00–17,557.00
Value of retail transactions to GDP (%)	289.85	241.89	215.16	153.89	151.82	145.55	130.68	116.29	0.54–5,067.78
RTGS concentration ratio (%)	n.a.	n.a.	47.60	39.42	49.70	43.99	48.35	45.42	37.70–84.00
Retail payments concentration ratio (%)	85.70	85.40	84.90	71.85	71.73	71.14	69.79	69.27	16.00–83.60
Savings mobilization									
Broad money supply (M2) to GDP (%)	32.03	32.26	31.87	32.90	33.55	33.80	32.10	29.07	39.15–412.65
Real deposit interest rate (%)	–3.42	–2.13	–1.03	–3.69	–4.80	–2.40	–5.49	–10.97	—
Gross domestic savings to GDP (%)	15.80	14.40	16.00	16.40	17.90	17.00	17.60	14.13	13.50–52.89
Reserve money to total deposits (%)	21.69	22.05	21.72	21.57	20.93	21.39	20.23	19.03	—
Loan to deposit ratio (%)	79.01	70.93	69.56	68.93	73.10	80.27	80.53	88.78	—
Worker remittances to GDP (%)	7.34	7.78	7.75	7.57	8.06	7.64	7.74	7.20	0.02–2.14

Sources: Central Bank of Sri Lanka; ADB 2009c (worker remittances to GDP for 2008); CBSL, *Annual Report,* 2008 (domestic bond market to equity market capitalization and domestic public bonds outstanding to GDP for 2007 and 2008 and reserve money to total deposits for 2008); Securities and Exchange Commission of Sri Lanka 2009 (domestic bond market to equity market capitalization and domestic public bonds outstanding to GDP for 2007 and 2008); CPSS 2004 (value of retail transactions to GDP for 2001 and 2002, RTGS concentration ratio for 2003, and retail payments concentration ratio for 2001–03).

Note: All benchmark indicators are for selected high-income OECD member countries and nonmember Asian economies (Australia; Canada; China; France; Germany; Hong Kong, China; Italy; Japan; the Republic of Korea; Malaysia; New Zealand; Singapore; Thailand; the United Kingdom; and the United States).

a. Basel guideline: not less than 8 percent of risk-weighted assets.

b. Accepted norms for HHI: less than 1,000, banking industry is unconcentrated; 1,000–1,800, moderately concentrated; more than 1,800, highly concentrated.

— = not available.

n.a. = not applicable.

Appendix 3A. Getting Finance Indicators for Benchmark Economies, 2001–08

Table A3a.1 Benchmark Indicators, 2001

Reference	Indicator	Australia	Canada	China	France	Germany	Hong Kong, China	Italy	Japan	Korea, Rep.	Malaysia	New Zealand	Singapore	Thailand	United Kingdom	United States	Range
	Access to finance																
1	Demographic branch penetration (branches per 100,000 people)	25	29	1[a]	44	69	26	51	30	10	—	21	12	5	25	24	5–69
2	Demographic ATM penetration (ATMs per100,000 people)	68	115	2[a]	62	60	—	64	112	—	—	47	43	—	62	114	43–115
3	Deposit accounts per 1,000 people	—	—	—	—	—	—	—	—	—	—	—	—	—	—	—	976–1,671[b]
4	Loan accounts per 1,000 people	—	—	—	—	—	—	—	—	—	—	—	—	—	—	—	248–513[c]
5	Geographic branch penetration (branches per 1,000 km^2)	1	1	1	47	159	1,766[a]	97	102	98	—	3	710[a]	6	61	8	1–159
6	Geographic ATM penetration (ATMs per 1,000 km^2)	1	4	2	67	139	—	122	378	—	—	7	2,632[a]	—	152	35	1–378
	Performance and efficiency																
7	Return on equity (%)	20.10	13.90	4.42	9.60	4.60	17.90	8.60	–14.30[a]	12.80	13.30	23.38	9.70	32.80	7.70	13.00	4.42–32.80
8	Return on assets (%)	1.30	0.70	0.21	0.50	0.20	1.40	0.60	–0.60[a]	0.70	1.00	1.06	1.00	1.47	0.50	1.10	0.20–1.47
9	Staff cost ratio (%)	41.98	44.55	4.62[a]	46.31	36.12	43.86	40.86	14.87	20.01	28.21	42.88	36.93	37.98	41.88	35.51	14.87–46.31
10	Operating cost ratio (%)	118.64	149.64	81.64	294.02	222.89	52.22	150.42	177.01	148.90	98.68	82.78	49.86	107.04	109.90	106.82	49.86–294.02
11	Net interest margin (%)	2.09	2.23	2.12	0.64	1.19	2.53	2.47	1.43	2.13	3.03	2.10	1.81	1.93	1.89	3.55	0.64–3.55
12	Recurring earning power (%)	1.55	1.29	0.57	0.45	0.10	1.93	0.88	0.79	1.92	2.29	1.52	1.31	0.54	1.21	2.22	0.10–2.29
	Financial stability																
13	Capital adequacy ratio (%)	10.40	12.30	5.89[a]	12.10	12.00	16.50	10.40	10.80	11.70	13.00	10.79	18.20	13.30	13.20	12.90	10.40–18.20
14	Leverage ratio (times)	9.32	7.08	4.72	4.74	5.05	9.50	5.96	4.11	4.95	8.45	6.58	15.01	5.44	8.64	10.74	4.11–15.01
15	Gross nonperforming loans ratio (%)	0.60	1.50	29.80	4.10	4.60	6.50	6.70	8.40	3.40	17.80	1.20	8.00	11.50	2.60	1.30	0.60–29.80
16	Provisions to nonperforming loans ratio (%)	107.10	44.00	—	59.90	—	59.20	—	36.50	—	37.60	25.40	60.10	47.10	72.20	128.80	25.40–128.80
17	Liquid assets ratio (%)	13.33	18.95	17.59	44.39	31.47	35.64	22.26	14.83	10.94	24.43	7.42	40.44	31.66	22.22	16.77	7.42–44.39
18	Liquid assets to liabilities ratio (%)	8.89	2.83	16.67	29.05	23.08	42.20	26.34	14.33	12.69	22.36	7.21	30.18	239.08[a]	22.28	21.24	2.83–42.20

	Capital market development																
19	Domestic bond market to equity market capitalization (%)	45.48	86.90	76.05	54.91	139.62	8.90	233.29	256.86	150.51	69.84	77.70	42.28	100.70	30.95	108.70	8.90–256.86
20	Domestic public bonds outstanding to GDP (%)	18.16	58.69	15.19	44.48	31.70	8.83	83.88	95.34	16.04	36.36	27.18	32.11	15.93	29.58	41.92	8.83–95.34
21	Trading value of top 10 stocks ratio (%)	50.40	37.30	6.04	29.10	61.90	44.70	60.90	23.53	37.50	10.70	57.00	27.90	23.20	37.00	15.55	6.04–61.90
22	Stock market capitalization to GDP (%)	102.22	110.52	40.00	141.03	56.68	350.02	51.23	55.29	40.35	135.20	35.58	160.80	31.13	169.59	145.98	35.58–350.02
23	Stock trading value to GDP (%)	65.31	65.53	37.27	156.18	75.27	120.25	56.73	44.79	78.78	27.14	16.21	74.68	26.68	130.77	290.00	16.21–290.00
24	Stock market turnover ratio (times)	0.64	0.59	0.93	1.01	1.22	0.34	0.95	1.42	2.21	0.21	0.46	0.47	0.95	0.77	1.99	0.34–2.21
	Market concentration and competitiveness																
25	Herfindahl-Hirschman Index (HHI)	952.49	1,375.15	918.00	1,487.22	1,044.49	1,192.77	505.07	326.66	427.10	544.39	924.28	1,658.53	629.54	514.28	498.54	427.10–1,658.53
26	K-bank concentration ratio (k=3), assets (%)	41.19	51.56	79.45	55.27	62.92	52.29	55.31	38.43	46.59	44.45	33.40	61.19	49.32	27.04	34.88	27.04–79.45
27	K-bank concentration ratio (k=3), deposits (%)	40.20	51.31	51.26	54.12	45.63	51.01	29.73	23.53	30.60	30.93	34.72	60.18	30.76	27.44	36.16	23.53–60.18
28	K-bank concentration ratio (k=3), loans (%)	37.54	50.19	52.46	29.49	41.06	45.10	29.66	22.28	34.11	31.73	34.73	66.30	27.29	27.02	30.41	22.28–66.30
29	Private credit extended by banks to GDP (%)	87.65	66.98	111.77	85.03	116.92	157.85	74.91	113.52	85.67	127.23	108.07	112.28	96.91	131.95	42.00	42.00–157.85
30	Commercial banking assets to GDP (%)	91.13	76.98	16.27	103.04	145.43	174.28	91.55	199.22	83.15	143.98	113.33	136.51	117.39	131.69	44.90	44.90–174.28
	Payment systems development																
31	Notes and coins in circulation to GDP (%)	15.62	3.41	28.97	1.98	3.22	7.82	4.61	13.40	3.72	7.09	1.93	7.72	9.98	3.26	5.78	1.98–28.97
32	Narrow money supply (M1) to GDP (%)	78.82	26.11	110.57	27.13	28.47	17.70	42.02	56.62	36.02	22.62	16.47	23.47	11.29	65.19	11.93	11.29–110.57
33	Value of RTGS transactions to GDP (%)	14,834.77	2,571.51	—	7,340.15	4,909.79	7,244.76	2,173.83	5,206.44	3,746.80	—	—	7,511.93	1,381.14	8,518.42	7,260.20	1,381.00–14,835.00
34	Value of retail transactions to GDP (%)	—	467.64	—	281.71	104.22	890.28	196.12	0.62	1,432.30	—	—	340.51	3.57	357.98	414.55	0.62–1,432.30

(Table continues on next page)

Table A3a.1 Benchmark Indicators, 2001 *(continued)*

Reference	Indicator	Australia	Canada	China	France	Germany	Hong Kong, China	Italy	Japan	Korea, Rep.	Malaysia	New Zealand	Singapore	Thailand	United Kingdom	United States	Range
35	RTGS concentration ratio (%)	—	82.90	—	43.60	—	—	38.70	—	—	—	—	—	—	84.00, 79.00[d]	—	38.70–84.00
36	Retail payments concentration ratio (%)	—	83.60	—	—	—	—	22.50	—	—	—	—	69.00–100.00[e]	—	81.00	—	22.50–83.60
	Savings mobilization																
37	Broad money supply (M2) to GDP (%)	286.09	48.81	171.78	68.46	68.46	273.33	68.46	132.87	127.31	101.81	40.91	117.65	127.82	88.32	53.94	48.81–286.09
38	Real deposit interest rate (%)	—	—	—	—	—	—	—	—	—	—	—	—	—	—	—	—
39	Gross domestic savings to GDP (%)	22.37	24.92	38.39	21.22	21.50	29.82	21.95	25.39	31.63	41.84	24.69	41.55	30.59	15.11	15.20	15.11–41.84
40	Reserve money to total deposits (%)	—	—	—	—	—	—	—	—	—	—	—	—	—	—	—	—
41	Loan to deposit ratio (%)	—	—	—	—	—	—	—	—	—	—	—	—	—	—	—	—
42	Worker remittances to GDP (%)	0.48	—	0.63	0.69	0.21	0.09	0.20	0.05	0.14	0.85	1.98	—	1.08	0.33	0.03	0.03–1.98

Sources: See appendix 3B.

a. Outlier not used in range.

b. Range is for 2002 (low value) and 2003 (high value).

c. Range is for 2004 (low value) and 2003 (high value).

d. The United Kingdom has two RTGS systems, and therefore, two different values are shown.

e. Singapore has more than one retail payment system, and therefore, a range of values is shown.

— = not available.

Table A3a.2 Benchmark Indicators, 2002

Reference	Indicator	Australia	Canada	China	France	Germany	Hong Kong, China	Italy	Japan	Korea, Rep.	Malaysia	New Zealand	Singapore	Thailand	United Kingdom	United States	Range
	Access to finance																
1	Demographic branch penetration (branches per 100,000 people)	25	29	4[a]	44	65	24	52	29	10	—	28	11	5	24	25	5–65
2	Demographic ATM penetration (ATMs per 100,000 people)	83	128	2[a]	65	61	—	69	110	—	—	48	37	—	69	122	37–128
3	Deposit accounts per 1,000 people	—	—	—	—	—	—	976	—	—	—	—	—	—	—	—	976–1,671[b]
4	Loan accounts per 1,000 people	—	—	—	—	—	—	328	—	—	—	—	—	—	—	—	248–513[c]
5	Geographic branch penetration (branches per 1,000 km^2)	1	1	5	47	149	1,640[a]	99	98	103	—	4	650[a]	6	60	8	1–149
6	Geographic ATM penetration (ATMs per 1,000 km^2)	2	4	2	71	141	—	132	371	—	—	7	2,266[a]	—	169	38	2–371
	Performance and efficiency																
7	Return on equity (%)	20.20	9.30	24.94	9.10	2.90	17.20	7.10	−19.50[a]	10.90	16.70	25.51	7.60	3.50	6.10	14.10	2.90–25.51
8	Return on assets (%)	1.40	0.40	0.10	0.50	0.10	1.50	0.50	−0.70[a]	0.60	1.30	1.25	0.80	0.20	0.40	1.30	0.10–1.50
9	Staff cost ratio (%)	41.91	43.05	16.39	47.27	34.43	43.59	32.62	19.73	23.58	31.02	44.36	33.35	24.20	39.19	35.62	16.39–47.27
10	Operating cost ratio (%)	115.74	138.44	75.74	217.40	238.96	53.39	185.95	158.02	121.15	87.83	75.00	62.27	141.77	106.29	102.21	53.39–238.96
11	Net interest margin (%)	2.09	2.45	2.30	0.84	1.21	2.36	2.02	1.32	2.53	2.86	2.26	2.01	2.11	1.83	3.55	0.84–3.55
12	Recurring earning power (%)	1.53	1.24	1.05	0.54	0.17	1.83	0.22	0.83	1.90	2.21	1.77	1.54	1.05	1.18	2.39	0.17–2.39
	Financial stability																
13	Capital adequacy ratio (%)	9.60	12.40	−12.10[a]	11.50	12.70	15.80	11.20	9.40	11.20	13.20	11.08	16.90	13.00	13.10	13.00	9.60–16.90
14	Leverage ratio (times)	9.18	6.92	1.21	4.56	4.24	9.79	6.32	3.57	4.67	8.77	7.19	14.64	5.77	8.47	10.66	1.21–14.64
15	Gross nonperforming loans ratio (%)	0.40	1.60	26.00	5.00	5.00	5.00	6.50	7.20	2.40	15.90	0.70	7.70	16.50	2.60	1.40	0.70–26.00
16	Provisions to nonperforming loans ratio (%)	106.20	41.10	—	60.40	—	62.93	—	24.50	89.60	38.10	37.50	61.20	62.90	75.00	123.70	24.50–123.70
17	Liquid assets ratio (%)	13.66	19.24	15.99	37.74	33.05	30.92	36.06	17.15	8.86	25.76	7.07	31.70	30.52	22.16	16.75	7.07–37.74
18	Liquid assets to liabilities ratio (%)	9.15	2.99	15.04	21.23	25.17	39.60	38.79	15.75	9.65	23.82	6.65	31.39	294.40[a]	22.61	21.34	2.99–39.60

(Table continues on next page)

Table A3a.2 Benchmark Indicators, 2002 *(continued)*

Reference	Indicator	Australia	Canada	China	France	Germany	Hong Kong, China	Italy	Japan	Korea, Rep.	Malaysia	New Zealand	Singapore	Thailand	United Kingdom	United States	Range
	Capital market development																
19	Domestic bond market to equity market capitalization (%)	55.10	109.42	103.74	92.62	254.50	10.06	347.68	322.15	176.25	68.68	84.40	52.99	104.17	40.99	145.00	10.06–347.68
20	Domestic public bonds outstanding to GDP (%)	16.55	56.57	16.71	52.69	38.72	9.33	91.27	123.46	17.50	35.71	26.99	35.53	22.77	28.52	42.26	9.33–123.46
21	Trading value of top 10 stocks ratio (%)	48.40	28.60	9.84	29.80	62.60	46.40	73.90	22.32	37.40	14.60	78.70	22.20	22.40	36.40	17.55	9.84–78.70
22	Stock market capitalization to GDP (%)	92.86	88.65	31.85	105.58	34.01	304.85	39.14	52.81	39.52	129.09	33.14	124.91	35.78	131.72	120.61	31.85–304.85
23	Stock trading value to GDP (%)	72.13	56.00	24.23	135.47	60.11	131.88	52.05	43.09	109.09	34.58	12.47	63.58	32.54	174.36	244.23	12.47–244.23
24	Stock market turnover ratio (times)	0.78	0.63	0.71	1.15	1.38	0.43	1.21	0.78	2.91	0.27	0.38	0.51	1.02	1.32	2.03	0.27–2.91
	Market concentration and competitiveness																
25	Herfindahl-Hirschman Index (HHI)	927.66	1,386.29	746.79	1,127.64	1,001.83	1,136.50	461.51	332.36	433.45	492.50	907.04	1,869.49	627.49	560.56	484.12	332.36–1,869.49
26	K-bank concentration ratio (k = 3), assets (%)	40.18	51.88	75.23	51.09	64.83	50.78	65.99	36.72	46.67	40.68	34.37	63.79	49.65	30.03	33.75	30.03–75.23
27	K-bank concentration ratio (k = 3), deposits (%)	39.56	51.14	41.81	71.59	44.11	49.03	25.69	22.38	29.02	28.25	35.09	62.26	30.34	29.72	36.17	22.38–71.59
28	K-bank concentration ratio (k = 3), loans (%)	37.56	50.34	44.26	59.68	41.90	43.11	28.46	21.16	32.35	28.14	35.47	62.38	28.08	30.95	28.95	21.16–62.38
29	Private credit extended by banks to GDP (%)	89.79	67.88	118.66	85.57	116.69	154.98	77.31	106.04	93.16	121.35	111.18	111.81	102.54	135.94	42.30	42.30–154.98
30	Commercial banking assets to GDP (%)	92.17	78.39	50.74	103.36	144.08	172.93	93.15	154.45	87.78	135.59	116.62	138.06	113.94	136.53	45.23	45.23–172.93

	Payment systems development																
31	Notes and coins in circulation to GDP (%)	15.52	3.49	29.25	4.71	4.71	8.86	4.71	14.52	3.76	7.21	1.97	7.80	10.70	3.22	6.02	1.97–29.25
32	Narrow money supply (M1) to GDP (%)	68.17	26.69	119.99	34.49	34.49	20.31	34.49	70.83	41.24	23.71	16.30	22.62	12.17	66.67	11.89	11.89–119.99
33	Value of RTGS transactions to GDP (%)	14,139.01	2,511.53	—	7,183.24	5,822.33	7,211.15	1,941.78	4,919.32	3,434.99	—	—	6,335.44	1,230.97	7,793.08	6,891.10	1,231.00–14,139.00
34	Value of retail transactions to GDP (%)	3,484.43	435.12	—	300.24	98.53	800.52	200.56	0.56	1528.68	—	1.17	314.41	5.03	354.85	439.85	0.56–3,484.43
35	RTGS concentration ratio (%)	—	81.30	—	46.10	54.00	—	37.70	—	—	—	—	—	—	84.00, 78.00[d]	—	37.70–84.00
36	Retail payments concentration ratio (%)	—	81.90	—	49.70	—	—	31.50	—	—	—	—	61.00–100.00[e]	—	80.00	—	31.50–81.90
	Savings mobilization																
37	Broad money supply (M2) to GDP (%)	282.88	49.43	190.20	68.74	68.74	275.45	68.74	137.52	135.68	102.37	41.08	113.84	121.95	87.47	55.46	41.08–282.88
38	Real deposit interest rate (%)	—	—	—	—	—	—	—	—	—	—	—	—	—	—	—	—
39	Gross domestic savings to GDP (%)	23.08	23.71	40.44	20.68	21.83	31.13	22.09	24.37	30.46	42.03	24.11	40.55	30.49	14.47	14.00	14.00–42.03
40	Reserve money to total deposits (%)	—	—	—	—	—	—	—	—	—	—	—	—	—	—	—	—
41	Loan to deposit ratio (%)	—	—	—	—	—	—	—	—	—	—	—	—	—	—	—	—
42	Worker remittances to GDP (%)	0.47	—	0.90	0.71	0.23	0.07	0.19	0.05	0.12	0.95	2.14	—	1.09	0.28	0.03	0.03–2.14

Sources: See appendix 3B.

a. Outlier not used in range.

b. Range is for 2002 (low value) and 2003 (high value).

c. Range is for 2004 (low value) and 2003 (high value).

d. The United Kingdom has two RTGS systems, and therefore, two different values are shown.

e. Singapore has more than one retail payment system, and therefore, a range of values is shown.

— = not available.

Table A3a.3 Benchmark Indicators, 2003

Reference	Indicator	Australia	Canada	China	France	Germany	Hong Kong, China	Italy	Japan	Korea, Rep.	Malaysia	New Zealand	Singapore	Thailand	United Kingdom	United States	Range
	Access to finance																
1	Demographic branch penetration (branches per 100,000 people)	24	29	5[a]	65	60	23	53	28	10	—	28	10	5	24	30	5–65
2	Demographic ATM penetration (ATMs per 100,000 people)	102	139	2[a]	70	62	—	68	108	—	—	47	37	—	78	128	37–139
3	Deposit accounts per 1,000 people	—	—	—	—	—	—	—	—	—	1,250		1,671	—	—	—	976–1,671[b]
4	Loan accounts per 1,000 people	—	—	—	—	—	—	—	—	—	329		513	—	—	—	248–513[c]
5	Geographic branch penetration (branches per 1,000 km²)	1	1	7	71	139	1,531[a]	101	94	104	—	4	592[a]	6	59	8	1–139
6	Geographic ATM penetration (ATMs per 1,000 km²)	3	5	2	76	143	—	130	364	—	—	7	2,275[a]	—	192	40	2–364
	Performance and efficiency																
7	Return on equity (%)	24.20	14.70	65.02	8.50	–1.50[a]	17.80	7.40	–2.70[a]	3.40	17.10	25.27	10.10	10.30	8.60	15.00	3.40–65.02
8	Return on assets (%)	1.60	0.70	0.30	0.40	–0.10[a]	1.90	0.50	–0.10[a]	0.20	1.30	1.15	1.10	0.60	0.60	1.40	0.20–1.90
9	Staff cost ratio (%)	43.44	45.76	21.42	49.50	38.85	44.30	27.48	23.05	18.89	32.70	40.59	36.65	26.94	39.90	38.29	18.89–45.76
10	Operating cost ratio (%)	113.93	146.08	74.92	183.22	200.73	57.21	232.90	153.59	144.00	81.43	76.14	49.20	120.49	106.24	105.72	49.20–200.73
11	Net interest margin (%)	2.02	2.36	2.33	0.98	1.24	2.11	1.82	1.29	2.83	2.67	2.28	2.08	2.29	1.70	3.37	0.98–3.37
12	Recurring earning power (%)	1.63	1.25	1.24	0.66	0.15	1.72	0.14	0.83	2.05	2.02	1.82	1.62	1.32	1.18	2.30	0.14–2.30
	Financial stability																
13	Capital adequacy ratio (%)	10.00	13.40	–5.90[a]	11.90	13.40	15.30	11.40	11.10	11.10	13.80	10.30	17.90	13.40	13.00	13.00	10.00–17.90
14	Leverage ratio (times)	9.71	6.63	0.75	4.95	4.50	8.88	8.27	4.05	4.46	8.53	6.01	15.39	7.18	8.64	10.57	0.75–15.39
15	Gross nonperforming loans ratio (%)	0.30	1.20	20.40	4.80	5.20	3.90	6.70	5.20	2.60	13.90	0.30	6.70	13.50	2.50	1.10	0.30–20.40
16	Provisions to nonperforming loans ratio (%)	131.80	43.50	—	59.60	—	64.03	—	25.50	84.00	38.90	45.40	64.90	72.80	71.20	140.40	25.50–140.40
17	Liquid assets ratio (%)	13.76	21.64	16.01	37.31	35.23	29.99	34.43	21.96	9.42	27.06	7.59	29.66	27.14	22.35	16.73	7.59–37.31
18	Liquid assets to liabilities ratio (%)	9.39	2.46	15.69	28.43	25.68	36.66	30.17	21.59	10.30	26.64	7.41	29.25	250.34[a]	24.87	21.46	2.46–36.66

	Capital market development																
19	Domestic bond market to equity market capitalization (%)	51.92	88.23	95.73	89.50	193.79	6.46	339.42	275.81	149.04	61.32	71.46	39.98	47.72	33.60	123.27	6.46–339.42
20	Domestic public bonds outstanding to GDP (%)	15.46	54.63	17.51	57.24	41.99	9.94	89.84	137.88	18.73	38.85	26.55	38.43	21.53	27.68	44.17	9.94–137.88
21	Trading value of top 10 stocks ratio (%)	44.80	26.00	17.73	29.70	59.00	38.20	64.70	23.56	38.10	11.90	74.00	31.70	25.30	35.50	16.42	11.90–74.00
22	Stock market capitalization to GDP (%)	93.04	86.18	31.26	115.36	44.23	382.10	40.80	69.83	49.05	154.78	34.61	134.49	83.46	120.03	117.25	31.26–382.10
23	Stock trading value to GDP (%)	70.88	54.61	24.15	107.59	53.26	214.19	54.45	52.52	75.49	50.22	13.17	95.12	71.82	120.11	142.20	13.17–214.19
24	Stock market turnover ratio (times)	0.76	0.63	0.81	1.07	1.47	0.56	1.50	0.88	1.78	0.37	0.38	0.71	1.25	1.00	1.21	0.37–1.50
	Market concentration and competitiveness																
25	Herfindahl-Hirschman Index (HHI)	926.74	1,470.51	636.75	1,068.85	1,004.01	1,140.87	431.69	341.51	479.40	476.98	898.85	1,864.85	639.82	553.58	459.53	341.51–1,864.85
26	K-bank concentration ratio ($k = 3$), assets (%)	39.43	53.50	72.31	53.59	65.11	50.69	66.45	37.08	46.94	40.09	34.43	64.41	50.38	29.64	32.58	29.64–72.31
27	K-bank concentration ratio ($k = 3$), deposits (%)	38.07	53.09	35.60	73.60	44.74	48.56	25.97	22.70	31.91	26.83	35.52	62.80	30.30	29.96	35.03	22.70–73.60
28	K-bank concentration ratio ($k = 3$), loans (%)	35.76	51.57	35.22	64.12	39.23	43.62	16.79	20.96	34.23	28.03	35.77	60.04	28.63	30.91	27.11	16.79–64.12
29	Private credit extended by banks to GDP (%)	95.43	67.96	126.46	85.88	115.51	153.39	80.41	101.66	95.63	118.59	113.13	107.83	93.22	140.53	43.11	43.11–153.39
30	Commercial banking assets to GDP (%)	96.59	78.28	120.15	104.06	142.57	172.10	96.25	153.07	94.70	130.42	119.00	135.21	110.49	141.35	45.80	45.80–172.10
	Payment systems development																
31	Notes and coins in circulation to GDP (%)	15.51	3.43	30.39	5.33	5.33	10.36	5.32	14.78	3.70	7.37	1.98	7.98	11.18	3.24	6.08	1.98–30.39
32	Narrow money supply (M1) to GDP (%)	70.54	26.88	129.45	36.49	36.49	28.73	36.49	74.14	42.77	25.65	16.90	24.06	12.96	69.51	12.15	12.15–129.45

(Table continues on next page)

Table A3a.3 Benchmark Indicators, 2003 *(continued)*

Reference	Indicator	Australia	Canada	China	France	Germany	Hong Kong, China	Italy	Japan	Korea, Rep.	Malaysia	New Zealand	Singapore	Thailand	United Kingdom	United States	Range
33	Value of RTGS transactions to GDP (%)	13,652.72	2,599.21	—	7,167.46	5,940.64	7,908.41	1,854.18	4,811.32	3,294.98	3,347.56	6,647.48	6,125.96	1,320.54	7,920.99	7,060.64	1,321.00–13,653.00
34	Value of retail transactions to GDP (%)	3,603.61	350.13	—	292.91	97.11	1,147.07	212.73	0.54	1,478.55	—	1.18	315.06	6.51	347.81	455.53	0.54–3,603.61
35	RTGS concentration ratio (%)	—	80.20	—	48.40	54.00	—	38.80	—	—	—	—	—	—	83.00, 77.00[d]	—	38.80–83.00
36	Retail payments concentration ratio (%)	—	81.10	—	50.70	20.00	—	33.30	—	—	—	—	63.00–100.00[e]	—	80.00	—	20.00–81.10
	Savings mobilization																
37	Broad money supply (M2) to GDP (%)	292.44	49.83	207.91	70.87	70.87	308.83	70.87	139.22	135.53	107.52	40.68	121.07	119.35	88.42	55.63	40.68–308.83
38	Real deposit interest rate (%)	—	—	—	—	—	—	—	—	—	—	—	—	—	—	—	—
39	Gross domestic savings to GDP (%)	22.97	23.75	43.40	19.84	21.37	31.16	21.22	24.48	32.34	42.46	23.84	43.55	31.75	14.42	13.50	13.50–43.55
40	Reserve money to total deposits (%)	—	—	—	—	—	—	—	—	—	—	—	—	—	—	—	—
41	Loan to deposit ratio (%)	—	—	—	—	—	—	—	—	—	—	—	—	—	—	—	—
42	Worker remittances to GDP (%)	0.51	—	1.09	0.63	0.24	0.08	0.14	0.03	0.14	0.90	1.25	—	1.13	0.28	0.03	0.03–1.25

Sources: See appendix 3B.

a. Outlier not used in range.

b. Range is for 2002 (low value) and 2003 (high value).

c. Range is for 2004 (low value) and 2003 (high value).

d. The United Kingdom has two RTGS systems, and therefore, two different values are shown.

e. Singapore has more than one retail payment system, and therefore, a range of values is shown.

— = not available.

Table A3a.4 Benchmark Indicators, 2004

Reference	Indicator	Australia	Canada	China	France	Germany	Hong Kong, China	Italy	Japan	Korea, Rep.	Malaysia	New Zealand	Singapore	Thailand	United Kingdom	United States	Range
	Access to finance																
1	Demographic branch penetration (branches per 100,000 people)	24	28	5[a]	66	58	22	53	27	10	—	28	9	5	23	25	5–66
2	Demographic ATM penetration (ATMs per 100,000 people)	107	152	2[a]	72	64	—	68	107		—	50	38	—	91	130	38–152
3	Deposit accounts per 1,000 people	—	—	—	—	—	—	—	—	—	—	—	—	1,423	—	—	976–1,671[b]
4	Loan accounts per 1,000 people	—	—	—	—	—	—	—	—	—	—	—	—	248	—	—	248–513[c]
5	Geographic branch penetration (branches per 1,000 km^2)	1	1	6	72	133	1,512[a]	103	91	104	—	4	583[a]	6	58	8	1–133
6	Geographic ATM penetration (ATMs per 1,000 km^2)	3	5	2	79	147	—	132	361		—	8	2357[a]	—	225	42	2–361
	Performance and efficiency																
7	Return on equity (%)	22.80	16.70	13.70	10.60	1.90	20.30	9.30	4.10	15.20	16.60	15.59	11.80	16.80	10.90	13.20	1.90–22.80
8	Return on assets (%)	1.50	0.80	0.50	0.50	0.10	1.70	0.60	0.20	0.90	1.40	0.98	1.30	1.20	0.70	1.30	0.20–1.70
9	Staff cost ratio (%)	44.98	48.36	22.44	41.27	38.75	56.30	47.30	24.34	26.29	34.79	39.68	43.85	30.96	43.05	38.44	22.44–56.30
10	Operating cost ratio (%)	126.78	154.30	69.23	162.67	172.59	63.01	138.38	133.21	105.00	87.49	78.19	59.57	94.76	106.25	109.56	59.57–172.59
11	Net interest margin (%)	1.85	2.19	2.27	1.01	1.12	1.78	2.26	1.24	3.04	2.36	2.04	1.82	2.77	1.45	3.12	1.01–3.12
12	Recurring earning power (%)	1.40	1.26	1.32	0.72	0.61	1.55	1.21	0.84	1.98	1.89	1.43	1.38	1.72	1.07	1.97	0.61–1.97
	Financial stability																
13	Capital adequacy ratio (%)	10.40	13.30	−4.70[a]	11.50	13.20	15.40	11.60	11.60	12.10	14.40	10.84	16.10	12.40	12.70	13.20	10.40–16.10
14	Leverage ratio (times)	10.12	6.41	0.68	3.78	3.37	8.38	6.27	4.44	5.37	8.10	8.16	15.18	7.65	7.89	10.93	0.68–15.18
15	Gross nonperforming loans ratio (%)	0.20	0.70	12.80	4.20	4.90	2.30	6.60	2.90	1.90	11.70	0.30	4.00	11.90	1.90	0.80	0.20–12.80
16	Provisions to nonperforming loans ratio (%)	182.90	47.70	—	61.30	—	88.43	—	29.90	104.50	41.00	34.20	76.00	79.80	64.50	168.10	29.90–182.90

(Table continues on next page)

Table A3a.4 Benchmark Indicators, 2004 *(continued)*

Reference	Indicator	Australia	Canada	China	France	Germany	Hong Kong, China	Italy	Japan	Korea, Rep.	Malaysia	New Zealand	Singapore	Thailand	United Kingdom	United States	Range
17	Liquid assets ratio (%)	12.99	21.04	14.45	32.70	34.98	31.53	28.22	25.88	8.82	30.03	7.50	31.54	22.59	27.22	16.45	7.50–34.98
18	Liquid assets to liabilities ratio (%)	8.45	2.49	13.89	8.89	24.93	24.43	2.47	24.71	10.07	29.42	7.55	21.89	217.92[a]	13.32	21.36	2.47–29.42
	Capital market development																
19	Domestic bond market to equity market capitalization (%)	45.85	74.57	117.86	86.18	187.04	5.58	299.09	248.98	146.02	60.90	56.55	38.58	57.54	36.96	118.07	5.58–299.09
20	Domestic public bonds outstanding to GDP (%)	14.65	55.10	22.45	57.02	43.57	9.67	86.59	148.43	46.94	37.93	24.40	38.22	27.40	27.82	45.38	9.67–148.43
21	Trading value of top 10 stocks ratio (%)	42.50	24.30	14.74	28.90	49.40	39.50	65.60	21.65	33.20	11.90	75.60	40.90	25.30	32.80	15.29	11.90–75.60
22	Stock market capitalization to GDP (%)	108.40	106.37	23.18	118.43	43.59	486.34	45.73	77.24	57.23	145.65	38.71	149.04	71.54	122.96	131.62	23.18–486.34
23	Stock trading value to GDP (%)	81.46	66.73	26.78	119.93	56.24	269.33	56.14	72.79	91.87	49.43	15.45	76.00	72.15	173.37	165.81	15.45–269.33
24	Stock market turnover ratio (times)	0.75	0.63	1.08	1.09	1.36	0.55	1.38	1.03	1.82	0.36	0.40	0.51	0.99	1.41	1.26	0.40–1.82
	Market concentration and competitiveness																
25	Herfindahl-Hirschman Index (HHI)	820.08	1,449.90	586.42	1,343.21	975.17	627.51	247.12	257.94	464.25	480.68	1,172.17	1,093.98	634.26	345.65	517.74	247.12–1,449.90
26	K-bank concentration ratio ($k = 3$), assets (%)	35.58	53.39	58.25	57.47	64.96	35.35	35.21	37.33	45.49	41.30	46.59	38.04	48.31	21.16	35.07	21.16–64.96
27	K-bank concentration ratio ($k = 3$), deposits (%)	34.97	52.37	31.92	61.90	44.76	34.73	18.25	22.80	29.27	26.74	44.08	38.96	30.19	21.84	37.20	18.25–61.90
28	K-bank concentration ratio ($k = 3$), loans (%)	33.19	50.16	30.56	50.45	39.64	31.97	16.79	26.03	31.03	27.31	44.66	37.03	27.93	21.90	28.39	16.79–50.45
29	Private credit extended by banks to GDP (%)	100.94	69.59	119.71	87.74	112.56	141.34	82.52	97.68	90.09	111.63	116.56	101.38	94.61	147.61	44.00	44.00–147.61
30	Commercial banking assets to GDP (%)	101.68	79.31	117.47	105.70	139.45	166.75	98.22	152.95	93.45	122.56	121.12	126.60	105.51	148.50	46.22	46.22–166.75

	Payment systems development																
31	Notes and coins in circulation to GDP (%)	15.85	3.38	30.01	6.04	6.04	10.90	6.02	14.71	3.59	7.59	1.96	7.58	11.44	3.27	6.01	1.96–30.01
32	Narrow money supply (M1) to GDP (%)	72.30	27.51	134.14	37.93	37.93	31.94	37.93	75.85	44.21	26.86	16.34	24.46	13.24	71.41	11.99	13.24–75.85
33	Value of RTGS transactions to GDP (%)	14,930.67	2,558.08	—	7,582.94	5,714.82	8,881.18	2,019.09	4,962.01	—	4,190.48	6,416.99	5,458.93	1,132.53	7,712.13	7,057.57	1,133.00–14,931.00
34	Value of retail transactions to GDP (%)	3,914.02	326.31	—	275.10	96.00	1,652.37	216.58	0.54	1,162.45	—	1.18	304.35	8.51	351.41	440.06	0.54–3,914.02
35	RTGS concentration ratio (%)	—	79.90	—	52.00	54.00	—	44.70	—	—	—	—	52.00	—	81.00, 78.00[d]	—	44.70–81.78
36	Retail payments concentration ratio (%)	—	81.10	—	60.50	19.00	—	36.60	—	—	—	—	65.00–100.00[e]	—	79.00	—	19.00–82.50
	Savings mobilization																
37	Broad money supply (M2) to GDP (%)	310.26	49.70	353.91	72.44	72.44	322.53	72.44	139.68	137.57	126.06	39.15	114.64	115.13	92.26	55.19	39.15–353.91
38	Real deposit interest rate (%)	—	—	—	—	—	—	—	—	—	—	—	—	—	—	—	—
39	Gross domestic savings to GDP (%)	23.57	24.93	45.81	19.66	22.07	30.70	21.52	24.97	34.63	43.42	23.77	47.10	31.65	14.53	13.67	13.67–47.10
40	Reserve money to total deposits (%)	—	—	—	—	—	—	—	—	—	—	—	—	—	—	—	—
41	Loan to deposit ratio (%)	—	—	—	—	—	—	—	—	—	—	—	—	—	—	—	—
42	Worker remittances to GDP (%)	0.47	—	0.98	0.60	0.24	0.14	0.13	0.02	0.12	0.90	0.96	—	1.01	0.29	0.02	0.02–1.01

Sources: See appendix 3B.

a. Outlier not used in range.

b. Range is for 2002 (low value) and 2003 (high value).

c. Range is for 2004 (low value) and 2003 (high value).

d. The United Kingdom has two RTGS systems, and therefore, two different values are shown.

e. Singapore has more than one retail payment system, and therefore, a range of values is shown.

— = not available.

Table A3a.5 Benchmark Indicators, 2005

Reference	Indicator	Australia	Canada	China	France	Germany	Hong Kong, China	Italy	Japan	Korea, Rep.	Malaysia	New Zealand	Singapore	Thailand	United Kingdom	United States	Range
	Access to finance																
1	Demographic branch penetration (branches per 100,000 people)	24	28	4[a]	66	56	22	54	26	13	10	28	9	5	23	26	5–66
2	Demographic ATM penetration (ATMs per 100,000 people)	115	158	4[a]	79	65	—	69	107	90	16	57	39	17	97	134	16–158
3	Deposit accounts per 1,000 people	—	—	—	—	—	—	—	—	—	—	—	—	—	—	—	976–1,671[b]
4	Loan accounts per 1,000 people	—	—	—	—	—	—	—	—	—	—	—	—	—	—	—	248–513[c]
5	Geographic branch penetration (branches per 1,000 km²)	1	1	6	73	129	1,502[a]	105	88	65	7	4	580[a]	6	57	8	1–129
6	Geographic ATM penetration (ATMs per 1,000 km²)	3	6	5	87	149	—	135	361	437	12	9	2,487[a]	21	241	43	3–437
	Performance and efficiency																
7	Return on equity (%)	25.30	14.90	15.10	11.80	9.20	19.10	9.70	11.30	18.40	14.10	14.54	11.10	14.20	11.80	12.70	9.20–25.30
8	Return on assets (%)	1.80	0.70	0.60	0.60	0.30	1.70	0.70	0.50	1.30	1.40	0.94	1.20	1.40	0.80	1.30	0.30–1.80
9	Staff cost ratio (%)	42.26	44.97	26.99	39.44	42.59	52.71	50.30	29.45	37.90	35.02	23.00	43.23	33.73	42.69	40.00	23.00–52.71
10	Operating cost ratio (%)	101.14	168.99	67.38	185.82	162.89	65.19	122.20	100.93	78.91	91.45	112.46	66.94	82.48	110.00	108.06	65.19–185.82
11	Net interest margin (%)	1.98	1.95	2.22	0.71	1.03	1.84	1.70	1.24	3.00	2.25	2.82	1.80	3.08	1.17	3.13	0.71–3.13
12	Recurring earning power (%)	1.51	1.09	1.32	0.65	0.57	1.49	1.11	0.81	1.71	1.94	1.39	1.33	1.80	0.82	2.06	0.57–2.06
	Financial stability																
13	Capital adequacy ratio (%)	10.40	12.90	2.50	11.40	12.20	15.30	10.60	12.20	13.00	13.70	10.91	15.80	13.20	12.80	13.00	2.50–15.80
14	Leverage ratio (times)	9.31	6.32	4.11	3.76	3.93	8.13	6.48	5.10	6.40	7.82	8.03	15.25	8.37	6.58	11.68	3.76–15.25
15	Gross nonperforming loans ratio (%)	0.20	0.50	9.80	3.50	4.00	1.40	6.20	1.80	1.20	9.60	0.30	3.00	9.10	1.00	0.70	0.20–9.80
16	Provisions to nonperforming loans ratio (%)	203.00	49.30	—	63.80	—	81.34	—	31.20	131.40	45.40	38.20	80.90	83.70	56.10	155.00	31.20–203.00
17	Liquid assets ratio (%)	10.10	22.59	14.34	36.59	35.50	31.26	21.52	22.71	8.89	29.37	7.30	29.87	20.58	30.94	15.81	7.30–36.59
18	Liquid assets to liabilities ratio (%)	5.65	2.47	13.06	9.36	23.34	23.26	4.24	21.73	10.86	25.90	5.81	13.21	172.58[a]	11.78	20.36	2.47–25.90
	Capital market development																
19	Domestic bond market to equity market capitalization (%)	45.84	63.76	150.63	69.63	156.55	4.95	274.27	175.68	91.32	68.41	57.43	32.78	63.77	32.79	123.66	4.95–274.27
20	Domestic public bonds outstanding to GDP (%)	15.25	57.38	27.45	50.55	38.47	10.07	74.82	145.19	48.57	37.75	25.40	39.78	30.42	28.95	47.23	10.07–145.19
21	Trading value of top 10 stocks ratio (%)	38.60	23.00	15.90	29.20	49.60	43.80	59.40	18.01	19.00	26.80	76.40	39.20	28.80	29.60	15.88	15.88–76.40

22	Stock market capitalization to GDP (%)	111.27	109.19	17.91	126.69	43.81	499.21	44.59	104.74	90.73	132.05	39.74	152.99	70.31	126.22	135.10	17.91–499.21
23	Stock trading value to GDP (%)	89.17	73.06	17.50	136.03	68.72	294.85	73.10	102.87	152.98	37.75	16.92	83.20	54.28	189.80	181.53	16.92–294.85
24	Stock market turnover ratio (times)	0.77	0.65	0.92	1.13	1.59	0.57	1.64	1.12	2.19	0.28	0.41	0.52	0.80	1.45	1.30	0.28–2.19
	Market concentration and competitiveness																
25	Herfindahl-Hirschman Index (HHI)	475.57	1,447.54	590.57	2,561.91	1,147.93	1,033.59	597.79	307.66	470.67	473.35	877.84	1,139.75	595.03	596.43	526.01	307.66–2,561.91
26	K-bank concentration ratio ($k = 3$), assets (%)	21.30	54.23	62.68	59.83	69.34	47.56	30.25	40.56	45.23	41.74	38.83	41.05	45.72	32.87	35.24	21.30–69.34
27	K-bank concentration ratio ($k = 3$), deposits (%)	19.93	53.53	31.42	53.37	46.46	48.75	35.43	27.13	27.99	26.83	37.05	42.32	28.50	35.10	37.26	19.93–53.53
28	K-bank concentration ratio ($k = 3$), loans (%)	18.39	50.48	29.38	43.65	41.12	42.37	36.62	24.74	29.58	28.03	36.72	40.35	26.60	30.54	28.72	18.39–50.48
29	Private credit extended by banks to GDP (%)	109.73	75.65	110.99	90.17	111.11	160.18	86.28	99.97	93.03	110.59	129.47	110.21	93.21	160.48	47.84	47.84–160.48
30	Commercial banking assets to GDP (%)	102.30	79.80	126.35	108.10	137.52	167.76	101.63	153.67	94.90	120.15	121.91	127.37	104.14	149.40	46.50	46.50–167.76
	Payment systems development																
31	Notes and coins in circulation to GDP (%)	16.19	3.32	30.42	6.64	6.64	10.29	6.61	15.01	3.61	7.68	1.97	7.50	11.02	3.31	5.86	1.97–30.42
32	Narrow money supply (M1) to GDP (%)	75.62	27.59	135.82	43.16	43.16	25.18	43.16	79.56	46.04	27.77	15.01	23.71	12.84	74.85	11.23	11.23–135.82
33	Value of RTGS transactions to GDP (%)	13,857.02	2,670.13	—	8,007.35	6,170.26	9,529.72	2,310.68	5,115.97	—	4,313.05	5,221.62	6,478.40	1,489.31	7,876.84	6,984.27	1,489.00–13,857.00
34	Value of retail transactions to GDP (%)	4,174.21	329.71	—	276.81	93.62	1,554.16	223.38	0.54	1,183.11	—	1.20	303.80	11.36	354.04	433.59	0.54–4,174.21
35	RTGS concentration ratio (%)	—	77.00	—	51.20	54.00	—	48.10	—	—	—	—	—	—	79.00, 78.00[d]	—	48.10–79.00
36	Retail payments concentration ratio (%)	—	81.30	—	59.30	17.00	—	38.70	—	—	—	—	66.00–100.00[e]	—	78.00	—	17.00–81.90
	Savings mobilization																
37	Broad money supply (M2) to GDP (%)	328.15	49.26	378.23	76.43	76.43	316.63	76.43	141.31	141.25	138.75	40.90	113.09	111.76	98.87	54.04	40.90–378.23
38	Real deposit interest rate (%)	—	—	—	—	—	—	—	—	—	—	—	—	—	—	—	—
39	Gross domestic savings to GDP (%)	23.85	25.54	49.60	19.46	22.13	33.00	20.68	24.95	32.42	42.82	22.26	48.65	30.13	13.89	13.73	13.73–49.60
40	Reserve money to total deposits (%)	—	—	—	—	—	—	—	—	—	—	—	—	—	—	—	—
41	Loan to deposit ratio (%)	—	—	—	—	—	—	—	—	—	—	—	—	—	—	—	—
42	Worker remittances to GDP (%)	0.44	—	0.91	0.56	0.24	0.17	0.13	0.02	0.11	0.93	0.68	—	0.67	0.28	0.02	0.02–0.93

Sources: See appendix 3B.
a. Outlier not used in range.
b. Range is for 2002 (low value) and 2003 (high value).
c. Range is for 2004 (low value) and 2003 (high value).
d. The United Kingdom has two RTGS systems, and therefore, two different values are shown.
e. Singapore has more than one retail payment system, and therefore, a range of values is shown.
— = not available.

Table A3a.6 Benchmark Indicators, 2006

Reference	Indicator	Australia	Canada	China	France	Germany	Hong Kong, China	Italy	Japan	Korea, Rep.	Malaysia	New Zealand	Singapore	Thailand	United Kingdom	United States	Range
	Access to finance																
1	Demographic branch penetration (branches per 100,000 people)	25	28	4[a]	65	51	22	55	25	10	—	28	9	5	23	26	5–65
2	Demographic ATM penetration (ATMs per 100,000 people)	120	167	5[a]	78	65	—	74	108	—	—	56	39	—	101	134	39–167
3	Deposit accounts per 1,000 people	—	—	—	—	—	—	—	—	—	—	—	—	—	—	—	976–1,671[b]
4	Loan accounts per 1,000 people	—	—	—	—	—	—	—	—	—	—	—	—	—	—	—	248–513[c]
5	Geographic branch penetration (branches per 1,000 km^2)	1	1	6	72	119	1,515[a]	107	85	99	—	4	580[a]	6	57	8	1–119
6	Geographic ATM penetration (ATMs per 1,000 km^2)	3	6	7	87	151	—	145	366	—	—	9	2,487[a]	—	252	43	3–366
	Performance and efficiency																
7	Return on equity (%)	27.00	20.90	14.80	15.60	7.50	18.17	11.50	8.50	14.60	13.43	14.88	13.70	8.80	8.09	12.80	7.50–27.00
8	Return on assets (%)	1.60	1.00	0.70	0.70	0.30	1.80	0.80	0.40	1.10	1.30	0.98	1.40	0.80	0.50	1.30	0.30–1.80
9	Staff cost ratio (%)	51.90	48.82	28.06	48.44	51.91	50.93	48.57	33.29	40.10	36.01	43.44	48.36	25.51	45.21	41.86	25.51–51.91
10	Operating cost ratio (%)	115.08	157.59	64.08	226.32	186.18	62.65	121.14	99.91	80.99	92.94	70.85	63.28	107.44	117.05	108.66	62.65–226.32
11	Net interest margin (%)	2.03	1.76	2.30	0.63	0.81	1.90	1.96	1.26	2.72	2.15	2.07	1.83	3.30	1.04	2.93	0.63–3.30
12	Recurring earning power (%)	1.46	1.30	1.45	0.75	0.58	1.65	1.29	0.81	1.67	1.89	1.44	1.62	1.80	0.81	2.03	0.58–2.03
	Financial stability																
13	Capital adequacy ratio (%)	10.60	12.60	4.90	10.90	12.50	15.00	10.70	13.10	12.80	13.50	10.67	15.40	13.60	12.90	13.10	4.90–15.40
14	Leverage ratio (times)	8.50	6.49	5.12	3.87	3.23	8.69	6.49	5.60	6.57	7.37	7.70	14.37	8.35	6.02	11.77	3.23–14.37
15	Gross nonperforming loans ratio (%)	0.20	0.40	7.50	3.00	3.40	1.10	5.30	1.50	0.80	8.50	0.20	2.40	8.10	0.90	0.70	0.20–8.50
16	Provisions to nonperforming loans ratio (%)	204.50	55.30	—	62.90	—	80.56	46.00	28.10	175.20	50.70	36.30	86.90	82.70	63.54	148.40	28.10–204.50
17	Liquid assets ratio (%)	10.88	23.96	15.23	38.73	34.31	30.80	25.66	20.13	8.31	30.76	9.41	29.61	21.48	34.13	16.65	8.31–38.73
18	Liquid assets to liabilities ratio (%)	3.48	1.82	14.23	11.07	13.83	22.31	2.53	19.16	10.12	26.62	6.39	8.47	182.25[a]	17.80	21.64	1.82–26.62
	Capital market development																
19	Domestic bond market to equity market capitalization (%)	41.67	57.90	103.33	60.50	137.30	2.97	250.87	171.21	121.04	62.06	45.56	20.61	78.27	32.62	145.36	2.97–250.87
20	Domestic public bonds outstanding to GDP (%)	12.95	48.52	29.70	53.79	42.21	9.49	83.14	154.47	51.79	39.28	19.69	43.03	35.34	35.84	48.57	9.49–154.47
21	Trading value of top 10 stocks ratio (%)	—	26.20	14.92	25.50	41.30	35.30	61.00	19.50	26.50	25.10	82.10	37.60	30.40	28.10	14.46	14.46–82.10

22	Stock market capitalization to GDP (%)	142.65	130.82	43.31	165.15	56.53	903.56	55.46	112.40	93.96	156.32	43.13	290.69	67.94	164.97	148.25	43.13–903.56
23	Stock trading value to GDP (%)	111.89	98.60	43.82	171.40	94.49	438.57	85.96	143.27	151.14	49.90	21.41	136.34	48.92	329.20	259.09	21.41–438.57
24	Stock market turnover ratio (times)	0.90	0.81	1.50	1.20	1.91	0.60	1.75	1.29	1.73	0.36	0.52	0.56	0.76	2.21	1.85	0.36–2.21
	Market concentration and competitiveness																
25	Herfindahl-Hirschman Index (HHI)	866.11	1,501.22	578.63	2,414.97	1,078.60	1,854.41	799.27	296.88	518.16	517.31	1,611.11	1,707.79	603.12	704.03	563.35	296.88–2,414.97
26	K-bank concentration ratio (k = 3), assets (%)	30.98	56.14	69.77	68.08	72.25	58.29	39.88	40.70	51.37	53.14	57.99	57.06	50.79	35.57	37.58	30.98–72.25
27	K-bank concentration ratio (k = 3), deposits (%)	36.51	55.91	30.97	56.39	50.31	58.05	44.93	26.32	26.49	28.01	57.49	58.58	27.33	39.12	39.55	26.32–58.58
28	K-bank concentration ratio (k = 3), loans (%)	34.10	52.26	28.38	45.08	37.21	50.93	42.86	24.26	27.51	29.01	56.07	56.93	26.14	35.83	31.01	24.26–56.93
29	Private credit extended by banks to GDP (%)	123.61	143.04	108.27	94.12	108.84	139.33	90.98	98.27	101.95	107.65	158.70	98.19	87.69	193.60	59.91	59.91–193.60
30	Commercial banking assets to GDP (%)	102.30	79.80	130.85	111.71	133.25	167.76	105.89	154.70	101.57	117.45	121.91	127.37	99.04	149.40	46.50	46.50–167.76
	Payment systems development																
31	Notes and coins in circulation to GDP (%)	16.71	3.36	30.85	7.05	7.05	10.19	7.01	15.05	3.66	7.99	1.95	7.28	10.28	3.30	5.72	1.95–30.85
32	Narrow money supply (M1) to GDP (%)	83.25	29.19	143.61	44.46	44.46	26.31	44.46	78.33	43.42	29.80	14.83	24.88	11.90	76.45	10.52	10.52–143.61
33	Value of RTGS transactions to GDP (%)	15,325.59	2,887.18	—	8,371.99	6,492.82	10,756.56	2,559.52	5,853.77	—	5,264.55	6,127.90	6,627.60	1,827.52	8,419.18	7,330.32	1,828.00–15,326.00
34	Value of retail transactions to GDP (%)	4,541.88	335.35	—	280.67	94.51	2,663.84	229.51	0.55	1,593.61	—	1.20	322.03	10.22	357.86	426.17	0.55–4,541.88
35	RTGS concentration ratio (%)	—	77.70	—	56.20	53.00	—	45.30	—	—	—	—	—	—	80.00, 78.00[d]	—	45.30–80.00
36	Retail payments concentration ratio (%)	—	80.90	—	60.30	17.00	—	38.60	—	—	—	—	69.00–100.00[e]	—	77.00	—	17.00–82.20
	Savings mobilization																
37	Broad money supply (M2) to GDP (%)	358.19	51.08	393.80	79.73	79.73	342.84	79.73	140.26	151.17	153.39	45.35	124.94	109.34	106.84	53.57	45.35–393.80
38	Real deposit interest rate (%)	—	—	—	—	—	—	—	—	—	—	—	—	—	—	—	—
39	Gross domestic savings to GDP (%)	25.52	25.10	52.41	19.87	23.20	33.09	20.71	25.20	30.77	43.19	21.44	49.87	32.04	14.42	13.80	13.80–52.41
40	Reserve money to total deposits (%)	—	—	—	—	—	—	—	—	—	—	—	—	—	—	—	—
41	Loan to deposit ratio (%)	—	—	—	—	—	—	—	—	—	—	—	—	—	—	—	—
42	Worker remittances to GDP (%)	0.43	—	0.88	0.54	0.25	0.15	0.14	0.03	0.11	0.99	0.60	—	0.64	0.29	0.02	0.02–0.99

Sources: See appendix 3B.

a. Outlier not used in range.

b. Range is for 2002 (low value) and 2003 (high value).

c. Range is for 2004 (low value) and 2003 (high value).

d. The United Kingdom has two RTGS systems, and therefore, two different values are shown.

e. Singapore has more than one retail payment system, and therefore, a range of values is shown.

— = not available.

Table A3a.7 Benchmark Indicators, 2007

Reference	Indicator	Australia	Canada	China	France	Germany	Hong Kong, China	Italy	Japan	Korea, Rep.	Malaysia	New Zealand	Singapore	Thailand	United Kingdom	United States	Range
	Access to finance																
1	Demographic branch penetration (branches per 100,000 people)	25	—	4[a]	—	—	18	56	—	—	—	27	11	5		22	5–56
2	Demographic ATM penetration (ATMs per 100,000 people)	122	—	4[a]	—	—	35	74	—	—	—	57	36	—	—	—	35–122
3	Deposit accounts per 1,000 people	—	—	—	—	—	—	—	—	—	—	—	—	—	—	—	976–1,671[b]
4	Loan accounts per 1,000 people	—	—	—	—	—	—	—	—	—	—	—	—	—	—	—	248–513[c]
5	Geographic branch penetration (branches per 1,000 km^2)	1	—	6	—	—	1,234[a]	110	—	—	—	4	487[a]	7	—	7	1–110
6	Geographic ATM penetration (ATMs per 1,000 km^2)	3	—	6	—	—	2,420[a]	146	—	—	—	9	1,658[a]	—	—	—	3–146
	Performance and efficiency																
7	Return on equity (%)	28.10	12.50	19.90	9.88	14.04	20.05	11.40	3.20	14.98	16.14	16.24	13.40	7.30	8.25	10.50	3.20–28.10
8	Return on assets (%)	1.60	0.60	1.00	0.31	0.44	1.90	0.76	0.20	1.00	1.40	1.06	1.40	0.30	0.51	1.10	0.20–1.90
9	Staff cost ratio (%)	54.63	48.64	40.78	36.23	53.08	48.84	47.50	—	41.48	38.79	48.66	46.06	23.47	43.11	38.02	23.47–54.63
10	Operating cost ratio (%)	115.72	169.92	55.82	313.18	170.75	71.76	115.88	101.36	76.91	88.04	66.14	77.64	122.62	135.13	130.92	55.82–313.18
11	Net interest margin (%)	1.65	1.72	2.68	0.40	0.76	1.94	1.84	1.23	2.77	2.16	2.14	2.01	3.61	1.03	2.93	0.40–3.61
12	Recurring earning power (%)	1.16	1.24	1.89	0.49	0.52	1.77	1.08	0.68	1.75	1.94	1.63	1.45	1.69	0.86	1.78	0.49–1.94
	Financial stability																
13	Capital adequacy ratio (%)	10.30	12.10	7.70	—	—	13.40	10.90	12.90	12.70	13.20	7.15	14.00	14.60	—	12.80	7.15–14.60
14	Leverage ratio (times)	5.76	4.60	6.23	3.18	3.10	7.90	6.71	4.91	6.53	7.13	6.50	10.06	9.45	3.53	10.08	3.10–10.08
15	Gross nonperforming loans ratio (%)	0.20	0.40	6.60	2.80	—	0.90	—	1.50	0.80	6.60	—	1.80	8.60	—	1.10	0.20–8.60
16	Provisions to nonperforming loans ratio (%)	188.90	44.90	37.50	—	—	—	—	28.80	180.00	62.60	—	105.90	80.10	—	104.80	28.80–188.90
17	Liquid assets ratio (%)	13.81	24.68	18.84	38.48	34.89	32.87	24.42	19.07	8.95	35.03	8.91	25.28	22.64	27.94	19.72	8.91–38.48
18	Liquid assets to liabilities ratio (%)	4.73	2.21	18.24	10.42	8.85	23.42	2.48	17.16	11.66	32.02	5.37	11.39	114.05[a]	9.87	25.10	2.21–32.02
	Capital market development																
19	Domestic bond market to equity market capitalization (%)	53.55	52.23	37.67	67.18	124.91	1.94	285.33	189.88	98.65	54.90	—	17.55	68.99	35.28	122.04	1.94–285.33
20	Domestic public bonds outstanding to GDP (%)	14.46	55.24	34.65	54.84	42.25	8.95	84.10	163.25	48.05	38.57	—	42.21	38.52	33.10	47.72	8.95–163.25

21	Trading value of top 10 stocks ratio (%)	34.70	28.00	13.50	25.60	42.90	35.90	69.20	17.20	21.40	24.80	74.10	35.00	38.80	29.60	12.50	12.50–74.10
22	Stock market capitalization to GDP (%)	158.00	164.85	136.55	164.80	63.85	1,284.15	50.89	106.56	115.76	180.00	36.70	334.17	80.19	141.20	144.25	36.70–1,284.15
23	Stock trading value to GDP (%)	166.94	123.26	188.18	220.11	131.17	1,033.79	109.73	156.04	206.85	93.92	18.68	236.32	47.97	378.83	332.34	18.68–1,033.79
24	Stock market turnover ratio (times)	1.15	0.84	2.19	1.42	2.31	0.98	2.20	1.43	2.05	0.61	0.52	0.83	0.70	2.70	2.32	0.52–2.70
	Market concentration and competitiveness																
25	Herfindahl-Hirschman Index (HHI)	873.69	1,576.82	637.87	2,015.42	1,764.93	1,796.16	2,080.86	280.88	556.97	637.13	1,522.85	1,894.89	735.79	817.30	653.92	280.88–2,080.86
26	K-bank concentration ratio ($k = 3$), assets (%)	35.60	57.13	35.01	57.17	64.30	56.87	66.89	25.21	29.01	32.37	55.25	64.11	31.99	39.51	40.47	25.21–66.89
27	K-bank concentration ratio ($k = 3$), deposits (%)	36.54	55.64	36.04	67.16	61.75	55.76	64.11	24.98	29.36	32.74	57.97	67.29	33.42	46.55	44.25	24.98–67.29
28	K-bank concentration ratio ($k = 3$), loans (%)	34.25	55.10	33.12	50.45	49.50	48.76	64.23	24.50	30.68	34.01	53.91	18.41	31.39	37.96	33.23	18.41–64.23
29	Private credit extended by banks to GDP (%)	122.81	127.26	115.83	—	—	139.58	—	96.92	107.81	105.13	149.49	95.72	84.10	189.58	62.44	62.44–189.58
30	Commercial banking assets to GDP (%)	138.67	—	138.23	376.27	197.97	—	187.97	182.79	103.64	175.13	—	—	94.54	—	78.34	138.67–376.27
	Payment systems development																
31	Notes and coins in circulation to GDP (%)	16.58	3.30	31.03	7.18	7.18	10.91	7.18	16.66	3.67	8.36	1.94	7.14	10.34	3.51	5.74	1.94–31.03
32	Narrow money supply (M1) to GDP (%)	89.30	28.39	156.02	43.84	43.84	26.68	43.84	96.78	39.20	33.51	14.29	27.41	11.77	66.69	10.05	10.05–156.02
33	Value of RTGS transactions to GDP (%)	17,557.12	3,186.06	—	8,658.22	9,621.95	15,069.65	2,749.44	6,815.76	—	5,923.89	5,658.53	6,546.88	2,147.19	9,159.75	8,382.42	2,147.00–17,557.00
34	Value of retail transactions to GDP (%)	5,067.78	358.43	—	277.80	93.66	4,945.51	220.33	0.57	1,748.76	—	—	374.42	7.42	355.07	422.78	0.57–5,067.78
35	RTGS concentration ratio (%)	—	76.79	—	58.20	62.00	—	50.70	—	—	—	—	—	—	80.00, 77.00[d]	—	50.70–80.00
36	Retail payments concentration ratio (%)	—	80.79	—	64.80	16.00	—	43.90	—	—	—	—	69.50–100.00[e]	—	77.00	—	16.00–83.60
	Savings mobilization																
37	Broad money supply (M2) to GDP (%)	406.36	51.32	412.65	83.68	83.68	388.97	83.68	141.38	159.59	157.99	42.03	127.54	107.26	112.47	54.14	42.03–412.65
38	Real deposit interest rate (%)	—	—	—	—	—	—	—	—	—	—	—	—	—	—	—	—
39	Gross domestic savings to GDP (%)	26.23	—	52.89	20.20	25.32	32.18	21.18	—	30.20	42.20	—	51.41	34.49	15.19	—	15.19–52.89
40	Reserve money to total deposits (%)	—	—	—	—	—	—	—	—	—	—	—	—	—	—	—	—
41	Loan to deposit ratio (%)	—	—	—	—	—	—	—	—	—	—	—	—	—	—	—	—
42	Worker remittances to GDP (%)	0.47	—	1.02	0.53	0.26	0.17	0.15	0.04	0.12	0.97	0.48	—	0.67	0.30	0.02	0.02–1.02

Sources: See appendix 3B.

a. Outlier not used in range.

b. Range is for 2002 (low value) and 2003 (high value).

c. Range is for 2004 (low value) and 2003 (high value).

d. The United Kingdom has two RTGS systems, and therefore, two different values are shown.

e. Singapore has more than one retail payment system, and therefore, a range of values is shown.

— = not available.

Table A3a.8 Benchmark Indicators, 2008

Reference	Indicator	Australia	Canada	China	France	Germany	Hong Kong, China	Italy	Japan	Korea, Rep.	Malaysia	New Zealand	Singapore	Thailand	United Kingdom	United States	Range
	Access to finance																
1	Demographic branch penetration (branches per 100,000 people)	25	—	4[a]	—	—	18	56	—	—	—	27	11	5		22	5–56
2	Demographic ATM penetration (ATMs per 100,000 people)	122	—	4[a]	—	—	35	74	—	—	—	57	36	—	—	—	35–122
3	Deposit accounts per 1,000 people	—	—	—	—	—	—	—	—	—	—	—	—	—	—	—	976–1,671[b]
4	Loan accounts per 1,000 people	—	—	—	—	—	—	—	—	—	—	—	—	—	—	—	248–513[c]
5	Geographic branch penetration (branches per 1,000 km^2)	1	—	6	—	—	1,234[a]	110	—	—	—	4	487[a]	7	—	7	1–110
6	Geographic ATM penetration (ATMs per 1,000 km^2)	3	—	6	—	—	2,420[a]	146	—	—	—	9	1,658[a]	—	—	—	3–146
	Performance and efficiency																
7	Return on equity (%)	28.10	12.50	19.90	9.88	14.04	20.05	11.40	3.20	14.98	16.14	16.24	13.40	7.30	8.25	10.50	3.20–28.10
8	Return on assets (%)	1.60	0.60	1.00	0.31	0.44	1.90	0.76	0.20	1.00	1.40	1.06	1.40	0.30	0.51	1.10	0.20–1.90
9	Staff cost ratio (%)	54.63	48.64	40.78	36.23	53.08	48.84	47.50	—	41.48	38.79	48.66	46.06	23.47	43.11	38.02	23.47–54.63
10	Operating cost ratio (%)	115.72	169.92	55.82	313.18	170.75	71.76	115.88	101.36	76.91	88.04	66.14	77.64	122.62	135.13	130.92	55.82–313.18
11	Net interest margin (%)	1.65	1.72	2.68	0.40	0.76	1.94	1.84	1.23	2.77	2.16	2.14	2.01	3.61	1.03	2.93	0.40–3.61
12	Recurring earning power (%)	1.16	1.24	1.89	0.49	0.52	1.77	1.08	0.68	1.75	1.94	1.63	1.45	1.69	0.86	1.78	0.49–1.94
	Financial stability																
13	Capital adequacy ratio (%)	10.30	12.10	7.70	—	—	13.40	10.90	12.90	12.70	13.20	7.15	14.00	14.60	—	12.80	7.15–14.60
14	Leverage ratio (times)	5.76	4.60	6.23	3.18	3.10	7.90	6.71	4.91	6.53	7.13	6.50	10.06	9.45	3.53	10.08	3.10–10.08
15	Gross nonperforming loans ratio (%)	0.20	0.40	6.60	2.80	—	0.90	—	1.50	0.80	6.60	—	1.80	8.60	—	1.10	0.20–8.60
16	Provisions to nonperforming loans ratio (%)	188.90	44.90	37.50	—	—	—	—	28.80	180.00	62.60	—	105.90	80.10	—	104.80	28.80–188.90
17	Liquid assets ratio (%)	13.81	24.68	18.84	38.48	34.89	32.87	24.42	19.07	8.95	35.03	8.91	25.28	22.64	27.94	19.72	8.91–38.48
18	Liquid assets to liabilities ratio (%)	4.73	2.21	18.24	10.42	8.85	23.42	2.48	17.16	11.66	32.02	5.37	11.39	114.05[a]	9.87	25.10	2.21–32.02
	Capital market development																
19	Domestic bond market to equity market capitalization (%)	53.55	52.23	37.67	67.18	124.91	1.94	285.33	189.88	98.65	54.90	—	17.55	68.99	35.28	122.04	1.94–285.33
20	Domestic public bonds outstanding to GDP (%)	14.46	55.24	34.65	54.84	42.25	8.95	84.10	163.25	48.05	38.57	—	42.21	38.52	33.10	47.72	8.95–163.25
21	Trading value of top 10 stocks ratio (%)	34.70	28.00	13.50	25.60	42.90	35.90	69.20	17.20	21.40	24.80	74.10	35.00	38.80	29.60	12.50	12.50–74.10
22	Stock market capitalization to GDP (%)	158.00	164.85	136.55	164.80	63.85	1,284.15	50.89	106.56	115.76	180.00	36.70	334.17	80.19	141.20	144.25	36.70–1,284.15

23	Stock trading value to GDP (%)	166.94	123.26	188.18	220.11	131.17	1,033.79	109.73	156.04	206.85	93.92	18.68	236.32	47.97	378.83	332.34	18.68–1,033.79
24	Stock market turnover ratio (times)	1.15	0.84	2.19	1.42	2.31	0.98	2.20	1.43	2.05	0.61	0.52	0.83	0.70	2.70	2.32	0.52–2.70
	Market concentration and competitiveness																
25	Herfindahl-Hirschman Index (HHI)	873.69	1,576.82	637.87	2,015.42	1,764.93	1,796.16	2,080.86	280.88	556.97	637.13	1,522.85	1,894.89	735.79	817.30	653.92	280.88–2,080.86
26	K-bank concentration ratio (k = 3), assets (%)	35.60	57.13	35.01	57.17	64.30	56.87	66.89	25.21	29.01	32.37	55.25	64.11	31.99	39.51	40.47	25.21–66.89
27	K-bank concentration ratio (k = 3), deposits (%)	36.54	55.64	36.04	67.16	61.75	55.76	64.11	24.98	29.36	32.74	57.97	67.29	33.42	46.55	44.25	24.98–67.29
28	K-bank concentration ratio (k = 3), loans (%)	34.25	55.10	33.12	50.45	49.50	48.76	64.23	24.50	30.68	34.01	53.91	18.41	31.39	37.96	33.23	18.41–64.23
29	Private credit extended by banks to GDP (%)	122.81	127.26	115.83	—	—	139.58	—	96.92	107.81	105.13	149.49	95.72	84.10	189.58	62.44	62.44–189.58
30	Commercial banking assets to GDP (%)	138.67	—	138.23	376.27	197.97	—	187.97	182.79	103.64	175.13	—	—	94.54	—	78.34	138.67–376.27
	Payment systems development																
31	Notes and coins in circulation to GDP (%)	16.58	3.30	31.03	7.18	7.18	10.91	7.18	16.66	3.67	8.36	1.94	7.14	10.34	3.51	5.74	1.94–31.03
32	Narrow money supply (M1) to GDP (%)	89.30	28.39	156.02	43.84	43.84	26.68	43.84	96.78	39.20	33.51	14.29	27.41[b]	11.77	66.69	10.05	10.05–156.02
33	Value of RTGS transactions to GDP (%)	17,557.12	3,186.06	—	8,658.22	9,621.95	15,069.65	2,749.44	6,815.76	—	5,923.89	5,658.53	6,546.88	2,147.19	9,159.75	8,382.42	2,147.00–17,557.00
34	Value of retail transactions to GDP (%)	5,067.78	358.43	—	277.80	93.66	4,945.51	220.33	0.57	1,748.76	—	—	374.42	7.42	355.07	422.78	0.57–5,067.78
35	RTGS concentration ratio (%)	—	76.79	—	58.20	62.00	—	50.70	—	—	—	—	—	—	80.00, 77.00[d]	—	50.70–80.00
36	Retail payments concentration ratio (%)	—	80.79	—	64.80	16.00	—	43.90	—	—	—	—	70.00–100.00[e]	—	77.00	—	16.00–83.60
	Savings mobilization																
37	Broad money supply (M2) to GDP (%)	406.36	51.32	412.65	83.68	83.68	388.97	83.68	141.38	159.59	157.99	42.03	127.54	107.26	112.47	54.14	42.03–412.65
38	Real deposit interest rate (%)	—	—	—	—	—	—	—	—	—	—	—	—	—	—	—	—
39	Gross domestic savings to GDP (%)	26.23	—	52.89	20.20	25.32	32.18	21.18	—	30.20	42.20	—	51.41	34.49	15.19	—	15.19–52.89
40	Reserve money to total deposits (%)	—	—	—	—	—	—	—	—	—	—	—	—	—	—	—	—
41	Loan to deposit ratio (%)	—	—	—	—	—	—	—	—	—	—	—	—	—	—	—	—
42	Worker remittances to GDP (%)	0.47	—	1.02	0.53	0.26	0.17	0.15	0.04	0.12	0.97	0.48	—	0.67	0.30	0.02	0.02–1.02

Sources: See appendix 3B.

Note: Because of data unavailability, data for 2007 are used for 2008.

a. Outlier not used in range.

b. Range is for 2002 (low value) and 2003 (high value).

c. Range is for 2004 (low value) and 2003 (high value).

d. The United Kingdom has two RTGS systems, and therefore, two different values are shown.

e. Singapore has more than one retail payment system, and therefore, a range of values is shown.

— = not available.

Table A3a.9 Benchmark Indicator Ranges, 2001–08

Reference	Indicator	2001	2002	2003	2004	2005	2006	2007	2008	Overall
	Access to finance									
1	Demographic branch penetration (branches per 100,000 people)	5–69	5–65	5–65	5–66	5–66	5–65	5–56	5–56	5–69
2	Demographic ATM penetration (ATMs per 100,000 people)	43–115	37–128	37–139	38–152	16–158	39–167	35–122	35–122	16–167
3	Deposit accounts per 1,000 people[a]	976–1,671	976–1,671	976–1,671	976–1,671	976–1,671	976–1,671	976–1,671	976–1,671	976–1,671
4	Loan accounts per 1,000 people[b]	248–513	248–513	248–513	248–513	248–513	248–513	248–513	248–513	248–513
5	Geographic branch penetration (branches per 1,000 km^2)	1–159	1–149	1–139	1–133	1–129	1–119	1–110	1–110	1–159
6	Geographic ATM penetration (ATMs per 1,000 km^2)	1–378	2–371	2–364	2–361	3–437	3–366	3–146	3–146	1–437
	Performance and efficiency									
7	Return on equity (%)	4.42–32.80	2.90–25.51	3.40–65.02	1.90–22.80	9.20–25.30	7.50–27.00	3.20–28.10	3.20–28.10	1.90–65.02
8	Return on assets (%)	0.20–1.47	0.10–1.50	0.20–1.90	0.20–1.70	0.30–1.80	0.30–1.80	0.20–1.90	0.20–1.90	0.10–1.90
9	Staff cost ratio (%)	14.87–46.31	16.39–47.27	18.89–45.76	22.44–56.30	23.00–52.71	25.51–51.91	23.47–54.63	23.47–54.63	14.87–56.30
10	Operating cost ratio (%)	49.86–294.02	53.39–238.96	49.20–200.73	59.57–172.59	65.19–185.82	62.65–226.32	55.82–313.18	55.82–313.18	49.20–313.18
11	Net interest margin (%)	0.64–3.55	0.84–3.55	0.98–3.37	1.01–3.12	0.71–3.13	0.63–3.30	0.40–3.61	0.40–3.61	0.40–3.61
12	Recurring earning power (%)	0.10–2.29	0.17–2.39	0.14–2.30	0.61–1.97	0.57–2.06	0.58–2.03	0.49–1.94	0.49–1.94	0.10–2.39
	Financial stability									
13	Capital adequacy ratio (%)	10.40–18.20	9.60–16.90	10.00–17.90	10.40–16.10	2.50–15.80	4.90–15.40	7.15–14.60	7.15–14.60	2.50–18.20
14	Leverage ratio (times)	4.11–15.01	1.21–14.64	0.75–15.39	0.68–15.18	3.76–15.25	3.23–14.37	3.10–10.08	3.10–10.08	0.68–15.39
15	Gross nonperforming loans ratio (%)	0.60–29.80	0.70–26.00	0.30–20.40	0.20–12.80	0.20–9.80	0.20–8.50	0.20–8.60	0.20–8.60	0.20–29.80
16	Provisions to nonperforming loans ratio (%)	25.40–128.80	24.50–123.70	25.50–140.40	29.90–182.90	31.20–203.00	28.10–204.50	28.80–188.90	28.80–188.90	24.50–204.50
17	Liquid assets ratio (%)	7.42–44.39	7.07–37.74	7.59–37.31	7.50–34.98	7.30–36.59	8.31–38.73	8.91–38.48	8.91–38.48	7.07–44.39
18	Liquid assets to liabilities ratio (%)	2.83–42.20	2.99–39.60	2.46–36.66	2.47–29.42	2.47–25.90	1.82–26.62	2.21–32.02	2.21–32.02	1.82–42.20
	Capital market development									
19	Domestic bond market to equity market capitalization (%)	8.90–256.86	10.06–347.68	6.46–339.42	5.58–299.09	4.95–274.27	2.97–250.87	1.94–285.33	1.94–285.33	1.94–347.68
20	Domestic public bonds outstanding to GDP (%)	8.83–95.34	9.33–123.46	9.94–137.88	9.67–148.43	10.07–145.19	9.49–154.47	8.95–163.25	8.95–163.25	8.83–163.25
21	Trading value of top 10 stocks ratio (%)	6.04 –61.90	9.84–78.70	11.90–74.00	11.90–75.60	15.88–76.40	14.46–82.10	12.50–74.10	12.50–74.10	6.04–82.10

22	Stock market capitalization to GDP (%)	35.58–350.02	31.85–304.85	31.26–382.10	23.18–486.34	17.91–499.21	43.13–903.56	36.70–1,284.15	36.70–1,284.15	17.91–1,284.15
23	Stock trading value to GDP (%)	16.21–290.00	12.47–244.23	13.17–214.19	15.45–269.33	16.92–294.85	21.41–438.57	18.68–1,033.79	18.68–1,033.79	12.47–1,033.79
24	Stock market turnover ratio (times)	0.34–2.21	0.27–2.91	0.37–1.50	0.40–1.82	0.28–2.19	0.36–2.21	0.52–2.70	0.52–2.70	0.27–2.91
	Market concentration and competitiveness									
25	Herfindahl-Hirschman Index (HHI)	427.10–1,658.53	332.36–1,869.49	341.51–1,864.85	247.12–1,449.90	307.66–2,561.91	296.88–2,414.97	280.88–2,080.86	280.88–2,080.86	247.12–2,561.91
26	K-bank concentration ratio (k = 3), assets (%)	27.04–79.45	30.03–75.23	29.64–72.31	21.16–64.96	21.30–69.34	30.98–72.25	25.21–66.89	25.21–66.89	21.16–79.45
27	K-bank concentration ratio (k = 3), deposits (%)	23.53–60.18	22.38–71.59	22.70–73.60	18.25–61.90	19.93–53.53	26.32–58.58	24.98–67.29	24.98–67.29	18.25–73.60
28	K-bank concentration ratio (k = 3), loans (%)	22.28–66.30	21.16–62.38	16.79–64.12	16.79–50.45	18.39–50.48	24.26–56.93	18.41–64.23	18.41–64.23	16.79–66.30
29	Private credit extended by banks to GDP (%)	42.00–157.85	42.30–154.98	43.11–153.39	44.00–147.61	47.84–160.48	59.91–193.60	62.44–189.58	62.44–189.58	42.00–193.60
30	Commercial banking assets to GDP (%)	44.90–174.28	45.23–172.93	45.80–172.10	46.22–166.75	46.50–167.76	46.50–167.76	138.67–376.27	138.67–376.27	44.90–376.27
	Payment systems development									
31	Notes and coins in circulation to GDP (%)	1.98–28.97	1.97–29.25	1.98–30.39	1.96–30.01	1.97–30.42	1.95–30.85	1.94–31.03	1.94–31.03	1.94–31.03
32	Narrow money supply (M1) to GDP (%)	11.29–110.57	11.89–119.99	12.15–129.45	13.24–75.85	11.23–135.82	10.52–143.61	10.05–156.02	10.05–156.02	10.05–156.02
33	Value of RTGS transactions to GDP (%)	1,381.00–14,835.00	1,231.00–14,139.00	1,321.00–13,653.00	1,133.00–14,931.00	1,489.00–13,857.00	1,828.00–15,326.00	2,147.00–17,557.00	2,147.00–17,557.00	1,133.00–17,557.00
34	Value of retail transactions to GDP (%)	0.62–1,432.30	0.56–3,484.43	0.54–3,603.61	0.54–3,914.02	0.54–4,174.21	0.55–4,541.88	0.57–5,067.78	0.57–5,067.78	0.54–5,067.78
35	RTGS concentration ratio (%)	38.70–84.00	37.70–84.00	38.80–83.00	44.70–81.78	48.10–79.00	45.30–80.00	50.70–80.00	50.70–80.00	37.70–84.00
36	Retail payments concentration ratio (%)	22.50–83.60	31.50–81.90	20.00–81.10	19.00–82.50	17.00–81.90	17.00–82.20	16.00–83.60	16.00–83.60	16.00–83.60
	Savings mobilization									
37	Broad money supply (M2) to GDP (%)	48.81–286.09	41.08–282.88	40.68–308.83	39.15–353.91	40.90–378.23	45.35–393.80	42.03–412.65	42.03–412.65	39.15–412.65
38	Real deposit interest rate (%)	—	—	—	—	—	—	—	—	—
39	Gross domestic savings to GDP (%)	15.11–41.84	14.00–42.03	13.50–43.55	13.67–47.10	13.73–49.60	13.80–52.41	15.19–52.89	15.19–52.89	13.50–52.89
40	Reserve money to total deposits (%)	—	—	—	—	—	—	—	—	—
41	Loan to deposit ratio (%)	—	—	—	—	—	—	—	—	—
42	Worker remittances to GDP (%)	0.03–1.98	0.03–2.14	0.03–1.25	0.02–1.01	0.02–0.93	0.02–0.99	0.02–1.02	0.02–1.02	0.02–2.14

Sources: See appendix 3B.
Note: Because of data unavailability, data for 2007 are used for 2008.
a. Ranges are for 2002 (low value) and 2003 (high value).
b. Ranges are for 2004 (low value) and 2003 (high value).
— = not available.

Appendix 3B. Data Sources and Notes for Benchmark Economies

Sources: By indicator.

1. World Bank, World Development Indicators database, 2006a, staff calculations; CPSS, *Statistics on Payment and Settlement Systems in Selected Countries* (various years); data from various central banks; Hong Kong Association of Banks 2007; New Zealand Bankers' Association data; Korea Federation of Banks data.
2. World Bank, World Development Indicators database, 2006a, staff calculations; CPSS, *Statistics on Payment and Settlement Systems in Selected Countries* (various years); data from various central banks; Hong Kong Association of Banks 2007; New Zealand Bankers' Association data; UK Payments Administration data.
3. World Bank, World Development Indicators database, 2006a, staff calculations.
4. World Bank, World Development Indicators database, 2006a, staff calculations.
5. World Bank, World Development Indicators database, 2006a, staff calculations; CPSS, *Statistics on Payment and Settlement Systems in Selected Countries* (various years); data from various central banks; Hong Kong Association of Banks 2007; New Zealand Bankers' Association data; Korea Federation of Banks data.
6. World Bank, World Development Indicators database, 2006a, staff calculations; CPSS, *Statistics on Payment and Settlement Systems in Selected Countries* (various years); data from various central banks; Hong Kong Association of Banks 2007; New Zealand Bankers' Association data; UK Payments Administration data.
7. International Monetary Fund (IMF), International Financial Statistics database, *Global Financial Stability Report* (various issues); Bureau van Dijk Electronic Publishing (BvDEP), Bankscope database; World Bank staff calculations.
8. IMF, International Financial Statistics database, *Global Financial Stability Report* (various issues); BvDEP, Bankscope database; World Bank staff calculations.
9. BvDEP, Bankscope database; World Bank staff calculations.
10. BvDEP, Bankscope database; World Bank staff calculations.
11. BvDEP, Bankscope database; World Bank staff calculations.
12. BvDEP, Bankscope database; World Bank staff calculations.
13. BvDEP, Bankscope database; IMF, International Financial Statistics database, *Global Financial Stability Report* (various issues); World Bank staff calculations.
14. BvDEP, Bankscope database; World Bank staff calculations.
15. IMF, International Financial Statistics database, *Global Financial Stability Report* (various issues); World Bank staff calculations.
16. IMF, International Financial Statistics database, *Global Financial Stability Report* (various issues); World Bank staff calculations.
17. BvDEP, Bankscope database; World Bank staff calculations.

18. BvDEP, Bankscope database; World Bank staff calculations.
19. World Federation of Exchanges data; IMF, *Global Financial Stability Report* (various issues); BIS 2007; World Bank staff calculations.
20. World Bank, World Development Indicators database, staff calculations; BIS 2007.
21. World Federation of Exchanges data; World Bank staff calculations.
22. World Federation of Exchanges data; IMF, *Global Financial Stability Report* (various issues); World Bank, World Development Indicators database, staff calculations.
23. World Bank, World Development Indicators database, staff calculations; World Federation of Exchanges data.
24. World Bank staff calculations using data for indicators 22 and 23.
25. BvDEP, Bankscope database; World Bank staff calculations.
26. BvDEP, Bankscope database; World Bank 2006b, staff calculations.
27. BvDEP, Bankscope database; World Bank staff calculations.
28. BvDEP, Bankscope database; World Bank staff calculations.
29. World Bank 2006b, staff calculations; IMF, International Financial Statistics database.
30. World Bank, World Development Indicators database, 2006b, staff calculations; IMF, International Financial Statistics database; data from various central banks; BvDEP, Bankscope database.
31. CPSS, *Statistics on Payment and Settlement Systems in Selected Countries* (various years); data from various central banks; Statistics New Zealand data; IMF, World Economic Outlook database; World Bank staff calculations.
32. CPSS, *Statistics on Payment and Settlement Systems in Selected Countries* (various years); data from various central banks; Statistics New Zealand data; IMF, World Economic Outlook database; World Bank staff calculations.
33. CPSS, *Statistics on Payment and Settlement Systems in Selected Countries* (various years); UK Payments Administration data; Statistics New Zealand data; data from various central banks; IMF, World Economic Outlook database; the Clearing House (CHIPS) data; World Bank staff calculations.
34. CPSS, *Statistics on Payment and Settlement Systems in Selected Countries* (various years); UK Payments Administration data; Statistics New Zealand data; data from various central banks; IMF, World Economic Outlook database; World Bank staff calculations.
35. CPSS, *Statistics on Payment and Settlement Systems in Selected Countries* (various years); World Bank staff calculations.
36. CPSS, *Statistics on Payment and Settlement Systems in Selected Countries* (various years); World Bank staff calculations.
37. CPSS, *Statistics on Payment and Settlement Systems in Selected Countries* (various years); data from various central banks; IMF, World Economic Outlook database; World Bank staff calculations.
38. Data from various central banks.
39. CPSS, *Statistics on Payment and Settlement Systems in Selected Countries* (various years); data from various central banks; IMF, World Economic Outlook database; World Bank, World Development Indicators database, staff calculations.
40. Data from various central banks.
41. Reserve Bank of Australia data.

42. CPSS, *Statistics on Payment and Settlement Systems in Selected Countries* (various years); data from various central banks; IMF, World Economic Outlook database; World Bank, World Development Indicators database, staff calculations.

Note: All benchmark indicators are for selected high-income OECD member countries and nonmember Asian economies (Australia; Canada; China; France; Germany; Hong Kong, China; Italy; Japan; the Republic of Korea; Malaysia; New Zealand; Singapore; Thailand; the United Kingdom; and the United States). Outliers noted in the tables are omitted in the calculation of ranges. Because of nonavailability of data, 2007 data are used as benchmarks for 2008 as well. No benchmarks are calculated for indicators 38, 40, and 41 because only partial data were available.

Appendix 4A. Corporate Governance Matrix: Questionnaire Responses for South Asian Countries, 2008

Table A4a.1 Ownership Structure and Influence of External Stakeholders

Question	Afghanistan	Bangladesh	Bhutan	India	Maldives	Nepal	Pakistan	Sri Lanka
1.1 Identification of substantial majority holders								
1.1.1 What are the rules that govern disclosure of share ownership? Is the ownership structure transparent?	✓ Need DAB approval	In articles of association (AA)	✓ Need RMA approval	✓	✓	x	✓	✓
• Top 10 shareholders and percentage of ownership to be disclosed?	—	✓	To regulator	✓	✓	To regulator	✓	Top 20
• Threshold of share ownership that needs to be disclosed (e.g., 5% and over)?	Need to report holdings to DAB	10%	10%	1%	5%	0.5%	10%; 3% to SBP	5%
• Is the government's ownership disclosed with its special privileges?	x	✓ In AA	x	✓	x	✓	✓	✓
• Does government control the nomination and remuneration process for the board of directors (BOD)?	✓	✓ Nomination for state-owned banks	✓	✓ Nomination for public banks	✓	x	✓ Nomination for government controlled banks	✓ Nomination for state banks
• Is there evidence of influence from external stakeholders such as labor unions or banking and securities regulators?	x	x But regulator can	x	✓ For public sector banks	✓	x	x	x
• Are the preemption rights of minority shareholders firmly protected (e.g., are they enshrined in the company law and requiring a supermajority [75%] to disapply them)?	x	✓	✓	x	x	x	x Encouraged; no rules	✓

(Table continues on next page)

Table A4a.1 Ownership Structure and Influence of External Stakeholders *(continued)*

Question	Afghanistan	Bangladesh	Bhutan	India	Maldives	Nepal	Pakistan	Sri Lanka
1.2 Indirect and beneficial ownership								
1.2.1 Are there rules that govern the disclosure by shareholders of ultimate beneficial ownership?	✓	✓	✓	✓	✓	x	✓	x No rules, but thresholds
• If so, please specify the threshold for disclosure of ownership.	20%	10%	No threshold	5%	5%		3%	15%
• Are shareholders required to disclose their ownership to an authority?	x	Only in indiv. tax returns	✓	✓	✓		✓	✓
• Where, when, by whom, and to whom are such disclosures to be made?	DAB keeps central registry	Banks to SEC	Dept of revenue & customs, tax returns	To bank	By shareholder to CMDA, 7 stock exchanges		Annual a/c and reports to SBP	To CBSL; for listed cos, also to CSE
• Do shareholders have access to this information?	✓	—	✓	✓	✓		✓	✓
• Does the market have access to this information?	✓	—	x	✓	✓		✓	✓
• Please specify monitoring and enforcement provisions, including penalties for noncompliance.	Warning letters, fines, removal of directors	—	None	Fines	Fines, imprisonment		Penalties per bank ordinance & prudential regulations	Shareholdings thru AR only for listed companies
• How many cases of noncompliance have been recorded in the past 5 years, and what actions were taken?	Many; not specified	—	None	—	1		Action taken case by case	None

Source: See appendix table A4a.4.
— = not available, ✓= yes, x = no.

Table A4a.2 Investor Rights

Question	Afghanistan	Bangladesh	Bhutan	India	Maldives	Nepal	Pakistan	Sri Lanka
2.1 Shareholder meetings and voting procedures								
2.1.1 Shareholder meetings								
• Are shareholders informed of shareholder meetings?	✓	✓	✓	✓	✓	✓	✓	✓
• How much notice is given (e.g., 4 weeks before the meeting)?	30 days	3 weeks	21 days	21 days	14 days	3 weeks	21 days	15 days
• Do banks provide detailed agendas and explanatory circulars along with the notice of meetings?	✓	✓	x	✓	—	✓	✓	✓
2.1.2 Voting procedures								
• Can shareholders vote by proxy, by post, or electronically?	Proxy	Proxy	x	Proxy, post	Proxy, post, electronic	Proxy, post	Proxy	Proxy
• Is the counting of votes verified by a third party?	x	x	x	✓	Depends on AA	✓	✓	x
• Can shareholders vote on a normal range of issues, including major and related-party transactions?	✓	✓	x	✓	Specified in AA	x	✓	x
• Are banks required to disclose special voting rights and caps on voting rights?	x	✓ 5% cap except for government	x	Specified in Banking Regulation Act; 10% private sector, 1% public sector	—	✓	✓	x

(Table continues on next page)

Table A4a.2 Investor Rights *(continued)*

Question	Afghanistan	Bangladesh	Bhutan	India	Maldives	Nepal	Pakistan	Sri Lanka
2.2 Basic ownership rights								
2.2.1 Are all directors' appointments and dismissals subject to a shareholder vote?	✓	✓	x	✓ only for private banks subject to RBI	✓ As in AA	x	✓ SBP has power to rule	x
• Can the government control such outcomes due to higher percentage of ownership (where applicable)?	✓	✓	✓	✓ For public banks	✓	x	By virtue of s/holding	Possible
2.2.2 Is there a clear dividend policy?	x	✓	✓	✓	Depends on annual general meeting (AA)	Decided by BOD at annual general meeting (AGM)	✓	✓
2.2.3 Are there structural takeover defenses that would prevent a legitimate takeover bid?	x	x	x	✓ RBI approval for above-threshold limits	x	x	✓ Purchases more than 5% need SBP approval	✓ Purchases more than 10% need CBSL/MOF approval (more than 30%, must make offer to all shareholders)
• Can the government or regulators reserve the right to approve such transactions?	✓	x	✓	✓	✓	x Promoters' share transfers need regulators' approval	Bank management changes need SBP approval	
2.2.4 Can minority shareholders easily nominate independent directors?	Depends on individual bank rules	x	x	x No right of nomination; only through election	Depends on individual bank rules	x	✓	Depends on internal bank rules

Source: See appendix table A4a.4.
— = not available, ✓= yes, x = no.

Table A4a.3 Transparency and Disclosure

Question	Afghanistan	Bangladesh	Bhutan	India	Maldives	Nepal	Pakistan	Sri Lanka
3.1 Adherence to internationally accepted accounting standards								
3.1.1 Do banks prepare their financial statements in accordance with local generally accepted accounting principles and provide reconciliation with international accounting standards?	x No local body; banking law says must comply with IAS	✓ ROSC[a]	✓ Conform to Indian GAAP	✓ (Local GAAP, but some do)	— Code says must comply with IAS	✓	x IAS as adopted by country	✓ No reconciliation with IAS
3.1.2 Are accounting standards in material conformity with international accounting standards?	x Somewhat compliant; see above	✓ ROSC[a]	✓ Conform to Indian GAAP	✓ Mostly	—	✓ ROSC[a]	✓ Except IAS 39 & 40	✓ Except IAS 32, 34 & IFRS, yet to be introduced
3.1.3 What is the frequency of reporting of financial statements (e.g., quarterly)?	Monthly, quarterly, & annually	Annually	Monthly, quarterly, & annually	Quarterly, semiannually, & annually	Quarterly	Quarterly	Quarterly, semiannually, & annually	Monthly, quarterly, & annually
3.1.4 Are bank financials available to the general public? If yes, how? On the Web, in newspapers, upon request?	✓ Upon request	✓ All	✓ Newspapers	✓ All	—	✓ All	✓ All	✓ All
3.1.5 Is disclosure of audit and nonaudit fees paid to the external auditor required?	✓	✓	✓	x	—	✓	✓	✓
3.1.6 Must the chief executive officer (CEO), chief financial officer (CFO), or directors sign and certify bank's annual accounts?	✓ CEO + CFO + directors	✓ CEO + 3 directors	✓ Chairman + CEO	✓ CEO + CFO	✓ Chairman + CEO + CFO	✓ CEO + CFO + directors	✓ CEO + 3 directors	✓

(Table continues on next page)

Table A4a.3 Transparency and Disclosure *(continued)*

Question	Afghanistan	Bangladesh	Bhutan	India	Maldives	Nepal	Pakistan	Sri Lanka
3.2 Independent internal and external auditors and audit committee								
3.2.1 Audit committee								
• Has the bank appointed an audit committee?	✓	✓	✓	✓	—	✓	✓	✓
• If banks appoint such a committee, is there a mandate or charter that clearly delineates its responsibilities?	✓	✓	✓	✓	—	✓	✓	✓
• How often does the committee meet?	Differs from bank to bank	3–4/yr min.	Quarterly	Quarterly	—	As required	Quarterly (min.)	Not specified (differs from bank to bank)
• Does the committee control the selection of auditors?	Not clearly stated; differs from bank to bank	x	✓	✓ For private banks	—	—	✓	
• Does the committee chair attend shareholder meetings, and is the chair available to address questions on the audit?	Not clearly stated; differs from bank to bank	✓ Not clearly stated but expected, as chair is a director	✓	✓ RBI has directed	—	✓	✓ Not clearly stated but expected, as chair is a director	✓ Not clear
3.2.2 External auditors								
• Has the bank appointed a reputed and experienced external auditor?	✓	✓	✓	✓	—	✓	✓	✓
• Does the bank's auditor rotation policy conform to the requirements set by the regulator?	✓	✓ 3 years, 3 times only	✓	✓ 3 years	—	✓ 3 years	✓ 5 years	✓
• Does the auditor perform any nonaudit services for the bank?	✓	✓ (under separate terms of reference)	x	x	—	x	x	x
• Are local auditing rules and practices in line with international standards and practices?	x Banks to comply with IAS; see 3.1.1	✓ ROSC[a]	✓	✓	—	✓ ROSC[a]	✓	✓ Update needed in certain areas

Question	Afghanistan	Bangladesh	Bhutan	India	Maldives	Nepal	Pakistan	Sri Lanka
3.2.3 Internal auditor								
• Has the bank appointed a qualified internal auditor?	✓	✓	✓	✓	—	✓	✓	✓
• Is the internal auditor independent? Does he report to the audit committee, board of directors, or other governing authorities?	✓	✓	✓	✓	—	✓	✓	✓
• Does the internal auditing program include clearly defined policies, processes, and metrics as performance benchmarks?	✓	✓ ROSC[a]	✓	✓	—	✓	✓	✓
• Does the internal auditor provide periodic reports on the risk management, control, and governance processes to the audit committee?	✓	✓	x	✓	—	✓	✓	✓
• If so, what is the frequency of such reports?	Depends on BOD of each bank	Quarterly	Depends on bank	Annual	—	Quarterly	Not specified	Differs from bank to bank

Source: See appendix table A4a.4.

a. ROSC = Report on the Observance of Standards and Codes.

GAAP = generally accepted accounting standards, IAS = International Accounting Standard, IFRS = International Financial Reporting Standard,
— = not available, ✓= yes, x = no.

Table A4a.4 Board Structure and Effectiveness

Question	Afghanistan	Bangladesh	Bhutan	India	Maldives	Nepal	Pakistan	Sri Lanka
4.1 Role and effectiveness								
4.1.1 Structure								
• What is the average structure of the board (unitary, two tier, or hybrid)?	Hybrid	Unitary	Unitary	Unitary	Unitary	Hybrid	Unitary	Hybrid
• What is the average size of the board?	3–9	13	Not less than 5	8–12	7–10	5–9	7 ministers	5–11
• Are there minimum qualification requirements for appointment of board members by law, regulation, and recommended practice?	✓	✓	✓	x	✓	✓	✓	✓
4.1.2 Role and responsibility								
• Is the scope of the powers and responsibilities of the board clearly defined?	✓	✓	✓	✓	✓	✓	✓	✓
• Are tasks and objectives individually allocated to board members, including the chair and the board secretary?	✓	✓	x	x	x	✓	✓ Defined by BOD	✓
• Does the board have a process to identify all the laws and regulations it must comply with?	✓	✓	x	✓	Depends on bank	✓	✓	✓
• Is there a process in place for director induction, training, and continuing education?	✓	✓	x	x	✓	x	✓ Orientation courses (SBP prior approval needed)	✓
4.1.3 For two-tier boards, do key responsibilities include the following? (Please specify whether required by law or regulation or recommended by a code.) • Reviewing and guiding corporate strategy and major plan of action • Developing risk policy • Drawing up business plans • Setting performance objectives • Monitoring implementation and corporate performance • Overseeing major capital expenditures, acquisitions, and divestitures	Corporate governance regulation and banking laws address these requirements	n.a.	n.a.	n.a.	n.a.	—	n.a.	Direction on corporate governance issued by CBSL requiring BOD to be responsible for these issues

Table A4a.4 Board Structure and Effectiveness

Question	Afghanistan	Bangladesh	Bhutan	India	Maldives	Nepal	Pakistan	Sri Lanka
4.2 Compensation								
4.2.1 Determination of board remuneration								
• Is there a law or regulation that sets board remuneration?	x	✓	x	✓	x	✓	✓	x
• What role do shareholders play in determining board remuneration?	Approve it at AGM	—	Depends on bank	Approve it in private sector banks	Not specified	Approve it at AGM	Approve it at AGM	Varies from bank to bank
• Who sets remuneration for the CEO?	BOD & shareholders	BOD, with BB approval	BOD	Government for public banks, shareholders for private banks	BOD	BOD, approve it at AGM	BOD	Varies from bank to bank
4.2.2 Does the board of directors receive some performance-based compensation in the form of an annual cash bonus, stock, or the like?	Varies from bank to bank	x	x	Executive directors get performance bonus for achieving targets from March 2006; public sector banks pay performance bonus only from 2006 and only to full-time executive directors	Corporate governance code specifies, but depends on bank	✓ As per company ordinance; approved at AGM	x	Varies from bank to bank
4.2.3 Do banks disclose the board's compensation?								
• If so, is disclosure aggregate or detailed?	✓ Aggregate	x	x	✓ Public, aggregate; private, detailed	—	✓ Detailed	✓ Detailed	✓ Aggregate

Sources: South Asian central banks, securities and exchange commissions and boards, and stock exchanges; RBI 2006a, 2006b, 2007a, 2007b, 2008a, 2008b, *Annual Report* (various years).

Note: For definitions of acronyms and abbreviations, see the list at the beginning of the report.

a. The ROSC Report provides information that is contradictory to questionnaire responses (for Bangladesh, see World Bank 2003; for Nepal, see World Bank 2005a).

— = not available.

n.a. = not applicable.

Appendix 4B. Status of Corporate Governance of Banks in South Asian Countries, 2008

Afghanistan	Da Afghanistan Bank issued a regulation on corporate governance in 2005, but it is limited to specifying responsibilities, qualifications, and the like for banks' boards of supervisors and management boards. Although most other areas are broadly covered by the banking law, comprehensive guidelines need to be issued to strengthen the institutional capacity of the banking sector. Moreover, while the banking law requires commercial banks to follow international accounting and auditing standards, the lack of local standard-setting bodies hampers transparency and enforceability.
Bangladesh	Bangladesh Bank has issued several key guidelines for banks, but they remain at the development stage. Corporate governance needs to be clearly defined and standardized so that market discipline would be improved. In particular, the guidelines need to be augmented by legal provisions governing beneficial ownership, minority shareholder rights, the remuneration of directors, and the roles and responsibilities of external and internal auditors. Bangladesh also needs to work toward full conformity with international accounting and auditing standards. And while the regulatory authorities have started moving ahead with the process of infusing the banking system with a corporate governance culture and educating shareholders about their rights and responsibilities, much more needs to be done in this area.
Bhutan	The Royal Monetary Authority of Bhutan (RMA) issued prudential regulations relating to corporate governance in 2002. These cover such areas as reporting requirements, submission of annual accounts, guidelines for compliance officers, dividends and reserves, regulations for directors and CEOs, and share ownership of banks and nonbank financial institutions. But Bhutan lacks a code of corporate governance or specific guidelines for banks. Developing a corporate governance code for banks and streamlining accounting and auditing procedures are key areas on which the RMA needs to focus.
India	The Reserve Bank of India has issued guidelines that are both comprehensive and laudable. Yet several areas need further review, including corporate governance issues relating to government ownership of banks as well as harmonization of standards and codes. Revision of statutes and guidelines should be undertaken to improve transparency and consistency. In addition, given recent events in the international arena, performance-based compensation mechanisms should be reviewed carefully, and the monitoring of performance levels discussed.
Maldives	Maldives has taken important steps by issuing a corporate governance code as well as corporate governance regulations for banks. Since these were issued very recently, it is still too early to assess their effectiveness. But among the issues that need to be addressed are the heavy government ownership, voting procedures, minority shareholder rights, compliance with guidelines and standards, and transparency and disclosure principles with an emphasis on accounting and auditing standards. The recently established local accounting body needs to be further strengthened, and compliance with international standards pursued. Developing governance practices and compliance would further improve transparency and accountability.
Nepal	Corporate governance is an area needing immediate attention in Nepal. While Nepal Rastra Bank has issued detailed guidelines for banks, the guidelines need to be broadened to include investor rights and disclosure requirements, beneficial ownership, and the responsibilities of auditors. A key improvement would be better adherence to international accounting and auditing standards. Weak corporate governance in some private sector banks is a matter of growing concern because of the intense competition and high-risk activity being observed in the market. And while guidelines have been issued, compliance by banks is low. Governance standards need to be improved, and compliance ensured through effective enforcement. And banks need be encouraged to undertake more meaningful implementation of the guidelines.
Pakistan	The State Bank of Pakistan has issued a comprehensive handbook on the code of corporate governance for banks. In addition, in late 2005 Pakistan established the Pakistan Institute of Corporate Governance to further strengthen the corporate governance culture by providing training and building awareness. Still, some areas need review, including disclosures on beneficial ownership, safeguards on stakeholders' rights, transfer of ownership and management, and competitive compensation packages. Compliance and enforcement are two other areas that need further review. Compliance is key, and the success of governance procedures depends largely on the commitment of banks, which should go beyond simple compliance with legal requirements. Regulatory surveillance and enforcement are equally important.
Sri Lanka	The Central Bank of Sri Lanka has issued a code of corporate governance for banks and other financial institutions. The guidelines are mandatory. But some areas need to be reviewed to make the guidelines more comprehensive and effective. Among these areas are stakeholder rights, special voting rights, minority shareholder rights, the rights of shareholders to vote on bank operations, and regulatory and government control of share transactions. In addition, disclosure requirements need to be expanded, and compliance and enforcement improved. Equally important is to encourage banks to incorporate the best practices of corporate governance. Sri Lanka has made credit rating mandatory for banks and implemented Basel II guidelines, moves that would also support better corporate governance.

Sources: Corporate governance questionnaire responses received from South Asian supervisory authorities; Indian Banks' Association 2006a, 2006b, 2006c, 2008a, 2008b, 2008c; RBI 2006a, 2006b, 2007a, 2007b, 2008a, 2008b, *Annual Report* (various years).

Appendix 5. Payment Systems in Place in South Asian Countries

	Real-time gross settlement (RTGS) system	Retail payment system
Afghanistan	*No RTGS system*	*One system for both large- and small-value transactions* *Partially automated gross settlement system* The Afghanistan Clearing and Settlement System is operated by Da Afghanistan Bank. Its services are offered to commercial banks and to banks' clients.
Bangladesh	*No RTGS system* Bangladesh Bank (BB) is working toward a strategy for modernizing the payment systems and implementing an RTGS system in the future. The National Payment Systems Council was formed in 2007.	*End-of-day net settlement system* *Manual clearing system* BB allows telegraphic transfer (TT) discounting facilities to scheduled banks against the collateral of government securities. Installation of the Bangladesh Automated Clearing House (BACH), with an automated check processing system and electronic fund transfer network, has started in BB.
Bhutan	*No RTGS system*	*One system for both large- and small-value transactions* *End-of-day net settlement system* *Automated clearing system* The Bhutan Electronic Clearing House is operated by the Royal Monetary Authority of Bhutan (RMA). A check truncation system using magnetic ink character recognition (MICR), operated through the clearinghouse, was launched in January 2007. The RMA, with financial assistance from the World Bank, is undertaking a project aimed at developing an efficient payment system for Bhutan.
India	The RTGS system, in operation since March 2004, is primarily for large-value transactions (the minimum threshold is Rs 1 lakh, or Rs 100,000). The number of RTGS-enabled bank branches stood at 55,006 on March 31, 2009, with 11,494 branches added to the RTGS network in 2008/09.	*Small- or retail-value payment systems* *End-of-day net settlement system* *Automated and manual clearing systems* The retail payment system includes automated check clearing (MICR and non-MICR), retail electronic fund transfer, and card payments. Some 71 MICR check processing centers operate in the country. Where setting up MICR check processing was found to be nonviable (the case in 1,064 clearinghouses), the settlement operations have been computerized so that settlement is done electronically even though the instruments are still sorted manually.

(Table continues on next page)

Appendix 5. Payment Systems in Place in South Asian Countries *(continued)*

	Real-time gross settlement (RTGS) system	Retail payment system
		High-value clearing is available at 24 major locations in the country. For enhancement of the efficiency of the paper-based clearing system, a check truncation system was implemented in February 2008 as a pilot project with the 10 banks in the National Capital Region. Electronic fund transfer systems include the electronic clearing service, electronic fund transfer, and national electronic fund transfer.
Maldives	*No RTGS system* The Maldives Monetary Authority (MMA) is working toward implementing an RTGS system as part of the mobile phone banking project, initiated in 2009 to introduce branchless banking.	*One system for both large- and small-value transactions* *End-of-day net settlement system* *Manual clearing system* In addition to an RTGS system, the mobile phone banking project is expected to implement several other systems: an automated clearinghouse (ACH) system, a mobile payment system, and an electronic fund transfer point-of-sale/ATM (EFTPOS/ATM) switch system.
Nepal	*No RTGS system* Nepal Rastra Bank (NRB) is working to formulate and implement a payment system master plan, including implementation of an RTGS system and a script security settlement system.	*One system for both large- and small-value transactions* *End-of-day net settlement system* *Manual clearing system* More than 10 check clearinghouses operate at regional and district levels for clearing and settling transactions relating to paper-based instruments such as checks, drafts, and payment orders. NRB manages all clearinghouses, which still run with entirely manual systems.
Pakistan	The State Bank of Pakistan (SBP) launched an RTGS system, the Pakistan Real Time Interbank Settlement Mechanism (PRISM), in July 2008. The system is designed to handle all large-value payments in Pakistan, including interbank money and securities market transactions, the domestic leg of foreign exchange transactions, and net settlement positions from retail and bank card clearings.	*Small- or retail-value payment systems* *End-of-day net settlement system* *Automated clearing system* The National Institutional Facilitation Technologies (NIFT) network serves more than 4,500 branches of 40 banks (including the SBP) in 100 major cities of Pakistan.
Sri Lanka	The Central Bank of Sri Lanka (CBSL) established an RTGS system, which it operates, in September 2003 for processing large-value, time-critical fund transfers. For securities settlement, the CBSL established and operates LankaSecure, which consists of a scripless securities settlement system and scripless securities depository system. LankaSecure maintains central records of ownership and transfers securities between security holders' accounts. It also handles government securities in scripless form. The CBSL operates the RTGS system and LankaSecure as an integrated system, known as LankaSettle.	*Small- or retail-value payment systems* *End-of-day net settlement system* *Automated clearing system* A check-based retail payment system is operated by LankaClear Pvt. Ltd. and jointly owned by the CBSL and commercial banks. The Sri Lanka Interbank Payment System (SLIPS, owned and operated by LankaClear) facilitates interbank transfer of retail payments. A U.S. dollar clearing system is operated by a commercial bank. A check imaging and truncation system automated retail payments, reducing the time for check payment and settlement from about T+10 to T+1.

Sources: South Asian central banks, securities and exchange commissions and boards, and stock exchanges.

Appendix 6. Annual Rankings on the Getting Finance Indicators for South Asian Countries, 2004–08

Table A6.1 Annual Ranking on the Getting Finance Indicators for South Asian Countries, 2004

Dimension	Afghanistan	Bangladesh	Bhutan	India	Maldives	Nepal	Pakistan	Sri Lanka
Access to finance	8	32	23	27	43	16	24	43
Rank	**8**	**3**	**6**	**4**	**1**	**7**	**5**	**1**
Performance and efficiency	6	12	27	33	46	21	34	33
Rank	**8**	**7**	**5**	**3**	**1**	**6**	**2**	**3**
Financial stability	9	25	34	42	30	12	35	27
Rank	**8**	**6**	**3**	**1**	**4**	**7**	**2**	**5**
Capital market development	6	28	19	46	15	27	38	35
Rank	**8**	**4**	**6**	**1**	**7**	**5**	**2**	**3**
Market concentration and competitiveness	6	36	15	43	26	35	28	27
Rank	**8**	**2**	**7**	**1**	**6**	**3**	**4**	**5**
Payment systems development	9	18	18	26	12	12	8	47
Rank	**7**	**3**	**3**	**2**	**5**	**5**	**8**	**1**
Savings mobilization	13	25	28	38	31	23	22	23
Rank	**8**	**4**	**3**	**1**	**2**	**5**	**7**	**5**
Total aggregate score	57	176	164	255	203	146	189	235
Overall rank	**8**	**5**	**6**	**1**	**3**	**7**	**4**	**2**

Source: Authors' calculations based on data from appendixes 2 and 4.
Note: No ranking is shown for corporate governance, as data for all eight countries are available only for 2008.

Table A6.2 Annual Ranking on the Getting Finance Indicators for South Asian Countries, 2005

Dimension	Afghanistan	Bangladesh	Bhutan	India	Maldives	Nepal	Pakistan	Sri Lanka
Access to finance	6	26	22	35	45	15	24	43
Rank	**8**	**4**	**6**	**3**	**1**	**7**	**5**	**2**
Performance and efficiency	6	22	25	26	46	23	39	29
Rank	**8**	**7**	**5**	**4**	**1**	**6**	**2**	**3**
Financial stability	8	24	38	42	26	11	35	30
Rank	**8**	**6**	**2**	**1**	**5**	**7**	**3**	**4**
Capital market development	6	30	17	47	16	26	36	36
Rank	**8**	**4**	**6**	**1**	**7**	**5**	**2**	**2**
Market concentration and competitiveness	6	36	14	45	28	31	28	28
Rank	**8**	**2**	**7**	**1**	**4**	**3**	**4**	**4**
Payment systems development	10	17	19	26	10	12	9	46
Rank	**6**	**4**	**3**	**2**	**6**	**5**	**8**	**1**
Savings mobilization	13	27	21	38	21	25	24	28
Rank	**8**	**3**	**6**	**1**	**6**	**4**	**5**	**2**
Total aggregate score	55	182	156	259	192	143	195	240
Overall rank	**8**	**5**	**6**	**1**	**4**	**7**	**3**	**2**

Source: Authors' calculations based on data from appendixes 2 and 4.
Note: No ranking is shown for corporate governance, as data for all eight countries are available only for 2008.

Table A6.3 Annual Ranking on the Getting Finance Indicators for South Asian Countries, 2006

Dimension	Afghanistan	Bangladesh	Bhutan	India	Maldives	Nepal	Pakistan	Sri Lanka
Access to finance	6	27	23	35	45	14	23	43
Rank	**8**	**4**	**5**	**3**	**1**	**7**	**5**	**2**
Performance and efficiency	15	23	21	21	46	24	37	29
Rank	**8**	**5**	**6**	**6**	**1**	**4**	**2**	**3**
Financial stability	15	22	34	37	32	10	34	30
Rank	**7**	**6**	**2**	**1**	**4**	**8**	**2**	**5**
Capital market development	6	30	18	46	15	28	35	37
Rank	**8**	**4**	**6**	**1**	**7**	**5**	**3**	**2**
Market concentration and competitiveness	6	36	15	44	28	33	28	26
Rank	**7**	**2**	**6**	**1**	**4**	**3**	**4**	**5**
Payment systems development	14	17	18	25	11	11	21	45
Rank	**6**	**5**	**4**	**2**	**7**	**7**	**3**	**1**
Savings mobilization	13	27	25	39	20	24	24	25
Rank	**8**	**2**	**3**	**1**	**7**	**5**	**5**	**3**
Total aggregate score	75	182	154	247	197	144	202	235
Overall rank	**8**	**5**	**6**	**1**	**4**	**7**	**3**	**2**

Source: Authors' calculations based on data from appendixes 2 and 4.
Note: No ranking is shown for corporate governance, as data for all eight countries are available only for 2008.

Table A6.4 Annual Ranking on the Getting Finance Indicators for South Asian Countries, 2007

Dimension	Afghanistan	Bangladesh	Bhutan	India	Maldives	Nepal	Pakistan	Sri Lanka
Access to finance	6	27	23	35	46	14	23	42
Rank	**8**	**4**	**5**	**3**	**1**	**7**	**5**	**2**
Performance and efficiency	13	26	28	18	42	20	35	33
Rank	**8**	**5**	**4**	**7**	**1**	**6**	**2**	**3**
Financial stability	30	21	32	36	28	8	34	27
Rank	**4**	**7**	**3**	**1**	**5**	**8**	**2**	**6**
Capital market development	6	29	16	47	22	29	35	32
Rank	**8**	**4**	**7**	**1**	**6**	**4**	**2**	**3**
Market concentration and competitiveness	6	40	13	44	28	33	26	21
Rank	**8**	**2**	**7**	**1**	**4**	**3**	**5**	**6**
Payment systems development	13	17	17	26	12	11	22	44
Rank	**6**	**4**	**4**	**2**	**7**	**8**	**3**	**1**
Savings mobilization	18	27	25	38	15	25	25	24
Rank	**7**	**2**	**3**	**1**	**8**	**3**	**3**	**6**
Total aggregate score	92	187	154	244	193	140	200	223
Overall rank	**8**	**5**	**6**	**1**	**4**	**7**	**3**	**2**

Source: Authors' calculations based on data from appendixes 2 and 4.
Note: No ranking is shown for corporate governance, as data for all eight countries are available only for 2008.

Table A6.5 **Annual Ranking on the Getting Finance Indicators for South Asian Countries, 2008**

Dimension	Afghanistan	Bangladesh	Bhutan	India	Maldives	Nepal	Pakistan	Sri Lanka
Access to finance	6	26	24	35	46	15	22	42
Rank	**8**	**4**	**5**	**3**	**1**	**7**	**6**	**2**
Performance and efficiency	22	24	21	17	43	31	29	29
Rank	**6**	**5**	**7**	**8**	**1**	**2**	**3**	**3**
Financial stability	37	22	29	40	19	12	31	26
Rank	**2**	**6**	**4**	**1**	**7**	**8**	**3**	**5**
Capital market development	6	30	17	47	22	30	33	29
Rank	**8**	**3**	**7**	**1**	**6**	**3**	**2**	**5**
Market concentration and competitiveness	6	40	19	42	28	33	25	23
Rank	**8**	**2**	**7**	**1**	**4**	**3**	**5**	**6**
Payment systems development	15	17	18	24	11	11	34	43
Rank	**6**	**5**	**4**	**3**	**7**	**7**	**2**	**1**
Savings mobilization	12	30	17	39	15	27	23	26
Rank	**8**	**2**	**6**	**1**	**7**	**3**	**5**	**4**
Corporate governance	25	28	24	31	21	27	35	31
Rank	**6**	**4**	**7**	**2**	**8**	**5**	**1**	**2**
Total aggregate score	129	217	169	275	205	186	232	249
Overall rank	**8**	**4**	**7**	**1**	**5**	**6**	**3**	**2**

Source: Authors' calculations based on data from appendixes 2 and 4.

References

ADB (Asian Development Bank). 2009a. *Asian Development Outlook 2009 Update.* Manila: ADB.

———. 2009b. *Global Financial Crisis and Proposed ADB Response.* Manila: ADB. http://www.adb.org/Documents/Others/in17-09.pdf.

———. 2009c. *Key Indicators for Asia and the Pacific, 2009.* Manila: ADB.

Al-Muharrami, Saeed, Kent Matthews, and Yusuf Khabari. 2006. "Market Structure and Competitive Conditions in the Arab GCC Banking System." *Journal of Banking and Finance* 30: 3487–501.

Baliamoune, M. N., and A. R. Chowdhury. 2003. "The Long-Run Behavior and Short-Run Dynamics of Private Savings in Morocco." *Savings and Development* 27 (2): 135–60.

Bangladesh Bank. 2007a. *Annual Report, 2006.* Dhaka: Bangladesh Bank.

———. 2007b. *Financial Sector Review, 2006.* Vol. 2, no. 2. Dhaka Bangladesh Bank.

Basel Committee on Banking Supervision. 2004a. *Implementation of Basel II: Practical Considerations.* Basel: Bank for International Settlements. http://www.bis.org/publ/bcbs109.htm.

———. 2004b. *International Convergence of Capital Measurement and Capital Standards: A Revised Framework.* Basel: Bank for International Settlements.

———. 2006. *Enhancing Corporate Governance for Banking Organizations.* Basel: Bank for International Settlements.

———. 2009. "Consultative Proposals to Strengthen the Resilience of the Banking Sector Announced by the Basel Committee." Press release, December 17. http://www.bis.org/press/p091217.htm.

Beck, Thorsten, Asli Demirgüç-Kunt, and Maria Soledad Martinez Peria. 2005. "Reaching Out: Access to and Use of Banking Services across Countries." Policy Research Working Paper 3754, World Bank, Washington, DC.

Bhutan, National Statistical Bureau. 2009. *Bhutan at a Glance, 2009.* Thimphu: National Statistical Bureau.

BIS (Bank for International Settlements). 2007. *BIS Quarterly Review, September 2007.* Basel: BIS.

CBSL (Central Bank of Sri Lanka). Various years. *Annual Report.* Colombo: CBSL.

———. Various years. *Financial System Stability Review.* Colombo: CBSL.

Cord, Louise, Marijn Verhoeven, Camilla Blomquist, and Bob Rijkers. 2009. "The Global Economic Crisis: Assessing Vulnerability with a Poverty Lens." Policy Note, World Bank, Washington, DC.

CPSS (Committee on Payment and Settlement Systems). 2001. *Core Principles for Systemically Important Payment Systems.* Basel: Bank for International Settlements.

———. 2004. *Payment Systems in Sri Lanka.* Basel: Bank for International Settlements.

———. Various years. *Statistics on Payment and Settlement Systems in Selected Countries.* Basel: Bank for International Settlements.

Djankov, Simeon, Darshini Manraj, Caralee McLiesh, and Rita Ramalho. 2005. "Doing Business Indicators: Why Aggregate and How to Do It." Resource Paper, World Bank and International Finance Corporation, Washington, DC. http://siteresources.worldbank.org/EXTAFRSUMAFTPS/Resources/db_indicators.pdf.

Enterprise Development Impact Assessment Information Service. 2003. "How to Promote Good Corporate Governance." http://www.enterprise-impact.org.uk/.

ESCAP (Economic and Social Commission for Asia and the Pacific of the United Nations). 2009. *Economic and Social Survey of Asia and the Pacific 2009: Addressing Triple Threats to Development.* New York: ESCAP.

eStandardsForum. 2007. "Best Practice Report: India." eStandards Forum, New York. http://www.estandardsforum.org/india/standards (accessed October 7, 2009).

———. 2009a. *Annual Globalization Report 2008–09.* New York: eStandardsForum, Financial Standards Foundation.

———. 2009b. "Best Practice Report: Bangladesh." eStandards Forum, New York. http://www.estandardsforum.org/bangladesh/standards (accessed October 7, 2009).

GTZ ProMis (German Agency for Technical Cooperation, Promotion of the Microfinance Sector). 2009. *Microfinance Industry Report: Sri Lanka 2009.* Produced in collaboration with the Banking with the Poor Network. http://www.bwtp.org/resources.html.

Hong Kong Association of Banks. 2007. Press release, April 2. http://www.hkab.org.hk/file/News/en/Peter_Legco_Presentation_Final.pdf.

IMF (International Monetary Fund). Various issues. *Global Financial Stability Report.* Washington, DC.

Indian Banks' Association. 2006a. *Performance Highlights of Foreign Banks 2005–06.* Mumbai: Indian Banks' Association.

———. 2006b. *Performance Highlights of Private Sector Banks 2005–06.* Mumbai: Indian Banks' Association.

———. 2006c. *Performance Highlights of Public Sector Banks 2005–06.* Mumbai: Indian Banks' Association.

———. 2008a. *Performance Highlights of Foreign Banks 2007–08.* Mumbai: Indian Banks' Association.

———. 2008b. *Performance Highlights of Private Sector Banks 2007–08.* Mumbai: Indian Banks' Association.

———. 2008c. *Performance Highlights of Public Sector Banks 2007–08.* Mumbai: Indian Banks' Association.

Jayamaha, Ranee. n.d. "Modernization of the National Payment System." Central Bank of Sri Lanka, Colombo. http://www.cbsl.gov.lk/pics_n_docs/05_fss/_docs/article1.pdf.

Leeladhar, Shri V. 2007. Special address delivered by deputy governor of the Reserve Bank of India during the panel discussion at the "FICCI-IBA Conference on Global Banking: Paradigm Shift," Mumbai, September 13. http://www.rbi.org.in/scripts/BS_ViewBulletin.aspx?Id=8778.

Levine, Ross. 1999. "Financial Development and Economic Growth: Views and Agenda." Policy Research Working Paper 1678, World Bank, Washington, DC.

Maldives, Ministry of Finance and Treasury. 2009. "Fiscal and Economic Outlook 2009–2011." Background paper prepared for the Maldives Partnership Forum, Male, March 23–24.

McKinnon, Ronald I. 1973. *Money and Capital in Economic Development.* Washington, DC: Brookings Institution.

Nanto, Dick K. 2009. "The Global Financial Crisis: Analysis and Policy Implications." Congressional Research Service Report for Congress, RL34742. http://www.fas.org/sgp/crs/misc/RL34742.pdf.

NRB (Nepal Rastra Bank). 2008. *Banking and Financial Statistics, No. 51.* Kathmandu: NRB.

———. Various years. *Annual Bank Supervision Report.* Kathmandu: Bank Supervision Department.

OECD (Organisation for Economic Co-operation and Development). 2004. *OECD Principles of Corporate Governance.* Paris: OECD.

Pakistan Microfinance Network. 2009. "Pakistan Microfinance Review, 2008: Mainstreaming Microfinance—Progress, Opportunities and Challenges." Islamabad: Pakistan Microfinance Network.

Pavlović, Jelena, and Joshua Charap. 2009. "Development of the Commercial Banking System in Afghanistan: Risks and Rewards." IMF Working Paper, Middle East and Central Asia Department, International Monetary Fund, Washington, DC.

Ratha, Dilip, and Zhimei Xu. 2008. *Migration and Remittances Factbook 2008.* Washington, DC: World Bank.

RBI (Reserve Bank of India). 2006a. *A Profile of Banks, 2005–06.* Mumbai: RBI.

———. 2006b. *Report on Trend and Progress of Banking in India, 2005–06.* Mumbai: RBI.

———. 2007a. *Basic Statistical Returns of Scheduled Commercial Banks in India.* Vol. 36, March. Mumbai: RBI.

———. 2007b. Reserve Bank of India database. http://www.rbi.org.in/scripts/Statistics.aspx (accessed in August 2007).

———. 2008a. *Handbook of Statistics on Indian Economy 2007–2008.* Mumbai: RBI.

———. 2008b. *Report on Trend and Progress of Banking in India, 2007–08.* Mumbai: RBI.

———. Various years. *Annual Report.* Mumbai: RBI. http://rbi.org.in/.

SBP (State Bank of Pakistan). 2008. *Quarterly Performance Review of the Banking System.* December. Karachi: Bank Surveillance Department.

———. 2009a. *Islamic Banking Bulletin, October–December 2008.* Karachi: Islamic Banking Department.

———. 2009b. *Pakistan 10-Year Strategy Paper for the Banking Sector Reforms.* Karachi: SDP. http://www.sbp.org.pk/bsd/10YearStrategyPaper.pdf.

Securities and Exchange Commission of Sri Lanka. 2009. *Annual Report, 2008.* Colombo: Securities and Exchange Commission of Sri Lanka.

SEMP (Suburban Emergency Management Project). 2009. "What Is Procyclicality?" Biot Report 604. http://www.semp.us/publications/biot_printview.php?BiotID=604 (accessed in November 2009).

Shaw, Edward. 1973. *Financial Deepening in Economic Development.* New York: Oxford University Press.

Sophastienphong, Kiatchai, and Anoma Kulathunga. 2008. "Getting Finance in South Asia 2009: Indicators and Analysis of the Commercial Banking Sector." Finance and Private Sector Development Unit, South Asia Region, World Bank, Washington, DC.

Standard & Poor's. 2004. *Corporate Governance Scores and Evaluations: Criteria, Methodology and Definitions.* New York: McGraw-Hill Companies.

Thirlwall, A. P. 2002. "The Mobilization of Savings for Growth and Development in Developing Countries." *IUP Journal of Applied Economics* 1 (1): 7–30.

U.S. Department of Justice and Federal Trade Commission. 1997. "Horizontal Merger Guidelines." U.S. Department of Justice and Federal Trade Commission, Washington, DC.

World Bank. 2003. *Report on the Observance of Standards and Codes (ROSC), Accounting and Auditing: Bangladesh*. Washington, DC: World Bank.

———. 2004. "South Asia Financial Performance and Soundness Indicators Phase I." Finance and Private Sector Development Unit, South Asia Region, Washington, DC.

———. 2005a. *Report on the Observance of Standards and Codes (ROSC), Corporate Governance Country Assessment: Nepal*. Washington, DC: World Bank.

———. 2005b. "South Asia Financial Performance and Soundness Indicators Phase II." Finance and Private Sector Development Unit, South Asia Region, Washington, DC.

———. 2006a. "Indicators of Access to and Use of Financial Services across Countries, Data Set 2001–04." World Bank, Washington, DC. http://go.worldbank.org/EZDOBVQT20 (accessed July 2008).

———. 2006b. "A New Database on Financial Development and Structure (Dataset)." World Bank, Washington, DC. http://go.worldbank.org/X23UD9QUX0.

———. 2006c. *Report on the Observance of Standards and Codes (ROSC), Corporate Governance Country Assessment: Bhutan*. Washington, DC: World Bank.

———. 2006d. "South Asia Financial Performance and Soundness Indicators Phase III: Getting Finance in South Asia—An Analysis of the Commercial Banking Sector." South Asia Region, Finance and Private Sector Development Unit, Washington, DC.

———. 2008a. *Finance for All? Policies and Pitfalls in Expanding Access*. Washington, DC: World Bank.

———. 2008b. "Global Financial Crisis: Implications for South Asia." South Asia Region, World Bank, Washington, DC.

———. 2008c. "Mobile Phone Banking Project." Project Appraisal Document, Finance and Private Sector Development Unit, South Asia Region, World Bank, Washington, DC.

———. 2009. "Crisis Hitting Poor Hard in Developing World, World Bank Says." Press Release 2009/220/EXC, World Bank, February 12.

World Bank and IMF (International Monetary Fund). 2005. *Financial Sector Assessment: A Handbook*. Washington, DC: World Bank.

Web Sites Consulted

Central Banks

Bangladesh Bank, http://www.bangladesh-bank.org/

Bank of Canada, http://www.bankofcanada.ca/en/index.html

Bank of England, http://www.bankofengland.co.uk/

Bank of Italy, http://www.bancaditalia.it/

Bank of Japan, http://www.boj.or.jp/en/index.htm

Bank of Korea, http://eng.bok.or.kr/eng/engMain.action

Bank of Thailand, http://www.bot.or.th/English/Pages/BOTDefault.aspx

Central Bank of Malaysia, http://www.bnm.gov.my/

Central Bank of Sri Lanka, http://www.cbsl.gov.lk/

Hong Kong [China] Monetary Authority, http://www.info.gov.hk/hkma/

Maldives Monetary Authority, http://www.mma.gov.mv/laws.php

Nepal Rastra Bank, http://www.nrb.org.np/

People's Bank of China, http://www.pbc.gov.cn/english/

Reserve Bank of Australia, http://www.rba.gov.au/

Reserve Bank of New Zealand, http://www.rbnz.govt.nz/

State Bank of Pakistan, http://www.sbp.org.pk/

U.S. Federal Reserve Board, http://www.federalreserve.gov/

Others

The Clearing House (CHIPS), http://www.chips.org/home.php

Colombo Stock Exchange, http://www.cse.lk

Hong Kong [China] Association of Banks, http://www.hkab.org.hk/index.jsp

Korea Federation of Banks, http://www.kfb.or.kr/kfb_eng_09/index.htm

Maldives Attorney General's Office, http://www.agoffice.gov.mv/V2/Dhivehi/IndexDhi.asp

Maldives Capital Market Development Authority, http://www.cmda.gov.mv/laws-and-regulations/

New Zealand Bankers' Association, http://www.nzba.org.nz/

Securities and Exchange Board of India, http://www.sebi.gov.in/

Securities and Exchange Commission of Bangladesh, http://www.secbd.org/

Securities and Exchange Commission of Pakistan, http://www.secp.gov.pk/

Securities and Exchange Commission of Sri Lanka, http://www.sec.gov.lk/

Securities Board of Nepal, http://www.sebonp.com/

Statistics New Zealand, http://www.stats.govt.nz/

UK Payments Administration, http://www.ukpayments.org.uk/

World Federation of Exchanges, http://www.world-exchanges.org/

Index

Boxes, figures, notes, and tables are indicated by *b*, *f*, *n*, and *t*, respectively.

A

access to finance, 2–3
- benchmark comparisons, 116*f*, 124*f*
- demographic penetration, 3, 139–140
- findings and observations regarding, 130
- geographic penetration, 3, 6*f*, 140–141
- guide to underlying data, 139–141
- in Afghanistan, 28
- in Bangladesh, 35–36
- in Bhutan, 42–43
- in India, 49–50
- in Maldives, 59–60, 107*f*, 113*n*1
- in Nepal, 68–69
- in Pakistan, 78
- in Sri Lanka, 89–90, 107*f*
- rankings, 9, 106, 107*f*

account ratios, 3, 140. *See also* access to finance

ADB (Asian Development Bank), 201*b*

Afghanistan, 26–33. *See also* specific topics, e.g. access to finance, which may contain general information pertinent to Afghanistan
- access to finance in, 28
- Basel II Capital Accord, 29
- capital market development in, 30
- corporate governance in, 31–33
- global financial crisis affecting, 202, 206, 210, 213
- in rankings, 8–10, 102, 103*t*, 104*f*, 105*f*
- inflation in, 26, 31
- key economic indicators, 27*t*
- market concentration and competitiveness in, 30
- microfinance in, 12*t*, 28
- opium trade, 26, 98*n*1
- payment systems development in, 30–31
- performance and efficiency in, 29*f*
- prudential regulations, 161–163
- savings mobilization in, 31
- stability, financial, 29–30

African Development Bank Group, 201*b*

annual rankings, 104–106, 105*t*

ASEAN (Association of Southeast Asian Nations), 201*b*

Asian Development Bank (ADB), 201*b*

assets and asset quality
- commercial banking assets to GDP ratio, 5, 148
- financial stability measured in terms of, 4, 144 (*See also* stability, financial)
- prudential regulations regarding, 21–22

Association of Southeast Asian Nations (ASEAN), 201*b*

ATMs (automated teller machines), access to finance via, 3, 12*n*1, 140, 141

Australia. *See* benchmark comparisons

automated teller machines (ATMs), access to finance via, 3, 12*n*1, 140, 141. *See also* access to finance

B

Bangladesh, 33–41. *See also* specific topics, e.g. access to finance, which may contain general information pertinent to Bangladesh
- access to finance in, 35–36
- Basel II Capital Accord, 35, 37
- capital market development in, 37
- corporate governance in, 39–41
- deposit insurance scheme in, 35, 213
- global financial crisis in, 201, 202, 206, 207*t*, 210, 213
- in rankings, 8–10, 102, 103*t*, 104*f*, 105*f*
- inflation in, 34, 38
- key economic indicators, 27*t*
- market concentration and competitiveness in, 35*f*, 37, 110*f*
- microfinance in, 12*t*, 36

payment systems development in, 38
performance and efficiency in, 36
prudential regulations, 163–170
savings mobilization in, 38–39
stability, financial, 36–37
bank branches, access to finance via, 3, 12*n*1, 139–141
Basel Committee principles on corporate governance, 7, 153*t*
Basel I Capital Accord, 18–19, 29, 50, 70, 210
Basel II Capital Accord
Afghanistan, 29
Bangladesh, 35, 37
benchmark comparisons, 118
Bhutan, 43
findings and observations regarding, 131
global financial crisis and, 210
implementation of framework, 7, 15, 16, 17–20
India, 50
Nepal, 68, 70, 74
Pakistan, 77, 80
SAARC and, 24*n*4
Sri Lanka, 88, 91, 98
benchmark comparisons, 115–127
access to finance, 116*f*, 124*f*
capital market development, 119*f*, 125*f*
development dimensions/getting finance indicators
data sources and notes, 296–298
tables, by country, 274–295*t*
expansion of economies used for, 7, 8*b*, xi
market concentration and competitiveness, 119–120, 120*f*, 126*f*
OECD economies, use of, 2, 7, 8*b*, 115, 122–127, 123*t*, 124–127*f*
of individual economies, 122–127, 123*t*, 124–127*f*
payment systems development, 120–121, 121*f*, 126*f*
performance and efficiency, 117*f*, 124*f*
remittances, 121, 122*f*, 123*t*, 127*f*
savings mobilization, 121–122, 122*f*, 127*f*
SEANZA group, use of, 8*b*, 115
selected Asian economies, use of, 7, 8*b*, 115, 122–127, 123*t*, 124–127*f*
stability, financial, 117–119, 118*f*, 125*f*
Bhutan, 41–47. *See also* specific topics, e.g. access to finance, which may contain general information pertinent to Bhutan
access to finance in, 42–43
capital market development in, 43–44
corporate governance in, 45–47
global financial crisis in, 202, 206, 210, 213
high liquidity position, 42*f*, 43
in rankings, 8–10, 102, 103*t*, 104*f*, 105*f*
Indian economy affecting, 41
inflation in, 41, 45
key economic indicators, 27*t*
market concentration and competitiveness in, 44
microfinance in, 43
payment systems development in, 38
performance and efficiency in, 43
prudential regulations, 170–173
savings mobilization in, 44–45
stability, financial, 43, 113*n*2
bond markets
capital market development, domestic bond market ratios as measure of, 4, 145 (*See also* capital market development)
in India, 51–52
in South Asia generally, 25
branches, access to finance via, 3, 12*n*1, 139–141. *See also* access to finance

C

Canada. *See* benchmark comparisons
capital adequacy
Basel II Framework, 7, 15, 18–20
financial stability, ratios as indicator of, 4, 143 (*See also* stability, financial)
global financial crisis and, 210, 211*f*
prudential regulations regarding, 16–18
capital market development, 4
benchmark comparisons, 119*f*, 125*f*
domestic bond market ratios as measure of, 4, 145
findings and observations regarding, 132
guide to underlying data, 145–146
in Afghanistan, 30
in Bangladesh, 37
in Bhutan, 43–44
in India, 51–52, 110*f*
in Maldives, 61
in Nepal, 71–72

in Pakistan, 81
in Sri Lanka, 92
rankings, 10, 102, 105*f*, 107, 110*f*
stock market ratios as measure of, 4, 146
CAR (capital adequacy ratios). *See* capital adequacy
China, 201*b*. *See also* benchmark comparisons
commercial banking assets to GDP ratio, 5, 148. *See also* market concentration and competitiveness
Committee on Payment and Settlement Systems (CPSS), Bank for International Settlements, 5
competition. *See* market concentration and competitiveness
Compilation Guide, definition and concepts of ratios, 139–153
compilation of data, 155
concentration of market. *See* market concentration and competitiveness
corporate governance, 6–7
Basel Committee principles, 7, 153*t*
findings and observations regarding, 134–135
guide to underlying data, 152–153
in Afghanistan, 31–33
in Bangladesh, 39–41
in Bhutan, 45–47
in India, 54–57
in Maldives, 63–65
in Nepal, 73–75
in Pakistan, 83–87, 112*f*
in Sri Lanka, 96–98
OECD good governance practices, 7, 152, 153*t*
questionnaire responses, by country, 299–307*t*
rankings, 11
five-year average, 109, 112*f*
methodology, 157
relative composite performance, 102, 105*f*
status, by country, 308*t*
Countercyclical Support Facility, 201*b*
CPSS (Committee on Payment and Settlement Systems), Bank for International Settlements, 5
credit
asset quality measured in terms of, 4, 144
Bangladesh, credit growth in, 38
exposure limits, 22
India, credit growth in, 52
private credit extended by banks
global financial crisis and, 208, 209*f*, 214
market concentration and competitiveness, as measure of, 5, 148 (*See also* market concentration and competitiveness)
Sri Lanka, credit growth in, 93
credit information bureaus
in Bangladesh, 35
in India, 48
in Maldives, 58–59, 61
in Nepal, 66
in Pakistan, 78
in Sri Lanka, 88

D

data compilation, 155
data presentation, 157
debt restructuring, prudential regulations for, 23–24
demographic penetration, 3, 139–140. *See also* access to finance
deposit insurance schemes
global financial crisis and, 213–214
in Bangladesh, 35, 213
in India, 48, 213
in Sri Lanka, 88–89
Nepal's lack of, 66
development dimensions/getting finance indicators, 2–7. *See also* specific dimensions and indicators
choice of, 155–156
ranking methodology and, 155–156
relative performance on, 102, 105*f*
tables
benchmark economies, by country, 274–295*t*
South Asian economies, by country and year, 242–273*t*
directed lending to priority sectors, 23
domestic bond market ratios, 4, 145
drug trade in Afghanistan, 26, 98*n*1

E

economic crisis and slowdown. *See* global financial crisis
efficiency. *See* performance and efficiency
electronic fund transfer (EFT)
in Bangladesh, 38
in Bhutan, 44

in India, 52–53
in Maldives, 62
European Bank for Reconstruction and Development, 201*b*
exposure limits, 22

F

financial systems in South Asia, 1–12, xi–xii
bank dominance of, 25
benchmarks (*See* benchmark comparisons)
country perspective on, 25–26 (*See also* specific countries)
development dimensions/getting finance indicators, 2–7 (*See also* development dimensions/getting finance indicators)
findings and observations regarding, 129–136
global financial crisis, repercussions of, 1, 161, 206–214, 209*f*, 211*f*, 212*f* (*See also* global financial crisis)
methodology for analyzing, 7–8, 101, 155–157, 158–160*t*
microfinance, 11–12, 12*t*
prudential regulations for, 15–24 (*See also* prudential regulations)
rankings, 8–11, 101–113 (*See also* rankings)
fiscal stimulus packages, 206, 207*t*
France. *See* benchmark comparisons

G

geographic penetration, 3, 6*f*, 140–141. *See also* access to finance
German Agency for Technical Cooperation, 90
Germany. *See* benchmark comparisons
getting finance indicators. *See* development dimensions/getting finance indicators
global financial crisis, 199–214
background and overview, 200
banking and, 208–212, 209*f*, 211–212*f*
fiscal stimulus packages, 206, 207*t*
growth deceleration due to, 201–202, 203–204*f*
impact on South Asia, 135–136, 200–206
in Afghanistan, 202, 206, 210, 213
in Bangladesh, 201, 202, 206, 207*t*, 210, 213
in Bhutan, 202, 206, 210, 213
in India, 47–48, 51, 56–57, 200, 202, 206, 207*t*, 210, 213
in Maldives, 57, 200, 201, 202, 206, 208, 210, 213
in Nepal, 202, 206, 208, 210
in Pakistan, 76, 200, 202, 206, 207*t*, 208, 210, 213
in Sri Lanka, 87, 200, 202, 204, 206, 207*t*, 208, 210, 213
institutional and donor response to, 201*b*
recovery from, 202–206, 205*f*
repercussions for financial systems and regulation, 1, 161, 206–214, 209*f*, 211*f*, 212*f*
governance. *See* corporate governance
Group of Twenty, 201*b*

H

Herfindahl-Hirschman Index (HHI). *See also* market concentration and competitiveness
as measure of market concentration and competitiveness, 5, 146–147 (*See also* market concentration and competitiveness)
benchmark comparisons, 120
defined, 12*n*2
in Bangladesh, 35*f*, 37
in Bhutan, 44
in India, 52
in Maldives, 61–62
in Nepal, 72
in Pakistan, 81
in Sri Lanka, 93
high-value clearing
in India, 53
in Pakistan, 82
Hong Kong, China. *See* benchmark comparisons

I

ICAB (Institute of Chartered Accountants of Bangladesh), 40
IFC (International Finance Corporation), 61, 66, 84
IMF (International Monetary Fund), 76, 87, 99*n*14, 200, 201*b*
income recognition, 22
India, 47–57. *See also* specific topics, e.g. access to finance, which may contain general information pertinent to India

access to finance in, 49–50
Basel II Capital Accord, 50
Bhutan economy affected by, 41
capital market development in, 51–52, 110*f*
corporate governance in, 54–57
deposit insurance scheme, 48, 213
economic growth in, 47
global financial crisis in, 47–48, 51, 56–57, 200, 202, 206, 207*t*, 210, 213
in rankings, 8–10, 102, 103*t*, 104*f*, 105*f*
inflation in, 41, 47, 54
key economic indicators, 27*t*
market concentration and competitiveness in, 52, 110*f*
microfinance in, 12*t*, 49–50
payment systems development in, 52–54
performance and efficiency in, 50
prudential regulations, 173–180
savings mobilization in, 54, 111*f*
stability, financial, 48*f*, 50–51, 109*f*
India-Nepal Remittance Corridor, 73
indicators. *See* development dimensions of financial systems in South Asia
inflation
in Afghanistan, 26, 31
in Bangladesh, 34, 38
in Bhutan, 41, 45
in India, 41, 47, 54
in Maldives, 57, 59, 62, 63
in Nepal, 23, 65–66, 73
in Pakistan, 76, 83, 99*n*14
in Sri Lanka, 87, 95–96
real deposit interest rates affected by, 11
Institute of Chartered Accountants of Bangladesh (ICAB), 40
Institute of Chartered Accountants of India, 56
Inter-American Development Bank, 201*b*
interest rates
global financial crisis and, 210
net interest margin, 3, 142, 210, 211*f* (*See also* performance and efficiency)
real deposit interest rate, 6, 11, 151 (*See also* savings mobilization)
International Accounting Standards, 15, 25
international benchmarking. *See* benchmark comparisons
International Finance Corporation (IFC), 61, 66, 84
International Financial Reporting Standards, 56
International Monetary Fund (IMF), 76, 87, 99*n*14, 200, 201*b*
Islamic banking in Pakistan, 78, 79*t*
Italy. *See* benchmark comparisons

J

Japan, 201*b*. *See also* benchmark comparisons

K

K-bank concentration ratios, 5, 147. *See also* market concentration and competitiveness
Korea, Republic of, 201*b*. *See also* benchmark comparisons

L

LankaClear, 94–95, 100*n*25
legislation and regulations, prudential. *See* prudential regulations
Lehman Brothers, collapse of, 200
leverage ratio, 4, 143. *See also* stability, financial
liquidity
Bhutan, high liquidity position in, 42*f*, 43
financial stability measured in terms of, 4, 144 (*See also* stability, financial)
global financial crisis and, 208, 209*f*
Maldives, high liquidity position in, 61, 98–99*n*7
prudential regulations regarding, 23
Liquidity Program for Growth Sustainability, 201*b*
loan to deposit ratio, 6, 151–152, 208. *See also* savings mobilization
loans, nonperforming. *See* nonperforming loans

M

magnetic ink character recognition (MICR), 44, 52
Malaysia. *See* benchmark comparisons
Maldives, 57–65. *See also* specific topics, e.g. access to finance, which may contain general information pertinent to Maldives
access to finance in, 59–60, 107*f*, 113*n*1
capital market development in, 61
corporate governance in, 63–65
global financial crisis affecting, 57, 200, 201, 202, 206, 208, 210, 213
high liquidity position in, 61, 98–99*n*7

in rankings, 8–10, 102, 103*t*, 104*f*, 105*f*
inflation in, 57, 59, 62, 63
key economic indicators, 27*t*
market concentration and competitiveness in, 61–62
payment systems development in, 62
performance and efficiency in, 60, 108*f*
prudential regulations, 180–182
savings mobilization in, 62–63
stability, financial, 58*f*, 60–61
tourism and fisheries sectors, dominance of, 57, 60
tsunami of 2004 affecting, 57

market concentration and competitiveness, 4–5
benchmark comparisons, 119–120, 120*f*, 126*f*
commercial banking assets to GDP ratio, 5, 148
findings and observations regarding, 132–133
guide to underlying data, 146–148
HHI as measure of, 5, 146–147
in Afghanistan, 30
in Bangladesh, 35*f*, 37, 110*f*
in Bhutan, 44
in India, 52, 109*f*
in Maldives, 61–62
in Nepal, 72, 113*n*3
in Pakistan, 81–82
in Sri Lanka, 93
K-bank concentration ratios, 5, 147
private credit extended by banks as measure of, 5, 148
rankings, 10, 107–108, 110*f*

May, Ernesto, xii
methodology, 7–8, 101, 155–157, 158–160*t*
MICR (magnetic ink character recognition), 44, 52
microfinance in South Asia, 11–12, 12*t*
Afghanistan, 12*t*, 28
Bangladesh, 12*t*, 36
Bhutan, 43
India, 12*t*, 49–50
Pakistan, 78
Sri Lanka, 90

money supply ratios
payment systems development, as indicator of, 5–6, 148–149 (*See also* payment systems development)
savings mobilization, as indicator of, 6, 150–151 (*See also* savings mobilization)

Multilateralised Chiang Mai Initiative, 201*b*

N

Nepal, 65–75. *See also* specific topics, e.g. access to finance, which may contain general information pertinent to Nepal
access to finance in, 68–69
Basel II Capital Accord, 68, 70, 74
capital market development in, 71–72
corporate governance in, 73–75
deposit insurance scheme, lack of, 66
global financial crisis in, 202, 206, 208, 210
in rankings, 8–10, 102, 103*t*, 104*f*, 105*f*
inflation in, 23, 65–66, 73
key economic indicators, 27*t*
market concentration and competitiveness in, 72, 113*n*3
microfinance in, 12*t*
payment systems development in, 72–73
performance and efficiency in, 57*f*, 69
prudential regulations, 182–185
savings mobilization in, 62–63
stability, financial, 69–70

net interest margin, 3, 142, 210, 211*f*. *See also* performance and efficiency
New Zealand. *See* benchmark comparisons
nonperforming loans
financial stability, measures of, 4, 143–144 (*See also* stability, financial)
global financial crisis and, 210, 212*f*
recognition of, 21

O

OECD. *See* Organisation for Economic Co-operation and Development
operating cost ratio, 3, 142. *See also* performance and efficiency
opium trade in Afghanistan, 26, 98*n*1
Organisation for Economic Co-operation and Development (OECD)
as benchmark economies, 2, 7, 8*b*, 115, 122–127, 123*t*, 124–127*f*
good governance practices, 7, 152, 153*t*

P

Pakistan, 75–87. *See also* specific topics, e.g. access to finance, which may contain general information pertinent to Pakistan
access to finance in, 78

Basel II Capital Accord, 77, 80
capital market development in, 81
corporate governance in, 83–87, 112*f*
global financial crisis affecting, 76, 200, 202, 206, 207*t*, 208, 210, 213
in rankings, 8–10, 102, 103*t*, 104*f*, 105*f*
inflation in, 76, 83, 99*n*14
Islamic banking in, 78, 79*t*
key economic indicators, 27*t*
market concentration and competitiveness in, 81–82
microfinance in, 11–12, 12*t*, 78
payment systems development in, 72–73
performance and efficiency in, 76, 77*f*, 78–79
prudential regulations, 185–192
savings mobilization in, 83
stability, financial, 80–81

payment systems development, 5–6
benchmark comparisons, 120–121, 121*f*, 126*f*
findings and observations regarding, 133
guide to underlying data, 148–150
in Afghanistan, 30–31
in Bangladesh, 38
in Bhutan, 38
in India, 52–54
in Maldives, 62
in Nepal, 72–73
in Pakistan, 72–73
in Sri Lanka, 88, 89*f*, 93–95, 100*n*25, 111*f*
money supply ratios, 5–6, 148–149
rankings, 11, 102, 105*f*, 108–109, 111*f*
retail transactions, 6, 149–150
RTGS system, 6, 149, 150
systems in place, by country, 309–310*t*

performance and efficiency, 3
benchmark comparisons, 117*f*, 124*f*
findings and observations regarding, 130
global financial crisis and, 208–210
guide to underlying data, 141–143
in Afghanistan, 29*f*
in Bangladesh, 36
in Bhutan, 43
in India, 50
in Maldives, 60, 108*f*
in Nepal, 57*f*, 69
in Pakistan, 76, 77*f*, 78–79
in Sri Lanka, 90–91
net interest margin, 3, 142, 210, 211*f*
operating cost ratio, 3, 142
rankings, 9, 102, 105*f*, 106, 108*f*
recurring earning power, 3, 142–143
return on assets, 3, 142, 208, 211*f*
return on equity, 3, 141
staff cost ratio, 3, 142

presentation of data, 157
priority sectors, directed lending to, 23
private credit extended by banks
global financial crisis and, 208, 209*f*, 214
market concentration and competitiveness, as measure of, 5, 148 (*See also* market concentration and competitiveness)

prudential regulations, 15–24
asset quality, 21–22
Basel II, implementation of, 7, 15, 16, 17–20 (*See also* Basel II Capital Accord)
capital adequacy, 16–18
commercial bank regulators, by country, 15, 16*t*
debt restructuring, 23–24
directed lending, 23
exposure limits, 22
global financial crisis, repercussions of, 1
income recognition, 22
liquidity requirements, 23
major policy developments, by country, 161–198
Afghanistan, 161–163
Bangladesh, 163–170
Bhutan, 170–173
India, 173–180
Maldives, 180–182
Nepal, 182–185
Pakistan, 185–192
Sri Lanka, 192–198
reform in, 25
table, country by country, 216–241*t*
write-off provisions, 22

R

rankings, 8–11, 101–113
annual, 104–106, 105*t*, 311–313*t*
composite, 102, 103*t*, 104*f*, 105*f*
five-year average
access to finance, 106, 107*f*
capital market development, 107, 110*f*
composite scores, 158–160*t*
corporate governance, 109, 112*f*

market concentration and competitiveness, 107–108, 110*f*
payment systems development, 108–109, 111*f*
performance and efficiency, 106, 108*f*
savings mobilization, 108–109, 111*f*
stability, financial, 106–107, 109*f*
methodology, 101, 156–157
real deposit interest rate, 6, 11, 151. *See also* savings mobilization
real-time gross settlement (RTGS) system
Afghanistan's lack of, 30
findings and observations regarding, 133
in Bangladesh, 38
in India, 53
in Maldives, 62
in Pakistan, 82–83
in Sri Lanka, 93–95
Nepal's lack of, 73
payment systems development, as indicator of, 6, 149, 150 (*See also* payment systems development)
recurring earning power, 3, 142–143. *See also* performance and efficiency
regulations, prudential. *See* prudential regulations
remittances
benchmark comparisons, 121, 122*f*, 123*t*, 127*f*
findings and observations regarding, 133–134
global financial crisis, recovery from, 204–206, 205*f*
in Bangladesh, 34, 38–39
in India, 47, 49, 54
in Maldives, 63
in Nepal, 65, 66, 67, 70, 71, 72, 73
in Pakistan, 76, 77, 78, 83
in Sri Lanka, 87, 95
savings mobilization, as indicator of, 6, 152 (*See also* savings mobilization)
Republic of Korea, 201*b*. *See also* benchmark comparisons
retail transactions, 6, 149–150. *See also* payment systems development
return on assets, 3, 142, 208, 211*f*. *See also* performance and efficiency
return on equity, 3, 141. *See also* performance and efficiency
RTGS. *See* real-time gross settlement (RTGS) system

S

SAARC (South Asian Association for Regional Cooperation), 24*n*4, 133
SAARCFINANCE network, 24*n*4
Samurdhi banking societies, 90, 100*n*19
Sanasa thrift and credit cooperatives, 90, 100*n*19
savings mobilization, 6
benchmark comparisons, 121–122, 122*f*, 127*f*
findings and observations regarding, 133–134
global financial crisis, recovery from, 204–206, 205*f*
guide to underlying data, 150–152
in Afghanistan, 31
in Bangladesh, 38–39
in Bhutan, 44–45
in India, 54, 111*f*
in Maldives, 62–63
in Nepal, 62–63
in Pakistan, 83
in Sri Lanka, 95–96
loan to deposit ratio, 6, 151–152, 208
money supply ratios, 6, 150–151
rankings, 11, 108–109, 111*f*
real deposit interest rate, 6, 11, 151
remittances as indicator of, 6, 152 (*See also* remittances)
SEANZA (South East Asia, New Zealand, and Australia) group, 8*b*, 115
Singapore. *See* benchmark comparisons
Society for Worldwide Interbank Financial Telecommunications (SWIFT), 30, 82, 94–95
South Asia
financial systems in (*See* financial systems in South Asia)
key economic indicators for countries in, 27*t*
South Asian Association for Regional Cooperation (SAARC), 24*n*4, 133
South East Asia, New Zealand, and Australia (SEANZA) group, 8*b*, 115
speed clearing, in India, 53
Sri Lanka, 87–98. *See also* specific topics, e.g. access to finance, which may contain general information pertinent to Sri Lanka
access to finance in, 89–90, 107*f*
Basel II Capital Accord, 88, 91, 98
capital market development in, 92
corporate governance in, 96–98

deposit insurance scheme, 88–89
global financial crisis affecting, 87, 200, 202, 204, 206, 207*t*, 208, 210, 213
in rankings, 8–10, 102, 103*t*, 104*f*, 105*f*
inflation in, 87, 95–96
key economic indicators, 27*t*
market concentration and competitiveness in, 93
microfinance in, 12*t*, 90
payment systems development in, 88, 89*f*, 93–95, 100*n*25, 111*f*
performance and efficiency in, 90–91
prudential regulations, 192–198
savings mobilization in, 95–96
stability, financial, 91–92
stability, financial, 3–4
assets and asset quality, measured in terms of, 4, 144
benchmark comparisons, 117–119, 118*f*, 125*f*
capital adequacy ratios as indicator of, 4, 143
findings and observations regarding, 130–132
global financial crisis and, 208–210
guide to underlying data, 143–144
in Afghanistan, 29–30
in Bangladesh, 36–37
in Bhutan, 43, 113*n*2
in India, 48*f*, 50–51, 109*f*
in Maldives, 58*f*, 60–61
in Nepal, 69–70
in Pakistan, 80–81
in Sri Lanka, 91–92
leverage ratio, 4, 143
liquidity, measured in terms of, 4, 144
nonperforming loans, 4, 143–144
rankings, 10, 106–107, 109*f*, 157
staff cost ratio, 3, 142. *See also* performance and efficiency
stimulus packages, 206, 207*t*
stock markets
capital market development, stock market ratios as measure of, 4, 146 (*See also* capital market development)
in India, 51–52
in South Asia generally, 25
SWIFT (Society for Worldwide Interbank Financial Telecommunications), 30, 82, 94–95

T

Thailand. *See* benchmark comparisons
tsunami of 2004, 57

U

United Kingdom. *See* benchmark comparisons
United States, 201*b*. *See also* benchmark comparisons

W

worker remittances to GDP ratio, 6
World Bank, 199, 201*b*, 203, xi
write-off provisions, 22

ECO-AUDIT

Environmental Benefits Statement

The World Bank is committed to preserving endangered forests and natural resources. The Office of the Publisher has chosen to print ***Getting Finance in South Asia 2010: Indicators and Analysis of the Commercial Banking Sector*** on recycled paper with 30 percent postconsumer fiber in accordance with the recommended standards for paper usage set by the Green Press Initiative, a nonprofit program supporting publishers in using fiber that is not sourced from endangered forests. For more information, visit www.greenpressinitiative.org.

Saved:

- 27 trees
- 4 million British thermal units of total energy
- 1,273 pounds of greenhouse gases (CO_2 equivalent)
- 6,131 pounds of waste water
- 372 pounds of solid waste

green press INITIATIVE